MW01634161

ISRAEL AND EMPIRE

ISRAEL AND EMPIRE

A Postcolonial History of Israel and Early Judaism

Leo G. Perdue and Warren Carter

Edited by
Coleman A. Baker

B L O O M S B U R Y
LONDON • NEW DELHI • NEW YORK • SYDNEY

Bloomsbury T&T Clark
An imprint of Bloomsbury Publishing Plc
Imprint previously known as T&T Clark

50 Bedford Square
London
WC1B 3DP
UK

1385 Broadway
New York
NY 10018
USA

www.bloomsbury.com

**Bloomsbury, T&T Clark and the Diana logo are trademarks
of Bloomsbury Publishing Plc**

First published 2015

© Leo G. Perdue, Warren Carter and Coleman A. Baker, 2015

All rights reserved. No part of this publication may be reproduced or transmitted in any form or by any means, electronic or mechanical, including photocopying, recording, or any information storage or retrieval system, without prior permission in writing from the publishers.

Leo G. Perdue, Warren Carter and Coleman A. Baker have asserted their rights under the Copyright, Designs and Patents Act, 1988, to be identified as Authors of this work.

No responsibility for loss caused to any individual or organization acting on or refraining from action as a result of the material in this publication can be accepted by Bloomsbury or the authors.

British Library Cataloguing-in-Publication Data
A catalogue record for this book is available from the British Library.

ISBN: HB: 978-0-56705-409-8
          PB: 978-0-56724-328-7
          ePDF: 978-0-56728-051-0

Library of Congress Cataloging-in-Publication Data
A catalogue record for this book is available from the British Library.

Typeset by Forthcoming Publications (www.forthpub.com)
Printed and bound in Great Britain

Contents

Abbreviations vii
Preface ix

**Introduction:
Empires, Colonies,
and Postcolonial Interpretation** 1
    I.   Sources of Social Power 2
    II.   The Power of Discourse 2
    III. The Discourse of Resistance 3

**1 Major Considerations in the Analysis
   of Imperial Rule and Postcolonial Criticism** 5
    I.   What Is Postcolonialism Criticism? Postcolonial Historiography and
        Biblical Interpretation 5
    II.   The Subaltern and Economic Exploitation 7
    III. Racism in the Ideology and Practice of Imperialism 8
    IV. *Orientalism*: The Subverting of Western Stereotypes of the East 9
    V.   The Location of Culture 15
    VI. Can the Subaltern Speak? 19
   VII. Postcolonial Historiography 22
  VIII. The Imperial Metanarrative 30
    IX. Colonial Resistance 32
    X.   The Diaspora 33

**2 The Assyrian Empire, the Conquest of Israel,
   and the Colonization of Judah** 37
    I.   Historical Introduction 37
    II.   The Metanarrative of the Assyrian Empire 40
    III. Israel/Judah and the Assyrian Empire: The Example of Hosea 49
    IV. The Colonization of Judah and Assyrian Domination 63

3 Judah under the Neo-Babylonian Empire 69
   I.   Historical Introduction 69
   II.   The Babylonian Metanarrative of Empire 72
   III.   Jewish Communities during the Exile 76
   IV.   The Prophetic Resistance to the Empires:
          Jeremiah and Second Isaiah 87

4 The Persian Empire and the Colony of Judah 107
   I.   Historical Introduction 107
   II.   Persian Culture and the Imperial Metanarrative 109
   III.   Judah as a Persian Colony 117
   IV.   Conclusion: Unity and Diversity in Judaism
          in the Persian Empire 127

5 Judea/Israel under the Greek Empires 129
   I.   Alexander the Macedonian (336–323),
          his Conquests, and Successors (*Diadochi*) 135
   II.   Ptolemaic Rule and Judea/Israel 147
   III.   Seleucid Rule of Judea/Israel 200–175 BCE 172
   IV.   Antiochus IV Epiphanes (175–164 BCE) 184
   V.   Post-164 BCE Rededication of the Temple
          and Independence 210

6 Judea/Israel under the Roman Empire 217
   I.   Historical Introduction 223
   II.   The Metanarrative of the Roman Empire 227
   III.   Rome and Judea: Roman Religious Acts
          and Imperial Cult Observance 235
   IV.   Imperial and Provincial Rule 241
   V.   Economics 251
   VI.   Judean/Israelite Religion 263
   VII.   Material Culture 273
   VIII. Decolonizing the Mind 279
   IX.   Conclusion 291

Bibliography 293
Index of References 313
Index of Authors 325

Abbreviations

ANET	Ancient Near Eastern Texts Relating to the Old Testament. Edited by J. B. Pritchard. 3rd ed. Princeton, 1969
COS	*The Context of Scripture.* Edited by W. W. Hallo. 3 vols. Leiden, 1997–2003
JB	Jerusalem Bible
KAI	*Kanaanäische und Aramäische Inscriften*, H. Donner and W. Röllig, 2nd ed. Wiesbaden, 1966–69
KJV	Kings James Version
NAB	New American Bible
NRSV	New Revised Standard Version
TEV	Today's English Version (= Good News Bible)
VAB	Vorderasiatische Bibliothek

Preface

It may seem strange to dedicate a book to one who has authored the book. But that's what we have done here. In dedicating this book to Leo Perdue, we honor a first-rate scholar, one of much learning, dedicated hard work, prolific scholarly productivity, and significant influence on scholarly discourse. Here is the backstory.

This book began as Leo's idea, another product of his fertile and creative scholarly mind. In his later scholarship, he became increasingly interested in matters of empire and especially in postcolonial approaches. He conceived this study of Israel and the empires spanning Israel's history from the Assyrians, through the Babylonians, Persians, and Greeks to the Romans. He planned for himself an opening chapter on postcolonial theory, and three chapters on Israel's negotiation of the Assyrian, Babylonian, and Persian empires. Typical of his enthusiasm and his humility, he recruited a co-writer to address Israel and the Greek and Roman empires, which he considered not to be in his purview.

Leo worked on the project and 'completed' a draft of his material for his chapters. Regrettably, he became ill before he was able to complete the project for publication. Dr. Coleman Baker, a former student of Leo's, became the editor for the volume, working on Leo's somewhat disordered manuscript and preparing it for publication. Dr. Warren Carter completed Chapters 5 and 6. We are both grateful to our student assistants, Zhenya Gurina-Rodriguez, Naiomi Gonzalez, and Hannah Galloway for their assistance in the book's preparation. We also express our gratitude to Dominic Mattos of T&T Clark/Bloomsbury for his encouragement and editorial assistance, and to Dr. Timothy Sandoval, Associate Professor of Hebrew Bible at Brite Divinity School, for his assistance on several points related to Hebrew language and literature.

Leo Perdue served Brite Divinity School at Texas Christian University in Fort Worth, Texas in various roles—Professor of Hebrew Bible, Dean, President—for more than twenty years. In dedicating this volume to Leo, we honor not only a fine scholar but also one who faithfully served and furthered the cause of theological education in this institution. Completing and publishing this volume expresses our appreciation for Leo's work as professor, scholar, and theological educator.

We dedicate this volume to Professor Leo G. Perdue.

Warren Carter
Coleman A. Baker
Fort Worth, Texas
March 2014

Introduction:
Empires, Colonies,
and Postcolonial Interpretation

Empires arose in recorded history as early as the third millennium BCE and have been generally understood as systems of international domination based on power, ideology, and control. They have existed globally, arising from limited tribal conflicts in small geographical regions and occasionally developing into rather large transnational spaces.

Not limited to the past, these tyrannical forms of political and economic rule have continued to the present. Metropoles, the capitals of empires, grow economically and militarily strong and launch efforts to conquer and rule not only their own but also foreign peoples and centers. They increase their suzerainty and influence through military invasion and the internal political administrations of the conquered peoples, which become colonies to support imperial demands that enhance the empire's attainment of power and wealth. In their gaining of supremacy over colonial populations, either kingdoms or tribes, empires rule their colonies not only through superior military might and the threat of its use, but also by the establishment of economic policies favorable to the metropole and the imposition of a culture that colonizes the minds of those who are ruled.

Martial force alone cannot maintain the sovereignty of an empire. Continued control requires the indoctrination of imperial values, beliefs, and concepts issuing from the defining traditions of empires used to socialize not only the metropolitan core, but also the peoples of the defeated. Furthermore, through a system of recompense that rewards loyal, indigenous leaders by giving them a measure of official and social status, the chances of successful colonizations are increased significantly.

I.
Sources of Social Power

The sociologist Michael Mann identifies four principal 'sources' of social power that intersect in a nation: ideology, military strength, economic resources, and socio-political administration.[1] When applied to the analysis of empire, the deployment and maintenance of these sources provides the means by which hegemony is gained and endures. Once these sources decline significantly and begin to fail, the imperial society that uses them deteriorates and, eventually, crumbles.

Yet even the colonized and their descendants among liberated peoples also possess at least a limited degree of social power in their status of subjection to empires. This colonial power is expressed in the form of resistance, ranging from subversion in speech to deeds of passive and active revolution. However, discourse among the subjugated becomes the most important means by which the subjugated resist the hegemony of imperial nations.

II.
The Power of Discourse

Michel Foucault's views of discourse are essential to understand his concept of the relationship between power and knowledge.[2] He argues that language is not simply the stringing together of words, but also embodies a creativity that creates and continues to shape the outside world, the value of nature, and human communities, all that embraces that which is intrinsic to self-identity. For Foucault, the concept of a single explanation, or grand narrative, is preposterous. Rather, new ideologies do not result from metanarratives of history and culture, but rather they develop from many disparate, unrelated causes. However, what drives the creation of grand narratives is the ambition of the powerful to maintain their status in the social hierarchy.

Foucault believes that so-called normative knowledge is connected to systems of social control. Sovereign powers in a society, including an empire, decide what is legitimate and true and punish those who differ in their definitions, decisions, and actions.

---

1.   Mann, *The Sources of Social Power*. Also see his 'The Autonomous Power'.
2.   Foucault, *L'archéologie du savoir*. Also see Foucault, *L'ordre du discours*.

In the application of Foucault's understanding of discourse, knowledge, and power to empire and colony, it becomes apparent that imperial dominion is largely founded on the conviction that its knowledge and right to rule are true. By contrast, those who are the objects of conquest are deemed inferior in knowledge. The defeat of imperial rule is in part due to a discourse of resistance that leads to revolution and, if successful, independence.

III.
The Discourse of Resistance

In his volume, *Domination and the Arts of Resistance*, James Scott concentrates on two types of discourse among both rulers and the ruled.[3] Scott contrasts *public transcript*, which describes openly the accessible interactions between imperial powers and those they control, and *hidden transcript*, which does not clearly reveal the communication of the empire and the colonized but is known primarily by the symbolic codes inherent in their respective discourse. He notes the symbolic meaning present in the language of both groups of people: the conquering metropole and the resisting colony. Ruling elites convey hegemony publicly through culture, language, state ceremonies, and many types of public transcripts (e.g., proclamations, laws, and rules) made known and implemented through forms of social and political control. Rulers use authority, culture, language, and the display of public ceremonies to enforce the components of their ideology of rule. Rituals of domination and subordination are public and provide symbolic expression of the rule of the metropole, both in formal celebrations and in informal observances, which occur in both the metropolitan core and in the colonies on the margins of culture and influence. Such displays not only maintain the subjugation of the colonized people, but also reinforce the self-understanding and identity of the colonizers as legitimate imposers of subjugation. In resistance to hegemonic rulers, marginalized peoples engage in a criticism of power in the variety of public and private discourse and activities at their disposal.

These two types of discourse propose to substantiate, in the first instance, the metanarrative of the empire and its so-called superior culture, and, to subvert, in the second case, the rulers' ideology of hegemony, particularly when submission and colonization of the mind is being forced upon the ruled. In their public discourse the dominated

3. Scott, *Domination*.

often engage in speech performance that is deceptive in the expression of feigned support for imperial superiority.

In masking their candor, symbolic twists of language and its performance weaken the force of imperial ideology. Confrontations between the powerful and the powerless (the conquered, slaves, workers, women, children, indigents, and feeble) include the latter's feigning of deference and obedience to their masters in public displays, since they are not allowed to engage publicly without punishing consequences. Yet their hidden transcripts express resistance to the conquerors through such things as folktales, songs, plays of the theater of the absurd, jokes of ridicule, and varieties of coded language known only to them. Even rituals serve to present the intent of resistance found in hidden transcripts. This coded language and its performance are central to the misrepresentation and disguising of the thoughts and views of the subordinated toward their masters. Because of threat from the powerful, the dominated seek anonymity behind the language of subversion as well as in actions that permit an innocuous understanding of who they are and what they mean to say. Once the hidden discourse is spoken publicly, the dominated experience the satisfaction of the expression of pent-up hostility, although the public expression may eventually lead to devastating results in their fortunes. The subordinates' views of the powerful come into the open and take the form of both passive and active violence. The objectives of the hidden discourse of the weak include decolonizing the minds of the dominated and the eventual driving out of their imperial powers and the foreign rule they enforce. Thus, the ruled have a measure of power, in particular discourse, in resisting and subverting both the empire and its after-effects in neocolonialism.

Following an introduction to postcolonialism and historiography in Chapter 1, this volume explores the major features of interactions between empires and colonies, along with confrontations, submissions, and fusions. This will be followed in the subsequent chapters by a postcolonial analysis of selected texts from Israel and Judah, beginning in the eighth century BCE, and continuing into the second century CE. In correspondence with the diaspora, some texts originating in Alexandria of Egypt and others from different locations of imperial Greece and Rome will be examined. Important to this study, throughout its various sections, is the role of religion in undergirding and channeling ideologies and actions of rule and resistance.

1

Major Considerations in the Analysis of Imperial Rule and Postcolonial Criticism

I.
What Is Postcolonialism Criticism?
Postcolonial Historiography and Biblical Interpretation

Slemon writes:

> Definitions of the 'post-colonial', of course, vary widely, but for me the concept proves most useful not when it is used synonymously with a post-independence historical period in once-colonized nations, but rather when it locates a specifically anti- or *post*-colonial *discursive* purchase in culture, one which begins in the moment that the colonizing power inscribes itself onto the body and space of its Others and which continues as an often occluded tradition into the modern theatre of neo-colonialist international relations.[1]

Sugirtharajah adds that postcolonial criticism is more of

> a style of enquiry, an insight or a perspective, a catalyst, a new way of life. As an enquiry, it instigates and creates possibilities, and provides a platform for the widest possible convergence of critical forces, of multi-ethnic, multi-religious, and multicultural voices, to assert their denied rights and rattle the centre.[2]

Postcolonial refers to a 'collection of critical and conceptual attitudes'.[3] Thus, it is a type of criticism, rather than a theory or method. Said notes that criticism is seen 'as life-enhancing and constitutively opposed to every form of tyranny, domination, and abuse; its social goals are non-coercive knowledge produced in the interests of human freedom'.[4] Homi

---

1. Slemon, 'Modernism's Last Post', 6.
2. Sugirtharajah, *Postcolonial Criticism and Biblical Interpretation*, 13.
3. Sugirtharajah, *Postcolonial Criticism and Biblical Interpretation*, 14.
4. Said, *The World, the Text, and the Critic*, 29.

Bhabha contends that postcolonial perspectives 'intervene in those ideological discourses of modernity that attempt to give a hegemonic "normality" to the uneven development and the differential, often disadvantaged, histories of nations, races, communities, people'. Cultural traditions and epistemologies developed in the Global South possess their own legitimacy and should be used to contest the notion of the intellectual and cultural superiority of nations and empires as normative.

What these postcolonial authors share is a view of postcolonialism that introduces the concepts of power and ideology into numerous arenas of interpretation, including literary criticism, the interpretation of the arts, social-critical analysis of institutions, historiography, and political-scientific inquiry. This critical undermining of imperial culture and rule seeks to detect stereotypical and colonial elements and then to eliminate them from both the writings of scholars and the colonized mind of former colonials. The postcolonial evaluation of history, official documents, and missionary reports strives to expose the significant levels of bias in Western writings and scholarship, including historiography, in their portrayal of the colonized. These writers engage in this critical analysis to legitimate colonial identity and value. Postcolonialists hold in common with schools of liberation, Marxists, and feminist/womanist discourses a resistance to any form of egregious oppression and the construction of truth claims that victimize the powerless.

While most postcolonial intellectuals are largely highly educated in metropolitan schools and steeped in the culture of the empire, they seek to recapture their own indigenous identity by returning to a sometimes mythological past and/or rediscovering and reinventing their own people's history to speak of their own achievements and accomplishments of distinction. These critics shape different narratives that radically resist and undo those of imperial systems. Postmodernism, which is a Eurocentric ideology, has often been embraced for ideological purposes in reshaping the consciousness of the indigenous people and in debunking the Western stories of domination. For diasporan and indigenous postcolonial intellectuals, theorists such as Freud, Marx, Derrida, Foucault, and their successors provide the theoretical grist for the mill that grounds new versions of understanding what is true and authentically real. Even intellectuals within the metropole, who are citizens of the dominating powers, at times turn against or heavily criticize the imperial exploitation of colonials, decrying imperialist inhumanity and fearing that the citizens of the empire themselves will mimic in their social and political arenas what has been done to exploit and suppress the weaker colonials.

II.
The Subaltern
and Economic Exploitation

Various terms are used to describe and define the colonials in the imperial system of domination, although they are not derived from the metanarratives of the empires. Subaltern is one of the most common and useful terms, meaning essentially 'of inferior or subordinated rank'.[5] This term, which equates with the *Other*, points to those who are unfamiliar to and unknown by the subjective knowledge of the conqueror. In the modern world, the West understood itself as the center of power and genuine knowledge, and thus superior, while the subalterns of colonies, former colonies, and the desperate countries of the Global South were construed to lack power, a critical and analytic self-consciousness, and the ability to reason and rule themselves. Authentic discourse, therefore, does not occur but rather a series of banal stereotypes of the *Other* are constructed. The term subaltern is not simply a sociological classification but also a psychological definition of the self. This understanding of self-identity, drawn from Freud and his disciples, derives from the view that it is constructed by the mind or the unconscious. In addition, in the views of some discourse theorists, subalterns require dialogue with the powerful in order to speak their views and understandings. In speech act theory, discourse requires both the participation of speaker and listener, otherwise authentic discourse does not take place. While their own experiences and understandings are generally ignored by imperialists, however, subalterns, who achieve self-realization from their own self-comprehension and discourse among themselves and find willing listeners among the imperial elite, continue to make themselves felt even in the consciousness and self-understanding of the metropole. Indeed, subalterns or the *Other* have the discursive ability to disturb, distort, and deconstruct the dominant representations of empire, due to their radical differences from what the empire considers normative identity, but only when an authentic speech act actually occurs. Otherwise, the subaltern is forced to dwell within the vacuous domain of unbroken silence.

5. For more on the history of this concept see Morton's 'The Subaltern: Genealogy of a Concept', in *Gayatri Spivak*, 96-97.

III.
Racism in the Ideology and Practice
of Imperialism

Racism directed against the conquered has been intrinsic to imperialism especially since the nineteenth century. With the age of Western empires continuing into the present, racism involves beliefs centering on the superiority of the conquering race's worth, abilities, and knowledge in contrast to the conquered, who are often of different ethnic identities and skin color. These latter are viewed as inferior and subhuman. This racist domination, based on widespread prejudice among the conquerors and their later generations, has continued to affect adversely the former colonies who have emerged since the Second World War to form their own independent states. Many in the populations of former colonies continue to suffer psychological damage from the effects of racism perpetuated among their former masters and from the difficulty of subverting its powers of definition. While racism may be prohibited by law codes of Western nations, its insidious capacity for discrimination and violence continues to effectuate its toll not only on the racial Other but also on the racists themselves.

While there are numerous critical theories of racism, a common recognition among these is the debilitating potency racism has continued to exert in the cultural, political, and social realms of former and present metropoles. Foucault's understanding of discourse is helpful in viewing racism as the social and imaginary construction by the offspring of conquering groups that emerges from imperialism, colonialism, and slavery. By knowing the colonized subject through these lenses, Europeans and their former *white* colonies have come to construct their identities by means of the construal of the superiority of their ethnicity and Eurocentric values of whiteness, culture, democracy, citizenship, and capitalism, while devaluing those whose identities were differently formed and held by peoples of non-white races.

Frantz Fanon was a leading voice in anti-colonial struggles in the 1950s, and he regarded racism as an intrinsic part of the colonial project. Fanon denounced imperial rule for teaching certain colonials that they were inferior, an aberration, and objects of ridicule because of the color of their skin.[6] Throughout his writings, he regarded racism as endemic to

---

6.   Fanon, *Black Skin, White Masks.*

imperialism, for it demeans the humanity of the dark-skinned colonized.[7] Fanon adapted the Marxist understanding of the distinction imperialism draws between the white colonizers who are wealthy and powerful and the non-white populations who are the dominated, exploited, and poor. Accordingly, the imperial negation of the personhood of the colonized denies them every attribute of humanity and respectability and creates a psychological structure that forms a 'colonized personality' identified by imperialists as savagery.

IV.

Orientalism:
The Subverting of Western Stereotypes of the East

Prior to his death, Edward Said (1935–2003) was one of the leading voices in the formation of modern postcolonialism as a political and cultural approach to the construction of world views that have shaped nations, ethnicities, and institutions since the end of the Second World War. Born in Jerusalem during the increasingly unsettled period of the British Mandate, Said grew up in the tumultuous world of the Middle East that witnessed the end of British rule, the formation of the State of Israel, and the early period of conflict between Arabs and Israelis. After immigrating to the United States, Said received his PhD at Harvard in 1964 and taught at Columbia University from 1963 until his death in 2003.

Said strongly emphasized the principle of contextuality, arguing that texts, like their authors, are intrinsically connected to their time, space, culture, language, social world, and political reality. Neither text nor author can be abstracted from these locations without doing harm to content and meaning. However, once indigenous individuals remove themselves or are forced to relocate from their original contexts to dwell in new ones, these latter contexts provide them with new settings in which part of their identity is formed. However, elements of their past cultures and spaces continue to influence them and shape their ever-changing identity. Exposure to displacement permeates the essence of Said's writings and is key to his ideas about imperialism and postcolonialism. While European immigrants have eventually been accepted by new cultures in Canada and the United States and are usually granted citizenship, those from the East who migrate to the West are not easily

---

7. For example, see Fanon's *Studies in a Dying Colonialism*; *Toward the African Revolution*; *The Wretched of the Earth*.

received and fully accepted in American society. This is due in large part
to Orientalism, a frame of ideological construal of the East by the West,
which was generated by the Western mind and imposed on the East.
Orientalism also happens to be the title of one of Said's best-known
works, which will be discussed below.[8]

In order to comprehend the insights of Said, it is important to remember that he wrote in the United States as a displaced exile, a Palestinian,
whose own personal history was tied to his experience and understanding of power and ideology in the United States. As a Palestinian who
migrated to the United States, Said's character and sense of self were
shaped by the recognition of his status as a marginal in exile. While
teaching at Columbia he wrote: 'Identity—who we are, where we come
from, what we are—is difficult to maintain in exile… We are the "other",
an opposite, a flaw in the geometry of resettlement, an exodus. Silence
and discretion veil the hurt, slow the body searches, soothe the sting of
loss.'[9]

The prominence of Said's thought for understanding postcolonialism
includes the fact that he demonstrated beyond question that colonialism
and imperialism were not simply carried out by military and economic
strategies of control and domination, but also by a discourse of imagined
knowledge that the empire viewed to be unquestionably true. Significantly influenced by Foucault, Said contended that discourse, whatever
the location, is ideologically shaped, for it contains cultural assumptions
about knowledge, its authority, and its construal through various forms
of power, both physical and epistemological. This contested knowledge
was used by imperialists to control the minds of the dominated or by the
colonized to deconstruct the cultural and political assumptions of the
controlling metropole. The metanarratives of the Western nations are
enmeshed in the political, social, and cultural features of their own
reality derived from their experiences and views of the world. At the
same time, postcolonial ideas, incorporated into speeches and writings,
became a way for the marginalized of empires and former empires to
respond to and undermine the metanarratives of their masters.

For Said, the postcolonial struggle is linked to what kind of future is
possible. Colonial resistance is not simply to the controlling domination
of the imperial past, but to the continuing obstacles to the liberation of
colonials and the former colonized who seek to experience a future in
which they are free to shape the social, political, economic, and ideological character of their own identity and national institutions. Said

8. Said, *Orientalism*.
9. Said, *After the Last Sky*, 16-17.

points to a variety of themes of resistance in which the oppressed participate, prior to liberation. One is the rejection of the remapping of the world drawn by colonial empires that led to the provincializing of countries, peoples, and cultures. Second, resistance also involves the return to earlier expressions of the separate boundaries of peoples and cultures. Third, resistance comprises the reshaping of former colonial identity by negating the imposed definitions given unilaterally by the empire. For Said, identity is crucial to the self-definition of a people, allowing them to reclaim their own norms, cultures, and social institutions and to continue to develop them unimpeded by outside forces. No longer are people held captive in their own lands or the regions of the diaspora to which they have migrated. Fourth, resistance also involves the reclaiming of a people's history seen through their own eyes, not those of the imperial rulers. Thus, resistance becomes an 'alternative way of conceiving human history', freed from the history of imperial superiority.[10] Fifth and finally, resistance enables the development of the understanding of a people's community and liberation in moving from colony, to nation, to solidarity and a shared culture, to a new socio-political reality.

Said also recognized that imperial power is not only expressed through military conquest and control, but also through the epistemic violence of spoken and written discourse done to the defining cultural traditions of a conquered people. Equally so, colonial resistance may be both physically and culturally brutal, possessing a destructive defiance as well as a deconstructive discourse. For empires, discourse is imbued with what passes for authoritative power and knowledge, leading to the mastery and control of their colonies, while for colonies semiotics promote resistance and construct a new linguistic paradigm that construes a fundamentally different cultural reality. Misogyny often enters into these Western portrayals in that the Orient is presented as feminine, exotic, and seductive. In addition, the Orient is further portrayed as wicked, untrustworthy, and uncivilized, posing then a threat to Western civility and moral standards. The Other is given a xenophobic twist, in that whatever is shaped by and embodies non-Western characteristics is judged to be inferior. The development of this imagined, falsely construed world and its people was important in the movements of imperialism in Europe and later in the United States. Orientalism is not only the product of Western imagination, but also an objectification of what is presumed to be real. Thus, the Orient may be scrutinized, studied, and analyzed in rational categories by Western thinkers who abstract themselves from the cultural impress of

10. Said, *Culture*, 216.

what they study. Westerners contended, however, that they knew intimately and understood in depth the various facets of the East through the lens of Orientalism. As shall be noted later, Orientalism has at times infused the academies of knowledge lodged in universities that offered programs in the study of Eastern peoples and cultures taught primarily by Europeans and Americans.

Orientalism thus was a Western discourse of power, combined with an ideology that distinguished between cultural realities of Euro-America and Asia and became an important feature of the world view that, in the guise of obvious subterfuge, compelled the West to move toward imperial domination of colonies in the East. Orientalism served as a discourse of legitimation for Western domination of others by means of a language of identity that defined both conquerors and conquered. The Other is alienated from the cultural and political reality that imperialists shape. Only by disassembling this myth of superiority through the avenues of various kinds of resistance, including revolution and epistemic violence, may liberation from the imperial powers occur.

Thus liberation begins by making the important transition from a culture of blame to a culture of resistance. Unlike Foucault, who lacks any political intentionality, Said's thought is imbued with it. Resistance to the empire by showing the weakness of its discourse and the falsity of many of its ideological assumptions and claims breaks its powerful grip on the colonized. Marginalized colonies and their descendants cannot be confined to and overpowered by the strategies of imperial representation of who and what they now are and must become to be truly civilized. Postcolonial thinkers express discursive world views, which are designed to give meaning and direction to the former colonies, to disassemble the ideology of the imperialists, and to persuade them to listen openly to dissent and thereby transform their erroneous conceptions of the East and its different world views. Yet, postcolonial scholars do not totally reject the world views or cultural vestiges of the dominant, since some of the elements of this cultural and political matrix continue in new forms of ever-changing hybridity. This creates the inner tension that exists within postcolonials, who are 'in the world, but not of the world'. This worldliness of texts and their interpreters means that neither may be geographically or politically isolated. This also means that texts do not contain simply an abstract truth, but rather are related to a network of contextual meanings, institutions, bodies, and cultures that produce a variety of possible understandings of what is thought by someone or some group to be true. Truth thus represents what the ideology of its formulators set forth, a view of reality that usually reflects their own self-interests.

Poststructuralism and postmodernism had already begun to undo the certitude of Western paradigms of knowledge. Thus, in his anticolonial writing and speaking, Said critically made use of existing theoretical models, in particular the writings of Michel Foucault, which had already developed in the West to deconstruct the certitude of Western political governance and cultural knowledge. Said borrowed a variety of his insights from Foucault, including the view that discourse creates a representation of the world. Discourse sets forth forms of knowledge that correspond to established paradigms of understanding. What is scandalous for Said is when any people's culture, usually that of the metropole of an empire, articulates its own ideology as authentic while another culture is prohibited or obstructed from articulating its own representative views. Thus the imperialists assume the hubristic position of speaking, writing, and acting for the colonials they seek to control. The rulers desire to shape the ideology of the colonials to match the imperial world's view of who they are.

By using these earlier linguistic and epistemological theories, Said shaped a version of anticolonial rhetoric that sought to end the dominance of Western mythic portrayals of the East and to begin to fashion new ones more representative of postcolonial cultures. To do so, he engaged postmodern critics and their ideas, along with the poststructuralist Foucault, without assuming a posture of blind obedience to their varied understandings. While he made use of some of the ideas emerging from this discourse, he did so selectively, choosing often to disagree when this differed from his own understanding of texts and experience of the world. He especially remained critical of deconstruction as advocated by Derrida, since he considered Derrida's understanding to eliminate the human freedom, necessity, and responsibility to decide, in this case, to oppose colonialism. In addition, Said does not allow language that takes form in a variety of texts to be extracted from its location in the world. He rejects the all too common academic approach to texts as reified objects open to external analysis by dispassionate literary critics. While strongly denying the view that texts are only humanly constructed objects, he chooses instead to regard them as cultural entities that, at times, reflect reality and still are imbued with the views of their creators and the worlds in which they and their audiences exist. Texts thus provide insight not merely into the external realm that is viewed and understood, but also into the internal world of their composers. Thus the world is not constructed simply by discourse. For his postcolonial insights, this view is fundamental. One cannot ignore the verisimilitude of political and social realities of texts in understanding those composed by both imperialists and postcolonialists. Therefore, texts, for Said, are worldly, but they are not understood only as reflective of the world in which they are written.[11] They also contain the entrance of the writer and audience into their interpretation. This worldliness infuses texts so that they are neither objects external to human involvement nor lifeless entities abstracted from the world that prevails external to writers and interpreters. Texts are not separate from, but rather are affiliated with, the various networks of ideas, interpretations, and relationships that are found in the larger world. The resulting interpretations produce a non-coercive social knowledge of the imagined reality in which the critics and their audiences mutually exist and engage the discourse of texts.

In addition to *Orientalism*, Said confronts *Eurocentrism* and particularly imperialism that exists not only in political policies but also in both the propaganda and the subconscious of Western thinking. Indeed the colonizers even produced vast amounts of knowledge about those they subjugated in order to legitimate their hegemony. Together these two forces, political policies and propaganda, have been especially important for the presence and advance of colonialism.[12] The postcolonial thinker is one who not only exposes the fallacy of this collusion, but also intervenes politically, including the retelling of the history of colonial peoples viewed through their own eyes. Yet the goal of the postcolonial is not simply to accomplish the return of the land and self-rule to the colonized; it seeks to replace the colonized mind with a new understanding of the world and to value its own traditions and culture. This is the moral imperative of the postcolonial writer. Opposing the powerful colonial world is difficult but necessary to create a new reality devoid of imperial oppression and racial and cultural stereotypes of the Other.

The importance of Said's thinking for biblical interpretation resides in three key points that may be extracted from his writings. First, biblical texts cannot be abstracted from the reality of their social, political, and cultural location. To do so is to remove the locality of texts necessary to their understanding. Contextuality is the key to understanding both texts and interpreters. Second, appropriate biblical texts should be read as part and parcel of intellectual resistance to imperial metanarratives and assimilation into the cultural worlds of the empires. Third, biblical

11. Said, *The World, the Text, and the Critic*.

12. See MacKenzie, *Propaganda and Empire*. In writing of British propaganda used to advance the empire, he notes that empire created 'for the British a world view which was central to their perceptions of themselves'. The elements of this propaganda included militarism, devotion to royalty, the identification and honoring of national heroes, a cult of personalities, and racism associated with Social Darwinism (p. 2). Most of these factors are present in other empires, including that of the United States.

writers who join in the resistance to the empires speak from the margins, a place distant from the imperial core. This placement on the periphery of imperial rule is not one of weakness, but of empowerment, as the prophets of Israel and Judah, for example, demonstrated in their influence on the streams and courses of Jewish history.

V.
The Location of Culture

Homi K. Bhabha openly acknowledges the fact that he writes from his own background, culture, and experiences, all of which shape his views. He describes himself as a 'Parsi, already a minority in the Indian context' who exists on the border between majority and minority cultures in the United States where he is now residing.[13] Bhabha uses psychoanalysis in his postmodern discussion of the differences between empires and their colonies. Like many other postcolonials, Bhabha notes that imperial discourse is an important means of maintaining dominion over the ruled. He argues that 'the objective of colonial discourse is to construe the colonized as a population of degenerate types on the basis of racial origins in order to justify both conquest and the establishment of systems of administration and instruction'.[14] While the colonized hold a deep-seated anger against their rulers, they may also shelter a desire to be like them. This conflict directs us to the three major concepts of Bhabha's postcolonial thought: ambivalence, hybridity, and mimicry, each of which may be used to provide insight into postcolonial historiography.

Ambivalence

The first of Bhabha's important ideas is ambivalence. Drawing on the insights of modern psychoanalysis, he contends that one's identity comes from establishing differences with the Other, i.e. the opposite of what one is not. For him the identity of the colonized is shaped by the conflict between the desire to be the ruler and the repulsiveness of domination. This is the attraction of Western modality for the Other. In imagining themselves as rulers, the colonized, however, still learn to look down on themselves. As the dominated, at least in their imagination, they come to despise themselves as would-be rulers. This is the internal fear of becoming what one despises and despising what one is becoming, and yet it continues to characterize the colonized even following liberation

13. Bhabha, 'Location, Intervention, Incommensurability', 64.
14. Bhabha, *The Location of Culture*.

from the empire. This concept may be applied to many of the prophets whose judgment, directed toward their imperial rulers and elitist holders of privilege, leads them to depict the coming destruction of the empires and the rise of a liberated Israel/Judah that will rule over the nations through the powerful acts of its God in history.

Hybridity

Bhabha rejects the simplistic polarizations of the world into distinct cultures and humans into self and others, speaking, instead, of hybridity. Cultures are mixtures and not discrete entities, while the self and the other are not disjoined but rather interrelated. For him, no culture, regardless of the degree of its uniformity, remains static but rather exists in a dynamic temporal and spatial sphere of constant reformulation as changes materialize, requiring adaptation of thinking and activity that become newly institutionalized. The causes of transformation are numerous, ranging from military conquest, to natural catastrophes, to economic developments, to migration, and to new or more intensive engagements with other civilizations. The symbiosis of new events and discourse leads to unavoidable cultural adaptations expressed through evolving tradition. One sees hybridity throughout the changing culture of Israel/Judah as it moves from a classless society, at least when it comes to males of the nation, in the pre-monarchic times to a class system of rulers, nobles, peasants, day laborers, and slaves, and finally to an exclusive community, at least in the views of the radical reactionaries like Ezra and Nehemiah, that discourages enculturation,[15] and excludes, among other things, the acceptance of and especially marriage with non-Jews.

In the formation of their imperial metanarratives, colonizing powers have attempted to forge polarized distinctions in cultures and ethnicities in order to justify the inequalities emerging from sovereignty. The goal of the imperialists has been to colonize the minds of the conquered by articulating and cultivating an ideology of the metropolitan core's cultural and ethnic superiority that would lead to the submission and control of marginalized colonials as alien inhabitants of the empire,

---

15. Enculturation is a social process by which group members are taught the norms, values, and customs of a changing culture so that they are able to function as full-fledged participants. Parental and educational instructions and cultural processes enable this to occur. Enculturation is an ongoing process brought about by such diverse happenings as conquestion, natural catastrophes, economic changes, migration to new territories, immigration, and encountering new civilizations. This leads to cultural adaptations and hybrids.

bearers of an inferior culture.[16] Domination depends on the perception of difference. For Bhabha, however, colonial discourse only seems successful in the domination of the colonized and the stranger. Beneath the claimed exceptional qualities of the colonizers and their cultural meanings resides anxiety about their aims, claims, and achievements. This emerges from the developing recognition of the sameness of the colonized population in regard to embedding imperial values, language, and culture and to their status as human beings. This equivalence opens up a gap between what is espoused and what is real, which the colonized can use to their advantage in resistance to the empire.

Hybridity, Bhabha argues, subverts the narratives of colonial power and dominant cultures. The series of inclusions and exclusions on which a dominant culture is premised is deconstructed by the very entry of the formerly excluded subjects, different cultures, and the reformulation of the dominant metanarrative into mainstream discourse and behavior. The dominant culture likes to think it is contaminated by the linguistic and racial differences of the native self and thus must guard itself from this threat of the Other by imposing barriers of resistance. These include racial profiling, cultural stereotypes, and xenophobic-inspired repudiation of what is different through cultural standards and legal norms. The colonized, by contrast, engage in mimicry (discussed more fully below), which has as its primary goal the establishment of their counter narrative that works to deconstruct the grand narrative of the empire through seeming to imitate, but in reality rejecting, the imperial culture through mockery and derision craftily shaped to avoid the empire's wrath. This counter narrative is present, for example, in postexilic psalms that praise YHWH as the true God of creation and salvation history in contradistinction to the empires god/s, and in the prophetic use of past traditions to reshape a new order that assumes the form of the coming Kingdom of God.

Bhabha contends that all cultures are constructed in the 'third space of enunciation',[17] which makes the construct of meaning and reference ambivalent. By this expression he means to challenge any sense of the historical identity of culture as a homogenizing, unifying force, authenticated by a mythical past residing in the national traditions of a social group considered to be changeless. In hybridization the cultures of the dominant power and the conquered continue to change. While the imbalance and inequity that result from domination cannot be ignored, the hybridity occasioned by the colonized challenges and resists a

---

16. Thiong'o, *Decolonising the Mind*.

17. Bhabha, *The Location of Culture*, 37.

controlling, imperial culture by depriving it of self-proclaimed superior-ity, legitimated dominance, and indisputable authority. Resistance does not take only the form of violence, but also includes a doubling process in which the similarities between the ruler and the ruled fabricate doubts about the authoritative rule and the self-proclaimed, superior culture of the conqueror.

Mimicry

The third of Bhabha's formative theories focuses on the colonized's adopting, adapting, and altering of the culture of the colonizer. While cultural representations were central to legitimating the domination of other lands by an empire, a similar process led to the opposition to the dominating power and the subsequent obtaining of independence from the metropolitan center. According to Bhabha, the colonized do not simply imitate the changing culture of the conquering power, since both the colonizer and colonized become interdependent and reflect the mutual and interrelated construction of their identities. For exam-ple, indigenous people are taught to speak the English language and to act out the views of British imperial rule, but they do not look English, speak properly the King's English, and find themselves as accepted as equals to the imperialists. The colonial culture inevitably assumes in different ways the culture of the imperialists that is presented to them, including especially the language of the colonizer. The loss of indige-nous languages only leads to a buttressing of the efforts to colonize the colonials by separating them from the native speech that defines their identities and gives a rich expression to their cultures and values. Hence, a form of resistance to the empire and its language is *Pidgin English* in which the pure form of the imperial language is distorted and its values rejected. Recapturing the indigenous languages and its symbols and the creating of a mixed imperial language become the means not only of resistance but also of transformation and subversion of the ruling culture in the locations of the colonized. Mimicry demonstrates the fragmented history of the colony and the demand for its own recognition of a rich culture and varied forms of expression.

Thus, mimicry is not simply servile imitation of the empire's culture and customs, but rather an exaggerated imitation of their language, manners, and ideas. Indeed the colonials wear the clothes, use the lan-guage, and perform the courtesies of their masters, but in ways that ultimately taunt the masters. The colonials may be unaware of this parody, although the effect is the same whether it is consciously known or a hidden issue of the subconscious. The colonized overstatement mocks the pretensions of colonialism and empire and becomes a form of resistance to colonial discourse. While the colonizer still wishes to affirm its so-called cultural superiority in order to signify and legitimate its domination, it is finally the colonials who determine the degree of that difference. This is done in a number of ways, including the imitation of the metanarrative of the empire, but restated with a decided twist to deconstruct its arguments for unchallenged superiority. Imitation takes on its own identity and disassembles the myth of the superiority of the colonizer. Further, the requirement of the colonizer to have indigenous intermediaries (mimic men) to influence the cultural dimensions of foreign rule, including such things as language and government, demonstrates similarity, not superiority. These intermediaries are in the unique position of finding themselves able to support or deconstruct the empire's cultural metanarratives. An important goal of the postcolonial, then, is to be a 'vernacular cosmopolitan' who is able to translate cultures and reinterpret traditions in ways that subvert the empire.[18]

One sees this subversion in numerous biblical texts composed during different imperial reigns. Thus, while Aramaic especially in the Neo-Babylonian and Persian Empires becomes increasingly the language of the Jewish population in Judah and in the Eastern diaspora, their composers and spokespersons continue to write and even on occasion speak in Hebrew and express a more colloquial form of royal Aramaic used in edicts and communiqués of the empire. Even the Jewish form of Aramaic is influenced by Hebrew. In addition, the exaggerated imitation of royal traditions of the Neo-Babylonian and Persian Empires in prophetic, apocalyptic, and liturgical texts subverts their metanarratives and visions of superiority.

VI.
Can the Subaltern Speak?[19]

Gayatri Spivak has been described as a Marxist and deconstructionist engaged in critiques of feminism, political theory, and postmodernism. She identifies herself as one who lives between postcolonial Indian

18. Bhabha, 'The Vernacular Cosmopolitan'.

19. Spivak, 'Can the Subaltern Speak?' (1988). Also see the following volumes she has composed and/or edited. *In Other Worlds: Essays in Cultural Politics*, edited with Ranajit Guha; *Selected Subaltern Studies*, edited with Sarah Harasym, 1988; *The Post-colonial Critic*, 1990; *A Critique of Postcolonial Reason*, 1999; *Death of a Discipline*, 2003. For a clearly written summary and evaluation of Spivak, see Moore-Gilbert, *Postcolonial Theory*, 74-113.

socialism and the Western teachings dominated by a colonial education. Among her prevalent subjects are British hierarchy, patriarchy, capitalism, British colonialism, and their continuing effect in the Global South.

Her reading and critique of Jacques Derrida have resulted in her use of postmodernism and deconstruction to dismantle Western ideology and imperial metanarratives.[20] She has shown that in spite of Western democracies' emphasis on liberalism and freedom, they have used imperial means to conquer, rule, oppress, and exploit the Global South both during the colonial and postcolonial periods. Critical of Derrida's apolitical relativism, she reshaped deconstruction into a political weapon and has used it to disassemble the ideology of the colonialism of empires and its rebirth economically in neocolonialism. She asserts that postmodernism cannot ethically ignore the political realities of human existence, but must open itself to the experiences of people, in particular subalterns or marginalized, by using the mode of discourse. Biblical scholars are learning from her that their work cannot avoid active and progressive efforts to negate the ideological and self-interested ambitions of the Global North. If scholars of Scripture are to engage in postmodernist interpretation, they are ethically required to deconstruct hierarchies based on patriarchy, classism, and imperial domination.

Subalterns, who comprise the oppressed and disempowered in both imperial and nationalist political systems, are to resist and attempt to overthrow systems of oppression. Her key admonition is that people, including in our case biblical scholars, must allow subalterns to speak with their own voice to break through the code of silence established by oppressors and be heard by the hierarchies of class, power, gender, economics, and knowledge if dialogue and transformation of the oppressive world of modernity are to take shape.

Spivak also recognizes the importance of the diversity of cultures in which subalterns carry on their lives. The geographical space of different indigenous peoples is intimately linked to their distinct experiences. This cannot be ignored in understanding a marginalized people either in the past or present. However, she is skeptical that scholars can rediscover the voices that imperialism has silenced, since they are lost forever to human memory. Even if imagined by writers in the past or present, these voices are only the fictional expression of an individual writer. What this means for historiography is the fact that biblical texts, which speak of even the heroes of Israel, are produced by human imagination. The biblical voices of the marginalized are fictional and written by intellectuals who rarely

20. Derrida, *Of Grammatology*. Spivak's translation of Derrida's classic was published in 1976.

can capture the thoughts, values, and views of the marginalized. This does not mean she denies history can be written, but it does imply that much in the biblical recreation of human beings in the past is historically irretrievable. Without subaltern discourse, which is rare in Israelite and Judean texts, great care has to be taken by historians who are attempting to reconstruct their lives, ideas, and beliefs. One perhaps may speak of possibilities, but these derive only from outsiders in the ancient world who were intellectuals and scholars in the present who cannot escape their own geographical space and culture.

She also adds her voice to the topic of epistemic violence that critiques the imperialist project of creating a metanarrative that legitimates the rule of an empire and forces upon the vanquished its world view, civilization, and claimed epistemological and racial superiority.[21] She notes that imperial metanarratives not only legitimate corporal violence but also epistemic savagery. Thus the imperialists invent the world for both themselves and those they rule. The colonized are forced through discourse and other means to see themselves as marginals in this imperialist world ruled by the metropolitan government and its citizens. Thus through their normative metanarrative, the imperialists create not only their own identity and role, but also those of the marginals in their sociopolitical cultural contexts. In addition the imperialists wrongly present themselves as the representatives of the colonized. To counter the imperialists and their metanarratives, Spivak admonishes the West not to read the rest of the world through Western eyes. Instead, Third World texts should be accepted as depicting proper representations of subalterns in different cultures, even if they are fictional persons.[22] Speaking to the nature and character of the depictions of women, Spivak criticizes those that reduce females to a one-dimensional character, thus negating individuality and difference. In discussing Third World women, Spivak argues that scholars are to disassemble the structures of epistemic violence of patriarchal imperialism that present a caricature of women, especially in the non-Western world.[23] Her insights entail the recognition that the depictions of Israelite and Jewish women by Western feminist biblical scholars should not be given the status of historical reconstructions, but are more the creation of modern scholars' own issues, interests, and cultures.

21. Spivak, 'Three Women's Texts'.
22. See Devi, *Imaginary Maps*.
23. Spivak, 'The Rani of Samir'.

VII.
Postcolonial Historiography

A clear summary of the interests and objectives of postcolonialism has been offered by R. S. Sugirtharajah. He has defined postcolonial interpretation of literature as

> signifying a reactive resistance discourse of the colonized who critically interrogate dominant knowledge systems in order to recover the past from Western slander and misinformation of the colonial period, and who also continue to interrogate neo colonializing tendencies after the declaration of independence.[24]

Postcolonialism is not a theory or method, but more a combination of shared attitudes inclusive of all peoples seeking to achieve new possibilities for a common public life. There are several views most postcolonial interpreters express in their writing, reading, and interpretations of texts. This will be true of the present effort to produce a postcolonial history of Israel.

First, postcolonialists seek to deconstruct the grand narratives of the colonizing and neocolonizing Western empires. In denying sole legitimacy to Western views and values in order to gain liberation from their dominant political, social, and cultural affirmations, postcolonialists understand that all social groups that are dominant have paradigms of meaning that are ideological. In an imperial culture, ideology is used to dominate the marginalized not only by socio-political and military means, but it also seeks to have them internalize these overarching metanarratives as the social construction of reality that is presented as universal and objectively true. Thus, education in the environment is part of the imperial agenda. Postcolonial writers argue for the value of their own cultural heritage and seek to resist efforts to present and define the conquered as cultural and intellectual inferiors. Scholars of the West, taught Graeco-Roman readings of ancient history, write history according to Greek models. Thus in the histories of Herodotus, Thucydides, Xenophon, Timaeus, Polybius, Livy, Tacitus, and Plutarch one discovers a common contention of superiority of their Western civilization and the inferiority of Eastern and African cultures. These classical histories came to support the features of the grand narratives of empires, as well as their epistemology, values, political institutions, and religion. This same type of metanarrative construction has often colored the histories of Israel,

24. Sugirtharajah, *Postcolonial Criticism and Biblical Interpretation*, 13.

especially when Christian interpreters exalt the virtues and religious teachings of Israel, Judah, and Judaism and demean those of other non-Western nations.

Postcolonialists reject the prejudices of those who engaged in empire building based on the imperial justification of possessing a superior civilization. They also construct their own interpretative narratives of their nation's or region's history and culture that lack Western biases. Too often Western historians and interpreters overlook the hidden transcripts of meaning composed by the historical and contemporary marginalized who seek to negate the grand narratives of their conquerors and exploiters.[25] Postcolonialists point to the connection between Western socio-economic and political power and the detrimental exploitation of the colonized for imperial self-interests.

When interpreting the cultural and socio-political history of their nations and regions, postcolonial writers view the world though the lens of their own culture and remembered traditions and history. History and culture are no longer seen only through the eyes of imperialists. Thus, there is a dialogically derived set of meanings that involves not simply the empires and colonies of the past, but also the First World and Third Worlds (or Global North and Global South) with an eye towards the liberation of the latter. Even those who share the cultural and political margins are themselves often agonistic in their histories and other types of cultural writings. Even so, the goal of postcolonial writing and reading of texts leads to inculturation (i.e. the traditions of the oppressed are included in a more expansive metanarrative) and liberation (or contextual philosophy) that become components of a new and different world view.

Second, postcolonialists often realize that multiple interpretations of culture, civilization, and history exist, not only in the global community of cultures, past and present, but also in their own nations and regions.

25. The expression 'hidden transcripts' was popularized by James Scott, especially in *Domination*. Scott uses the term 'public transcript' to describe the open, public interactions between rulers and the subjugated and the term 'hidden transcript' for the critique of power that goes on offstage, which power holders do not see or hear. Different systems of domination, containing various social, economic, and political elements, have covert aspects that are not expressed in their public dimensions. Scott emphasized the importance of what lay underneath the public discourse and actions. Publicly, the dominated appear to accept their inferior positions, but in a variety of more secretive ways, they question the rulers and their systems of hegemony. If this hidden discourse becomes public, there may be the resultant psychological feeling of liberation by the oppressed, but they may well face the wrath of the empire and the disaster this could rain down upon them. Also see the discussion of Scott in the Introduction to this volume.

Diversity is not limited to different nations or widely separate geographical spaces, but it is also present within the nation and its indigenous culture in geographical space. A multiplicity of interpretations is present, but they originate among indigenous writers whose own views are different from former conquerors. Thus, postcolonialists stress readings that are both dialogical and pluralistic in the construal of meanings. Dialogue should occur not only between colonizer and colonized, colonialist and post-colonialist, rich and poor, powerful and impotent, those in the center and those on the margins, but also between different genders, races, and ethnicities.

As a biblical scholar, Sugirtharajah has criticized biblical scholarship in the West for shaping an interpretative tradition that reflects the values of these nations and for failing to listen to scholars from among the geographical margins. Their voices, whether through narrative fiction or poetry, should be heard. In addition to this, there has often been little ethical criticism of the ravages of imperialism practiced by the kings of Israel and Judah as depicted in narratives and especially the poetry of the prophets. This means that a critical hermeneutic often does not emerge from biblical scholars that challenges and even undercuts the oppressive elements of biblical institutions and of the later church and synagogue. Why? One reason is the hesitancy of many biblical scholars to question the exegetical and hermeneutical methods of interpretation that they have mastered. To admit their shortcomings and biases means that a critical new look at the methods of interpretation must occur that could lead to their radical transformation or even discontinuance. Another is the reluctance to admit that their own world views and results of scholarship are often supportive, not critical, of empires. And a third reason is that the hermeneutical task in Africa, Asia, and Latin America is extremely different from that pursued in the West, due to the widely dissimilar contexts of modern global cultures. Much church history and Western theology is not interested in liberating oppressed margins, and they either often fail to point to the church's own participation in imperial conquest, rule, and exploitation or do not engage in a strong criticism. Many biblical scholars are ministers whose churches profited directly and indirectly from the empires in extending their own reach into other countries in the drive for members. This often has been done without admitting the travesty of injustice that has characterized imperial rule.

These are some of the significant points of interest in a postcolonial interpretation of the Bible. Not only does this approach allow for a new historical reading of Scripture, but it also presents a different hermeneutic that permits the voices from the margins to speak, to be heard, and to challenge Western understandings. Thus, in this history postcolonialism will be used to gain insight into these two areas: the social history and world views of the cultures of the Bible and the engagement of these with the interests of marginalized peoples in later periods, including especially the contemporary world and those who speak largely from the Third World or Global South.

Postcolonial historiography did not simply appear during the period since the end of World War II and the breakup of major European empires. Rather, its approaches and insights are based on earlier types of history writing, most of which continue to have influence in scholarly interpretations of the past. A brief overview of historiography should provide us with some insight into the writing of postcolonial history in the modern period.

Historiography and the Writing of Israelite History

The writing of Israelite history is a complicated task, due in part to the lack of sufficient sources in the form of cultural data (archaeology, written sources, and epigraphic inscriptions). Historiography is the use and application of historical critical methods to uncover and then analyze oral discourse, written texts, and archaeological data (material and written) in order to reconstruct and describe the history of the development, duration, and end of human civilizations. Culture is not monolithic, for there is constant interaction and even merger with others, while change and transformation is inherent to the historical process. Past cultures engaged in and experienced events, produced distinctive ideologies, and occupied temporal and spatial locations. Historiography, in its various forms, seeks to record and then interpret distinct cultures and their social forms particularly with regard to institutions, political arrangements, religions, and ideologies by using psychological, anthropological, and philosophical theories.[26] The interpretative process involves the use of what is called historical imagination to shape the forms, events, and images of a culture in order to set forth plausible reconstructions of history.[27]

26. Schwartz, *Imperialism and Jewish Society*, 2-3. Also see Huizanga, 'A Definition of the Concept of History', Krentz, *The Historical Critical Method*, and Van Seters, *In Search of History*.

27. 'Historical Imagination' is what Collingwood calls a 'moral engagement with the past'. It suggests a dynamic interaction or better a dialogue between history and the past or the present and cultural memory that leads to the possibility of the reconstruction of the past through historical narrative (Collingwood, *The Historical Imagination*).

Historiography seeks to trace a collage of sequential events, inter-active and distinct ideologies of various, interactive cultures, and their temporal and spatial locations. Data, of course, do not interpret them-selves, and, regardless of the methodology or orientation of an historian, his/her imagination is drawn upon to shape a collage of images that, taken together, comprise the representation of the history of a past culture. Due to the limits of the data and the varieties and subtleties, which these elements may represent, the most an historian can hope to attain is plausibility, on occasion probability, but not certainty. New data, different historiographical methods, and contemporary world views lead to new and at times different reconstructions of a people's past.

Historiography involves three major concerns. The first is to discover the material and cultural data of past civilizations and to reconstruct the human thought and behavior that produced them in particular times and places. The second is to examine the ways that the various pasts of these civilizations have been reconstructed and interpreted by later historians from antiquity to the present. And the third is the informed attempt of the modern historian to interpret the peoples and events of civilizations in order to comprehend their past experiences and preeminent under-standings and events by using current theories that shape the histories of the contemporary period.

Contemporary Approaches to Historiography and Postcolonialism

Postcolonialism did not arise in a vacuum without influence from earlier approaches to historiography. Since the Enlightenment, the major philosophies used in historiography in general and historical criticism in biblical studies in particular have included a variety of alternative ways of conceiving history. To understand historical criticism and the more recent approach of postcolonialism that has taken shape in the post-imperial world since World War II, it is important to become aware of the philosophies of history which have been used by biblical scholars in shaping their interpretation of ancient Israel and early Judaism. The major philosophies of history that have led to and influenced postcolonial interpretation include idealism, romanticism, realism, positivism, Marx-ism and neo-Marxism, and now, more recently, feminism and postmod-ernism. Most historians write from a vantage point of using insights and principles drawn from a variety of philosophies of history, even though one predominates in each of their reconstructions. This includes those scholars who write from postcolonial perspectives. Postcolonial histories are especially dependent on (neo-)Marxism and postmodernism.

Marxist and Neo-Marxist Interpretation of History

Marxism, and its later reshaping, Neo-Marxism, is a philosophy of history based upon a fundamental important assumption that no object, including literature, can exist independently. Literature can only be understood in the fullness of its relations with ideology, class, and economic substructures. Truth is ideological and is created by human institutions and articulated in language (oral and written). An inherent materialism also is present in this method, leading then to the rejection of the notion of eternal ideas that transcend material labor. In the consideration of anthropology, human beings shape themselves through their work, including through the creation of art (philosophy, culture, and world views) that is a branch of production. Class struggle is the inner dynamic of history, and literature encapsulates this endeavor. Literature reflects the self-interests of the group that writes it.

Another central component of Marxist and Neo-Marxist philosophy is that exploitation has been an enduring feature of history, in which the wealthy and powerful were pitted against the poor and vulnerable. The former profited from the labor of the latter, who did not receive just compensation for their work. Instead the ruling class appropriated their wealth for their own profit and use. According to Marx and his followers, in the beginning was an idyllic time in which simplicity, equality, and communal sharing predominated. But with the advent of private property, this idyll was shattered. In ancient times class struggle took place in city-states in which owners of property were pitted against serfs and slaves. Yet in the final birth of the communist world at the end of capitalist-dominated history, the coming great revolution will overcome injustice and oppression through the abolition of private property and usher in a new age in which there would be fair distribution of the rewards of human labor.

Following the end of World War II and the death of Stalin in 1953, Marxism was freed from the domination of the state. This allowed reformers to shape new developments and specific schools of thought that collectively are identified as neo-Marxism. The Frankfurt school, consisting of such scholars as Max Horkheimer, Theodor Adorno, Herbert Marcuse, and Jürgen Habermas, was one such new development that held to individualism, the ideals of democracy, the integration of the proletariat into the main stream of social life, and spontaneity, all the while rejecting an unbending view of a rigid, historical determinism. These scholars, while varied in many of their views, were united in their opposition to the essential views of positivism and materialism and made use of Kant's critical philosophy and its development. Social change was configured in the mode of German Idealism (e.g. Hegel), with ideas playing a dominant role. For the Frankfurt school, cultural Marxism analyzes the roles of the media, art, theater, film, and other artistic institutions in a society, often with an added emphasis on race and gender in addition to class.[28] Among postcolonial scholars are neo-Marxists who are strongly opposed to capitalism and its inevitable exploitation of labor.[29] Marxism and what were considered to be improvements over its limitations provided, for them, a different way to read history and to understand the present. History was no longer the sole property of imperial states whose scholars vaunted their achievements and civilizations. Several prominent biblical scholars have made use of neo-Marxism in writing social-scientific studies of the Bible, including Norman K. Gottwald and Roland Boer.[30] Their work strongly criticizes the empires and their metanarratives as biased, self-serving, and reductionistic in that the marginalized in the metropoles and among the conquered are either erased from history or belittled as uncivilized people who require the culture and values of the empires to become fully human.

Postmodernism

The emergence of postmodernism at approximately the same time as postcolonialism, i.e. the period following the end of World War II, is not simply a coincidence. In noting this connection, Robert Young views postcolonialism as Europe's explanation that it is no longer the center of the world.[31] The growing interest of postcolonialism in the United States has the same objective. Subsequently, due to this removal of the West from the center of meaning and culture, many postcolonialists have embraced various facets of postmodernism in their resistance to the grand narratives of former empires and in the construction of their

28.   Held, *Introduction to Critical Theory*.

29.   For example, see the writings of Frantz Fanon, including his *Black Skin, White Masks*.

30.   Boer, *Marxist Criticism of the Bible*.

31.   Young, *Postcolonialism*. Also see Young, *White Mythologies*, and Jameson, *Postmodernism*. A Marxist critic of postmodernism, Jameson notes that the features of late capitalism include mass culture, mass media, multinational corporations, and information technology as well as massive global debt, huge structural divides between social and global communities, the neo-liberal view of Wall Street that leads to the lust for economic and therefore socio-political power, and the death of traditional cultures that have shaped identities. Postmodernism should not be identified simply with postcolonialism, but also with neocolonialism. Jameson concludes that political postmodernism, if it should exist, will necessarily have to invent and project a global cognitive mapping on a social and spatial scale.

own theories and strategies for the determination of meanings. Since postcolonialism embraces postmodernism's primary argument that there is no single meaning or reality or objective free interpretation, but rather there are multitudes of meanings or realities, usually based on the self-interests of texts and interpreters,[32] interpretation becomes the function and outlook of a particular perspective, something that is both historically and culturally located and yet in constant flux. This does not mean that interpretation or reality is solipsistic, thus denying the concrete existence of data (temporal, physical, active, and spatial), but rather that meaning is construed in large measure by the imagination of the historiographers or other types of interpreters working within their own social locations and out of their own ideological framework.

Postcolonialism

To this point, most Western historiography has evolved within a paradigm that is produced by and resonates with the very ideology that has shaped Western European and Northern American social and humanitarian research since the Enlightenment. The hegemony of this ideology has not diminished in its powerful expression made possible by the economic wealth and paradigms of knowledge of the Western academy and its publishing houses, both secular and religious. Western historiography is largely grounded philosophically in positivism and is written by historians who dwell within and are shaped by the cultural and social forces of the Global North in which they live and work. This cultural bias is one of the greatest weaknesses of Western historiography in that it projects an assumed cultural superiority over nations and cultures of the East and the Global South. Furthermore, the influence of classical Greek and the Roman Empires on the education and world views of the West only adds to this stance of cultural eminence.

In opposing features of Western historiography, in particular Orientalism, postcolonialism is designed not only to indicate how colonies resisted the empires that ruled them, but also to demonstrate how its insights may be used to oppose the continued imperial domination of non-Western nations, not only through the economic and military policies and activities of the elite nations and the urban metropoles, but also by means of undercutting what the West considers to be the canons of normative knowledge. Postcolonial interpretation not only resists the cultural domination of the West, but also provides new insights into ways that allow oppressed peoples to inhabit a diversity of global and

---

32. Segovia, 'In the World but Not of It', 198.

cultural spaces and to produce their own metanarratives of meaning. Indeed, postcolonialism may be used to assist in the creation of a new global order based on values different from those currently in operation in neoliberal, capitalist ideology.

VIII.
The Imperial Metanarrative

The dominant imperial narrative that may be expressed in a variety of forms from instruction in the schools to the governmental rule of colonies to hymns and celebrations contains an ideology that is hierarchical, consisting of masters who dominate and rule the conquered and exploit their countries natural resources. By these means, empires attempt to control the diverse reality over which they rule. The desire is to inculcate among the colonials values conducive to the interests of the metropole and the importance of mimicking their civilization. Creators of metanarratives imagine and generate a national mythology that speaks of their origins, superior civilization, and accomplishments.

From their internal desire for identity that leads them to seek and accomplish integration into social groups and even nations, humans acquire a sense of commonality and belonging. Once conquered, human communities are usually forced to redirect their identity to come into conformity with the values and other elements of civilization of the empire. Imperial grand narratives celebrate and re-awaken the memory of the members of both the empire and the peoples conquered. These narratives point to the shared awareness of a conquering people to take delight in the power of being chosen by fate, a divine pantheon, or in the West the Christian God, in order to civilize and rule the world. The celebrations of formative events and achievements establish the bonds of the people in the metropole of belonging to land, home, and community.[33]

Religion assisted in the empire's quest to shape a common culture and system of control for the peoples ruled by legitimating violence, the hierarchy, and its so-called divinely chosen rulers. In addition, religion also authenticates the sources of social power that were put into effect either by willing conversion or by coercion to the imperial deity or

---

33. McLeod, *Beginning Postcolonialism*, 68-75.

deities and the acknowledgment of their divine status. Religious propaganda in the empire teaches that human challenges could be successfully met by the aid of transcendent power and sacred authority, an assumption that could be disproven only by the empire's collapse.

Paideia, or education, and the moral character of an educated person controlled by the empire is another important means for colonizing the mind. It involves two related features: the process of education that culminates in a young person eventually taking his/her place in society, and the character of the educated person. Imperialists argued that the cultivated mind, received through what the empire considered proper schooling in subjects based on imperial knowledge and values, enables a person to become virtuous and civilized. Teachers from the metropolitan centers are often employed to teach the students of the colonies in order to superintend and instruct indigenous students. These students are taught that the empire reflects the natural or mythic order of reality and that their highest ambition should be to serve the empire. They become colonized colonials who learn to abhor their own culture.

In addition to military force and the colonization of the minds of the subjugated, empires also utilize the loyalty and services of local leaders among the colonies. These native leaders, usually hailing from the upper class, collude with the empires and are often appointed to represent imperial interests while assuming the administrative, legal, and economic responsibilities of the colonies. They implement the laws, education, and local administration imposed by the metropoles. Their task is to provide and support the imperial elite in maintaining political and social control, economic gain, and power. These intermediaries are largely former leaders who now receive their authority and positions through their selection by imperial administrations. What these local officials gain are social and political status, substantial opportunities for wealth, tax breaks, and a measure of power. Financially they may receive grants of estates and shares in the revenues generated by institutions in exchange for faithful service to the empires. Their profits come from the exploitation of their fellows.[34] Yet they were never considered to be the social, political, and racial equals of the empire's own citizens, particularly its aristocracy.

Colonies also were settled and at times even governed by citizens of the imperial metropole seeking to make their fortunes in the new territories.[35] While establishing their political and economic control on the colonial level, settlers came to regard indigenous peoples as

34. Lenski, *Power and Privilege*, 219-30.
35. Boer, *Last Stop before Antarctica*, 7-8.

subhuman, a view that, if allowed to go unchallenged, leads native colonials to adopt self-perceptions of inferiority and self-debasement. At times the intermediary class of indigenous leadership gives way to a new ruling class of previously foreign settlers.

IX.
Colonial Resistance

Resistance to colonization, and its culmination in liberation, are achieved by constructive ideology and actions of intervention.[36] These take on a variety of forms, including the affirmation of an indigenous discourse of culture as well as labor strikes and revolts to undermine the dominating rule of empires.[37] In the process of decolonization, prior to the recovery of colonial geographical space and modes of self-rule, principal beliefs and cultural resistance are sought by recovering the re-imagined history, world views, knowledge, and culture of the former colony in new and transformed configurations.[38] Through discourse, behavior, and works of the imagination, postcolonialism resists and rejects the continuation of Western hegemony, which seeks not only to dominate but also to exploit the peoples of weaker and poorer nations. This hegemony is built upon a twisted ideology of violence, both physical and psychological, that promotes as authentic only the views and understandings of the empire. Resistance involves subverting the empire's metanarrative through mimicry, i.e. imitation that mocks, derides, and misshapes imperial language, ideas, and values. In addition, the undercutting of grand narratives is undertaken through discourse to demonstrate the falsity of imperialist ideologies that seek to legitimate their civilization's pre-eminence and the incontrovertible truth of its world views.[39] This requires a new rhetoric that espouses the values and ideas of the ever-changing colony by the indigenous intelligentsia set on contravening the absurdity of imperial metanarratives. Of course, violent opposition often occurred in revolutions that included pacts with other colonies to throw off the shackles of imperial force. The goal of postcolonialism is for nations, formerly subjected, to gain their own self-identity and means of rule by casting off the oppressive domination of the empire.

36. Young, *Postcolonialism*, 57.
37. Thiong'o, *Moving the Centre*.
38. Said, *Culture and Imperialism*, 209-20.
39. Lyotard's rejection of metanarratives is set forth in his volume *The Postmodern Condition*.

X.
The Diaspora

Postcolonialism also examines displaced populations which continue the native traditions of the past but also forge new memory and history among the displaced, while not dispensing with the degrees of diversity inherent to their cultures. Postcolonialism unveils the probable reasons for a displaced ethnic community's uprootedness, examines how its literature responds to a new and strange geographical and cultural space, and points to various ideological and cultural adaptations of people who have been transplanted to live in an alien environment. The interpretative goal is to identify the cultural and ethnic bonds of solidarity that enable them to exist as an identifiable population in communities in new locations.

Postcolonialism also studies and seeks to describe the displaced people's culture and their reinterpretation of formative traditions within new contexts. These postcolonial 'translated writings', as Salman Rushdie describes them, arise from displaced communities, tend to be anti-authoritarian, and even set forth a multicultural presentation of egalitarianism that negates the provincialism of metropolitan communities and their cultural ideology.[40] Becoming marginals in their new dwellings, displaced peoples settle into communities of their own ethnic identities and find themselves in the interstices of the larger culture of the location in which they now dwell. While earlier generations may long for existence in the former homelands, this desire gradually fades as adaptations are made by subsequent generations. Instead of seeing the margins as areas of bondage, postcolonial scholars regard exiles in new communities in the metropole as important creators of new understandings arising from their resistance to the forces of hierarchy, uniformity, and hegemony in different geographical spaces. To function in the new world they learn the culture and the nature of those who dominate the larger space, but without completely dispensing with their past traditions. They form a hybridity of traditions and ways of existence in their new locations.

40. Rushdie, *Imaginary Homelands*, 9-21. He asserts that everyone is a migrant from a past that is lost, a time of experiences which one wishes to reclaim, but cannot due to an imperfect memory and relocation. Also see Gilroy, 'Diaspora'.

People who have migrated to other lands by choice or by force live border lives in their new contexts.[41] Indeed, as Rushdie asserts, the immigrant is perhaps 'the defining figure of the twentieth', and now the early twenty-first, centuries.[42] This was also true, however, of ancient civilizations, including the culture and religion of Judaism. Rushdie contends that all of us are migrants who become immigrants, from our past to the present, from our homes to new locations, from a culture that is known and comfortable to one that is new, unknown, and often disconcerting. Transitory groups of migrants find themselves separated by time (past and present), location (the former land of dwelling and present space in the metropole), and culture (majority and minority). In the early generation, the longing for the past leads to the continuation of the former language, literature, religion, and ritual that provided cultural identity in the homeland, even though these begin to be reshaped by the new features of the present location. Border crossings to new locations lead to writings and other cultural forms that may be highly imaginative, adaptive cases of hybridity. These crossings interrupt traditional understandings of knowledge, community, and culture, for they require blending and contrasting the past with the present. These migrations are liminal in that location, culture, and experience are betwixt and between. They are not binary separations of people into classes of slaves and masters or outsider and insider, but rather are hybrids in which the mingling together of populations with their differences reshapes both those who cross the border into a different reality and the metropole's earlier inhabitants. The traditions of the past are not abandoned by migrants, but rather are interwoven with new understandings within a different culture to which they must adapt. Those who cross the threshold and enter the diaspora begin to form for themselves a new identity in which they are part of a strange and different culture and geographical space. People of the diaspora are required to reshape and reinterpret the world into which they enter, thereby shaping a new cultural hybridity that adapts older traditions to new circumstances and may threaten to disturb and change conventional understandings of the existing culture in which they enter. In addition the culture they enter often experiences hybridity. All of this does not mean that conflicted differences and understandings of the formative elements of their changing identities do not exist among diaspora. The diaspora community, however, experiences ideological, ethnic, and often geographical isolation from the majority population and its culture.

41. Bhabha, *The Location of Culture*.
42. Rushdie, *Imaginary Homelands*, 177.

* * *

This chapter has sought to raise the central methodological issues in postcolonial criticism by summarizing key scholars and noting the interconnections to history, historiography, and postmodernism. With this theoretical framework in place, we now turn to consider the conquest of Israel and the colonization of Judah by the Assyrian Empire.

2

The Assyrian Empire,
the Conquest of Israel,
and the Colonization of Judah

I.
Historical Introduction[1]

When the installation of a new monarch in the temple of Ashur occurs during the Akitu festival, the Sangu priest of the high god proclaims when the human ruler enters the temple: 'Ashur is King! Ashur is King!' The ruler now is invested with the responsibilities of the sovereignty, power, and oversight of the Assyrian Empire. The Assyrian Empire has been described as 'a heterogeneous multi-national power directed by a superhuman, autocratic king, who was conceived of as the representative of God on earth'.[2] As early as Naram-Sin of Assyria (ca. 1872–1845 BCE), two important royal titulars continued and were part of the larger titulary of Assyrian rulers: 'King of the Four Quarters' and 'King of All Things'.[3]

Assyria began its military advances west to the Euphrates in the ninth century BCE. In the ninth and eighth centuries BCE, Syria and Israel were brought to heel and the Assyrian troops continued their march beyond the Tigris and Euphrates rivers. Tiglath-pileser III (745–727 BCE), likely a usurper, was one of the greatest of the military

---

1. Larsen, 'The Tradition of Empire in Mesopotamia'. Also see his definition of empire: 'a supernational system of political control, and such a system may have either a city-state or a territorial state as its center'. Empires in Mesopotamia engaged in a series of typical imperial efforts: (1) a methodical and permanent occupation of conquered territory, (2) the implantation of military garrisons, and (3) a division of the territory into provinces.

2. Parpola, *Assyrian Prophecies*, xxi. See also p. lxxxii n. 25: 'This analogy is not accidental, for the empire was conceived of as the counterpart (*tamšilu*) of the divine world, referred to as the "kingdom of heaven" in oracle 2.5'.

3. Seux, *Épithetes royales akkadiennes et sumériennes*.

conquerors. He seized the Assyrian throne during a civil war, having killed the royal family. To secure his power against internal and external sedition, he downsized the provinces and appointed loyal governors to gain provincial support. He turned southward to defeat its most powerful cities: Aram, Tyre, Biblos, Samaria, and Hamath.

While revolts and other forms of resistance occurred, they were crushed, including Israel in the Syro-Ephraimitic War (736 BCE–732 BCE). This war, in which Pekah the king of Northern Israel participated, included an anti-Assyrian coalition of states: Kashpuna, Tyre, Ashkelon, and Damascus. Joash of Judah, along with the Transjordan states of Moab and Ammon, rejected the overtures from the rebel states to join in the revolution, a wise decision since Tiglath-pileser III responded with a crushing invasion. The armies of Rezin of Damascus and Pekah of Israel invaded Judah in an attempt to force Judah to join the coalition (735 BCE). Philistines and Edomites began to make incursions into Judah, seeing it as an opportune time to expand their territories and take their wealth. To save his hide and prevent the destruction of much of his nation, Ahaz, in spite of Isaiah's opposition, called on the Assyrians for help. Tiglath-pileser III was only too happy to take advantage of the situation, defeated the coalition, and wreaked havoc with Edom and Philistia. Though Judah was forced to provide the Assyrian court with tribute, it was able to survive the Assyrian destruction of Israel to the north in 722 BCE. In 733 BCE, Tiglath-pileser III wreaked havoc in Israel and forced it to surrender large amounts of its territory. In 732, he advanced against Damascus, first ruining the gardens outside the city and then conquering the capital and killing its king. In his invasion of the Northern kingdom in 733 BCE, Tiglath-pileser III left behind him numerous destroyed towns and cities and took some of the Israelite population into exile. Judah also fell under the foot of Assyrian military might.

The Babylonians proved to be the most serious nemesis to Tiglath-pileser III. Prior to his reign they enjoyed a relative amount of independence, since they paid to their overlords an annual tribute and offered no resistance. On one occasion, the vast Assyrian military rescued from revolt a loyal Babylonian ruler, Nabu-nasir; however, a Babylonian ruler named Mukin-zer rebelled. His forces were quickly dispatched. But the fires of resistance and even revolt would continue to flare.

Shalmaneser V succeeded Tiglath-pileser III as king in 726 BCE, although he accomplished little of note according to the Akkadian sources. The Babylonian Chronicle mentions as significant only his sacking of Samaria (cf. 2 Kgs 17:1-41; 18:1-12). When he was killed during an internal Assyrian power struggle, a new ruler and usurper, Sargon II, came to the throne (721 BCE). The other Assyrian rulers who figure prominently in the history of Israel and Judah included Sennacherib (704–681 BCE), Esarhaddon (680–669 BCE), and Ashurbanipal (668/9–631 BCE).

In the internal struggles for power in Assyria developing at the time of succession from Shalmaneser V to Sargon II, states within the empire began to form alliances in Aprad, Syria, and Samaria to revolt against the empire. Each of these would eventually fail. Sargon II first defeated Syria and then subdued the rebel armies at Qarqar in 720 BCE. Gaza, on the Philistine coast, was defeated as was an Egyptian force on the borders of the kingdom of the Nile. The cities of the Philistine league on the coast of Southern Israel were also brought into submission. This Assyrian monarch then engaged in a substantial deportation of leaders of the rebellion, moving upper-level officials to be administrators and skilled workers to other locations within the empire.

In 704 BCE, Hezekiah of Judah, who reigned ca. 715–686 BCE, foolishly chose to rebel against the Assyrians, with the promise of Egyptian and Ethiopian military assistance. After defeating these armies in Israel, Sennacherib unleashed a brutal retaliation upon many cities and villages of Judah and then laid a threatening siege of Jerusalem in 701 BCE, which ended abruptly for unknown reasons. According to 2 Kings 18:13–19:36, the end of the siege is attributed to an angel of YHWH, who slaughtered 185,000 of the Assyrian forces. Other possibilities include a plague of mice or an internal revolt at home that required Sennacherib to withdraw his forces and return to Assyria. While the victory stela, Sennacherib's prism, proclaimed his conquest of forty-six walled cities and the town of Jerusalem and boasted that Hezekiah was 'locked up like a bird in a cage' in his stronghold in Jerusalem, he did not actually take the city.[4] In addition, Merodach-Baladan of Babylonia was finally defeated in 689 BCE, and the Assyrians rested for a time from their conflict with Babylonia.

Sennacherib appears to have been assassinated by one of his sons, Esarhaddon, who took the throne. He eventually defeated the Egyptian forces in 671 BCE and conquered the capital, Memphis. In his attempt to bring a continuously contentious Egypt completely to its knees, he died while leading his forces to confront the Egyptians. With the exception of Sidon and Tyre, the lands of Coele-Palestine were largely passive in not resisting Assyrian domination. While Sidon was eventually forced into submission, Tyre's location enabled the city to continue to be independent of Assyrian control. Esarhaddon unwisely designated two of his

---

4. This is found in the Neo-Assyrian monumental inscriptions (*COS* 2:303).

sons as his successors; Ashurbanipal was to gain the throne in Assyria, while his brother, Shamash-Shuma-Ukin, was given the position of king over Babylonia. This eventually led to an internal struggle and civil war.

Prior to the fall of the empire, the last significant, and most capable king was Ashurbanipal. Military struggles with Egypt finally led to expelling the Assyrians from Egypt, and this nation ceased being the object of Assyrian invasion. His contest with his brother, Shamash-Shuma-Ukin, led to an intense civil war, with Babylonia's temporary defeat in 648 BCE. These struggles began to lay the foundation for unrest throughout the empire, leading to its eventual demise.

The final rulers of Assyria were largely unimpressive: Ashur-etil-ilani (631–627 BCE), Sin-shumu-lisher (626 BCE), and Sin-shar-ishkun (627–612 BCE). The combined forces of Babylonia and the Medes led to the sacking of Asshur in 614 BCE, with the capital of Assyria, Nineveh, falling in 612 BCE. While the Assyrians attempted to regroup in Harran, this effort was brought to an end by Babylonian and Median forces in 609 BCE.

II.
The Metanarrative
of the Assyrian Empire[5]

The Assyrian Empire sought to legitimize its rule in various ways: the divine commission to expand the imperial boundaries in order to establish order in the cosmos, the emphasis placed on the superiority of Assyrian culture, and the xenophobic views expressed toward non-Assyrians. The titulary of two Assyrian kings, both of whom bore the name of Sargon, imitated the Sargonic titular. It expressed conscious Assyrian emulation of the empire of the 'Great King', Sargon of Akkad (2334–2154 BCE), who was remembered in Mesopotamian tradition as having conquered and ruled over the city-states of Sumer and then expanded his empire to include other regions of Mesopotamia, parts of Persia and Syria, and even some regions in Anatolia and Arabia. He became the paradigm of the great ruler of an empire well into the period of the Achaemenids.[6]

---

5. Holloway articulates a well-known point: 'All empires construct flattering portraits of themselves through officially sanctioned media and political theater aimed primarily at their own elites, secondarily directed towards the sea of subject kingdoms and population groups' (Holloway, *Aššur Is King!*, xvii).

6. Westenholz, 'The Old Akkadian Empire in Contemporary Opinion'.

Assyria's imperial metanarrative is found in numerous texts, monuments, and inscriptions and in artistic representations. Some of these were public while others were not accessible to the general population. Many of these were created to serve the ideology of the empire. Even false projections of knowledge served propagandistic functions. These especially included the royal claims of divine knowledge that embraced wisdom, divination, the interpretation of omens, prophecies, and astrology. Visual sources include brief narratives on palace and temple reliefs, stelae, obelisks, sculptures, frieze works in glazed bricks or glass, and glyptics.

Political and military narratives contain the official history of the empire and are dependent on the official narrative texts and visual sources of individual monarchs.[7] These narratives, which were stamped with the court's approval, also included inscriptions on palace and temple walls, gates, sculptures, statues, and royal stelae. Some also included epics, such as the letter of the king to a deity, which include an articulation of the king's achievements.[8] The content of these official narratives usually portrays Assyrian victories (real or claimed), making them appear to be invincible.[9] This perception of invincibility was psychologically significant in colonizing the minds of colonials and thus was used to rule over a huge empire of client states and provincial colonies that were scattered over a huge geographical region.[10] In addition, this portrayal of Assyrian power served to sanction the invasion of other nations and empires.

7.   Liverani, 'The Ideology of the Assyrian Empire'; and Tadmor, 'History and Ideology in the Assyrian Royal Inscriptions'.

8.   Assyrian historical inscriptions are ideological and incorporate the empire's ideology. Royal scribes for obvious reasons provided the official description and interpretation of royal achievements and events. For a discussion, see Tadmor, 'Propaganda, Literature, Historiography'.

9.   See Brinkman, 'Political Covenants, Treaties, and Loyalty Oaths', 85. There were some, however, that presented losses in battle or the failure to gain success in military engagements.

10.   Thomas Richards succinctly states: 'An empire is partly a fiction. No nation can close its hand around the world; the reach of any nation's empire always exceeds its final grasp. An empire is by definition and default a nation in overreach, one nation that has gone too far, a nation that has taken over too many countries too far away from home to control them effectively. All of the great historical empires, ancient and modern, have had to come to terms with the problems of control at a distance... The narratives of the late nineteenth century are full of fantasies about an empire united not by force but by information' (Richards, *The Imperial Archive*, 1).

Assyrian Kingship[11]

The emperor was the central force of the Assyrian Empire and its
metanarrative. In royal propaganda, he is the subject of many of the
official Assyrian texts and is often depicted visually in images, monuments, bas-reliefs, glyptics, and coins.[12] His roles include his representation of the gods, in particular the high god Ashur, possession of divine
powers, awareness of divine desires and directions, service as the intermediary between the gods and the people, the shepherd of his people and
their protector, issuing decrees as the righteous judge and legislator,
having the skills and bravery of the hunter and warrior, the possessor of
great wisdom, and the one divinely chosen to establish order and peace
in the cosmos.

Assyrian religion, which evolved from Sumerian and earlier Akkadian
religion, centered on the worship of one supreme deity, Ashur, who was
the king among the divine council and the lord of the cosmos.[13] The
Assyrian king, though, was not divine, but he possessed the powers and
wisdom equivalent to those exhibited by the gods. While the gods are
depicted as wearing a distinctive crown that is found on the heads of
bulls with human heads that guard the entrances to royal palaces and
wearing tunics that do not reach the knees, these features are not found in
the portrayals of kings. The emperor did not build temples for his own
worship, and there was no imperial cult that honored his deceased fore-
bears. Instead they built and renovated temples for the Assyrian pantheon
of gods and other privileged deities. There were no prayers uttered to
ruling or deceased kings, but rather addresses were limited to such things
as petitions for various needs or desires.[14] The gods at times are presented
as standing on animal mounts, a feature lacking in royal depictions. The
king is portrayed in some representations as a worshipper of the gods, in
particular Ashur, and is often characterized as one who serves the gods.

However, there are instances in which the images of kings were placed
in Mesopotamian temples (e.g. in Ashur, Harran, and Babylon).[15] These

11.   Westenholz, 'The King, the Emperor, and the Empire'.
12.   Brinkman, 'Political Covenants, Treaties, and Loyalty Oaths', 85. Brinkman
points to features of royal propaganda found in these different genres.
13.   See especially the important volume of Holloway, *Aššur Is King!*
14.   Craig, *Assyrian and Babylonian Religious Texts*.
15.   The Balawat gates and the Nimrud liturgical setting point to visual relics of
limited divine honors commissioned and received by the kings of the Neo-Assyrian
Empire. While not gods, these kings still have divinized images that receive sacrifice
in temples and abroad (Barnett and Forman, *Assyrian Palace Reliefs*; Curtis and
Tallis, *The Balawat Gates of Ashurnasirpal II*).

images were even the recipients of sacrifices.[16] These likely serve as a votary in the temple of the gods, thus representing the king's special relation to the world of the divine, as the chosen recipient of divine favor, and his unique capacity of being the intermediator of heaven and earth.

In royal texts allegedly uttered by the emperor, the king speaks in the first person, making them an early form of pseudo-autobiography. His skills in the hunt against a lion and occasionally a bear or bull not only portray him as a mighty and fearless hunter, but also suggest his control of the forces of chaos in mythical and military forms.

Great, even divine, wisdom and the knowledge of omens were given by the gods to the rulers.[17] These gifts enabled the ruler to know the will of the gods and to bring order and well-being to the empire.[18] Sennacherib praises himself:

> But I Sennacherib, foremost among princes, expert in all craftsmanship (*mude sipri kalama*), great bronze pillars, striding lion colossi, (the like of) which no king before me had ever cast, with the ingenuity (*ina uzni nikilit*) which the noble DN has granted me, (and) taking counsel with myself (*ina situlti ramaniya*) regarding this artistic work I deliberated deeply (*rabis amtallik*): out of my own intelligence and knowledge of my mind (*ina milik temiya u meres kabattiya*), I fashioned (the objects) by casting bronze and did it with consummate skill (*unakkila niklasu*).[19]

The ruler who especially extols his own wisdom was Ashurbanipal (668–627 BCE). He states that he learned the divine wisdom (*nemequ*) of Nabû while studying in the crown prince's quarters and that he was instructed in the omens to learn the divine plans often secret to all but him. He tells of later receiving understanding and intelligence from Marduk as well as Nabû. He speaks of having learned the art of the *apkallu* (antedeluvian and early postdiluvian sages), that of Adapa, and that, being the possessor of all scribal learning, he could, among other things, read inscriptions from the time prior to the Flood as well as unfathomable texts that escape understanding. One singer of dirges, Marduk-šum-ukīn, addresses the king in a dream as 'the offspring of a

16. Dalley, 'The God Ṣalmu and the Winged Disk'.

17. Seux, *Épithètes royales akkadiennes et sumériennes*, 22.

18. Sargon calls himself 'the wisest prince in the world' (TCL 3, 115).

19. Luckenbill, *Annals of Sennacherib*, 109 vi 89-vii 8. The codification of centuries of omens occurred during the reign of the Sargonid kings. These included the celestial omen series. Like the control of information and the development of what was thought to be superior knowledge and insight, omens and other types of information were used to enhance the control of Assyrian power.

sage and Adapa'.[20] His great love for wisdom led him to construct a great library in Nineveh where he housed numerous cuneiform texts from throughout Mesopotamia.

Imperial Administrative and Provincial Rule[21]

The Neo-Assyrians were the first in the ancient Near East to establish a system for conquest and rule of the provinces that involved communications, military logistics, and an efficient administrative structure. The political rule of the empire consisted of the metropole (the land of Assyria), provinces, and client states. Its geographical reach at its height extended south to Nubia, north to the Empire of Urartu, east to Western Iran, and west to the Phrygian Empire. Client states largely enjoyed autonomy, were allowed to have indigenous rulers, and paid tribute usually through the taxation of landholders. The provinces outside the metropole were under direct Assyrian control, had Assyrian governors, and were the location for Assyrian garrisons to offer a measure of imperial presence and oversight. The land of Assyria, the center of the empire, was divided into provincial districts ruled by court-appointed governors. The court in the metropolitan center oversaw their economy and military. Perhaps beginning with Tiglath-pileser III, the autonomy of client nations ended, and a new provincial system was created that was placed under Assyrian governors supported by their garrisons. Assyrian control became more direct throughout the empire. Tiglath-pileser also replaced the political roles in powerful aristocracy with his own people. To lessen the power of local governors, the central bureaucracy oversaw the army and the administration of each province. Any hint of disloyalty led to the removal and deportation of the leadership. If rebellion continued or flared up again, the indigenous leadership was executed or exiled along with a significant number of the population, especially skilled laborers, who were deported with them to another location within the empire.[22] This provincial system of client states and conquered kingdoms could be more directly and much more easily controlled by the central administration.

20.   Adapa was one of the antediluvian *apkallus*, a king, a priest of Ea, and a man of holiness, piety, and wisdom. Ea, the god of fresh water and wisdom, endowed him with great intelligence in order to instruct humans about the ordinances of the earth and the arts of civilization.

21.   Postgate, 'Assyria: the Home Provinces'; PeCiikova, 'The Administrative Methods of Assyrian Imperialism'; and Parker, *The Mechanics of Empire*.

22.   Donner, *Israel unter den Volkern*, 1-3; and 'The Separate States of Israel and Judah', 418-21.

This new system also permitted a more efficient movement of large armies over hundreds of miles, especially because it was conducive to their free movement and to logistical support. These provinces provided conscripts, tribute, and taxes to support the ambitions of the political metropole. Nevertheless, this pattern was frequently altered by later emperors.

Assyrian Economics[23]

The economic relationship of the Assyrian metropole, particularly the court and the provinces under its control, was largely parasitic. Wealth in the forms of tribute, taxes, soldiers, workers, and different types of commodities were extracted from other nations in exchange for peace from invasion.[24] Local non-Assyrian nobles living in these nations, who were forced to cower before Assyrian power, were rewarded with status and wealth often in the form of large estates that enriched them. However, more wealth was created from the Assyrian provinces of the metropole than was received from military conquests. There is no evidence that the economic conditions of the Assyrian peasants improved, and indeed, may have deteriorated as the empire expanded.

Much of the need for Assyrian expansion by military force and mutual trade with powerful nations was due to the lack of the core's sufficient natural resources. The establishment of Assyrian garrisons guarded vital routes and protected trade so that commerce and tribute could flow easily into the metropole and the court. Yet in controlling land trade, the Assyrians faced rivals in other empires and states, as well as nomadic tribes, also seeking a piece of this economic pie. This rivalry led to a constant state of military activity necessary to protect the empire.

The use of seaports, made possible through treaties with sea-faring peoples, especially the Phoenicians, was also critical to Assyrian interests, as was the conquest of coastal seaports. This military action became another way that vital foodstuffs, building commodities, and even items of luxury for the wealthy increased. The need for resources explains to some extent why the movements into the Levant and the conquest of coastal port cities of Syro-Palestine and Egypt were essential.

The Assyrian economy may be divided into palace, temple, and a private sector. The palace economy included the king's establishments and families in different cities, and similar households belonging to near relatives (queen mother, crown prince, and officials and courtiers whose

23. Postgate, 'The Economic Structure of the Assyrian Empire'.
24. Postgate, *Taxation and Conscription*.

remuneration came from the royal purse). On the income side there was immense wealth that flowed to the imperial coffers for the emperor's own personal use. He could, of course, provide profits for the larger economy and engage in building projects that included palaces, temples, and fortifications of cities. Due to conquests and exiles, the emperor also owned a large number of slaves, vast quantities of precious metals, and could afford large numbers of conscripts for needed labor. To some extent, although on a far lesser scale, temple economies functioned in similar ways.[25]

State Religion in Assyria[26]

Assyrian priesthoods devoted to various gods, cultic activities of sacrifice and festivals, and temples and their worship were crucial to legitimate royal rule. The emperors were involved in these activities and supported those theological affirmations that included divine selection and support for rulers. As for the conquered, their temples often were destroyed and their gods (referred to by the colonizers as idols) taken into exile. There were, though, instances of the Assyrians rebuilding temples in areas outside of Assyria proper, placing in them the idols of local deities, and even providing support for sacrifices and other necessary materials to function as long as the provinces and cities were loyal. There are also instances in the court annals of Assyrian kings participating in the important cultic functions of foreign nations. Among others, Tiglath-pileser, Sargon II, Esarhaddon, and Ashurbanipal claimed to have participated in the rituals of temples in Babylonia and elsewhere. This participation was important to claim that the Assyrian ruler was not simply the worshipper of the foreign deities, but also received their divine approval for ruling their colonies.[27]

While the Assyrians were noted for their destruction of towns and cities located in states they attacked and often conquered, there is little mention of the destruction of foreign temples in the court annals and none in the royal inscriptions. The major examples of the pillaging and

25. Postgate, 'The Economic Structure of the Assyrian Empire', 202.

26. Robertson, 'The Social and Economic Organization of Ancient Mesopotamian Temples', 447; Postgate, 'The Role of the Temple in the Mesopotamian Secular Community'; George, *House Most High*.

27. 'Religious imperialism is defined as deliberate, coercive involvement in the affairs of a foreign and subordinate polity with the intention of either manipulating the internal affairs of the foreign cult, or of imposing cultic dues and obligations consciously understood by both polities for the support of the cult(s) of the imperial polity, or both' (Holloway, *Aššur Is King!*, 98).

devastation of foreign temples are those of Susa by Ashurbanipal[28] and Babylonia by Sennacherib.[29] The idols of foreign gods were usually not destroyed, although they were often taken from their temples and included among the booty carted back to the court. Assyrian propaganda benefited by claiming that Ashur and other members of the pantheon were more powerful than the gods of other nations and empires.[30] Even so there was no requirement that the foreign states in the empire had to cease the cultic activities of local religions. The foreign provinces and states were allowed to worship their gods and were not forced to engage in the Assyrian cults.[31] The indigenous gods, for example Marduk, are at times presented as having become angry at the rulers of foreign nations and required that they and their country be punished.[32]

Assyrian Culture[33]

The literary sources for this period of Assyrian history are substantial. There are important material sources, including sculptures. Assyria proper was itself comprised of numerous ethnicities, meaning that this filtered into cultural variations. A common written language, royal ideology, artistic canons of architecture, monuments, and reliefs, and a religion placed into a hierarchy of gods provided the major means for forging something of a common, though still diverse, civilization.

An Assyrian artistic style distinct from that of Babylonian art, which was the dominant contemporary art in Mesopotamia, began to emerge ca. 1500 BCE and lasted until the fall of Nineveh in 612 BCE. The characteristic Assyrian art form was the polychrome carved stone relief that decorated imperial monuments. The precisely delineated reliefs concern royal affairs, chiefly hunting and war making. Predominance is given to animal forms, particularly horses and lions, which are magnificently represented in great detail. Human figures are comparatively rigid and static but are also minutely detailed, as in triumphal scenes of sieges, battles, and individual combat. Among the best-known of Assyrian reliefs are the lion-hunt alabaster carvings showing Ashurnasirpal II (9th century BCE) and Ashurbanipal (7th century BCE), both of which

28. Brinkman, *Prelude to an Empire*, 102; also see her *A Political History of Post-Kassite Babylonia*.

29. Brinkman, 'Sennacherib's Babylonian Problem: An Interpretation'.

30. Holloway, *Aššur Is King!*, 123-44.

31. Cogan, *Imperialism and Religion*, 9-21.

32. See Brinkman, 'Through a Glass Darkly: Esarhaddon's Restrospects on the Downfall of Babylon'.

33. Oppenheim, *Ancient Mesopotamia*.

are in the British Museum. Guardian animals, usually lions and winged
beasts with bearded human heads, were sculpted partially in the round
for fortified royal gateways, an architectural form common throughout
Asia Minor. At Nimrud, carved ivories and bronze bowls were found that
are decorated in the Assyrian style but which were produced by
Phoenician and Aramaean artisans.[34]

Assyria and Terror

Empires use terror not only in conquest. They also used terror to establish and maintain control through the psychology of fear. While garrisons
of Assyrian soldiers and mercenaries were established in strategic places
throughout the empire, rebellion against Assyrian sovereignty was
frequent, thus requiring military campaigns against offenders who were
often many hundreds of miles from the metropole. The threat and actual
deportation of the ruling elite and the indigenous images of gods, the
destruction of cities, palaces, and on occasion temples struck terror into
nations. Such realities made foreign populations compliant to the new
power. Mythic images were used in the bullying of a nation's leadership
and population, especially the danger of returning the resisting nation to
chaos. Deportation of kings, the aristocracy, divine images, and other
booty spelled the end of the symbols of statehood, leaving a void that
could be filled by obedience to the new Assyrian power and rule.[35] The
flaying of traitorous vassals taken in capital cities, the mutilations of
enemy populations and particularly their leaders, and the forced marches
to other locations evoked perturbation among the populace and rulers
of a client state or province. Symbols of forced sovereignty, including
the presence of an Assyrian garrison, stelae, and menacing diplomatic
warnings, were means of keeping nations in control.

Colonization

As noted earlier, colonization is an imperial process of inculturation into
Assyrian art, literature, and ideology by a variety of means. The last
resort was military campaigns against an unruly or revolting colony.
Garrisons were established to provide not simply protection of the
Assyrian governor, whether from the metropole or a local ruler, but also
to signify Assyrian power. Of course, other activities designed to
maintain dominance included the control of food in the colony, annual

---

34. See Collins, *Assyrian Palace Structures*; Parrot, *The Arts of Assyria*; and
Groenewegen-Frankfort, *Arrest and Movement*.
35. Oded, *Mass Deportations and Deportees in the Neo-Assyrian Empire*.

tribute raised through taxes, and divine and royal symbols of pillars, flags, and celebration of important Assyrian days of observance, religious and political. Indigenous intermediaries introduced to Assyrian culture, language, and power also could quell the fires of revolt. Finally, local Assyrian authorities issued warnings of economic decline, the lack of sufficient food, and in the worst-case scenario, invasion leading to the total devastation of a city and even villages and walled towns. Following these actions, examples of what happened to revolutionaries were made, consisting of the execution of rebel leaders, deporting part of the population of the nation or city that revolted, and turning captives into slaves.

Having summarized the historical context of the Assyrian Empire and strategies by which it asserted and maintained its rule, we turn now to examine the eighth- and seventh-century BCE prophets from Israel and Judah, particularly Hosea, and their negotiation of the Assyrian Empire.

III.
Israel/Judah and the Assyrian Empire:
The Example of Hosea

It was especially the prophets of YHWH during this period that made use of their hidden discourse that sought to subvert the Assyrian metanarrative and its ideology of hegemony. This discourse, which was grounded in Israel's and Judah's own traditions and drew on the past conventions of salvation, burned within their memories. Thus, two cores of narratives of past salvation became the theological basis of their discourse: (1) the Mosaic tradition that included the Exodus, wilderness wandering, the giving of the law at Sinai, and entrance into Canaan, and (2) the David–Zion tradition encompassing authentic kingship and the one legitimate temple in Jerusalem.

The Historical Context of Hosea[36]

The prophet Hosea, son of Beeri, is the single Northern prophet whose prophecies were collected and redacted into a single book. We know nothing of his family and little about his own life. He likely prophesized

---

36. Brueggemann, 'The Recovering God of Hosea'; Daniels, *Hosea and Salvation History*. Dearman, *Hosea*; Landy, *Hosea*; Macintosh, *A Critical and Exegetical Commentary on Hosea*; Kwakkel, 'The Land in the Book of Hosea'; and Yee, *Composition and Tradition in the Book of Hosea*.

sometime from the middle of the eighth century BCE, that is, in the time
before Tiglath-pileser III and no later than shortly before the fall of the
Northern kingdom to Shalmaneser V in 722 BCE. The superscription
(1:1) places his prophecies in the reigns of Judean kings Uzziah (783–
742 BCE), Jotham (742–735 BCE), Ahaz (735–715 BCE), and Hezekiah
(715–687 BCE), but only Jeroboam II (786–746 BCE) is mentioned
among the kings from the Northern kingdom of Israel. From 746 BCE to
721 BCE, six different kings reigned in the Northern kingdom in a period
of growing instability (all but one died violently). Several of Hosea's
oracles reflect the unstable conditions of Israel's last years and the state
of turmoil that plagued the nation (5:1; 7:5-7; 8:4; 9:15; 13:10-11).

King Menahem (745–738 BCE) of Israel, recognizing the power of
Assyria when Tiglath-pileser III began his Western campaign in 743
BCE and recognizing the futility of resistance even with alliances with
neighboring states, willingly submitted to the Assyrian Empire and paid
tribute. However, King Pekah of Israel (739?–732), who was an officer
to Menahem's son King Pekahiah, joined the coalition of the Arameans
and the Philistines in their futile attempt to gain their freedom from the
Assyrians. This led to the Syro-Ephraimite war pitting Israel, the
Aramaeans, and the Philistines against Judah in order to depose King
Ahaz of Judah and force the Southern Kingdom to join the rebellion
(735–733 BCE). When the troops of Judah were being roundly defeated,
Ahaz, who had been a loyal vassal to the empire, called upon Tiglath-
pileser III for assistance (2 Kings 16) against the pleading of the prophet
Isaiah (Isaiah 7). This led to Tiglath-pileser's march southward to put
down the rebellion, which was carried out with brutality and with mass
destruction in Syro-Palestine. Among the states ravaged by the Assyrian
army was the Northern kingdom in 733 BCE, which included laying
waste to many of its cities and towns. Hosea's phrase, 'breaking the
bow' of Israel (Hos. 1:5; 2:18), likely refers to the final battle in the
Valley of Jezreel that resulted in the submission of the Northern kingdom to Assyrian sovereignty (733 BCE). This defeat was followed by
the deportation of many of its citizens to different regions of the empire,
leaving behind a ravaged kingdom, with Israel being reduced to the
northern hill country and the capital of Samaria. Succeeding Tiglath-
pileser III, Shalmaneser V launched his punitive expedition against Israel
in 725 BCE. The oracles about the demise of Israel's king (10:7; 13:10-
11) are commonly taken to be allusions to the punishment of Hoshea
the last king of the Northern kingdom (732–724 BCE) by the Assyrians.
The mention of Shalman who destroyed Beth-arbel (10:14) is sometimes taken to be a reference to Shalmaneser V, who was supposed to
have destroyed Beth-arbel en route to Samaria. With the kingship of

Pekah and Israel's rebellion, the forces of Shalmaneser V invaded and destroyed much of Israel and sacked the capital of Samaria, although the campaign may have been concluded by Sennacherib due to the death of his predecessor. There are several probable allusions in Hosea to the last days of Samaria (9:1-9; 10:3-10; 11:5-7). But there is no mention of the actual destruction of Samaria anywhere. Indeed, in the conclusion of the book, Samaria is apparently still standing, but her end is near (13:16). This would put the oracle sometime just before the fall of Samaria in 721 BCE. The deportation of much of the population of Samaria and their scattering throughout the empire ultimately led to its demise.

Hosea may have prophesized in or near Samaria as a marginal prophet who did not have privileged access to the royal court. His proclamations, though, may have been delivered at important sanctuaries like those in Bethel and Gilgal, both of which the book mentions. Cult prophets often spoke at such sanctuaries but Hosea's message was not one of salvation, the normal type of prophecy by these prophets, but rather one of judgment and coming devastation. Hosea appears to have uttered several oracles that allude to the capital city's final days, but he does not mention its fall (9:1-9; 10:3-10; 11:5-7; 14:1).

The Yahwistic Metanarrative of Hosea

In shaping his metanarrative to subvert that of the Neo-Assyrian Empire, Hosea speaks of YHWH as the one who controls history. The prophet makes important use of the Mosaic tradition as it had been formulated in Northern Israel by the eighth century BCE. Fundamental to this theological tradition is the understanding that the validity of the covenant was conditional upon the faithfulness of the covenant partners. Drawing on the past, especially the traditions of Israel's early formation as a people, Hosea presents YHWH as the God who led Israel out of Egypt in the Exodus (2:15; 11:1; 12:9, 13; 13:4) and guided them through the Sinai (2:14). Particularly important is his view that the wilderness period in Israel's relationship with YHWH was one of faithfulness. There are allusions in the book to the Sinai revelation. The very name 'not my people' suggests the Mosaic tradition in which YHWH called Israel 'my people' (cf. Exod. 6:7; 3:7, 10). That relationship assumed that the nation would obey the command of YHWH and 'keep the covenant' (Exod. 19:5); failure to do so would result in covenant curses and invalidation of the relationship. Only after the entrance into Canaan did apostasy and disloyalty to YHWH, the God of the covenant, begin to develop. Israel's most significant sins were her rebellion against YHWH (Hos. 5:7; 6:7; 7:1, 13, 14; 8:1-2; 9:15; 14:1), the worship of other gods (5:13; 7:8-13;

8:9-10) and the idols they had fashioned (8:4-5; 13:2), transgressions against the commandments incorporated within the covenant (4:1-3; 6:7; 7:1; 8:1), the dependence on their own military strength, and the turning both to Assyria and Egypt, not YHWH, for aid. YHWH has, according to Hosea, abandoned Israel. The prophet uses the metaphor of divorce. YHWH has divorced Israel as indicated by the decree of divorce 'I am not her husband, and she is not my wife' in 2:2. Due to the disloyalty of Israel and its worship of other gods, YHWH will send divorced Israel away stripped and naked as in the day she was born and expose her, i.e., leave her to die uncovered (2:3), and she will go into exile wandering among the nations (9:3, 17).[37] Hosea's marriage to Gomer, a prostitute, illustrates symbolically YHWH's relationship to Israel (14:9). But YHWH will take Israel back into the wilderness where the relationship will be restored (2:14) and once again the chosen nation shall become as it was in the days of its youth when it came forth out of Egypt in the Exodus (2:15).

Hosea and Gomer's children receive symbolic names that illustrate the brokenness of the bond between YHWH and Israel. The first-born is a son named Jezreel ('God sows', 1:4-5). The second child, a daughter, is given the name *Lo-ruhamam* ('not pitied', 1:6-7). The third child, a second son, receives the name *Lo-ammi* ('not my people', 1:9).

The name of the first born, Jezreel, refers to the central plain of Israel which is a west–east corridor that stretches from the coastal 'Way of the Sea'[38] to the 'King's Highway', the trade route that leads north from Egypt through the Transjordan to Syria. This valley was protected by two fortress cities, Megiddo and Taanach, the major military route of armies from Mesopotamia to the south into the Levant and Egypt and from Egypt north to the different kingdoms and empires in the Land of the Two Rivers. This valley is the place where many important battles

37. This dreadful metaphor of YHWH as abusive husband has been critiqued by feminist scholars. For discussion see Baumann, *Love and Violence*; Day, 'The Bitch Had It Coming to Her; Dijk-Hemmes, 'Imagination of Power and the Power of Imagination'; Keefe, 'The Female Body, the Body Politic, and the Land: A Sociopolitical Reading of Hosea 1–2'; Landy, 'Fantasy and the Displacement of Pleasure: Hosea 2:4-17'; Setel, 'Prophets and Pornography: Female Sexual Imagery in Hosea'; Sherwood, *The Prostitute and the Prophet*; Tornkvist, *The Use and Abuse of Female Sexual Imagery in the Book of Hosea*; Wacker, *Figurationen des Weiblichen im Hosea-Buch*; Weems, 'Gomer: Victim of Violence or Victim of Metaphor?'; Weems, *Battered Love*; Yee, 'Hosea', in *The New Interpreter's Bible* and *The Women's Bible Commentary*.

38. An important trade road along the coastal cities of Israel and the major military route of armies from Mesopotamia to Egypt and vice-versa.

were fought, including Josiah's subsequent disastrous defeat and death in 609 BCE. Josiah tried unsuccessfully to block Necho II's Egyptian army from joining the Assyrians in resisting the Babylonian invasion that was drawing close to its final conclusion in the sacking of Harran, the last stronghold of Ashur-uballit II. Hosea uses the name Jezreel to refer to Jehu's bloody seizure of the throne of Israel, thus ending the Omride dynasty (1:4). The blood spilled in this *coup d'état* included Jehu's personal assassination of Joram, king of Israel, who was in the town of Jezreel recovering from wounds suffered at the hands of the Syrian army in a battle at Ramoth-Gilead. The king of Judah, Ahaziah, who was present in Jezreel, attempted to escape but was fatally wounded by one of the soldiers of Jehu (2 Kgs 9:14-29). Jehu terminated the Phoenican alliance fashioned earlier by Omri and Ahab and ordered the death of Jezebel, residing in Jezreel. She was the daughter of the king of Sidon and the wife of Ahab, and was thrown from the upper story to the street below by her own eunuchs according Jehu's instructions (2 Kgs 9:30-37). The royal assassinations were then followed by the murder of the Northern kingdom's princes (Ahab's sons), whose seventy heads were brought and placed in two heaps before the new king in Jezreel. Finally, Jehu and his troops slaughtered some forty-two relatives of King Ahaziah because they were coming to visit the royal princes at Samaria (2 Kgs 10:1-17). This may have been designed to pave the way for Jehu's taking of Judah and ending the Davidic dynasty. Then, in Samaria, he eliminated Ahab's remaining relatives. Hosea's naming of his first born, Jezreel, indicates that Israel will be repaid for this bloody slaughter and bring an end to the Northern kingdom and its dynasty (Jeroboam II was a descendant of Jehu).

The names of the second and third child are symbolic and have no narrative references. The first of the two (*Lo-ruhaman*, 'not pitied') means that YHWH no longer has motherly compassion on Israel. The second of the two (*Lo-'ammi*, 'not my people') declares that Israel is no longer the 'people' of YHWH. But the prophet promises that Israel will be restored (following its devastation and the exile of the people of the capital city, Samaria) to areas throughout Assyria. They then will join Judah, who will have one 'head'; not a king but more likely a deliverer or judge like the temporary leaders of a united Israel who fought against and defeated common enemies. Hosea, then, is rejecting the dynasty created by David, who established the state, and evoking the tradition of the judges.[39]

39. If this is correct, then returning to 'David their king' (3:5) is a scribal addition.

Hosea was concerned with YHWH, the God of Israel, who led the Israelites out of Egypt and preserved them in the wilderness (12:13, 14). Israel knew 'no other God' but YHWH; there was no other savior (13:4; Exod. 20:3). Throughout the book there are specific references and allusions to the Exodus event (2:15; 11:1; 12:9, 13; 13:4) and the wilderness experience (2:14; 9:10; 13:4). Hosea romanticized the early days of Israel's history as a time of Israel's faithfulness (2:15).

Against this background one must understand the sins of Israel. The vassal had betrayed the suzerain; the people of Israel had rebelled (5:7; 6:7; 7:1, 13-14; 8:1-2; 9:15; 13:16). Israel (the figuration as a woman surfaces repeatedly) had transgressed the covenant and violated its stipulations (4:1-3; 6:7; 7:1; 8:1). This Israel did by showing allegiance to other gods, turning to foreign military power and relying on its own military prowess. Sharing the same world view as the predecessors of the Deuteronomistic school, Hosea condemned any deviation from the Yahwistic cult. The people had made molten images of silver and gold, just as they did in the days of Moses and Aaron (8:4-5; 13:2). Israel had violated the covenant relationship with YHWH by turning to the Canaanite gods and participating in their sexual rituals (2:5b-14; 9:10). The prophet described this unfaithfulness in sexual terms, as harlotry and adultery (2:2-13; 4:10-19; 5:3-4; 6:10; 7:4; 9:1). Here again is an allusion to the covenant at Sinai where the proliferation of altars and the worship of other gods are regarded as acts of harlotry (Exod. 34:12-16; cf. Judg. 8:33). The people of Israel rejected the love of YHWH and turned to the Canaanite gods. Like the later Deuteronomists, Hosea condemned the proliferation of altars and local sanctuaries (10:1-2, 8; 12:11). He regarded the temple in Jerusalem as the sole legitimate sanctuary in which to worship YHWH, and he condemned those who worshipped at the Northern shrines at Gilgal and Bethel (4:15; 9:15). He attributed the apostasy of Israel to what the Deuteronomist called 'the sin of Jeroboam', namely, the erection of the golden calf at Bethel (10:5).

In spite of YHWH's faithfulness as evident in history, Israel's people did not trust in YHWH's power to protect and deliver them. Instead, they turned to Assyria and Egypt (5:13; 7:8, 11; 8:9-10; 12:1), precisely the oppressive nations from which they had to be rescued. Thus Israel acted treacherously against YHWH her suzerain. Hence Israel's sacrifices and offerings were of no use to YHWH (6:6; 8:13).

Because of Israel's violations of the covenant, YHWH brought a lawsuit against Israel (4:1; 5:1). YHWH charged that Israel lacked faithfulness, loyalty, and knowledge of God (cf. 4:1). Knowledge and loyalty are two key theological concepts in Hosea. They occur together again in 6:6, where it is emphasized that YHWH preferred loyalty and knowledge of God to sacrifice.

The 'knowledge of God' marked Israel's special relationship with YHWH. People and priest alike are rejected by YHWH because of their lack of knowledge (4:1, 6; 5:4). The Hebrew verb 'to know' indicates intimate knowledge as of partners in a covenant or marriage. Israel's relationship with YHWH was once correct: they *knew* no other God but YHWH, and YHWH knew them in their wilderness wandering (13:4). But as soon as they were satiated with the nourishment that YHWH had provided them, they forgot the benevolence of YHWH (13:6). They claimed to know YHWH (8:2), but they had flagrantly broken the covenant with YHWH and violated the law (8:1).

In fact, they did not know YHWH. They did not even know that it was YHWH who provided them with grain, wine, and oil (2:8). Instead, they attributed these products of the land to other gods (2:5). They reckoned that vines and fig trees were their payment for their devotion to their 'lovers' (2:12). For the sake of grain and wine they participated in the fertility rites associated with Baal (7:14). They gashed themselves even though it was explicitly forbidden for them to do so (1 Kgs 18:28). It was YHWH who cared for them and healed them, but they did not know it (11:3). They did not know YHWH because they were possessed by the 'spirit of harlotry' (5:4).

But YHWH knew them (5:3). They had rejected knowledge, the absence of which was evident in their violation of the commandment of God (4:1-3, 6). The lack of knowledge is taken to be synonymous with treachery (5:7; 6:6-7), and for this treachery Israel was to go into exile (4:1, 6). But beyond the judgment Hosea saw hope for a new relationship established by YHWH and based on faithfulness, loyalty, justice, and mercy. Then would Israel truly know YHWH (2:20). To that end, Hosea urged his audience to 'know YHWH and pursue the knowledge of YHWH' (6:3).

For their transgressions, the people would be punished. Covenant curses would be upon them. They would be cursed with hunger (4:10). Their threshing floors and wine vats would cease to be operational (9:2). Though they were engaged in all sorts of rites to bring fertility, they would experience barrenness and dryness of breasts instead (9:11, 14). They and their princes would die by the sword (7:16; 9:13; 11:6). Their children would be dashed in pieces and their pregnant women would be cut open (13:16). War would overtake them (10:9, 14). Their cities would be destroyed by fire (8:14). Parents would be bereft of their

children (9:11-14, 16). Worst of all, there would be a reversal of the
Exodus; they would be brought back to Egypt whence they had been
delivered (8:13; 9:3; 11:5) or be in exile (9:3, 17; 11:5, 11). Thus the
unfaithful nation would receive the same punishment as the unfaithful
Gomer: they would be cast out of their home (land) and left to fend for
themselves in foreign territories. Through this experience of punishment
Israel would learn, even as the unfaithful wife did, that life was better
with its first husband, namely YHWH (2:7). Israel will, indeed, be punished for the abandonment of covenant responsibilities.

For Hosea, 'loyalty' marked the covenant of mutuality. Both covenant
partners were expected to demonstrate this quality. There was inequality.
YHWH's reliability was likened to the predictability of dawn and the
spring rain (6:1-3). Israel's loyalty, on the other hand, was as fleeting as
the morning cloud and the dew that evaporates all too quickly (6:4).
Israel must repent and sow righteousness in order to reap the fruits of
'loyalty' (10:12). The people must keep loyalty and justice (12:6). But
beyond judgment there is hope. Eventually, God will take Israel back as
a bride in righteousness, justice, mercy, faithfulness, and loyalty, and
Israel will truly know YHWH (2:19-20).

According to Hosea, there was, then, still hope. Due to YHWH's grace
and forgiveness, Israel will be taken back (2:19-20) and the Valley of
Achor (the valley just north of Jericho that the Israelites used to invade
Canaan in Joshua 7) shall become the door of hope (2:15). Then YHWH
shall once again become Israel's husband (not Baal) and Israel will
become YHWH's faithful wife. This relationship is substantiated and
exemplified in Hosea's own relationship with his wife. Divine love is
shown in the microcosm of Hosea's marriage. Love, indeed, is the central theme that unifies the book. The relationship between Hosea and his
beloved (chaps. 1–3), which mirrors the relationship between YHWH and
Israel (chaps. 4–14), is one of love on the part of the gracious husband.
As with loyalty and knowledge, so love may be understood in terms of
the covenant. In the ancient Near East, the ties between the vassal and
suzerain were said to be marked by 'love'. The vassal was supposed to
'love' the suzerain by observing the treaty stipulations, honoring its
responsibilities, and being loyal to the suzerain. Hosea was commanded
to love a harlotrous woman as a symbol of YHWH's love for the people
in spite of their unfaithfulness (3:1). God is also said to have loved Israel
like a child, even though Israel kept gravitating toward other gods (11:1-
4). That same love would be freely given with the eventual reconciliation
(14:5 [Eng. 14:4]). By the same token, the invalidation of the covenant is
expressed as the withdrawal of love (9:15). Eventually YHWH would heal

sickness and bind wounds so that his people would live again (6:1-2). Their fortunes would be restored (6:11). The exiles would return home (11:10-11; cf. 3:5). They would be healed (6:1, 11). YHWH would correct their apostasy and love them freely again (14:5 [Eng. 14:4]). They would return home and dwell under YHWH's shade (14:7).

Hybridity, Foreign Culture, and Religion in Israel[40]

The prophet condemns the nation for mixing with the peoples who devour its strength (7:8-9). Yahwism apparently did not dominate in the Northern kingdom as it did in Judah. There seems to have been a variety of religious devotion in Israel where hybridity, including the integration of Canaanite fertility cults into Yahwistic religion or the abandonment of the latter and its replacement with other cults, was well represented in state and private/family religions. The Samaritan ostraca contain a large number of Baal theophoric names, that is, personal names that either embed the name of a deity within them, such as *Theophilos* (one who loves God), or are themselves divine names, such as Diana. The ostraca of Samaria are also inscribed with the names of persons or towns that delivered oil or wine to the king's palace, much of which likely comprised tribute to the empire. They are dated 'in the ninth year', 'in the tenth year', and 'in the seventeenth year' of the king, although the name of the king is not mentioned.[41] Another key example of the adaption of Canaanite religion is in Kuntillet 'Ajrud, a traveler's way station in the Sinai. The pithos (large storage container) found here that depicts a couple with bovine features points to the presence of a Yahwistic cult. The inscription reads: 'May you be blessed by YHWH of Samarai and by his Asherah'.[42]

It is sometimes argued that Gomer bat-Diblaim was a cultic prostitute who participated in the ritual sexual acts of Canaanite religions (2:5-13). It has also been suggested that the name Diblaim, which may be taken to mean 'Two Figs' or the like, is a veiled reference to Gomer's partaking of the 'raisin cakes' (3:1). The latter is possibly an aphrodisiac associated with Canaanite fertility cults.

---

40. McKay, *Religion in Judah under the Assyrians*; Cogan, *Imperialism and Religion*; Spieckermann, *Juda unter Assur in der Sargonidenzeit*; Cogan, 'Judah under Assyrian Hegemony'.

41. Rollston, *The Script of Hebrew Ostraca*.

42. For a detailed discussion of the location and pithos of Kuntillet 'Ajrud see, Zevit, *The Religions of Ancient Israel*, 370-405.

According to Hosea, the people consecrated themselves at Baal-peor, soon after they had made the covenant with YHWH (9:10; Num 25:1-18). They were brought by YHWH to the land which YHWH had blessed, but they turned to the Canaanite gods instead, and attributed blessings and success to Baal (2:5, 8-9). The polemic against Canaanite religion is clear here. Baal was thought to be the god of nature and fertility, but it was really YHWH who gave and took away.

Among the practices of Canaanite religion, none bothered Hosea more than their attempt to induce fertility by sympathetic magic. Since fertility was thought to have been generated by sexual intercourse between the deities (specifically between Baal and Anat), certain men and women were set apart for cultic coitus. But Hosea insisted that the Canaanite gods could not deliver on their promise. The people participated in such sexual rites to ensure rich harvests and fecundity, but they would 'eat but not be satisfied, prostitute themselves but not multiply' (4:10).

Enculturation

Israel's prophets, like Hosea, read the present through the lens of past traditions of salvation, including the Mosaic tradition and that of David and Zion. This conservative and reactionary response to new elements taken from foreign religions and cultural expressions attempts to re-establish a romanticized past as the time of YHWH and the chosen's relationship. Hosea attempted to recall the Mosaic tradition that speaks of Israel's beginnings and especially the wilderness tradition. For Hosea, the trouble for Israel began after they entered Canaan and began to adopt traditional Canaanite language for Yhwh and/or actually worshipped Baal. In 4:12, people seek oracles from 'wood', which is likely a reference to the sacred tree that represents Asherah, wife of the Canaanite god. Since elements of Canaanite religion, as understood by the prophet, were incorporated into Israelite religious practices, this religious aspect of hybridity was placed in motion (7:8). This process of enculturation, in which new gods are worshipped or the former one (in this case YHWH) is identified with Baal and perhaps given Asherah as his consort, is common in the movements of people who come into contact with different cultures. But for Hosea, the worship of Baal was tantamount to apostasy. He included in this the worship of the multiple locations of Baal, sexual rites to Canaanite deities (2:5b-14; cf. 1:2; 4:10-19; 7:4; 9:1), worship at high places (4:13; 10:8), and the reference to Jeroboam's construction of golden calves which Israel continued to worship in Bethel (10:5, 8) and Gilgal (4:15; 9:15). The calf at Bethel will be carried as a piece of booty into exile (10:5-6). These sins of apostasy and idolatrous worship of Baal led to YHWH's lawsuit against the people (12:2; 4:1; 5:1). Their punishment would be hunger (4:10, 9:2), the inability to produce offspring, and especially the horrors of invasion and destruction, a reference to the future destruction of the state. Their alliances with Egypt and tribute to Assyria that was raised by taxing landholders (2 Kgs 15:19-20; *ANET*, 283) would not divert their eventual destruction (7:11-12, 16; 8:8-10; 12:1; 14:3).[43] Their efforts to build up their internal defenses, including the multiplication of fortified cities, were both futile and misguided. Instead they should have depended on YHWH for deliverance and protection. The prophet proclaimed for YHWH an indictment and judgment that indicated Israel would be devastated by invasion: war would overtake them (5:8-12; 10:9, 14), cities would be destroyed by fire (8:14), its people would die by the sword (7:16; 9:13; 11:6), children were to be dashed in pieces while pregnant women would be cut open (13:16). In a reverse Exodus, Israel would be brought back to Egypt (8:13; 9:3; 11:5) and go into Assyrian exile where they shall have to eat 'unclean food' (9:3; 11:5, 11). In Assyrian exile they will 'wander among the nations' (9:17). There they will remain without their false gods and idols, until YHWH liberates them and allows them to return home (3:4-5; 11:11).

Judgment leads eventually to hope, for YHWH will take Israel back (2:19-20). Divine forgiveness is exemplified in Hosea's willingness to accept once again his unfaithful wife, Gomer, and YHWH's love for Israel as a child. Divine compassion would lead to Israel's restoration, even as Ephraim the child would be taken back (11:8-9); in the end the people would be pitied (14:3). Thus, they were implored to return to YHWH (6:1; 12:6; 14:1-2), recognize their foolishness, live again (6:1-2), and be restored and healed (6:11). The exiles would return home again (11:10-11; 6:11; cf. 3:5) and be loved once more by their God (14:4, 7). Subsequently, the past traditions of salvation, especially that of Moses (Exodus, Wilderness, Sinai, Law, and Conquest), are used by the prophet to provide hope to a people, soon to experience the ravages of conquest and exile to different parts of the empire. This hoped-for deliverance, however, never materialized, since Israel disappeared into various Assyrian cultures.

---

43. Perhaps Hosea made use of suzerainty treaties common to the nations and empires of the ancient Near East, although this seems highly unlikely. It is doubtful that the prophet knew of these treaties since he gives no evidence of serving in the court where such treaties would have been known and there is no clear outline and features typical for this kind of treaty. See McCarthy, *Treaty and Covenant*, and Baltzer, *The Covenant Formulary*.

Ambivalence

Another element of Hosea's resistance is ambivalence, which is the view that identity derives in part from differences with the Other.[44] The Other, in the case of the Assyrians and the practitioners of Canaanite religion, is the opposite of what Israel should be. For Hosea, the identity of Israel is shaped by the conflict of traditional Yahwism and the religion of Canaan. This sharp dichotomy in this prophet's pronouncements is common throughout his writings. Israel can again become the chosen people by repudiating Canaanite religion and ceasing the practice of many of its features.

The prophet also makes an internal, political contrast. Kingship is also the Other. He condemns the acts of kings in the formulation of treaties with other nations and their quest for security by strengthening the state's military installations. He seems to suggest that Israel's true identity is not only in returning to the tradition of Moses and rejecting foreign religious incursions into their religion, but also in recognizing that their own kings were either not selected by YHWH or were given to them out of divine wrath. The implication is they were leading the nation to its conquest and deportation. He may even be suggesting that kingship from its beginning was not established by YHWH and that Israel's future governance should be that of tribal elders and charismatic leaders.

Decolonizing the Mind

There is little doubt that the Assyrian invasions of Israel led to the transformation of some of its leaders and less important people by their adoption of the imperial metanarrative, which included three key elements. First was the worship of Assyrian gods, in particular Ashur, who likely was believed to possess the power to control history, including the history of Israel. Second, related to the first, was the invincibility of the Assyrian Empire whose forces controlled large parts of the ancient Near East, including the Levant. Third was the power of the Assyrian rulers, beginning with Tiglath-pileser III (2 Kings 15)

The powerful force of these three elements is found in the reigns of the last seven kings of Israel, including Jeroboam II. The Deuteronomistic history condemned these rulers especially for religious infidelity by worshiping other gods (especially Baal, Asherah), building them high places and altars and engaging in their sacred rituals (including the

---

44. Identity that derives from distinguishing between *us* and *them* is an important aspect of social identity theory, which has been employed by several scholars in recent years. See Baker, 'Social Identity Theory and Biblical Interpretation'.

burning of their children to Molech). Idols, an Asherah, and the two calves fashioned originally by Jeroboam I are mentioned. The Deuteronomistic history repeated the denunciation used of many of the Northern kings: 'he did not depart from the sins of Jeroboam the son of Nebat, which he made Israel to sin' (2 Kgs 15:9, 18, 24, 28). Like Hosea, the Deuteronomistic history, as noted earlier, refers to both the Exodus and the commandments of YHWH in the covenant of Sinai, as the two primary traditions that were violated by Israel and its rulers (2 Kgs 17:7-18). By this memory of its salvific past, Israel's worship of foreign gods would come to an end.

Hosea, who likely prophesized during the early formation of the Deuteronomistic history, makes similar accusations. To decolonize the minds of the Northern populace, he speaks of returning to the Wilderness, before they yielded to the worship of foreign gods, to renew the pristine relationship with YHWH where it was first established and to repudiate the violation of divine commandments by religious duplicity. He also refers to the Exodus in which YHWH delivered his people from slavery (12:9, 13). The Exodus and Sinai traditions become central to Hosea's theology as he seeks to remind Israel of their earlier salvation (13:4, 5). The power of the Assyrians could not be denied, and he mentions the payment to them of tribute and costly oil to Egypt (12:1). Yet the prophet does promise the hope of divine deliverance of Israel from exile. Finally, depending on the support of the power of the Assyrians is a useless enterprise (5:13; 8:9; 9:6; 12:1; 14:3), while the build-up of their fortifications to resist invasion is also useless and will not succeed (8:14). In addition Hosea rejects the efforts to establish treaties with other nations to build up their strength (8:10). Indeed, the population will be taken to Assyria and to Egypt (11:5). For the prophet, YHWH controls history, not other gods (especially Ashur), for he is the one who sends into exile his people and will return them to their homeland. The prophet anticipates this empire will fall.

It is also important to note that in decolonizing the mind of the population from the legitimation and power of their own rulers, the prophet rejects Israel's choosing of kings by either denying they were chosen by YHWH (8:4) or indicating that they were given to them by YHWH due to his wrath for their sins (13:11). While this is likely a reference to the Northern rulers and treaties, including that between Israel and Syria in the Syro-Ephraimitic war, it may be that the prophet intends to encompass in this oracle all rulers, including the House of David. He certainly does not mention this sacred tradition of the selection of David and the establishment of Zion as the holy mountain.

To decolonize the mind of the population of the North the prophet repudiates the Northern rulers, if not all rulers, for they led Israel into religious apostasy, the making of treaties with other nations, and the building of an army for conquest and defense. Yet these will not have the power to defend them from their enemies (13:10). It may well be that Hosea envisions a nation that does not have future kings, but, like the period of the judges, only charismatic leaders chosen by YHWH through the prophets.

Hosea and Imperial Economics

Hosea's references to Assyria may allude to Israel's tribute gathered through the local payment of taxes in exchange for their favor and protection from invasion (5:13; 7:11; 8:9; 12:1; 14:3). Nevertheless, the nation (at least the upper class and skilled laborers) shall go into Assyrian captivity (9:3, 6; 10:6; 11:5). Among the losses endured by Israel for religious and political apostasy will be the lack of food and wine (9:2) endured by being a subject to Assyria and the heavy tribute required of them. In addition, Israelite families, the majority of which consisted of farming households depending on the labor of offspring, will be punished by the loss of their children (9:12, 16). Indeed, even the cattle used to plow and thresh will be lost, resulting in the people themselves having to do the plowing and reaping by the labor of their own hands. Siroccos, or hot air from the desert filled with sand, will blow across the land, parching the soil of the nation (12:1; 13:15). Thus, farming, the major industry of the Northern kingdom, will be ravaged by desert winds, the loss of children, and the tribute paid to Assyria. Indeed, Assyria's poor farmland meant that they depended heavily on the food, wine, and oil produced by the nations they conquered.

Power, Discourse, and Knowledge in Hosea[45]

Hosea's speeches suggest they are directed only to Israel, likely given in a royal sanctuary, and directed against the nation and its official state and private forms of religion. Prophets believed that as the spokesperson for YHWH their words were imbued with power for they contained what was revealed to them by the God of history. This means, then, that both oracles of judgment and salvation were powerful discourses that express YHWH's power of ruling not only Israel, but also the entire cosmos.

45. See Foucault, *The Order of Things*, and Scott, *Hidden Transcripts*.

The knowledge of YHWH is a major theme in Hosea. The lack of knowledge, especially due to the abandonment of the commandments by the priests that infected the populace, will lead to their destruction. For the prophet, the knowledge of God is found in the law (4:1-3, 6; 6:6; 8:12; 13:16) and by implication not in the sciences of the empire that include monumental inscriptions, royal annals, divination, omenology, augury, and astrology.[46] While Israel, the kings, and the priests are blamed, this movement into foreign religion is the reason for the coming devastation.

IV.
The Colonization of Judah and Assyrian Domination

Following the appeal of Ahaz to Tiglath-pileser III for help and the subsequent collapse of the Syro-Ephraimitic coalition in 732 BCE, the king of Judah was summoned to Damascus to meet this fearsome warrior (2 Kgs 16:10-16). Perhaps overwhelmed by what he saw of the power and the consequence of rebellion in the devastated city, he returned to Judah with the firm intent of assuring the Assyrian emperor that he was a loyal vassal. This loyalty included the raising of funds for tribute by taxation of land holders, taking treasure from the temple treasury, and likely the willingness to engage in the recognition and perhaps even worship of Assyrian gods.

The Metanarrative of Judah in Judah

In Judah, Asherah, the Queen of heaven, was worshipped along with YHWH and other gods. This henotheistic form of devotion was expressive of the hybridity that was central to the worship of Judah. The gods were important to Judah's discourse of prophetic opposition to and subversion of the Assyrian world view. In the place of the Assyrian metanarrative, Judah established a grand narrative that emphasized Judah's theology, in which YHWH was superior among the deities. Other important elements of Judah's grand narrative were the understanding of the Mosaic tradition of the Exodus, the wandering through the wilderness, the giving of the law of Sinai, the entrance into the land, and the David and Zion tradition. These past traditions were the basis of Israel's metanarrative. Calling on other deities added to Judah's religious world view.

46. See Oppenheim, *Mesopotamia*.

Religion in Judah during the Assyrian Empire[47]

Cultic innovations in Israel and Judah's new religious elements exemplify the hybridity that was in process in both nations. While the Deuteronomistic history and the prophets emphasize religious apostasy as the major reason for YHWH's abandonment of both states, leading to the Assyrian destruction of Israel and domination of Judah, it is likely that other elements of culture were also changing. Religion, culture, and politics are entwined in the ancient Near East, meaning that changes in religious concepts, rituals, temporality, and sacred space tell us a great deal about the political landscape of an empire and its colonies. The political upheavals in Judah occasioned by the presence of Assyrian troops located in garrisons, the engagement with Assyrian culture, and changes in the economy resulting from heavy tribute, were likely reasons for hybridity.

In the Deuteronomistic history, the religion of Judah during the period of Assyria's control unfolds in 2 Kings 16–23. While two kings, Ahaz and Manasseh, are condemned by the Deuteronomistic history for leading the nation into a posture of apostasy, there is no evidence that the Assyrians forced their vassals to engage in Assyrian religion. No Assyrian text states or implies that conquered peoples were required to worship the gods of Assyria. The symbols of Ashur, though, especially stelae representing both the power of Ashur and the Assyrian monarch, and the 'weapon of Ashur', were placed in strategic places, including on occasion in temples, in order to stress the greatness and power of the Assyrian god who controlled history and overpowered both a conquered nation and a willing vassal and their gods. This elevation likely was the case in Judah. The 'host of heaven' refers to the stars that the Assyrians worshipped and that Manasseh placed for them in the temple and built altars (2 Kgs 21:1-5). In Judah, as was true in Israel, religious apostasy was the focus of the Deuteronomistic history and prophetic texts during this period. This focus would suggest that the country was inundated by sacred places, priests, and sacrifices to other gods, especially those of Canaan, although other deities and certain religious acts that reflect their presence and worship were also a part of Judah's hybridity.

Economics in Judah during the Assyrian Empire

The heavy tribute paid to the Assyrians added to the economic decline of Judah's financial status. Judah continued to reap its harvest from the fields that made survival of the nation possible. Judah's trade to other

47. See McKay, *Religion in Judah under the Assyrians*.

nations depended on the exchange of its agricultural produce for their goods. Without these agricultural transactions, Judah would have not survived.

Ahaz, Manasseh, and Religion of Judah

Judean kings Ahaz (735–715 BCE) and Manasseh (687–642 BCE) engaged in syncretistic practices, including some reflecting Canaanite religion, as well as that of the Assyrians, to please their masters in order to gain some measure of security for their country. However, there may have been other factors at work, including efforts to reduce the power of the traditionalists, which include the priesthood operating in the temple and marginal prophets. Thus other cultic sites were not disallowed, in order to make the Zadokites in Jerusalem more receptive to cultural changes and to reject resisting the transformation of sacred traditions that included the kingship of the House of David and Zion as the inviolable city of God. This seems to have worked and becomes one reason why the Deuteronomistic history is so critical of these two kings. As religious conservatists who sought to reduce the power of the kings of Judah, to assume control of the law and worship in the temple, and to resist the social and economic power of others belonging to the powerful elite, the Deuteronomistic school demanded complete, unrivalled loyalty to the God of Israel. For those in Judah who viewed the nation's destiny as lying in the hands of the pure practice of the YHWH cult and expected total loyalty to YHWH, religious hybridity—understood as apostasy—and the disintegration of Judah's past traditions threatened a loss of identity.

Those who were syncretistic, however, saw things differently. By worshipping other gods, the future of the nation would be secured. Religion, culture, and politics in the ancient world could not be separated, meaning that any religious feature or change was also political in nature. These two kings, Ahaz and Manasseh, understood that the repudiation of other religions, especially that of Assyria, would create an intransigency that was dangerous to Judah's political survival.

Ahaz is reported to be the first king of Judah who 'made his son pass through fire' (a rite of Molech in the Valley of Hinnom, 2 Kgs 16:3). He also constructed an altar in Jerusalem like the one in Damascus (2 Kgs 16:10-16). While this was perhaps a copy of an altar of Hadad, the chief God of the Syrians, it is possible that it was an Assyrian one constructed earlier to please their masters. In either case, this was a further example of religious hybridity, since the worship of YHWH, the gods of Canaan, and the worship of Ashur and other Assyrian deities, including Ishtar, was integrated into a new form of polytheistic or henotheistic devotion in Judah. Further, Ahaz moved the old altar from its original place and situated it to the north of the new one. Uriah the priest was commanded to carry out the traditional acts of sacrifice, which included the morning burnt offering, the king's burnt offering, the evening grain offering, and the sprinkling of the blood of the morning sacrifice on the altar. The old bronze altar was used by the king to inquire of a deity, probably YHWH, although this could include omens, a common religious undertaking in Assyria to determine the will of the gods. Other actions were taken, including removing the sea from its placement on the bronze oxen and locating it on a stone pedestal. Ahaz removed the covered portal of the temple for use on the Sabbath and the outer entrance to the temple for the king at the command of the Assyrian king. The latter was likely used for grand processionals celebrating the reign of the king. Finally, the mention of the altar of Ahaz's upper chamber was likely the place where he engaged in the worship of the Host of Heaven (2 Kgs 23:12), Assyrian astral deities. The effect of these actions was to transform YHWH into a minor deity (2 Kings 22) due to his inability to protect Judah from the powerful Assyrians and Tiglath-pileser's defeat of Israel in 732 BCE.

The king of Judah most vilified by the Deuteronomistic history is Manasseh. He reconstructed the high places, erected altars for Baal, and made an Asherah which was an idol shaped in an anthropomorphic form (designated as a *semel*, found in a Phonician inscription)[48] and placed it in the temple. He built altars for the Host of Heaven in the two courts of the temple and forced his son to pass through the fire (2 Kgs 21:6). Taken together these actions are a mixture of the Assyrian state religion, Canaanite fertility religion, and worship of Molech (likely a Phoenician deity). In addition, he engaged in soothsaying and augury and had dealings with mediums and wizards (2 Kgs 21:6). These were actions of omenology that were condemned by the Deuteronomistic history (Deut. 18:9-14). In 2 Kings 21:7, there is a report of a carved image of Asherah that may have been introduced to Israel by the marriage of Ahab to Jezebel, a Phoenician princess. The worship of his goddess would have eventually made its way into Judah during the reign of Manasseh, who established her cult in Judah. In opposing his enemies, likely traditionalists who were averse to his religious and political actions, the king engaged in a massive bloodletting. All of this should come as no surprise during a period in Judah's history when the state concluded that YHWH was impotent and that it was impossible to gain liberation from a cruel and powerful enemy.

48.   *KAI* 26:C, IV.13ff.

The Reforms of Hezekiah and Josiah

Hezekiah (715–687 BCE), who ruled Judah between the reigns of Ahaz and Manasseh, carried out religious reform in order to signal his rejection of Assyrian sovereignty. The implication is that the return to the singular worship of YHWH displaces other gods such as Ashur and makes YHWH once again the supreme deity. The high places were eliminated and the standing pillars and wooden poles of the Asherim were broken into pieces. He also cut into pieces the bronze serpent (Nehustan) made by Moses, since it had become the object of sacrifices. These elements of non-Yahwistic religion go back to Rehoboam (1 Kgs 14:23) and include ones that are Canaanite. Even the serpent was an element of the mother goddess (Asherah) in different deities' artistic representation. In 2 Kings 18:5-8, 2 Chronicles 29–32, and Sennacherib's account of Hezekiah defeat[49] there is no mention of the removal of Assyrian deities. In spite of his efforts, Hezekiah's reforms did not last during the reign of Manasseh.

The reform of Josiah, who reigned as king in Judah from 641–609 BCE, renewed the earlier reform of Hezekiah by removing Assyrian symbols from the temple as an element of revolutionary activity directed against imperial domination. The discovery of the law in the temple (2 Kings 22 and 2 Chronicles 33–34), likely an early form of Deuteronomy, if not merely a literary fiction written by the Deuteronomists, would point to Josiah's support of the Levitical priesthood and their social, political, and religious conservatism. The discovery of this book also helped legitimate Josiah's reign as king. While his royal power was threatened by reduction, the support of the Deuteronomistic traditionalists and others residing especially in the villages and towns would emphasize the shift from the foundation of the David–Zion complex to that of the Mosaic traditions. Thus the cults of Ashur and Ishtar were removed from the temple, including their idols, along with male prostitutes and women who wove garments for Asherah in Canaanite fertility religion. The altars on the roof of the upper chamber of Ahaz and the two courts of the temple were broken into pieces. Josiah pulled down that altar at Bethel and its high place, burned it, and crushed the high place into dust. He also removed the bones of the tombs on the mount and burned them on the altar, defiling it. The horses dedicated to Shamash (the sun god) that kings rode were removed from the temple and burned (2 Kgs 23:11).[50] He also broke the pillars and sacred poles on which he

---

49. *COS* 2:303.

50. Small clay models of horses, chariots, and on occasion riders were likely votive offerings found in Palestine in the late bronze age at Lachish, Megiddo, and Beth-Shan. Ninth- and eighth-century specimens were found in Jerusalem and Hazor.

cast human bones. In addition, the centralization of worship in Jerusalem, the desacralization of high places, and the removal of priesthoods and their high places and sanctuaries were central undertakings. These priests of the high places were slaughtered on the altars and human bones were burned on them. The mediums, wizards, teraphim, and idols were put away. Finally, the Passover, which celebrated the Hebrews' liberation from Egyptian slavery, was instituted as a temple festival. This would have reminded people of an earlier (2 Kings 23) experience of freedom which the collapsing Assyrian Empire promised to the people of Judah.

Perhaps Josiah thought these efforts would not only gain YHWH's favor and lead to divine support for revolution, but also would actualize the enthusiasm and support of those dwelling in the countryside who had suffered under the often oppressive yoke of the monarchy. The reforms of both Hezekiah and Josiah represent an element of revolutionary activity against Assyrian domination.[51]

There were several attempts, first by Israel and later by Judah, to throw off the Assyrian yoke to gain independence, all of which failed until the effective end of the Assyrian Empire in the Babylonian conquest of the last stronghold in 609 BCE. On his way to join forces with Assyria against the Babylonians, the Egyptian king, Neco II, defeated the forces of Josiah who died in the confrontation. From 609–605 BCE Judah was a colony of Egypt, although this sovereignty was assumed by Nebuchadnezzar II of Babylonia, with the defeat of the Egyptians at the battle of Carchemish, resulting in the withdrawal of the Egyptian forces to the borders of Egypt. From the eighth century BCE onward, many of the classical prophets and their editors, including their apocalyptic heirs, sought to move beyond the destructiveness of imperial rule towards a peaceful kingdom that would allow all nations to worship the true God, YHWH, and to cease the making of war.

51. Based upon Assyrian suzerainty treaties, the presence of the 'weapon of Ashur', and the frequent deportation of the gods of the conquered peoples, Spieckermann presents a contrary position and argued that the Assyrians did force their vassals to recognize Ashur and forced their provinces and vassals to engage in Assyrian royal religion (Spieckermann, *Juda under Assur*).

3

Judah under
the Neo-Babylonian Empire

I.
Historical Introduction

When Assurbanipal died in 627 BCE, Assyria was still an imperial power that stretched throughout Mesopotamia into the Levant. But struggles over succession led to a weakening of centralized power. In the course of a decade, Babylon revolted and went on the offensive against Assyria. While the Medes from the north of Iran and the Babylonians conquered the old capital cities in the North, the total collapse of empire came with the conquest of Nineveh in 612 BCE and the final defeat of the Assyrians at Harran in 609 BCE.

The Emergence of the Babylonian Empire and the Colonization of Judah

The new imperial power, Babylonia, emerged from an alliance between the Chaldean kings and those of Media and the sealands. Nabopolassar (625–605 BCE) founded this Neo-Babylonian Empire (626–539 BCE), which came to rule most of Mesopotamia and the Levant for a century.[1] The Babylonian and Median victory in 609 BCE at Harran resulted not only in the scattering of the remaining Assyrian forces and the fall of Harran but also in the defeat of the armies of the Egyptians who were driven south to their own borders. The final deathblow to the Assyrians took place four years later in the battle at Carchemish (605 BCE) and Egypt fled beyond its borders. Judah passed from being a vassal kingdom of Egypt following Josiah's defeat by Necho II and became subject to the Babylonians following the battle of Carchemish. All of the nations of Syria-Israel had become colonies of the Neo-Babylonian Empire by 601 BCE.

---

1.   See Müller, *Babylonien und Israel*, and Albertz, *Israel in Exile*.

The Babylonian Empire's most important ruler was Nebuchadnezzar II, who followed his father, Nabopolassar, to the throne in 605 BCE. Nebuchadnezzar led his army in the conquest of areas including Syria and part of Asia Minor. In 605 he launched a surprise attack against the Egyptians at Carchemish and defeated them (Jer. 46:2). According to the Babylonian Chronicle, a second victory over Egypt occurred at Hamath, leading to Babylonian control of Syria.[2] Jehoiakim of Judah then transferred his allegiance to this new empire and became its vassal for three years (2 Kgs 24:1). However, when Nebuchadnezzar's forces were stalemated and possibly even defeated at the Egyptian border in 601 BCE, Jehoiakim followed the pro-Egyptian party's counsel in his court to rebel against Babylon (2 Kgs 24:1), leading to the attack of Judah by Babylonian allies (Syrians, Moabites, and Ammonites).

Then, in 598 BCE, Nebuchadnezzar led his army to destroy Judah and threatened the sacking of Jerusalem. Only the assassination of Jehoiakim (Jer. 22:18-19; 36:30) and the city's surrender saved it from annihilation. A large contingent of leaders, including the royal successor Jehoichin, was taken into exile and Nebuchadnezzar placed Zedekiah on the throne. The unrest that occurred during his reign threatened his kingship, for many still considered the exiled king in Babylonia the legitimate ruler and anticipated his return. The trip undertaken to Babylon by Zedekiah in 594 BCE may well have been to declare his loyalty to the Babylonian king. Finally, rebellion against Babylonia, with the expectation of Egyptian support, occurred in 589 BCE. However, in 587 BCE Nebuchadnezzar's forces took and destroyed Jerusalem. Gedaliah, the grandson of Shaphan, was chosen by Nebuchadnezzar to be governor of Judah at the city of Mizpah, but was soon assassinated by Judahite zealots, led by a descendant of David, Ishmael. Other Jews and a number of Babylonian soldiers stationed in the city were also murdered. While the rebels fled to Egypt for refuge, Nebuchadnezzar likely sent his forces back to Judah and took a number of Judahites into a third exile. The last king, Nabonidus, spent the final ten years of his reign in the desert oasis of Teman in Arabia, while his son ruled on his behalf in Babylon. He returned to fight the Persians, but lost in his resistance to the army of Cyrus, leading to the fall of Babylon in 539 BCE.

Zedekiah in the Empire

Zedekiah, the successor appointed by the Babylonians, encouraged by a pro-Egyptian faction at his court, foolishly refused Babylonian tribute in 589 BCE, and prepared for war by having formed an alliance with

2. Malamat, 'The Twilight of Judah', 130.

Psammetichus II in 593 BCE. With promised Egyptian support, he thought he had sufficient means to withdraw from the Babylonian Empire. However, just at the decisive time of rebellion, this Egyptian king died and military aid from Egypt did not materialize to save Jerusalem. The city was sacked in 586 BCE and the countryside was devastated. The royal princes along with numerous other high-ranking officials, priests, and administrators were executed, and a blinded Zedekiah and other ranking leaders of the nation were taken into exile. The Babylonians continued the earlier Assyrian policy of mass deportations. As a political policy, the exile of leaders to distant locations was designed to weaken resistance in the colonies.

Having devastated Judah, the Babylonians chose not to rebuild its destroyed towns and cities, and did little to occupy or station garrisons in Judah. The provincial capital at Mispah (Tell en-Nasbeh), which had a small Babylonian garrison, was attacked, and the Judahite rebels loyal to the House of David assassinated the governor and fled to Egypt, forcing the prophet Jeremiah to accompany them. This may have led to a third invasion and deportation, while Judah eventually was annexed to the old Assyrian province of Samaria (Jer. 52:30).

Colonization of the mind became the tool of control. Foreigners began to infiltrate Judah to set up their own fiefdoms. The Neo-Babylonian Empire began to weaken after the death of Nebuchadnezzar II with a quick succession of three rulers, followed by the last ruler, Nabonidus (555–539 BCE), a usurper and former court official who led a religious revival in Babylonia by restoring ancient cults and their temples and chose to worship as his primary deity the moon god Sîn, although he claimed the legitimacy of his rule through the former high god Marduk. By placing a new deity of the head of the Babylonian pantheon, he sought to gain religious power and to break the power of the priesthood of Marduk. He also withdrew to the desert to live in Teman for a decade to insure control of the significant trade route that passed through this area. His efforts to defeat the Persians, under Cyrus the Great, were not successful, and soon the army of Cyrus invaded Babylonia and took, unopposed, the city of Babylon in 539 BCE. The exiles from Judah, those who remained in the homeland, and various colonies of Babylonia now found themselves part of an expanding Persian Empire.[3]

3. See especially Lipschits and Blenkinsopp, *Judah and the Judeans*; Smith-Christopher, *The Religion of the Landless*; Oded, 'Observations on the Israelite/ Judaean Exiles in Mesopotamia'; and Barstad, *The Myth of the Empty Land.*

Neo-Babylonian Culture

Nebuchadnezzar II developed a sophisticated civilization aided by the activity of an advanced scribal culture. The literature, composed in both the complex Akkadian cuneiform as well as alphabetic Aramaic that had become the *lingua franca* of the ancient Near East, included codified laws, religious texts, chronicles for the history of kings and important events, and scholarly and religious texts that included a rich wisdom tradition and ancient mythological writings that continued to be redacted and passed down. Even Jewish exiled scribes began to shape a hybridity with the new culture and learned to communicate primarily in Aramaic.

The lower echelons of Babylonian scribal officials recorded temple gifts, tributes from the colonies, taxes from citizens and the sale of their products, and the distribution of materials and rations to laborers and skilled workers for building extensive monuments, palaces, temples, city fortifications and neighborhoods, and canals. They also kept records of the military munitions, supplies, and numbers of different armies and garrisons. Schools for the training of scribes, of all levels, were attached to palaces and temples to archive documents for libraries and educate in the arts. These schools also trained literary officials to record the data of sacrifices, priestly orders, produce from the fields, the goods sold by merchants, and objects produced for daily life.

Important artistic works included not only architectural buildings, but also decorative works such as Babylon's processional way and hanging garden, beautiful metal works made of cast bronze, iron, gold, and silver, and elegant pottery. The gods, who were dressed in expensive clothing, dwelt in luxurious temples and received the daily care of priests who had overseen their crafting and engaged in the rites of 'opening the mouth' to bring them life. The Babylonian cities, which were known by the Jewish exiles, must have been astonishing to behold and seductive for a people exiled there.[4]

II.
The Babylonian Metanarrative of Empire

Like empires in general, the Babylonian metanarrative includes language of the supremacy of culture, religion, and the military, and justification for conquest in a variety of its historical, mythical, and literary texts.

---

4. See Oppenheim, *Ancient Mesopotamia*, and Sasson, *Civilizations of the Ancient Near East*. Sasson's work includes lengthy essays that provide a detailed overview of Neo-Babylonian society, economy, and culture.

Especially important are the royal titulars that speak of the divine formation, call, and commissioning of the king. The king possessed two roles claiming divine authority: the rule over specific peoples and the restoration of major temples and cities. Thus one reads texts like the following 'uttered by Nebuchadnezzar II': 'Marduk sublimely commanded me to lead the land aright, to shepherd the people, to provide for cult centers, (and) to renew temples'.[5] Similarly, this king proclaimed: 'Marduk... entrusted me with the rule of the totality of peoples, Nabu...placed in my hands a just scepter to lead all populated regions aright and to make humanity thrive'.[6] It is interesting to note that Babylonian power and knowledge in these texts and similar ones, while obviously propaganda, is for rule of less civilized peoples and not for exploitation. The empire through its king is commissioned to protect the conquered nations and to treat them with justice. This is why the gods appointed him to rule the empire of the metropole and its colonies.

Early imperial metanarratives of Babylonia from the eighteenth century BCE were expressed, for example, in both the prologue to Hammurabi's law code for ordering society[7] and in the Creation Epic in which Marduk becomes the god of creation following his defeat of the chaos monster, Tiamat.[8] In the first, the high gods Anum and Enlil choose Babylon to be supreme among nations in the world while Marduk selects Hammurabi to rule over Babylonia and its empire. In the second, the origins of the cosmos, which finds its center in Babylon, are related in the narrative of Marduk's defeat of chaos leading to his rule of the divine pantheon and the heavens and the earth.

The metanarrative, then, includes the religious contention that Babylonia is the center of the world and protected by the high pantheon of gods, especially Marduk, whose temple, the Esagila, was located in the capital city of Babylon. Marduk, as the head of the Babylonian pantheon, chooses the ruling monarchs and oversees their rule. Tribute from the conquered nations flows into the capital, while defeated royalty come to the city to honor the Babylonian emperor. Numerous royal inscriptions end with a hymn or prayer to grant the king well-being, a long rule, and powerful weapons to defeat his enemies. These displays argue that resistance to the chosen monarch is rebellion against the high

---

5.   VAB 4 72 (Nbk 1=Zyl III,3) I 11-14; identical is VAB 4 104 (Nbk 13=III,7) I 22-25.

6.   VAB 4 112 (Nbk 12=Zyl III,5) I 13-17; the same language occurs in VAB 4 122 (Nbk 15=Stein-Tafel X) I 40-46.

7.   *ANET*, 163-65.

8.   *ANET*, 60-72, 501-503.

god's sovereignty over creation. Rebels can only expect destruction. Nebuchadnezzar II in particular is depicted as the new Hammurabi.[9] These ancient texts provide the basis for Neo-Babylonian royal ideology. The Old Babylonian lapidary script was used in royal inscriptions as were archaizing orthographies to emphasize this ideological connection with the past. This Neo-Babylonian narrative was celebrated in colonial spheres in order to colonize the mind of those who were in subjection to the empire. This meant that the subjugated were to recognize Babylonian superiority and their own inferiority.[10]

The Divine Legitimation of Empire

Still linking his reign to the religious traditions of the past for reasons of justifying his rule over the Neo-Babylonian Empire, the Cylinder of Nabonidus (556–539 BCE) contains Marduk's command to rebuild the Ehulhu, the temple of Sîn in Harran:

> I, Nabonidus, the great king, the strong king, the king of the universe, the king of Babylon, the king of the four corners, the caretaker of Esagil and Ezida, for whom Sîn and Ningal in his mother's womb decreed a royal fate as his destiny, the son of Nabû-balāssu-iqbi, the wise prince, the worshipper of the great gods.
>
> Ehulhu, the temple of Sîn in Harran, where since days of yore Sîn, the great lord, had established his favorite residence—(then) his heart became angry against that city and temple and he aroused the Mede, destroyed that temple and turned it into ruins—in my legitimate reign Bēl (i.e. Marduk, and) the great lord, for the love of my kingship, became reconciled with that city and temple and showed compassion. In the beginning of my everlasting reign they sent me a dream, Marduk, the great lord, and Sîn, the luminary of heaven and the nether-world, stood together. Marduk spoke with me: 'Nabonidus, king of Babylon, carry bricks on your riding horse, rebuild Ehulhu and cause Sîn, the great lord, to establish his residence in its midst'. Reverently I spoke to the Enlil of the gods, Marduk: 'That temple which you ordered (me) to build, the Mede surrounds it and his might is excessive'. But Marduk spoke with me: 'The Mede whom you mentioned, he, his country and the kings who march at his side will be no more' (*COS* 2:310-11).

In the imperial metanarrative of Nabonidus, new topics are taken up that were previously unmentioned in earlier ones: dialogues between king and architects, dream reports, and stories of the installation of his daughter as an *entu* priestess of Sîn at Ur.

9.　Berger, *Die neubabylonischen Königinschriften*, 371-75.

10.　Thiong'o, *Decolonising the Mind*.

The Babylonian Political Order

The Neo-Babylonian administration of the empire consisted of provincial governments required to pay tribute and taxation. As long as order in the province continued, the provinces were left alone. With Jerusalem and many of the towns and villages having been laid waste and with the exile of its leaders to Babylonia, Judah provided little threat to the empire. It had little to offer as tribute and taxes to the metropole and its ruler. Judah became a Babylonian province under the governorship of Gedaliah in the new capital of Mizpah (Tell Bet Mirsim) following the sacking of Jerusalem and the exile in 586 BCE. He was a political appointee by the Babylonian court and had a prominent ancestry: his father (Ahikam) and grandfather (Shaphan) had been leading officials in the court of the Davidic kings, since Josiah and the reform (2 Kgs 25:22). However, due to the fanaticism of rebels led by Ishmael, a descendant of David, Gedaliah was assassinated for collaboration with the Babylonians.

The financial structure of the Neo-Babylonian and Achaemenid periods consisted of three sectors: the palace, the temples, and private households, which would support the empire's needs for treasure and loyalty.[11] Redistribution of resources required that an institution not only had sizable wealth, but also provided land and goods to those holding important offices and members of the aristocracy.[12] Private archives point chiefly to the ownership of property, especially estates, by the upper class involved in the state's public institutions.

Public archives identify two important institutions, both the palace and temple, which held the primary positions in the economic history of the first millennium of ancient Babylonia.[13] The house of the king was primary. The palace raised cattle, controlled mining operations for silver, and oversaw trade, both within Babylonia and colonies and other nations. The palace also made and oversaw loans and distributed rations to the nation's poor who needed food, oil, and clothing to survive. To do so intimated that the palace owned or controlled the majority of the land within the state. Of course, there was a 'middle class' of merchants and

11.   Dandamayev, 'An Age of Privatization in Ancient Mesopotamia'. A different view of the temples' economic clout is offered by Jursa, 'Debts and Indebtedness in the Neo-Babylonian Period'. Jursa sees the temples during the Neo-Babylonian period as far more economically anemic.

12.   Van De Mieroop, 'Economic Theories and the Ancient Near East', 59.

13.   Jursa, 'Grundzüge der Wirtschaftsformen Babyloniens im Ersten Jahrtausend v. Chr.'; Renger, 'On Economic Structures of Ancient Mesopotamia'; and Lipiński, *State and Temple Economy*.

artisans. The making of various items, including pottery and idols and the crafting of valuable items including jewelry, were important skills. These goods contributed to the economic wealth of palace and temple.

The military was also important not only in fighting the empire's wars, but also economically, in that spoils of war and gifts were given to the soldiers, especially the high-ranking officers, for their success. The army also secured foreign workers for imperial projects. This also led to the integration of communities of non-Babylonians into the empire.

Of course, the palace's taxation of goods and the temple gifts and sacrifices were substantial sources of revenue for the two great political and economic engines of the empire. Beginning in the seventh century BCE, the palace moved the metropole into market exchange, which led to specialization in trade between the various social classes and between different countries. A more entrepreneurial spirit during this period was at work in trade and commerce, leading to the aristocracy's increased accumulation of wealth. In addition, rentier life was possible from patrimonies inherited by descendants. Noteworthy for the Judahite exiles who remained in Mesopotamia following the Persian conquest is the development of financial houses that provided loans to various ethnicities needing funds for the startup and continuation of businesses. The Murashû documents of Nippur, dating from the end of the fifth century BCE, contain many Hebrew personal names, indicating the presence of one very influential Jewish business family in the local economy during the Achaemenid period.[14]

III.
Jewish Communities during the Exile

The destruction of Samaria ultimately led to the end of any continuing Israelite identity and statehood, leaving Judah alone after 722 BCE to continue its existence as a nation. After the fall of Jerusalem and the ravaging of much of the territory of Judah in 586 BCE, two different groups of Judahite communities continued in different geographical locations: those who remained in a decimated Judah and those who went into exile in Babylonia. The destruction of Judah was extensive, as is demonstrated by the evidence of both archaeology and texts. Extensive archaeological data points to the extent of the destruction of the

---

14. See Zadok, *The Jews in Babylonia*.

kingdom.[15] The decline in the local economy of Judah is indicated by the near disappearance of Greek ceramics and the diminution of pottery types, indicating decline in trade that would arise from a weakened economy.[16] The important cities in Judah that were destroyed included Jerusalem, Ramat Rahel, Lachish, Gezer, Beth-Shemesh, Ein Gedi, Arad, Kadesh Barnea, Mesad Hashavyahu, Tell Keisan, Megiddo, Dor, Akko, Tell 'Erani, Tell el-Hesi, Tell Jemmeh, Tell Malhata, and Tell er-Ruqeish, along with many of the Philistine coastal cities. These cities were left in ruins throughout the time of the Neo-Babylonian Empire. Only a few urban sites escaped destruction: Tell en-Nasbeh, Tell el-Fûl, and Bethel, along with the towns in the tribal area of Benjamin and in the southern region of the Negev. Following the assassination of Gedaliah, Israel appears to have been divided into two regions: the northern province of Samaria and the southern area, which would become partially occupied and controlled locally by the Edomites. The Edomites had been allies of the Babylonians against Judah. The Samaritan governors simply transferred their province from the Assyrians to the Babylonians. However, Judah was not inserted into a heavily organized administrative system, since the new Judahite governors gave their primary attention to Babylonia and regions in the vicinity.[17] The devastation of Judah offered little to exploit. Its inhabitants were burdened with the requirement of annual taxes and lived lives of desperation as more and more non-Judahite groups migrated into the land and took up residence (see Lam. 2:2; 5:2-5, 9-11).[18]

The leaders of Judah in Jerusalem, who survived the conquest of the city and were not among the executed, were sent into exile. Members of the royal family, courtiers, administrators, chiefs of clans, the wealthy, high-ranking priests, and skilled artisans made the journey to Babylonia. They were the *'am haggōlâ*, 'the people of the exile', who were considered by the Chronist, Jeremiah (24:1-10), and by Ezekiel (33:23-29) as the legitimate descendants of the covenant people. They were in contention during and after the exile with the *'am hā'āreṣ* ('people of the land') who remained behind and mixed with those who migrated into the

15.   Ephraim Stern points to the archaeological evidence from this period, and concludes that the nation experienced 'a state of total destruction and near abandonment' (Stern, *Archaeology of the Land of the Bible*, 2:321-26).

16.   Lehmann, *Untersuchungen zur späten Eisenzeit in Syrien und Libanon*.

17.   See Stern, *Archaeology of the Land of the Bible*, 2:308-309.

18.   See Smith-Christopher, 'Reassessing the Historical and Sociological Impact of the Babylonian Exile'.

country. The exiles considered themselves the truly chosen (the good figs in Jer. 24:1-7) who would one day return to inherit once again the land, rebuild the temple, and reestablish the Davidic monarchy (Jeremiah 30–31). The bad figs were the 'people of the land' who would be scattered, mercilessly treated, and no longer allowed to occupy the land (Jer. 24:8-10). This view likely had the support of the followers of Jehoiachin and his surviving courtiers, who had been imprisoned in Babylon in 598 (2 Kgs 25:27-30) and certainly became dominant in Judah once the several returns took place.

Due to lack of evidence, it is not possible to know much about the exiles in Babylonia.[19] Peter Ackroyd argued that while their conditions were 'uncongenial', he still thought they lived together in their own communities, were allowed to carry out a normal life of agricultural existence and to experience a good deal of freedom in their livelihoods and traditions, and were loyal to their captors.[20] Bustenay Oded contends that the exiles were not imperial slaves made to engage in a state of permanent physical labor; yet, they were still forced to work on projects on occasion.[21] Some Babylonian economic records indicate that the exiles and other non-Babylonians also served the military settlements of the state. Thus, when needed, the exiles performed services for the palace, temple, large estates, and soldiers. It therefore appears more likely that the exiles would have had the status of slaves (foreigners and those captured in war) who performed the labor of the empire (see Isa. 52:3) and yet were still otherwise allowed to conduct their livelihoods. It is no coincidence that metaphors of slavery and imprisonment are numerous in biblical texts dating from the exilic and early post-exilic periods (Isa. 43:6; 45:14; 52:2; Jer. 34:13; Mic. 6:4; Pss. 105:18; 107:14; and frequently Job). At least some Jewish captives became corvée laborers as well as craftsmen for royal and temple projects.[22] This situation would have continued throughout the entire period of their captivity under Babylonian hegemony.[23]

19. See Zadok, *The Jews in Babylonia*; Bickerman, 'The Babylonian Captivity'.

20. Ackroyd, *Exile and Restoration*, 32.

21. Oded, 'Observations on the Israelite/Judean Exiles in Mesopotamia'. The Murashû documents indicate that some, although not all, exiles were slaves while others at least during the following Persian period achieved economic prosperity. See Dandamayev, *Slavery in Babylonia*.

22. Oded, 'Judah and the Exile', 483. See, for example, the Etemenanki cylinder that lists the lands within the Babylonian Empire that contributed works and lumber for the building of the ziggurat of Marduk in Babylon (Unger, *Babylon*).

23. Oded, 'Observations on the Israelite/Judean Exiles in Mesopotamia'.

The merging of communities of non-Babylonians into roles that promoted the well-being of the empire would have led to the enculturation of some of them into the ideology of the Babylonian metanarrative. Thus, many found their minds colonized by the traditions of their conquerors. There is no indication that all of the exiles would have lived in their own communities and carried on their particular legal, religious, and economic activities. Rather they mostly would have been laborers of the state working for the palace and temples or in helping to develop fallow lands possessed by these institutions and the upper class.[24] Their labor would have been largely agricultural, although those with important skills would have found positions within the appropriate guilds of scribes and artisans and some would even have been involved in entrepreneurial business enterprises. It would have been difficult for the exiles to maintain their own cultural and religious traditions, especially if they wished to achieve a higher status in the empire.

Some of the exiles of Judah perhaps lived in their own villages located on state lands in Babylonia and were even allowed to form their own communal worship of YHWH without direct interference (Psalm 137). The Babylonians did not engage in religious intolerance and persecution or require those conquered to worship their deities. Subsequently the exiles could practice their own religion dedicated to YHWH, although now they had to transform their theology to focus on a universal deity who did not have to have a temple, to be present and worshipped (since the one in Jerusalem had been destroyed).

Babylonian contracts from the Neo-Babylonian period[25] contain the names of 2500 persons. Some of these names, as many as 70, are clearly Jewish, although there could have been others, because a number of Babylonian and West Semitic names are closely related to Jewish ones. For example, in addition to those in the Bible like Zerubbabel (Zer-Babili), son of Saltier (Šalti-ilu, Ezra 2:2; 3:2), Mordecai (Ezra 2:2), Bilshan (Bel-šunu), Shenazzar (Sin-šar-user), son of Jehoiachin (1 Chr. 3:17), Mordecai, son of Yair (Est. 2:5, etc.), and Sheshbazar (Ezra 1:11), the Babylonian texts include West Semitic names like ᶠTaba-ᵈIš-šar, daughter of Ya-še-ʿ-a-ma, Ni-ri-ya-a-ma, son of Bel-zera-ibni, Šá-ab-ba-ta-a-a, son of Nabu-šarra-bullit, Ig-da-al-ya-a-ma, son of Naniddina, and Baniya, son of Amel-Nana.[26]

---

24. One of the building inscriptions of Nebuchadnezzar states that he required 'lands of the Hattim' to engage in forced labor in building the Etemenanki (cf. Schmid, *Der Tempelturm Etemenanki in Babylon*).

25. Zadok, *The Jews in Babylonia*, 38-40, and 'Some Jews in Babylonian Documents'.

26. Dijkstra, 'Religious Crisis and Inculturation', 103.

It would have been likely that the exiles included scribes and teachers who would have settled in Babylonia. Certainly administrative officials and a well-educated aristocracy, all of whom would probably have been literate in Hebrew and Aramaic, were taken into exile. Thus, education was probably significant among this group. The meager written and material evidence makes it impossible to know if any schools were established among the exilic communities. Yet the large number of texts likely written, redacted, and preserved during this period and in the early post-exilic times points to the necessity of some type of education due to the lengthy period of exile (more than two generations).

Did some of the Jewish intelligentsia have access to any Neo-Babylonian literature? This, of course, is impossible to know conclusively, but the literary themes of this culture seem to be well known to Jewish exiles as evidenced by the books of Second Isaiah and Job. The knowledge of Neo-Babylonian royal ideology and religious mythology intimates that some of the educated captives eventually had access to and perhaps could read the scribal texts in Aramaic and perhaps even Akkadian. It is not unthinkable that some of the Jewish scribes among the captives may have served in the Babylonian administration.

Cuneiform was known by some scribes in Israel and Judah from the early Assyrian period even into the early Hellenistic age.[27] In addition, Isaiah 28:11 possibly refers to Akkadian ('an alien tongue'). The exiles' knowledge of Akkadian likely would have been necessary, although the uneducated might have relied only on Aramaic, leaving it up to Jewish scribes to master this difficult language. This was possible due to the fact that Aramaic was the alphabetic language becoming the *lingua franca* of the empire, while Akkadian would have been known in the Levant since the Late Bronze Age. That Jewish scribes knew Aramaic well is evidenced by its considerable influence on later Hebrew texts.[28]

Contextualization in Babylonia would have been pursued by the intelligentsia of the Jewish exiles whose exposure to a vastly different civilization provided them the opportunity to have first-hand knowledge of Babylonian culture, including its literature. Contextualization connotes a means of interpretation based on the understanding that texts and authors are integrally linked to their culture, time, space, social institutions, and political structures. If removed from these locations, due to

27. Horowitz, Oshia, and Sanders, 'A Bibliographical List of Cuneiform Inscriptions', and *Cuneiform in Canaan.*

28. Horowitz, Oshia, and Sanders note that a few Neo-Babylonian texts have been found ('A Bibliographical List of Cuneiform Inscriptions').

such things as immigration, prior interpretation of reality becomes twisted, leading to the necessity of adapting earlier knowledge to a new world. In Babylonian captivity, the exiles would necessarily have to readjust their past written and oral records to understand the present and to cultivate hope for the future. Most important among the exiles were the prophetic voices of Habakkuk, Ezekiel, and especially Second Isaiah.

The Exile and Cultural Transformation

Cultures constantly change, but behavioral and intellectual adjustments and reformulations become even more precipitate when a nation with its own customs, ideas, and social behavior suddenly encounters a new and substantially different setting. The symbiosis of new events that a people experiences with the emerging discourse results in necessary cultural and behavioral adaptations reflected in an ever-evolving tradition. Cultural imperialism engulfed the exiles who had witnessed and endured the fall of what they had been taught was the inviolable sacred city of Jerusalem and, when accompanied by slaughter, execution of many leaders of the rebellion, and the exile of the skilled and elite leadership, the danger was the end of their own civilization that would dissolve among the components of what was said by the imperialists to be a superior expression of life. This crisis of ethnicity, identity, and survival would been a threat to the continuation of the exiled people of Judah. Many likely merged into the surrounding peoples and traditions.

In addition, if the conquered Judahites in Babylonia could not reshape their theological traditions of election and providence to allow for a new understanding of God's activity in the life of the imperiled nation and the larger world, then the exiles would be lost to history as a distinct ethnos and world view. Their colonized minds would have lost an active resistance to the empire with the result of the loss of their distinctiveness as a culture and a people. The challenge was not only that of deportation, but also in resisting a vast empire with an advanced cultural tradition in the form of literature, architecture, military power, economic development, and religious symbols.

The colonized exiles do not simply adopt the culture of the empire, since their colonial orientations inevitably merge in different ways with the civilization of the imperialists. Yet, even in adopting the major cultural features of the ruling metropole, the exiles are never accepted as equals by the Babylonian imperialists. The loss of the indigenous language and defining traditions from the past would result in separating colonials from their native language (from Hebrew to Aramaic) and from defining traditions that express their culture and values.

While the claim of cultural superiority was critical for imperial domination, strategies of resistance were necessary to oppose and gain at least some independence from the dominating power. These strategies emerged from identifiable groups in exile: prophets, priests, and royals. Hence forms of resistance to the empire and its culture result in a less than 'pure' form of such things as the imperial language and traditions. This distortion leads to the rejection of imperial culture and its ideology of rule.[29]

Interculturalism in Judah

Dikstra has lamented the fact that investigations of the Babylonian crisis confronting Judah around 600 BCE have not been utilized through the lens of interculturalism that occurred when the exiles entered into captivity.[30] Empires transform the cultures of the conquered through metanarratives, art, literature, and colonization of the mind. Imperialism rejects any expression of egalitarianism, since the privileged in the metropole rule the majority who dwell in marginal spaces and in the subjugated territories. Through the systematic penetration and domination of the cultural life of the conquered, including the values and behaviors orchestrated through imperial institutions (e.g., schools, temples, and royal administration), there is the imperial attempt to create a new colonial consciousness.[31] While culture, including art, literature, and religious symbols, plays a role in this domination, the major tools are discourse and education.[32]

Control and exploitation produce an angry response among a segment of the colonized who then seek to subvert the empire's domination. In addition to conquest by empires and the indoctrination into imperial knowledge and culture, enculturation is also intensified when peoples migrate into new cultural regions, leaving them bereft of many of their former cultural roots associated with their homelands. This migration may come as a result of necessity (e.g. famine and the new sources

29. Bhabha, *The Location*, 85-92.

30. As pertains to the Babylonian exile, enculturation involves introducing and conditioning the people of Judah as forced immigrants to a new culture in order that they may become functioning members within it. Similar is contextualization which involves the process of the interpretation of texts. Texts, like their authors, are intrinsically connected to their temporal space, culture, language, social world, geographical location, and political reality. See Dijkstra, 'Religious Crisis and Inculturation', 99.

31. Petras, 'Cultural Imperialism in the Late 20th Century', 139-40.

32. Kieh, 'The Roots of Western Influence in Africa'.

needed for additional food) or of force (conquest). In imperialism the center dominates the periphery and holds sway over all of its dependents.[33]

One way that migrants who form diaspora communities attempt to maintain their identity is to remember their important traditions of the past. Edward Said has observed that 'appeals to the past are among the commonest of strategies in interpretations of the present'.[34] Of course there are as many views of the past as there are of the present. In responding to empires, colonial leaders, who come to resist imperial pressure, often act to shape social groups by an appeal to past traditions that have been formative in indigenous cultural expressions and then alter them to allow either assimilation into the new context or to resist the imperial cultural power. This means that colonial spokespersons revise the values and ways of behaving in their own past traditions, leading to new views that confront the empire and its affirmations transmitted through sources of indoctrination, like colonial education. Colonial leaders set about the task of forming social groups that will become those who transmit the emended conceptualities and actions to a larger public, whether their views are compliant or resistant. Obviously, conflict among the colonialists themselves will emerge, since competing groups among the conquered will have alternative visions of cultural engagement with the empire.

The Exiles and Enculturation

One of the most challenging difficulties facing the exiles, then, was continuing enculturation of the emerging generations in native beliefs and customs, now that the temple and worship centers were no longer present to serve as the symbols needed for traditional socialization. In addition, the schools of scribes and children of the elite had to be replaced with some form of educational institution, possibly that of family scribal guilds. This becomes obvious from the literature that is written or redacted in the exile. Furthermore, meeting places for worship and community activities may have been structured within informal assemblies that eventually led to what we know as synagogues, although the first archaeological evidence for this institution comes from the latter part of the third century BCE in the environs of Alexandria. The preservation of past conventions and observances would have required some public interaction of the exiles in worship and discourse.

33. Petras, 'Cultural Imperialism in the Late 20th Century'.
34. Said, *Culture and Imperialism*, 3.

Diversity of Exilic Communities

While the explicit evidence for these communities is often limited, one
nonetheless may posit the existence of several competing groups within
the exiled community of Judah in Babylonia and the early Persian
period.

The Prophetic Party of Second Isaiah

This group consisted of a prophetic leader and his followers who, during
the exile, committed acts of sedition against the Babylonians and supported the new power arising in the east in the form of Cyrus II. Following the exile they constituted a party of outward accommodation to the
leading empire that controlled them, but eventually were transformed
into apocalyptic seers who saw the endtime as imminent and the destruction of the ruling empire as inevitable. While still under the domination
of foreign empires, they spoke and wrote a 'hidden transcript', composed
by marginals who sought to dissemble the privileged positions of their
foreign and native oppressors and exploiters. Apocalyptic language
allowed them to use a code that communicated to insiders, but appeared
to be nonsense to the uninitiated.

The Zadokite Priestly Party of the Priestly Code

With the death of Josiah, the dreams of the Levites to achieve the status
of priests, who were active in and perhaps even controlled for a brief
time the Jerusalem temple, ended. Yet the struggles of Zadokites and
Levites for legitimacy and power were not to end until the restoration
and perhaps even as late as the middle of the Hellenistic period. Each
had its scribes who redacted priestly and Deuteronomic traditions that
cast them in a favorable light. The Zadokites, who perhaps had already
achieved control of the temple prior to the Babylonian conquest, achieved
their status and authority through the Priestly Code. They were the ones
who descended from Phinehas and ultimately Aaron and received the
right to preside as priests in the sanctuary. Ezekiel, a former priest turned
prophet of judgment, had been a Zadokite.

The Nationalistic Party of the Royal Families and Courtiers

Two kings in exile and their surviving families (Jehoiachin and blind
Zedekiah) also contended for the legitimacy of dynastic succession.
Their descendants were to include after the exile Sheshbazzar and
Zerubbabel, two of the first governors following the early returns to
Judah.

The Party of Traditional Sages

Job's three opponents and even the imposter Elihu are presented as traditional sages seeking to reaffirm the older teachings of the wise: the justice of God, retribution, the discipline of suffering, and divine deliverance of the sufferer. The political implications of these views are a part of the desire that this group had to achieve for its members coveted positions of power and influence within the reconstituted community by the patronage of dominant priests and governors.

The Party of Radical Sages

This group of sages disputed the teachings of the ancestors and traditional YHWH religion in the effort to reconstitute anew the restored community. The stakes were high for them, for failure surely would lead to their decimation. However, success would mean a new order which they would shape and undoubtedly lead.

Apostates

There is textual evidence that some of the exiles worshipped other gods. In Jeremiah 44:16-18 (post-Jeremiah) the exiles respond to Jeremiah's accusation of their apostasy, that they and their ancestors worshipped the 'Queen of Heaven' (likely Ishtar) and received food and protection from their enemies. But when they returned to the worship of YHWH they knew only disaster.

Another community, led by the 'People of the Land' had been left behind when the groups of the elite were exiled. This group, who did not go into captivity, consisted largely of not only commoners (mainly unskilled and untutored) but also of outsiders who had moved within the land to take up residence in an unprotected country.

Emigrants

Finally, there was the group of emigrants who, following their assassination of Gedaliah, left to seek refuge in Egypt, forcing Jeremiah to accompany them. It is likely that Jeohoahaz and his family, exiled in Egypt, were regarded as the legitimate descendants of David.

The Exile as the Diaspora

What does the word 'diaspora' entail? The differences and complexities in understanding this term are significant. However, diaspora is best understood to refer to an 'exilic or nostalgic dislocation from homeland'. Interpreted in this manner, the term points to ideological and socio-political features for a community existing away from its homeland.[35]

As noted earlier, postcolonial interpretation seeks to discover a people's comparable experiences of past and present to assess the psychological and cultural difficulties occasioned by being uprooted from familiar settings and transitioning to a new situation. Postcolonial biblical interpretation's diasporan hermeneutics examine the many literatures and oral traditions of peoples who have been transplanted elsewhere to live in an alien environment. For Homi Bhabha, the goal of the diasporan interpreter is to be a 'vernacular cosmopolitan' able to translate between cultures and to reinterpret traditions. In the taking up of residence and existence under a dominant power, exiles became marginals who had no place to dwell except in the interstices of cultures, caught betwixt and between past and present locations and experience. Thus they participate in intercultural exchange, but become wanderers in the world. The hope exists, however, to maintain elements of older tradition with new interpretations that adapt to new situations and resist the forces of imperial hierarchy, cultural uniformity, and political hegemony that would extinguish a people's ethnic and cultural identity. Postcolonial scholars direct their attention to the interrelationship of those moving across borders and dwelling in a new world that is completely alien to their previous experience.

Exile, a policy used to relocate colonial leaders to various and different locations by the Neo-Assyrian and Neo-BabylonianEempires, is the forced movement of people from their homelands to another geographical location.[36] During the dominance of these two metropoles (Assyria and Babylonia), those transported to Assyria and Babylonia were primarily the upper class leadership and nobility as well as skilled artisans, scribes, and others with special skills that could be of assistance to imperial rulers. Further, the term 'exile' suggests the results of hybridity as the culture and language of resettled communities change due to engagement with the majority civilization.[37] Inevitably this involuntary relocation transforms the exiled community into a disadvantaged minority. As marginalized people, exiles dwell on the periphery of culture, governments, and economics. They are the Other whose voice is silenced by the majority culture. The colonized in new spaces must learn to speak to the majority in ways that express their loyalty to them without

---

35. Braziel and Mannur, 'Nation, Migration, Globalization', 4.
36. Segovia, 'Postcolonial and Diasporic Criticism in Biblical Studies', 187.
37. Ashcroft, Griffiths, and Tiffin, *Key Concepts in Post-Colonial Studies*, 68-70.

denying their own interests, with the goal, however, of maintaining their defiance towards the empire and their hopes for liberation and a new beginning.[38] As the voice of otherness, diasporan theology calls out for liberation from oppression; uses hidden transcripts to expose, critique, and provide an alternative vision and narrative to the metropole; values the diasporan experience as the crucible for solidarity and community, giving expression to hope; and engages in hybridity as fundamental to cultural life without requiring the complete abandonment of formative, past tradition.

IV.
The Prophetic Resistance to the Empires:
Jeremiah and Second Isaiah

The exilic and post-exilic prophets of Judah not only directed messages of judgment against their own rulers and other leaders of the nation for social oppression, but also often spoke messages of condemnation against the colonizers who had brought the small country into subjection. Postcolonial features of hybridity, mimicry, the 'other', migration, and 'translated writings' are featured in many of their oracles. While cultural adaptation among the exiles would have necessarily taken place in Babylon and even in Egypt where some survivors sought refuge, the texts of the exilic and early post-exilic periods that reflect on the exile and current situations point to resistance of the empire.

Jeremiah and the Babylonian Exile[39]

Jeremiah was the son of Hilkiah, a levitical priest in Anathoth of the former tribe of Benjamin, located only two to three miles north of Jerusalem, and yet in a very different culture from the former kingdom of Israel. As the son of a Levitical priest in the old northern territory, Jeremiah inherited no love for the Davidic Dynasty and the Zadokite priests who controlled the temple of Jerusalem and sought to end the

38. Segovia, 'Toward Intercultural Criticism', 322. Also see his essay, 'Toward a Hermeneutics of the Diaspora'.

39. Among the important studies of Jeremiah, see Mowinckel, *Zur Komposition des Buches Jeremias*. Also see Hyatt, 'The Deuteronomic Edition of Jeremiah'; Nicholson, *The Book of the Prophet Jeremiah*; Thiel, *Die Deuteronomistische Redaction of Jeremiah*; Holladay, *Jeremiah 1 & 2*; Clements, *Jeremiah*; and Lundbom, *Jeremiah 1–20, 21–36, and 37–52*.

existence of rival temples and sacred high places.[40] Jeremiah disputed the
David–Zion traditions that were heralded in Jerusalem and among those
loyal to their leaders (for example, the oracles concerning the House of
David in 21:11–23:8;[41] 'The Temple Sermon' in 7:1-15, 26:1-24; and the
'inhabitant of the valley' or Jerusalem, 21:13; cf. 22:6-7). Instead, he
turned to the older traditions of the Exodus, Wilderness Wandering, and
Entrance into the Land (e.g. the collection of oracles in 2:1–4:4) to shape
his theological discourse.

The prophet Jeremiah, who was active in the late seventh and early
sixth centuries BCE, lived in one of the most chaotic and destructive
periods in the history of Judah and early Judaism. According to the
superscription (1:1-3), he began to prophesy in the thirteenth year of the
reign of Josiah (627 BCE), and some forty years later was forced to go to
Egypt with the assassins of Gedaliah, the governor of Mizpah, perhaps
only a short time after the fall of Jerusalem in 586 BCE. From there, he
disappeared from history.

Traditions from the North, particularly those associated with Moses,
predominate in the call and in the earliest preaching of Jeremiah.
Jeremiah reflects upon the Exodus, Wilderness Wanderings, and Settlement in 2:2-9, where his indebtedness to the Song of Moses is clear.
From this song, Jeremiah learned that YHWH's grace toward Israel
frames the entire sweep of world history. Within this frame, however,
lies Israel's ingratitude, her corrupting ways with other gods, which
result from settled and agrarian living, and YHWH's punishment of Israel
for what in his eyes is wrongdoing. YHWH stays the hand of the enemy
only as Israel is about to be completely destroyed, then with a remnant
YHWH begins a new work of salvation, at which time the enemy is
defeated. Jeremiah follows the Song of Moses in depicting the Mosaic
Age as the idyllic period of national history, a time of purity when Israel

40.   Stevens, *Temples, Tithes, and Taxes*.

41.   Zedekiah ('Righteous of YHWH' or 'Righteous is YHWH'), in contrast with
the future Davidic king whose name—and entire being—will be 'YHWH is our
righteousness' (23:5-6). The oracle concerning 'a righteous branch' (23:5-6), a later
addition by an editor of this collection, is similar to Assyrian and Babylonian oracles
pronouncing the future reign of kings and the results of their reign (*ANET*, 606, and
Grayson, *Assyrian and Babylonian Chronicles*, 24-37). The name of the 'righteous
branch' is *ṣidiqîyāhû*, which means 'YHWH is my righteousness'. This future king,
unlike the preceding rulers in the collection save for Josiah (22:15-16), will exemplify what the royal house should have been but only rarely was. Another addition,
perhaps from the same editor, also attributes to Jeremiah an oracle concerning a
'righteous branch' who will execute justice in the land (33:15).

was YHWH's 'devoted bride' or 'first fruits' (2:2-3; cf. Deut. 32:10-12). He also views Israel's settlement in the land as the time when things began to go bad (2:7; cf. 2:21; 8:13; Deut. 32:13-18).

From Deuteronomy 1–28, which was originally a Northern document, Jeremiah learned that the Mosaic covenant was conditional in nature, and that obedience to this covenant was the basis on which land tenure rested. Though the Mosaic covenant could be broken—as it repeatedly was by Israel—at the same time it could also be reconstituted. Jeremiah preached both messages—the brokenness of the covenant and YHWH's decision to remake it—more clearly than any other prophet (2:20; 5:5; 7:5-10; 31:31-34; 32:37-41).

Jeremiah's preaching betrays indebtedness to the Northern prophet Hosea, whom we discussed in the previous chapter. From Hosea, Jeremiah learned that the covenant is like a familial bond—between husband and wife or between father and son; that sin is rooted in a lack of the knowledge of YHWH; and that a breach of covenant amounts to religious harlotry or adultery. Jeremiah follows Hosea in representing YHWH as a deeply compassionate God, one who experiences personal hurt by having to vent his wrath, and one who wants, after the punishment is over, to receive his wayward child home again (31:16-20; cf. Hos. 11:8-9).

During his long ministry in Jerusalem, Jeremiah also appropriated theology from Southern traditions associated with Abraham and David. One event associated with Abraham loomed very large for Jeremiah, as it did also for Isaiah and certain other prophets, and that was Sodom and Gomorrah's destruction (Genesis 18–19). From this, Jeremiah realized that YHWH punishes entire cities for unrighteous living (5:1-8), and that a point can be reached where mediation for such cities is no longer possible (7:16-20; 11:14-17; 14:11-12; 15:1-2). Not only immoral prophets, but also seemingly innocent people, such as the man who brought the news of Jeremiah's birth to his father, are likened by Jeremiah to the inhabitants of these proverbial cities (23:14; 20:15-16) and must suffer a similar fate when Jerusalem is destroyed. In his early preaching, Jeremiah stated that the blessings of the Abrahamic covenant were contingent upon Israel's repentance (4:1-2), but later he affirmed that YHWH's covenants to Abraham and David were eternal and remained intact. YHWH in future days would make good his promise to bless the nations through Israel, and Israel could count on David's royal line surviving, despite the nation's demise. This is fully in keeping with the basic tenets of Southern theology.

During his lengthy prophetic ministry, catastrophic events occurred. These events included the death of Josiah at Megiddo at the hands of Necho II of Egypt in 609 BCE, the fall of Assyria in its last stand at the battle of Carchemish (605 BCE), the rise of the Neo-Babylonian Empire (626 BCE), the incorporation of Judah into this empire (605 BCE), the first invasion of Judah due to the rebellion of King Jehoiakim, likely resulting in his assassination, the surrender of Jerusalem to the besieging imperial army (597 BCE) followed shortly by the exile of Jehoiachin and an entourage of the leaders of the revolt (597 BCE), and finally the devastation of Judah and the destruction of Jerusalem in 586 BCE resulting in the exile of the skilled workers and upper-class leadership to Babylonia.

In the collection of the 'Oracles against the Nations' (Jeremiah 46–51), most of which appear to have been post-Jeremiah oracles of judgment and spoken and composed by later prophets, perhaps within his 'school', there are several that betray the exilic experience. The two principle targets of prophetic judgment are Egypt and Babylonia.

The explanation of Jeremiah's presence in Egypt, where he disappears from history, incorporates the narrative explanation of the assassination of Gedaliah at Mizpah by Ishmael, whose band of rebels flees to Egypt to escape Babylonian retribution. According to the narrative, Jeremiah, together with Baruch, are forced to accompany them. This story became the necessary link for Jeremiah's oracles against Egypt in the 'Oracles against the Nations' (chaps. 46–51). The oracle against Egypt occurs in 46:13-26 and is followed by an oracle of salvation to Jacob in 46:27-28 that speaks of deliverance after the time of punishment. The speech of judgment against Egypt is placed within the context of Nebuchadnezzar's coming invasion of Egypt. Imitating the language of the oracles concerning the 'Foe from the North', this prophet issues warnings in Migdol, Memphis, and Tahpanhes to prepare for the sword that shall devour them. The Egyptians may not expect protection from the Apis bull[42] who has already fled the coming destruction, because King YHWH

_____

42. The Apis bull was the animal manifestation of the god Ptah of Memphis. This bull represented the god's fertility and power. He also was the representation of the divine Nile and the god of the annual flooding of the river, Hapy. Treated as a divine being, only one such bull lived at a time. Up to the time of the XIIth Dynasty Amon was a Theban god of no more than local importance, but as soon as the princes of Thebes had conquered their rival claimants to the rule of Egypt, and had succeeded in making their city a new capital of the country, their god Amon became a prominent god in Upper Egypt. It was probably under that dynasty that the attempt was made to assign to him the proud position, which was afterwards claimed for him of 'king of the gods'. In spite of Amon's political ascension, he also enjoyed

has 'thrust him down' and directed the Babylonian invasion. YHWH is the one who makes impotent the high god, Amon of Thebes,[43] the Egyptian kings, and their gods. Even the hired mercenaries of Egypt provide no defense against the invaders. A great multitude of Egyptians have already fallen, and those who survived spoke of returning to their own people, 'the land of their birth', to escape the invading army. Using the language of exile, the Egyptians, like Israel of old during the Exodus, are to prepare their baggage, not for liberation, but rather for exile. Memphis, like Jerusalem before, will become a 'waste, a ruin, without inhabitant'.

The very long section of oracles against Babylon (Jeremiah 50–51) depicts the fall and destruction of what the prophets of Judah considered the great destroyer of nations. The greatest of Judah's enemies that wreaked great havoc among its villages and towns, and finally destroyed Jerusalem and took its captives into exile was Babylonia (586 BCE). Zedekiah, who foolishly rebelled against Nebuchadnezzar in 589 BCE, had hoped in vain for Egyptian support. However, this never materialized even though in 587 an Egyptian army did set out to confront the Babylonians. For whatever reason, the army returned to Egypt, leaving hapless Zedekiah and the pro-Egyptian party to face the wrath of the great king.

During this second invasion, the Babylonian ruler showed no mercy. Many of the leaders were executed, including Zedekiah's own children. He was then led away to captivity where he died without a successor. He was the last king to sit on David's throne.

The savagery of the invaders who will come to destroy Babylonia is mentioned, although Cyrus the Persian is not mentioned by name, only the Medes. The gods, especially Marduk, who commissioned the king to rule by building new temples and refurbishing the old, as well as to extend his empire on their behalf, are mentioned first. In 50:2, the prophet utters the following:

popularity among the common people of Egypt. He was called the vizier of the poor. It was said that he protected the weak from the strong and was an upholder of justice. Those who requested favors from Amon were required to demonstrate their worthiness or to confess their sins first.

43.   Amon was the Egyptian high god of Amun and became identified with the chief deity who was worshipped in other areas during that period, *Ra-Herakhty*, the merged identities of *Ra* and *Horus*. This identification led to another merger of identities, with Amun becoming Amun-Ra. In the *Hymn to Amun-Ra* he is described as 'Lord of truth, father of the gods, maker of men, creator of all animals, Lord of things that are, creator of the staff of life'.

> Declare among the nations and proclaim,
> set up a banner and proclaim,
> conceal it not, and say:
> 'Babylon is taken,
> Bel is put to shame,
> Mer'odach is dismayed.
> Her images are put to shame,
> her idols are dismayed'.

Babylonia's enemies are also described as the Foe from the North. They will be devastated by their invaders. The empire that caused great destruction and death to many in Judah and beyond will now face the same ruin. The earth will quake with the fall of the mighty empire, while wild animals will traverse its ruins.

With the fall of Babylonia, the people of Judah shall come weeping and seeking YHWH. They ask the way home to Zion, promising now to join an everlasting covenant that will never be forgotten. Now they give praise to YHWH for his vindication.

Serai'ah, the son of Neri'ah, son of Mahsei'ah, is commissioned by Jeremiah to take these words and read them to the captives in Babylon so that they may know that Babylonia, one day, will fall and they will be redeemed. 'The word which Jeremiah the prophet commanded Serai' the son of Neri'ah, son of Mahsei'ah, when he went with Zedeki'ah king of Judah to Babylon, in the fourth year of his reign. Serai'ah was the quartermaster' (Jer. 51:59).

Second Isaiah and the Babylonian Exile

The text known as Second Isaiah occurs in Isaiah chapters 40–55, following the oracles and their additions in chapters 1–39. The book concludes with oracles composed and possibly spoken by Second Isaiah's school of followers who lasted into the Persian period of the post-exilic age. The empire that subdues Judah is the Neo-Babylonian one (626–539 BCE; cf. chaps. 46; 47; 48:20-21). Furthermore, in Second Isaiah, a new foreign king, given the title of Messiah, is Cyrus of Persia (560–530 BCE; cf. 41:2-3, 25; 44:24–45:13; 48:14). The leaders and skilled laborers of Judah were taken into Babylonian captivity. Second Isaiah composes and likely speaks the message to the exiles to leave Babylon, cross the desert, and return to Zion.

Second Isaiah's interpretation of sixth-century national and international events draws heavily on First Isaiah's interpretation of the nation and the great empires. An understanding of the eighth century and of First Isaiah's interpretation is therefore essential.

When the prophet behind First Isaiah was young, the Neo-Assyrian Empire began to intrude into the territory of Israel and Judah. Tiglath-pileser III (745–728 BCE) made his first great western campaign in 743–738 BCE. A coalition of western states under Uzziah of Judah was defeated, leading to the payment of tribute. A second campaign in 734–732 BCE resulted in Gilead, Galilee, and Damascus becoming Assyrian provinces. Pro- and anti-Assyrian parties thereafter entangled the politics of Israel. Menahem of Israel paid tribute to Tiglath-pileser in 738 BCE. The anti-Assyrian Pekah (736–732 BCE) assassinated Pekahiah and then, in 734 BCE, joined with Rezin, king of Aram, in an unsuccessful attempt to force neutral Judah to join their anti-Assyrian coalition. Consequently, Hoshea (732–723 BCE) was appointed king of Samaria by the Assyrians. Relying on Egyptian aid, he rebelled in 725 BCE, which precipitated the destruction of Samaria in 722 BCE by Sargon II, and the deportation of 27,290 Israelites.[44]

In the south, Judah managed to carry out a religious reform under the strong Hezekiah. Like the renaissance under Josiah a century later, it sought a revival of national life and a restoration of the boundaries of the ancient Davidic empire. Hezekiah's own coalition against Assyria, how-ever, did not prove long lasting. In 701 BCE, he found himself besieged in Jerusalem, 'like a bird in a cage', according to Assyrian annals.[45] Though Jerusalem was not destroyed, Hezekiah had to capitulate, his heavy tribute ending dreams of a return to the glorious days of old.

As Babylon declined, a new figure came to the fore, Cyrus the Persian. The Persians were an Indo-European tribe who settled in the ancient territory of Elam. Their name is derived from Persua (modern Fars), one of their first strongholds. The Persian prince Cambyses had married the daughter of the Median king Astyages, from which union with Cyrus was born. The Median army revolted against Astyages and handed him over to Cyrus around 550 BCE. Having consolidated his position in the east, Cyrus then led a campaign into Asia Minor against Croesus of Lydia, taking Sardis and making Lydia a Persian province in 546 BCE. His propaganda depicted him as liberal toward those whom he defeated. He treated Croesus well and won over the Greek colonies in Asia Minor. Nabonidus' unpopularity contrasted with Cyrus' popularity. Nabonidus' return to Babylon in 539 BCE made possible the celebration of the New Year Festival, apparently for the first time since he had left for Teman ten years before, but the king's sacrilegious behavior in the ceremonies

44. *ANET*, 284.
45. *ANET*, 288.

alienated the priests. The famous 'Cyrus Cylinder' shows how their allegiance had shifted to Cyrus. In language akin to Second Isaiah's about Cyrus (cf. 41:2, 25; 44:24–45:13), it declares, '[Marduk] pronounced the name Cyrus, king of Anshan, declared him to be (come) the ruler of the world... Marduk beheld with pleasure his good deeds and upright mind (lit. heart) (and therefore) ordered him to march against his city Babylon.'[46] Second Isaiah shared this view of Cyrus as liberator and respecter of native religions, declaring him to be the anointed of YHWH (45:1). In the fall of 539 BCE, Nabonidus fled and Cyrus' army entered Babylon without a battle. Cyrus himself later entered, forbade looting, and appointed a Persian governor, leaving native institutions and traditions undisturbed.

Soon after, Cyrus issued a decree, preserved in Ezra 6:3-5, allowing the temple of Jerusalem to be rebuilt, with the funds to come from the royal treasury. Judah became the province of Abr Nahara in the Persian Empire, under a Persian governor.

The Yahwistic Metanarrative of Second Isaiah

The message of Second Isaiah seeks to convince the exiles that the time of languishing in exile is at an end. There is to be imminent liberation from Babylonia, due to the coming conquest of Cyrus of Persia. Thus, as in the Exodus from Egypt, the Babylonian captives are to prepare to return to their homeland. The gods and kings of Babylon cannot keep the captives from leaving, for they are about to fall to the new empire of Persia. Israel in exile and after the return will be the heir of the covenant formerly made with the House of David (2 Samuel 7 and Psalm 89). Second Isaiah also argues that the exile to Babylonia enables Judah to become a 'light to the nations', the proclaimer of YHWH as the true God who all peoples are to worship.

The prophet is commissioned in 40:1-11 in a heavenly ceremony, which recalls other call narratives in Exodus 3–4, Jeremiah 2–10, Isaiah 6, and Ezekiel 1–2. The distinctiveness of Second Isaiah's call is the importance placed on the new Exodus-Conquest, which culminates in the journey to the homeland. The book then subverts the popular discouragement obstructing the new Exodus (40:12-31) in a disputation, which contains a series of questions that show that nothing can hinder YHWH's intent to save the people from exile, including the nations (vv. 12-17), the gods represented by Babylonia and kings (vv. 18-24), and members of the divine court (vv. 25-31). This is followed by a trial

46. *ANET*, 315-16.

scene that pits YHWH against the gods, and Israel against the nations (41:1–42:9). In two parallel scenes (41:1-20 = 41:21–42:9), YHWH judges the nations and their gods to be in the wrong, and upholds Israel as his image and servant. Chapters 42:10–43:8 describe YHWH's victory over chaotic waters and primordial night (vv. 10-16); Israel made blind by the darkness will have light for the journey (vv. 18-20). While Israel's punishment is deserved (vv. 21-25), the people have been forgiven but now are allowed to return to Zion (43:1-8).

The next major section, 43:9–44:5, reminds Israel that it is God's witness to the nations of YHWH's supremacy by its reenactment of the Exodus-Conquest. In 44:6-23, Israel is called to witness to the living and victorious YHWH, in contrast to the statues of the gods that represent powerless deities.

In 44:24–45:13, Cyrus, the Persian king, becomes the center of attention. First mentioned in 41:2-3 and 41:25 as YHWH's instrument, he is called by name in 45:1 and is identified as the anointed (messiah) of the one God. He is divinely commissioned to carry out God's plan for Israel's liberation and new beginning as a nation. In 45:14-25 (also 44:26-28), Cyrus is to rebuild the temple city of Zion.

In chapters 46–47, Second Isaiah announces that the city of Babylon will be destroyed and its departing inhabitants will carry with them the statues of its helpless gods. Chapter 48 admonishes the exiles to make preparations for leaving Babylon and the return home. How many Jewish exiles left is unclear, but they did face the challenge of rebuilding the temple city to fulfill Second Isaiah's visions of the imminent future.

In chapters 49–55, Zion and the servant become the focus of the prophet's interest. The servant recalls Moses the prophet who speaks to Israel in captivity, promising that they will journey to the land of promise (chap. 49). In 50:1–51:8 God once again will be present to his people in captivity and liberation even as he was with their ancestors in Egypt. He will bring to their knees their current enemy, the power of the raging sea of chaos, and all nations who threaten to oppress Zion. Chapters 54 extols Zion, the goal of the Exile, now restored with husband, children, and buildings. Chapter 55 invites all to come to Zion to the banquet, and from that holy shrine, to witness to YHWH's victory that brought them there.

Though they provide little biographical information, the speeches do permit fairly precise dating. They assume that the readers or hearers know that Cyrus, king of Persia, will soon conquer the Babylonian Empire. Such an assumption was only possible after Cyrus deposed his sovereign Astyages in 550 BCE, incorporating Media into the Persian Empire, and conquered Lydia in 546 BCE. That conquest, along with the palpable decline of the Babylonian Empire, signaled one of those great changes of fortune that every so often reshaped the ancient Near East. The speeches do not mention the entry of Cyrus' army into Babylon in 539 BCE. All of this points to a likely dating of the speeches during the 540s BCE.

It is clear that the prophetic composer of Second Isaiah was aware of Neo-Babylonian culture: the imperial world view, military conquest, economic policies, which adversely affected the victims of conquest, some indication of a possible knowledge of cuneiform,[47] and some knowledge of royal inscriptions.[48] In particular, in his effort to resist the empire and to negate the colonization of the minds of his fellow captives from Judah, his attack on cult images points to his concerted efforts to subvert the authenticity of Babylonian cosmology and imperial greatness that, among other things, presented Babylon as the center of the cosmos. In his own likely hidden transcript that eventually became public, the author of Second Isaiah satirizes the animation and knowledge of crafted idols.[49] The idol satires also undermined an important industry that especially profited Babylonian priesthoods, but this, once known, would have raised the ire of the temple priesthoods. Even so his would prove to be an important strategy of resistance to Babylonian imperialism and would reaffirm the sovereignty of YHWH that would pave the way for several returns to the Jewish homeland during the early Persian period.

The Subversion of the Babylonian Metanarrative

According to its metanarrative, Babylon is the center of the earth and holds together the created order. In addition, it is the sacred metropole of an ever-enduring empire that will not fall to invaders. In his theology of resistance, Second Isaiah seeks to undermine the major features of their imperial world view by means of an intentional mimicry that expresses both the rage of the exiles against their captors as well as the internal desire to become like them.

The exile's rage and mimicry constituted a vision of themselves as rulers and members of a new Jewish empire to which all nations would flow. Second Isaiah's prophetic composer speaks of the fall of those nations who have fought against Israel (41:11-13; 49:25; 51:22-23;

---

47.   Note Paul, 'Deutero-Isaiah and Cuneiform Royal Inscriptions'.

48.   Behr, *The Writings of Deutero-Isaiah*; and Vanderhooft, *The Neo-Babylonian Empire and Babylon in the Latter Prophets*, 170. See Berger, *Die neubabylonischen Königsinschriften*.

49.   See especially Berlejung, *Die Theologie der Bilder*.

54:15-17) and will even be a ransom for the exiles (43:3-4). Eventually they will come to their former victims in chains, lick the dust from their feet, and even devour their own flesh (45:14; 49:23, 26a). Even so, YHWH, the sovereign Lord of the world, will address these nations (42:6; 49:6) and announce that his salvation will reach all who turn to him and wait for his redemption. Recognizing the redemption YHWH has brought to the exiles (41:5; 42:10-12), they will turn to him of their own choosing, recognize YHWH as the true God, and serve Israel. Israel's role will be that of becoming a 'light to the nations' (49:6). Thus the subjugated nation will one day replace the empire and become the universal sovereign over all other peoples.

One sees another part of this cultural and religious subversion in the composer's description of the divinely chosen ruler or Messiah. In the first of the major sections of the text chapters (Isaiah 40–48), the prophet adapts the language of cuneiform royal inscriptions. Shalom Paul outlines a variety of phrases in these inscriptions, which Second Isaiah would likely have known, based on his language use.[50] One is the predestination and subsequent affirmation of the king's legitimacy by a divine call. Others include the royal terms, 'shepherd', 'servant', and 'beloved', common to Mesopotamian titulars. Second Isaiah utilizes these to speak of Cyrus II and the servant in the Servant Songs (42:1-4; 49:1-6; 50:4-9; 52:13–53:12).[51] Subsequent to the divine calling of the

50.   Paul, 'Deutero-Isaiah and Cuneiform Royal Inscriptions'.

51.   See Hallo, *Early Mesopotamian Royal Titles*, 132-42. In Sumer the phrase is 'called by the god by name' (*Sum.mu.pàd.da DN*). Other similar titulars were 'named with a (good) name by the god' (*Sum.mu.[du10].sa4.a DN*), 'beloved of the god' (*Sum.ki.ág DN*), 'favorite of the god' (*Sum.še.ga DN*), 'servant' (*Sum.arad₂*), and 'shepherd' (*Sum.sipa*). These were later found in the Akkadian royal instructions. For example: 'name had been called or designated' by the gods, Akkadian *šumšu/zikiršu/nibíssu/nibīt šumišu nabû* and *šumišu/zakār šumišu/nibīt sumišu zakāru*. These are identical to the calling of Cyrus and the 'servant' in Second Isaiah ('I have called you by your name, 43:1; and 'he designated my name', 49:1). Other Akkadian expressions of royal titles include 'the beloved of the god' (*nāram ili*), 'the favorite of the god' (*migar ili*), and 'the chosen of the god' (*itût [kūn libbi] ili*). These correspond to two titles in Second Isaiah: 'my beloved' (41:8) and 'my chosen one whom I desire' (42:1). A number of kings in Assyria and Babylonia are said to be predestined by the gods to a particular task, while they were still in the womb of the mother. This expression occurs not only in reference to the call and commissioning of Jeremiah (Jer. 1:5) but also to the 'Servant' (42:6; 49:1, 5-6, 8). However, in Second Isaiah it is only the 'Servant'. Additionally, the Akkadian terms for 'shepherd' (*rē'ûm*) and 'servant' (*wardum*) are found in reference to Cyrus ('my shepherd', 44:28) and the 'servant' in speaking of YHWH's chosen one throughout the Servant Songs (42:1-4; 49:1-6; 50:4-9; 52:13–53:12).

ruler, the Mesopotamian king is given his primary duty to perform, namely the protection and well-being of those within his empire, including colonials. This is quite similar to the mission of the servant who will 'set the captives free' (cf. Isa. 42:7), that is, liberate them to experience a new beginning.[52]

Second Isaiah also seeks to undermine the Babylonian metanarrative by identifying Cyrus II as the chosen savior of the exiles in Babylon (44:24-28). In Second Isaiah he is both 'my shepherd' (Isa. 44:28) and 'my anointed' one (Isa. 45:1). The first title is taken from the ideology of kingship in the ancient Near East[53] ('shepherd' as a royal title is also found in Jer. 17:16; Zech. 10:2; 11:16; 13:7), while the second is limited to Israel/Judah. Powerful kings including Hammurabi in the eighteenth century and Assurbanipal in the seventh century BCE, were two who bore the title 'shepherd'. Shepherd, in Mesopotamian royal language, referred first to the king's cultic authority as the head of the priesthood and the mediator between humans and the gods; and second to the task of the ruler to protect and provide for his people.[54] The 'anointed one' is not found in the ancient Near Eastern ideology outside of Israel. In Israel it refers to a prophet's ritual anointing of the one whom YHWH has chosen to rule (1 Sam. 16:6; 24:6-7, 10-11; 26:9, 11, 16, 23; 2 Sam. 1:14, 16; 19:21-22; 23:1; Pss. 20:6-7; 28:8; 84:9; 89:38, 51; 105:15 par. 1 Chr. 16:22; Ps. 132:10 par. 2 Chr. 6:42; Ps.132:17; 1 Sam. 2:10; Lam. 4:20; and Hab. 3:13). It is not used of the kings of Northern Israel, but rather of those in the line of David. The responsibility of the Davidic king to build and maintain the temple is now passed on to Cyrus II who will follow the direction of YHWH and rebuild the temple, beginning with the laying of foundations. Thus, Cyrus II becomes the heir of the Davidic and Zion traditions in their revision by Second Isaiah. Jerusalem and the temple will be rebuilt, although no mention is made of the reconstitution of the Davidic monarchy. Now it is Judah who will enjoy God's eternal covenant, not the Davidic dynasty, while Cyrus is the 'anointed one'

52. See the inscription: 'The people of Sippar, Nippur, Babylon, and Borsippa who, through no fault of theirs, have been kept imprisoned in it (i.e. the conquered city of Dur-Yakin), I destroyed their prison and let them see the light' (Paul, 'Deutero-Isaiah and Cuneiform Royal Inscriptions', 182).

53. Gadd, *Ideas of Divine Rule*, 38-39. Also see Bernhardt, *Das Problem der altorientalischen Königsideologie*, 68 n. 1. For 'shepherd' in Akkadian and Sumerian, see Seux, *Epithètes royales* akkadiennes *et sumériennes*: *nāgidu* (p. 189), *re'u/rē'û* (pp. 243-50), *utulla* (p. 356), and Sumerian *sipa* (pp. 441-45).

54. See Soggin, 'רועה *r'h* to tend'.

chosen to carry out Judah's redemption. The identification of Cyrus II with the messiah reshapes the meaning of the Jewish tradition to point to any deliverer sent by God to redeem the oppressed, elect people.

As Bhabha's discussion of ambivalence and mimicry suggests, one sees in Second Isaiah one of the colonized who resists the imperial meta-narrative. In so doing, he is shaped by the conflict between the desire to be the ruler (or at least the representative of the sovereign YHWH who directs history), the view of Cyrus as the new messiah, and the repulsiveness of domination. Assuming he is the 'Servant' in the Servant Songs, the royal imagery embedded in the language of these psalms points to the prophet's assuming the role of the ruler. In imagining himself as the dominant ruler, the colonized servant comes to look down on his conquerors, but as the dominated, he negated the possibility of becoming what is despised. The author's overstatement found in the use of imperial imagery of rule mocks the pretensions of colonialism and becomes a form of resistance to colonial discourse. Mimicry in colonial and postcolonial literature is most commonly seen when members of a colonized society imitate the language, dress, politics, or cultural attitude of their colonizers, but often with a disdain and mockery that subverts their false attitudes of superiority and legitimate rule. Yet Second Isaiah's mimicry allows him to assume a role that rejects the conqueror's expressions of power. Under colonialism and in the context of immigration, mimicry is seen as a pattern of behavior: one copies the person in power, because of the desire to have access to that same power oneself. In the case of the prophetic composer of Second Isaiah, likely the Servant, he mimics the Babylonian tradition of rule and adds that YHWH (not Marduk who is implied but not mentioned by name) providentially controls human destiny.[55]

The proclamation of Second Isaiah also gives expression to the diasporan experience in Babylonian captivity.[56] Second Isaiah's meta-narrative of Judah has the primary purpose of forging a shared memory and history among his fellows in exile to give them hope for a future and to prepare them for the approaching journey home to Judah. He accomplishes this by setting forth a message of liberation from Babylonian captivity that YHWH is bringing about through the Persian invasion. This portrait of liberation is informed by the language and events of the primal story of the freeing of Jewish ancestors from Egypt

---

55. See Bhabha, *The Location*, 85-92.
56. Segovia, *Decolonizing Biblical Studies*.

narrated particularly in the first twenty chapters of the book of Exodus and poetically presented in the texts of Psalms 78:12-54, 105:16-45, 106:7-33, and 136:10-16. Second, his metanarrative of new beginnings adapts the formative traditions of Judah's past to a new geographical location that represents an alien environment. The contemporary diasporan experiences may suggest themes and questions that require a new amalgam of cultural hybridity and different traditions with which to interpret life in the exile.[57] Third, Second Isaiah's metanarrative uncovers comparable experiences in the traditions of Israel's past which aid in understanding the terror of being removed from the familiarity of situations to new and different ones. He especially draws on the Exodus and the David–Zion traditions in accomplishing this understanding. And fourth, the imperial metanarrative of Babylonia is used by the prophet of the exile to offer symbols and understandings that may be integrated with Judah's past traditions.[58] Second Isaiah does this, for example, with the use of 'wilderness' (40:3) and 'passing through the waters' (43:1-7) to recall the Exodus experience.

In Second Isaiah's poetic narrative of cultural resistance, it is apparent from the fourth Servant Song that the hidden transcript of the prophet of the exile becomes public and leads to his execution. The fourth servant song (52:13–53:12) indicates that the servant is an individual, likely the prophet himself, who was executed, dying a vicarious death for his people in exile. It is certainly possible that this servant was a prophetic leader like Moses during the Exodus from Egypt who pronounces a proclamation of freedom from foreign slavery. If this is an accurate portrayal of the servant, then it would be possible that his message of deliverance, coupled with the approaching conquest of Babylonia and its empire by Cyrus and his army, would have been considered damaging to Babylonian efforts to repel Cyrus' invasion, once it was heard and reported to the authorities. The Babylonians knew they could not successfully resist invasion from without and at the same time rebellion from within. The more radical exiles among the subjugated saw the coming of the Persians as the Jewish community's means of liberation from an oppressive rule.

57.   Smith-Christopher, *The Religion of the Landless*, 11; and Cuellar, *Voices of Marginality*.

58.   See Kim D. Butler's study of diasporas that focuses on three key elements: exile and return, relationships with the host lands, and interrelationships within the diasporan group: 'Defining Diaspora', 191.

Second Isaiah's Cultural Hermeneutics and the Transformation of Tradition

Making use of fundamental theological traditions and their language that permeated Israel's earlier culture and faith, the prophet speaks of the creation of the cosmos (Genesis 1–2; Psalm 104) and the individual (Gen. 2:5-8, 18-24; 22:8-10; Job 10:8-12), the Exodus (Exod. 12:29–15:19), Zion (2 Sam. 7; Psalms 46; 48), and the covenant with the House of David (2 Sam. 7:1-17; Psalms 2; 89; 110). His expansive Exodus tradition includes not only the departure from Egypt, but also the journey through the wilderness (Exod. 15:22–19:1) and the entrance into the land (Joshua 1–12; Judges 1). These traditions were celebrated in Israelite liturgy in the First and Second Temple periods. In using and adapting these to the exile, the prophet would have drawn from rituals of resistance that would have occurred secretly within the context of a private assembly or communal worship.[59]

The danger to the prophet, of course, was the exposure of his secret transcripts to the Babylonian authorities, something that appears to have happened, if he indeed is the Servant.

Second Isaiah is important because of the transformative, intercultural theology present in his speeches. This is present in particular in his understanding of YHWH, the reshaping of older prophetic speech consisting largely of brief oracles of judgment and salvation to present a fluid discourse that incorporated the theological metamorphosis of ideology, the reformulation of traditions that included circumcision now becoming a rite of passage into the Jewish community and to signify social identity, and the resistance to and subversion of the Babylonian imperial metanarrative, the purpose of which was to legitimate this empire.

Especially in the first large section (chaps. 40–48), Second Isaiah urges his fellow exiles to regard Babylon as the Egypt of old that their ancestors had known. In recalling the narratives of the old Exodus, wandering in the Sinai wilderness, and entrance into the land of Canaan, the prophet used these salvific traditions to speak in similar terms of the new Exodus from Babylon, God's coming to nurture his people in the desert during the Wilderness migration, and then the divinely guided return to the homeland in Judah. These would be the divine acts by which the Judahites will become the true Israel once again. Cyrus is the instrument of YHWH who will bring about the destruction of Babylon, the liberation of the exiles, and the rebuilding of the cities of Judah and especially Zion. In the ancient Near East, the rebuilding of the temple

---

59. Scott, *Hidden Transcripts*, xi; and Young, *Rituals of Resistance*.

city was the task of the victorious deity. Zion will not be left in ruins. The rebuilding of the temple city and its sanctuary is central to Babylonian religion, particularly carried out by the high god Marduk, who the Babylonians believed to be the creator, the guide of history, and one who chose them to rule what became the Neo-Babylonian Empire. Marduk was also the arbiter of human destiny in Babylonian religion.

In the second large section (chaps. 49–55), the prophet who perhaps is the Servant in all of the Servant Songs, announces the defeat of Babylon to be followed by the journey homeward to Zion. Once there, in a city made of jewels (54:11-12), a great banquet will be held for all to celebrate this new-found redemption. While the exiles are collectively identified as the Servant in 44:21, this is likely a later editorial insertion. The Servant, who is called to a mission to Judah and through it the world, appears in the songs to be the prophet (Jer. 1:3-10; Isaiah 6) who is the individual subject or speaker: 42:1-4 (5-9); 49:1-6; 50:4-9; 52:13–53:12. Furthermore, the mythic tradition of YHWH's defeat of chaos is used to speak of the liberation of the exiles (52:9-11).

While there are numerous examples of hybridity and cultural transformation by means of new ideas and manners of behavior in the formulation of the tradition of the new Exodus to Zion, three are especially important: first, the trial speeches (41:1–42:9); second, which will be discussed in a subsequent section, the idol satires; and third, the language of the supremacy of YHWH. In Second Isaiah the trial speeches are not only directed against a sinful Israel of the past but also against the foreign nations, particularly Babylonia and its deities. In these speeches, the prophet states clearly for the first time in the history of Israel the affirmation of YHWH as the one God (41:4; 43:1-10; 44:6, 8; 45:21-22).[60] As the creator and redeemer throughout the prophet's disquisition, YHWH becomes the sovereign ruler of the cosmos (see, e.g., Isa. 40:12-18, 21-26; 41:2-6; 45:5-8; and 51:9-10). Monotheism has now entered into Israel's theological discourse of faith.

Second Isaiah and the Divine Warrior

Second Isaiah also appropriates and then transforms one of the earliest theological designations of YHWH: he is the Divine Warrior who fights on Israel's behalf in undoing the Canaanites and especially Baal, their god of War. YHWH is now the one who will defeat the rulers of the earth and bring their kingdoms to an end (40:23-26), and in particular he will destroy Daughter Babylon, the 'mistress' of an empire that its people

---

60.   Machinist, 'Mesopotamian Imperialism and Israelite Religion', 238-58.

thought would endure forever (47:1-15). As the Divine Warrior, he provides liberation for the weak and renews their strength, while he also brings the powerful nations to their end (40:29; 41:1). As the providential God who directs human history, YHWH brings from the east a victor to trample nations, some of which comprise those of the extended Babylonian Empire (41:1-6). This chosen liberator is Cyrus, king of Persia (44:28; 45:1).

Economics in Second Isaiah and Resistance

Resistance to the empire was not simply through cultural hermeneutics that led to the reshaping of past theological traditions to revitalize the faith and to resist the empire, but also included economic features best understood through the application of social-scientific studies, including Marxist and Neo-Marxist formulations of product, ownership, classes, and alienation. Second Isaiah's continuous proclamation of the exile's return from exile threatened one source of foreign laborers for the economic institutions of the palace and temples in ancient Babylonia. Indeed, this declaration, if private, was the captives' major hope for liberation and, if it became known in a public transcript, it would have threatened to collapse the entire Babylonian economy dependent on foreign workers to survive. In addition, God's freeing of captives would also bring to an end the supply of resources in the empire that enabled its major institutions of palace and temples to continue. An empire based on the exploitation of its foreign slaves and captured artisans and scribes would suffer enormous economic decline if the transcript became public and was affirmed by different conquered groups in exile.

The strong emphasis on monotheism (40:18; 44:6-8) in opposition to Babylonian polytheism also had revolutionary consequences, especially in regard to economic considerations and royal ideology that pointed to divine and legitimate earthly locations.[61] According to Second Isaiah, YHWH is both the creator and director of history, not Marduk.[62] As creator, Marduk in Babylonian religion is the one who provides the food necessary for consumption, and as the one who directs history he establishes the empire by supporting the Babylonian kings' conquest and rule of the nations who become the imperial colonies. By transferring these two roles to YHWH and denying the existence of other gods, including

61. See the relevant essays in Pongratz-Leisten, *Reconsidering the Concept of Revolutionary Monotheism*.

62. For Marduk's myth of creation see the 'Enuma Elish', *ANET*, 60-72, 501-503; and for his role as the god of history, see *ANET*, 308-309.

Marduk, the prophet attempts to decolonize the minds of the Jewish captives who were in exile. The rule of Persia is seen to be more benign and less intrusive, while establishing a context in both Babylonia and in the homeland in which the religion and nation of Judah are able to thrive.

In addition, the idol of Nabu (46:1), the scribe and minister of Marduk and in some texts his son, resided in the temple of Ezida, located in Borsippa. Nabu is especially the god of wisdom, which includes knowing the secrecy of divination and sorcery (47:9-13). Further, the attribution of counsel to YHWH (46:10) demonstrates that YHWH is the God of wisdom, not Nabu, and through strategic planning will bring destruction to the empire. The weakness of the Babylonian gods is demonstrated by their being taken as plunder in captivity by Cyrus (46:1-2).

The idol satires were directed not only against the gods of Babylonia in a merely theological dispute to deny they were indeed deities, but also, more importantly, against the imperial ideology that stressed Babylonian kings ruled by means of the decision of the gods, in particular Marduk (40:18-20; 41:5-7, 21-29; 42:8, 17b; 44:9-20; 45:16, 20-21; 46:1-2, 5-7; and 48:5). This attack against the idols had the major objective of undermining the divine legitimation of Babylonian power and cultural supremacy and at the same time damaged the vitality of idol crafting in the Babylonian temples. Isaiah 40:18-20 demonstrates the prophet was familiar with the Babylonian 'mouth washing' ritual (*mīs pî*).[63] This ritual pointed to priestly participation in awakening the idol, crafted by skilled artisans, to life.[64] In this passage, *misken* is likely identified with Akkadian *muskkannus* used in Mesopotamia for ornamental purposes in the making of furniture. Nebuchadnezzar's Wadi Brisk inscription reads: 'A canopy of *musukkannu*-wood, the durable wood, I had covered with real gold' (for the goddess Gula).[65] The pericope in 40:18-20 indicates the prophet's awareness of the Neo-Babylonian skillful making of votive objects and idols.

Further, as demonstrated in 46:1-2, the prophet parodies the procession of the statues of Bel (Marduk) and his son Nebo (Nabu) who go, not along the processional way to be enthroned in their sanctuaries, but rather into exile, lacking the power to resist their captivity. This captivity, to be carried out by the Persians under Cyrus II, echoes the

63. Berlejung, *Die Theologie del Bilder*, 369-91; and Williamson, 'Isaiah 40, 20'.

64. See Walker and Dick, 'The Induction of the Cult Image'; and Jacobsen, 'The Graven Image'.

65. VAB 4 164 [Nbk 19-WBr] B vi 12-13.

Babylonian taking of Israel's cultic paraphernalia into captivity, including the ark of the covenant. During the Babylonian *akitu* festival, the most important festival in the Babylonian year, Nabu's statue would travel by boat up the Euphrates from the Ezida temple in Borsippa to enter Marduk's temple complex, Esagil. Nabu would join the statue of Marduk in the ritual procession through the Ishtar Gate along Babylon's sacred way. Marduk would then be carried to the Esagil located next to the E-temen-an-ki, 'the House of the Foundation of Heaven and Earth'. These cult statues proceeded together, drawn in chariots by ceremonial animals, to the temple complex.[66] While these idols are to be taken into exile, YHWH is heralded as the one true God (46:1-7). In Babylonia, the making of idols with gold overlay, silver chains, and mulberry wood that resists rot by skilled craftsmen was an economic necessity for the temples' wealth and provided an income for an important guild of workers. Consequently, the condemnation of this business was another way of undermining the Babylonian economy (44:9-20).

The Persians, to whom we turn in the following chapter, treated with respect the cults of the conquered nations, even returning cult images and sacred treasures to their original temples. With the Persian king Cyrus' rise to power, the Judeans are permitted to return to their land, rebuild their temple, and resume life there, albeit life as a colony of the Persian Empire.

66. See Hallo, 'Cult Statue and Divine Image', 14-15; and Midmead, *The Akitu Festival*.

4

The Persian Empire and the Colony of Judah

I.
Historical Introduction[1]

Cyrus II and the March to Empire

Establishing the Achaemenid dynasty that was to endure until the conquest of Persia by Alexander the Great in 332 BCE, Cyrus II, the Achaemenid King of Persia (559–530 BCE), entered unopposed the city of Babylon in 539 BCE, where he was hailed as the new ruler of the former capital of the Neo-Babylonian Empire. According to the Babylonian Chronicle: 'In the month of Arahshamnu, the 3rd day, Cyrus entered Babylon, green twigs were spread in front of him—the state of "peace" (*šulmu*) was imposed upon the city'.[2] Persia became the metropole of a vast empire that ruled most of the ancient Near East and even Egypt for some two centuries.

The road to this imperial status was a long and winding one that took years to travel before reaching its destination. Defeating the Medes by 550 BCE whose king, Astyages, was killed in battle, Cyrus then moved east, taking control of Lydia in 546 BCE. For the next six years (546–540 BCE) he extended his empire in the east. The Behistun inscription, dating from 520 BCE, indicates that Parthia, Drangiana, Aria, Chorasmia, Bactria, Sogdiana, Gandara, Scythis, Sattagydia, Arachosia, and

---

1. For a review of Persian history and list of sources, see Curtis and Tallis, *Forgotten Empire*; Sancisi-Weerdenburg, Kuhrt, and Root, *Achaemenid History VIII: Continuity and Change.* Also see Allen, *The Persian Empire*; Briant, *From Cyrus to Alexander*. For the literary sources, Kuhrt, *The Persian Empire*. Much of our information about the history, religion, and political organization of the Persians was supplied by Greek historians, not indigenous writers, due to the fact that many Persian sources have not survived.

2. *ANET* (3) 306.

Maka were eventually absorbed, although the historicity of their being taken by Cyrus is questioned. It is likely that Cyrus himself led the army that defeated many of the nations that came within the Persian Empire.

Following the conquest of the Babylonian Empire and the nations of Asia Minor, the Persians conquered the different states of the Levant. Most of Egypt was later conquered by Cambyses II (530–522 BCE) when Persian forces carried the day at the battle of Pelusium in the eastern Nile Delta in 525 BCE. Thus Persia came to include most of southwest and central Asia and extended south to Egypt, westward to the Hellespont, and eastward to the Indus river. Its only significant military failure before Alexander was the defeat by the Greek city-states of the European mainland at Marathon in 490 BCE and the sea battle of Salamis in 480 BCE. This halted the Persian Empire's extension into Europe.

The enormity of this empire (in excess of 3000 km on its east–west axis and more than 1500 km from north to south) made it the largest in world history to this point. Its geographical, environmental, and cultural diversity were of epic proportions. For example, while Aramaic was the *lingua franca* of the empire and served as the language of most official correspondence, other official languages of the empire included Elamite, Akkadian, Old Persian Greek, Aramaic, and hieratic Egyptian. Thus, wide differences in language and culture presented formidable obstacles to a centralized and direct form of rule. Instead, the Achaemenids came to establish a system of provinces overseen by Persian governors and yet permitted large measures of local autonomy to loyal kingdoms and tribes through the practice of their own political, social, and religious traditions. In a loosely knit system of satrapies, given initial shape by Darius I (522–486 BCE), Persian sovereignty was recognized by means of tribute, taxes, and treaty. In its foreign rule, the Achaemenids were not the tolerant and benign rulers their propaganda depicted. However, there were major changes brought about by the necessity of ruling this huge area of land and sea that called for forbearance in the areas of local constitutions and religion.[3]

From the Death of Cyrus to Alexander

Cambyses II (530–522 BCE) followed his father, Cyrus II, to the throne after Cyrus' death in 530 BCE during a battle against an Iranian people, the Massagetae, along the banks of the Syr Darya river. The new king was soon successful in conquering Egypt in 525 BCE. However, he died during his journey from Egypt back to Persia to quell a local revolt

3. Grabbe, *A History of the Jews and Judaism*, 133-66.

leading to an extensive rebellion that greeted the accession of Darius I (522–486 BCE), a member of the Achaemenid royal house. The putting down of this rebellion led to Darius' desire to spread the Persian presence eastward into Eastern Europe against the states in Anatolia and Greece and westward into India. He subdued Thrace in 512 BCE and engaged the Scythians at the mouth of the River Danube. When allied with the states in Anatolia and Cyprus, however, the Greek states proved to be a cohesive military power that resisted successfully the Persians. Hostilities between Athens and other Greek nations led to the defeat of the Persian forces at Marathon in 490 and later at the naval battle of Salamis.

Darius has been given the credit for the development of an imperial bureaucracy resulting in twenty satrapies administered by governors appointed by the royal court. The new system allowed for the reformation and practice of indigenous laws codified to allow for the specificity of legal requirements at a local level, but also to guarantee that the administration of each satrapy had a conduit for taxation and tribute. This likely propelled Judah's efforts at codification of civil and religious legislation in the Priestly document, giving increased significance to the Torah, temple, and Zadokite priesthood. When Alexander defeated the forces of Darius III (336–330 BCE) at Issus, the new Hellenistic empire and its later divisions controlled an enormous land mass that included not only the land mass of the Persian Empire but also extended west into Eastern Europe.

II.
Persian Culture and the Imperial Metanarrative

The Achaemenid rulers, like most emperors, conceived of a unified world order under their hegemonic control. However, cultural unification was not a part of this ideology. By allowing local peoples to continue their traditional social institutions and culture, coupled with the propaganda of the Persian monarchs being chosen to rule by the gods of their conquered colonies, the Persian kings projected for reasons of propaganda the image of religious tolerance that they hoped would dampen the desire to revolt among most colonies. They evolved an administrative system of governing their colonies (satrapies), flexible enough to cater to the variety of colonial languages, races, and religions, while also maintaining enough unity of government necessary to maintain the empire. Local rulers were allowed to preside over their kingdoms, although a Persian satrap was appointed to insure loyalty that would not allow revolt, civil order, and the payment of taxes.

The propaganda of the peaceful kingdom and the faithful worshipper chosen by the gods of the nations to rule the colonies cannot logically be reconciled with Persian religion and Avestan belief in Ahura Mazda as God and Creator and Zarathustra, his prophet. Ahura Mazda's nemesis, Angra Manyu, was the evil spirit, who opposed him. Even so it would have been unwise to attempt to impose Avestan religious beliefs and practices on the numerous and ancient peoples conquered and formed into provinces. In addition, the attempt to force Persian religion on the colonialists would compromise the integrity of the principle of stability. Thus, the Great Kings referred to themselves as the supporters of their colonies' temples and priesthoods and even contributed to their upkeep and renovation from the royal treasury. This meant that if the Achaemenids were worshippers of Avestan religion and Zoroastrian teachings, this religion remained limited to the Persian metropole and was not extended to the colonies. It is possible, although it cannot be proven, that the colonials were expected to honor Ahura Mazda as an act of loyalty to the empire.

Cessation of Exile

Beginning with Cyrus, the Achaemenid rulers brought to an end the policy of deportation and allowed conquered nations to continue having their own native rulers, although Persians were appointed to rule the satrapies established by Darius I. In the Cyrus Cylinder, to which we will return below, Cyrus blamed the Babylonian king Nabonidus for being an oppressive ruler, while he presented himself as the 'king of the world, great king, legitimate king, king of Babylon, king of Sumer and Akkad, and king of the four rims (of the earth)', whose rule was loved by Bel (Marduk) and Nebu (Nabu). Indeed, Marduk, so the cylinder proclaims, chose Cyrus to rule Babylon after the misrule of Nabonidus. In return for the support of Marduk, Nabonidus became his faithful devotee.

In addition, the Great Kings returned to the pillaged temples and sanctuaries the idols that had been taken as booty by the Babylonians, established new temples, and rebuilt sanctuaries that had fallen into disrepair. While tolerant of those nations who recognized their sovereignty, the Persian kings were brutal in their treatment of nations that were disloyal. The Achaemenids did not suppress local religions as long as they did not foment and advance revolutionary activities. It should not be overlooked that the support of local temples, if carried out, was a way to ensure the collection and payment of taxes. Regardless of seeking political advantages with their 'humane' policies, it is fair to say that hybridity in the general sense of the transformation of Persian culture due to its contact with that of others and the changing of colonial cultures due to exposure to other native traditions was an extremely important feature of this empire.[4] Indeed, for the Jews, the contest between two spirits, one evil and the other good, as elements of apocalyptic thinking, may have resulted in part from this period of Persian cultural hegemony.

Divine Sanction for Rulers

As previously noted, the Persian rulers considered themselves as the ones chosen by the gods of the nations they conquered to be their rulers.

> He (i.e. Marduk) scrutinized all the countries; he looked around among his friends; a just prince after his own heart he took by his hand: Cyrus, the king of Anšan he appointed, he called his name to be ruler over all... Marduk, the great Lord who cares for his people, looked at his good works and his righteous heart with joy. He commanded him to move to his city Babylon... The 'liberated'... knelt before him, kissed his feet, rejoiced in his rule, his face was aglow.[5]

The Great King was the only bona fide king, meaning that there were no true vassal kings, only client vassals and dependent satraps approved by the royal administration to act on behalf of the Persian king himself. In addition, the Great King, while not divine, was chosen by the god Ahura Mazda and ruled at his pleasure.[6] As is true in other empires, kingship was the greatest source of power in ancient Persia. One reason for adopting some of the cultural traditions of their Mesopotamian predecessors in imperial rule was to legitimize Achaemenid hegemony over the world and the kings themselves as the embodiments of imperial power. The use and reworking of Mesopotamian imagery into Persian symbolism produced a new, legitimizing iconography.[7]

4. Hybridity is also noticed in other areas: the coinage of the realm, the gold daric in which a running archer with a crown could be connected to the trading networks linking Persia to all of Asia Minor and even Greece; royal roads and stations which followed the Assyrian pattern; and the cavalry and infantry, armed with spears and bows, borrowed from the Greek Hoplite military tradition. Even the navies of Phoenicia and eastern Greek city-states were used to sailing the Mediterranean and other bodies of water, providing a new feature of economic life and the expansion of the empire and its metanarrative of superiority.

5. Galling, *TGI*, 83; cf. *TUAT* 1:408-10.

6. Whether or not the Achaemenid rulers were Zoroastrians is debated (see Boyce, *Zoroastrians* and *A History of Zoroastrianism*). The argument that Zoroastrianism was practiced by the Achaemenids is largely based on the presence of stone fire-holders, distinct to the religion. The prophet regarded fire to be the icon before which worshippers should stand and pray to Ahura Mazda.

7. Root, 'Lifting the Veil' in *Achaemenid History VIII*, 9-37; and Root, *The King and Kingship in Achaemenid Art*.

One important example of the reworking of tradition and its cultural refashioning is the 'autobiographical' inscription attributed to Darius I, located on a cliff of the mountain of Behistun (*bagastana*, 'place of the gods'), which bordered the highway from Babylon to Ecbatana. The Behistun Inscription includes both a written and visual representation of Darius' rise to power and the consolidation of his empire, and is a prime example of the Persian metanarrative. The narrative composition is exceptional among the different Achaemenid reliefs in emphasizing the motifs of victory, triumph, and the humiliating subjection of the enemy. Darius' image stands above the conquered rulers to indicate his status as the Great King. Gautama, the pretender, who led the revolution in Babylon, lies prostrate while the other rulers are standing with neck collars. The divine legitimation of Darius is emphasized by the symbol of the god Ahura Mazda above him. Written in three versions (Akkadian, Old Persian, and Islamite), the narrative speaks of Ahura Mazda's election of Darius I to gain his historical victories and to rule the colonies subjugated by invasion and conquest:

> I.7. King Darius says: These are the countries which are subject to me; by the grace of Ahura Mazda they became subject to me; they brought tribute unto me. Whatsoever commands have been laid on them by me, by night or by day, have been performed by them.
> I.9. King Darius says: Ahura Mazda has granted unto me this empire. Ahura Mazda brought me help, until I gained this empire; by the grace of Ahura Mazda do I hold this empire.
> IV.56. King Darius says: This is what I have done, by the grace of Ahura Mazda have I always acted. Whosoever shall read this inscription hereafter, let that which I have done be believed. You must not hold it to be lies.
> IV.58. King Darius says: By the grace of Ahura Mazda I did much more, which is not graven in this inscription.
> IV.63. King Darius says: On this account Ahura Mazda brought me help, and all the other gods, all that there are, because I was not wicked, nor was I a liar, nor was I a despot, neither I nor any of my family. I have ruled according to righteousness. Neither to the weak nor to the powerful did I do wrong. Whosoever helped my house, him I favored; he who was hostile, him I destroyed.
> IV.70. King Darius says: By the grace of Ahura Mazda this is the inscription which I have made. Besides, it was in Aryan script, and it was composed on clay tablets and on parchment. Besides, a sculptured figure of myself I made. Besides, I made my lineage. And it was inscribed and was read off before me. Afterwards this inscription I sent off everywhere among the provinces. The people united worked upon it.[8]

---

8.   King and Thompson, *The Sculptures and Inscription of Darius the Great.*

The formulation of a cylinder narrative was typically Babylonian and stands within a Mesopotamian tradition that may be traced back to the third millennium BCE. Mesopotamian kings spoke of their divine election and righteousness when beginning their reigns. The Cyrus Cylinder, mentioned previously, is an example of a specific Mesopotamian literary genre, the royal building inscription, which was unknown in Old Persian literature. The narrative illustrates how Cyrus' scribes co-opted local Mesopotamian traditions and symbols to legitimize his control of Babylon. Many elements of the text of this cylinder were drawn from traditional Mesopotamian themes: the indictment of the wicked predecessor whom the gods have abandoned; the new king has been chosen by the gods; he rules justly and rectifies the wrongs of his predecessor; he addresses the welfare of the people for which he has been chosen; the sanctuaries of the gods are rebuilt or restored while offerings to the gods are provided or even increased; divine blessings are solicited; and repairs are to be made to the city which has come under his rule.

The Cyrus Cylinder demonstrates the divine legitimation of the first Persian ruler over Babylon and follows the typical form of dedication:

An incompetent person (Nabonidus) was installed to exercise lordship over his country. […] he imposed upon them. An imitation of Esagila he ma[de], for Ur and the rest of the sacred centers, improper rituals [ ] daily he recited. Irreverently, he put an end to the regular offerings; he established in the sacred centers. By his own plan, he did away with the worship of Marduk, the king of the gods; he continually did evil against his (Marduk's) city… Upon (hearing) their cries, the lord of the gods became furiously angry [and he left] their borders…He surveyed and looked throughout all the lands, searching for a righteous king whom he would support. He called out his name: Cyrus, king of Anshan; he pronounced his names to be king over all (the world). He (Marduk) made the land of Gutium and all the Umman-manda bow in submission at his feet. And he (Cyrus) shepherded with justice and righteousness all the black-headed people, over whom he (Marduk) had given him victory… He ordered him to march to his city Babylon… His vast army, whose number, like the water of the rivers, cannot be known, marched at his side fully armed. He made him enter his city Babylon without fighting or battle; he saved Babylon from hardship. He delivered Nabonidus, the king who did not revere him, into his hands.

I am Cyrus, king of the world, great king, mighty king, king of Babylon, king of Sumer and Akkad, king of the four quarters, son of Cambyses, great king, king of Anshan, descendant of Teispes, great king, king of Anshan, (of an) eternal line of kingship, whose rule Bel (i.e., Marduk) and Nabu love, whose kingship they desire for their hearts' pleasure.[9]

9. *ANET* (3) 315-15.

From these and other historical texts, one may catch a glimpse of one of the oldest strands of Avestan religion. It is also interesting that the call of Cyrus in Second Isaiah contains some of the features embedded in this cylinder (Isa. 44:28–45:1).

Persian Culture

The Persians adopted many of the customs of other peoples of the region, initially taking on those of the Elamites, one of the first people they had conquered. Later, they also incorporated aspects of customs from the Medes, Assyrians, Babylonians, and Egyptians. While the many cultures of the empire indicate that there was no attempt to force Persian values and standards on those they conquered, there are some indications of influence that lead to the ever-developing hybridity of Judah's forms of literature, art, and religious ideology. Due to the presence of Persians in commerce and trade, the location of Persian garrisons of troops, and the necessity to write and speak Aramaic, changes were occurring in which cultural traditions from Judah's past were necessarily reformulated. However, these changes were not simply for reasons of accommodation, but also included the subversive dimension of disassembling Persian rule.

Persian Military Power

The Persian army was one of considerable size and power, able to defeat the national armies of the east and those of the west, with the exception of the Greek city-states in Europe where imperial expansion ground to a halt. Consisting of a metropole and a confederation of client states organized since Darius I into a system of satrapies with their Persian overlords and the authority of the Great King, the Persian Empire could field a very large army. It comprised a multicultural military composed of the combination of many conscripted troops from the colonies, hired mercenaries from outside the empire, and the Persian army itself with each satrapy having a thousand Persian troops. The weakness of this army, however, when convened for battle, was in its inability to form a cohesive force, which, joined with new conscripts and hired mercenaries, was unable to defeat the well-coordinated armies of the Greek city-states and later to withstand the invasion of the Macedonian army of Alexander the Great. The Persians used the Phoenician and eastern Greek navies to create a formidable force for waging battles on the high seas, although again this fleet was outperformed by the combined navies of the Western Greeks, beginning with the decisive Persian defeat at Salamis.

The size of the Persian professional army itself was rather small. The regular army of the Persian Empire contained an elite corps known as the Immortals, since theoretically when one died another replaced him. The Immortals numbered 10,000. At the heart of this 10,000 was an even more elite royal bodyguard of 1,000 whose primary duty was to protect the Great King. The army followed a decimal pattern. Divisions of 10,000 were divided into battalions of 1,000, companies of 100, and squads of 10. The bow was the chief Persian weapon, fired over what was known as a 'shield wall' formed by battalions of Persian troops, while chariots were often outfitted with rotating scythes making them a fearsome contingent of military power. It was, though, plagued by disunity due to the large number of conscripts, different battle tactics, and many different languages. Nevertheless, the Great King's military power was enormous and was itself an intimidating force that would discourage internal rebellion, defeat any outbreaks, and bring to heel most foreign armies. The exception was the hoplites of the Greek city-states who were equipped with heavy armor and used the battle formation of the phalanxes, which provided maximum power for the infantry armed with metal shields, short swords, and spears. The hoplite infantry was supplemented by cavalry and archers.

To maintain order in the dependent satrapies, the empire established garrisons of Persian and hired soldiers in strategic locations to discourage any rebellions within the local populations. In the southern part of the satrapy of Abar Nahara, which included tiny Judah, garrisons and fortresses were not only positioned in or near significantly located cities and towns, but also especially on the coastal plain and the Way of the Sea to defend against any possible Egyptian incursions into Judah. Indeed Egyptian uprisings did occur during the fifth and fourth centuries BCE that led to temporary independence. While these small fortresses and garrisons were not large enough to resist an Egyptian invasion, they would have controlled any local uprisings in the villages and towns of Judah and served the first line of defense against possible Egyptian incursions.[10]

The Economics of the Persian Empire

From the surviving records of Achaemenid Persia, Darius I is identified as the Great King who realized that the success of his empire was based on building a strong economy requiring standardization of coinage and measurements, a system of international trade that would produce wealth

10. Betlyon, 'Neo-Babylonian Military Operations Other Than War', 276-77.

not only for Persian citizens but also for the royal treasury, a system of interconnecting roads that allowed for the movement of troops and caravans of commerce, and the use of Phoenician and eastern Greek shipping under the empire's control to expedite trade and on occasion for the conducting of war throughout the Mediterranean world.

The standardization of measurements for weight, volume, and length, which included the 'royal' cubit, some 33.6 cm in length, is attributed to Darius I. The royal cubit was slightly lengthened in the reigns of later rulers, since Herodotus indicates the length for the Persian cubit is three fingers longer than the common cubit (*Histories* 1.178). The coinage of the empire made use of silver and gold precious metals along with copper, while banking houses were established under Darius' initiative. Canals were also built in order to irrigate fields in agricultural areas that included arable land in remote places throughout the empire. A large canal that connected the Nile and the Red Sea for the movement of boats and ships was constructed during the reign of Darius I.

Tribute from defeated kingdoms and tribes as well as a system that led to the collection of taxes from the different satrapies provided a substantial amount of the wealth enjoyed by the Persian court. While satrapies could issue coinage in copper and silver, only the Great King had the authority to issue gold coins (the daric). Satrapies foolish enough to mint and use golden coinage were considered defiant to the rule of the royal court and would suffer the full brunt of royal military force.

Political Administration and Struggle during the Persian Period

Although Persian propaganda tells of a universal rule, the empire itself was organized into a system of satrapies by Darius I (521–486 BCE), the son-in-law of Cyrus II. As long as loyalty to the Achaemenid court was demonstrably evident and taxes were paid, each satrapy possessed a significant amount of local freedom and responsibility in its own military and civil affairs. Although the Persian king and his court sat atop the hierarchic structure of the empire, the traditions of local nations who submitted to Persian rule were generally respected. The position of satrap was held by a Persian and was hereditary. Local administrators for the most part carried out the local matters of civil and social institutions of the different ethnic groups within each satrapy. During the administrative overhaul of the empire, orchestrated by Darius I (Herodotus 3.88-95), Judah was situated within the satrapy of Abar Nahara (Ezra 4:10-11, 16-17, 20; 8:36; Neh. 2:7, 9). The political, administrative changes came to have important implications for the social history of Judah. The states of

Judah, Gaza, Ashdod, Samaria, and Arabia were the provinces (*medînôt*) of the satrapy along with their smaller national divisions (*pĕlakîm*) throughout the history of the later Persian Empire.

III.
Judah as a Persian Colony[11]

The lack of extensive literary sources and archaeological data pertaining to Judah makes it difficult to reconstruct historically this period of Jewish history and to be precise in interpreting the different responses of various political groups to Persian hegemony and cultural influence. The Priestly document's final redaction, the completion of the composition and redaction of Deuteronomy and the Deuteronomistic History, Chronicles, Ezra–Nehemiah, several prophetic texts (Third Isaiah, Haggai, Zechariah, and Malachi), an emerging apocalyptic (e.g., Isaiah 24–27), and some of the writings, in particular the Psalter and the final form of the book of Proverbs, provide some suggestive indications of the social and religious life of this period of the Second Temple. The ideological agenda of these texts highlights Jerusalem, the high priesthood, the Torah, scribalism, and anticipate a rebirth of the Davidic dynasty and independence from the empire. The books of Ezra and Nehemiah, which among the four Chronistic writings appear to have been finalized during the later Persian period, offer at times different scenarios and dates, leading to increased difficulty in reconstructing even the major events of the Persian period. We are limited to generalizations that represent Jewish life in Persia, the significant returns from exile in the late sixth century mentioned in the Deuteronomistic History and I Chronicles, the commissioning of Ezra and Nehemiah, and several prophetic proclamations. Yet there are some cultural materials in the forms of Persian inscriptions, papyri (especially from Elephantine), and coins that, when combined with the writings of Ezra, Nehemiah, and a few other biblical texts, allow an imperfect picture to emerge, at least of resistance versus accommodation.

The question to address to these texts and archaeological data here concerns the Jewish response to Persian imperial control and cultural influence. Save for the possibility of an early attempt at insurrection during the time of the contested transfer of power to Darius I, acquiescence to Persian rule was the norm. At issue were resistance and cultural hybridity in Judaism during these two centuries of imperial rule.

11. Carter, *The Emergence of Yehud in the Persian Period.*

The Economy of Judah

Upon his conquest of Babylon and the collapse of the entire Babylonian Empire, Cyrus II gave the exiles who had languished for a half century in Babylonia permission to return home to reoccupy and eventually rebuild Judah and Jerusalem, if they chose to do so. They began in 538 BCE, the first of several journeys homeward, possessing limited Persian support and that of Jews in other regions for rebuilding the temple and reinstituting the sacrificial cult after the return. Jewish villages and farms were reestablished, with ownership given to the heirs of the exiles and not to either the 'people of the land' or the foreigners who had settled in Judah during the period of the Babylonian captivity. The economy was largely agricultural, providing food for the local population and trade items for manufactured goods. The Persians returned to the policy of the Assyrians by rebuilding the destroyed cities and temples of their satrapies, and they added the policy permitting the establishment of local constitutions for the different countries comprising the colonies of the empire. This resulted not only in a rebuilt temple that became part of the economic engine of the Jewish colony, but also the establishment of the Priestly code as a significant part of the official constitution for Judaism.

The temple in the post-exilic period was an important institution for economic stimulus, especially for the city of Jerusalem. The rebuilding of the sanctuary would have involved employing numerous laborers and skilled craftsmen and a substantial number of priests for its operations, but the temple would also have generated economic activity in the form of merchants and shops selling wares to visiting pilgrims and of farms producing animals, grains, and wine for sacrifices and gifts. Further, the temple tax that came from all communities, including those located in the diaspora, would have added much-needed revenue. Indeed, the temple seems eventually to have become something of a national bank and treasury, evidenced by foreign rulers occasionally looting it to enhance their treasures and pay for the burden of military campaigns.

One historical factor leading to the growth in significance of the temple in Jerusalem occurred when Darius II gained the throne in 423 BCE and ruled until 404 BCE. Facing rebellions in Media, Anatolia, and Syria, the satrap of Egypt left the country to quell these revolts. This led to scattered resistance in Egypt. Two letters from the military colony of Elephantine sent to the governor of Judah and the two sons of Sanballat, governor of Samaria, complain of the destruction of the YHWH temple in the colony by Egyptian rebels. This led to an increased role of the high priest of Jerusalem's temple, since the Persians, ending this pogrom, required that only he could preside at the offering of animal sacrifices.

This in effect ended the prominence of this Egyptian Jewish temple and led to the elimination of the most important rival sanctuary to the international one in Jerusalem.

However, there were also instances of recorded social injustices during the Persian period. The wealthy failed in their social responsibilities to provide adequate support for the small landowners, tenant farmers, and day workers. Owners of small farms often faced the necessity of mortgaging and even selling their farms. The wealthy Jews required these working poor to pay high interest rates who at times even had to sell their children into slavery in order to exist (Neh. 5:2-5). The additional Persian taxation, when added to local poverty, often resulted in the break-up of households. Meanwhile, vast accumulations of wealth, especially in the Persian court, but also among the wealthy in the local satrapies, including Abar Nahara and its *medînôt*, were an economic reality in Persia. Nehemiah's reform was an attempt to confront these injustices. He required that lands be returned to the original owners who had been forced to sell them and that large debts were to be cancelled. How much of this actually occurred is a matter of contention among interpreters.

Persian Rule of Judah

The Persian court in ruling its empire also required the service of intermediaries who would enjoy a more privileged social rank, greater authority, and financial rewards for their activities that facilitated imperial rule. Thus, the Great Kings allowed Jewish governors (at first descendants of the royal house of David) to administer the internal operations of Judah as part of the larger satrapy. This governor was directly under the oversight and authority of a Persian satrap backed by a military unit stationed near the capital. In addition to the Jewish governor who dealt with civil matters, the high priest and the Zadokite hierarchy also held enviable positions in both shaping internal legal matters through the interpretation of the Torah and in the economic power of the temple generated through gifts, sacrifices, tithes, and festivals. Prior to the reform of Ezra, Malachi (during the fifth century BCE) indicates that sacrificial worship and the giving of tithes had declined and that divorce and the intermarriage of Jewish men with foreign women had increased, resulting in a crisis for the tiny state's identity as a Jewish nation (2:10-17). The leadership of the Judean community after the series of late sixth-century returns of the exiles was divided between a political leader, initially Zerubbabel who was clearly a Jewish resident in Babylon prior to his return, and the 'high priest' Jeshua or Joshua ben

Jehozadak (the name varies in the texts but refers to the same individual). The title *hakkohen haggadol* (high priest, chief priest; Hag. 1:1; Zech. 3:1) appears for the first time here and indicates the extraordinary significance of the priesthood in its role during the Second Temple period. Sheshbazzar, a 'prince of Judah' and presumably a descendant of David, led the first returnees to Judah following the decree of liberation by Cyrus (Ezra 1:8).

The fictionalized narrative of the Chronistic literature stresses the unity of Judaism, for Ezra sought to eliminate foreign intrusions into Yahwistic national religion. Historically, however, Judaism likely was far more fragmented as different groups competed socially and religiously for internal influence. These groups included the *Zadokite* priesthood and the local administration headed by a Persian appointed governor, both of which were loyal to the Persian metropole; *scribes* who worked within the local administration as well as teachers likely paid by the wealthy; *prophets* who addressed internal social and religious issues and imperial matters that would have included inciting some political resistance (Haggai, Zechariah, and elements of Malachi); and finally *apocalyptic seers* (e.g., Isaiah 24–27). The more radical opponents to Persian rule used a hidden transcript to address the woeful conditions suffered under the empire and thus pointed to a new future in which liberation and independence from foreign power would be divinely granted. If one were to step outside the people of Judah to the locals of the diaspora a far greater diversity would be encountered.

The Persians supported the governorships of local leaders (including several descended from the dynasty of David) as long as they were loyal to the Persians, Zadokite control of religious affairs especially associated with the temple, and the codification of the Priestly source as the basis for the reform of Ezra. Thus a conservative religious tradition of Torah, the Zadokite priesthood, the Jerusalem temple, and indigenous leadership on a local level were the pillars of the political structure of Second Temple Judah. The Chronicler indicates that the official and priestly leaders after Haggai and Zechariah apparently gave allegiance to the Persians by being content to accept foreign rule in exchange for economic, social, and political rewards. Opposition to this came from the undercurrent of some revolutionary prophets and apocalyptic seers (see discussion below).

However, there are indications that Jewish leaders who accommodated themselves to their master's domination still raged at their position as 'slaves' to the Great King. In a public proclamation, in his great prayer of repentance in Nehemiah 9 presented before the assembled Jews on the twenty-fourth day of the seventh month (perhaps Yom Kippur), Ezra, bristling from the effects of Persian oppression and colonizing images of imperial superiority, protests to YHWH, 'Here we are, slaves to this day—slaves in the land you gave to our ancestors' (Neh. 9:36). This suggests that the composers and editors of the Chronistic literature considered the Persians to be oppressive rulers, and this may have been a consistent theme throughout the period.

When Alexander's army entered Egypt, it met limited resistance. This was likely true of Judah, save for the opposition of Gaza commanded by a Persian ruler (Josephus, *Ant.* 11.8). If Josephus is at least partially correct in his summary, there was generally widespread Jewish enthusiasm when Alexander's Greeks conquered the Levant, especially, if this account is to be believed, when he acknowledged the deity represented by the high priest who came with a priestly delegation to pay him homage and to attempt to keep him from destroying Jerusalem and the temple. Josephus also presents Alexander as one who allowed the Jews in Judah and in other countries to practice their own customs. Inviting any Jews to join his army, many did and fought against the king's enemies (*Ant.* 11.326-339).

Militarism and Colonial Power

The reinstitution of a small Jewish military fortress for protection against local enemies and to oversee civil order along with strategically located Persian fortresses garrisons maintained stability throughout the period, although the Persians held the upper hand even in local military affairs. Persian garrisons were needed to protect the highways along the Way of the Sea and the King's Highway, especially due to the continuing threat of the Egyptians who continued their efforts to drive out the Persians from the Land of the Nile. While these small outposts were not large enough to contain for long a well armed, large Egyptian invasion force, they could fight a delaying action until more substantial Persian forces and conscripts would quell the revolt. However well equipped a Jewish army may have been, its small size meant that Judah's only hope for a successful revolution depended on a restless, colonial Egypt seeking to drive the Persians back into Mesopotamia.

Haggai and Zechariah do suggest that in 519 BCE Judah may have joined the rebellion against the Persians that followed the death of Cambyses in 522 BCE and the contested accession to the throne by Darius I in the same year. His ascension was met with stiff resistance led internally by Gautama, a Median priest who pretended to be the dead younger brother of Cambyses II, Smerda, who had apparently been assassinated three years earlier by the Median sacerdotal leaders opposing the Achaemenid dynasty. This civil war was accompanied by the rebellion of governors of several satrapies including those of Elam, Babylon, and Egypt, before Darius I was finally able to put down the attempted revolution. While the texts of these two Jewish prophets lack some clarity in regard to revolutionary activity, it is possible that Jewish zealots, inspired by prophetic prediction, may have pushed Judah to rebel in order to establish an independent state under a restored dynasty of David. Indeed the ability to communicate in Hebrew may have encouraged the rebels to compose hidden transcripts that were less susceptible to interception and reading. In Hag. 2:23, Zerubbabel was the original 'signet ring', a royal symbol, and zealots may have seized their opportunity during the power struggle following the demise of Cambyses. This may have been the motivation these two nationalistic prophets used to push for the completion of the temple, since they regarded this as a prerequisite for independence. What happened to this governor, who never again is mentioned, and to the assumed rebels can only be imagined, but the Persians were known to deal harshly with disloyal subject nations and their leaders.

When Xerxes I (486–465 BCE) ascended the Persian throne, he soon faced an Egyptian rebellion that ultimately was put down by 483 BCE. The letter of accusation against Judah and Jerusalem in Ezra 4:6-16 suggests Jewish participation in this revolt. This is a further indication that loyalty to the Great King was not always a constant feature of Jewish life in the empire. Eventually, the walls of Jerusalem were rebuilt by Governor Nehemiah sometime near the end of the fifth and the early part of the fourth century BCE.

Presented in the Jewish metanarrative as the cupbearer of Artaxerxes II (Neh. 1:11; cf. Gen. 40:1, 2, 5, 9, 13, 20, 21, 23; 41:9; 2 Kgs 10:5; 2 Chr. 9:4), Nehemiah may reflect the roles of the legendary Ahiqar, a sage who was said to be the cupbearer and keeper of the signet ring and the financial secretary of Sennacherib and Esarhaddon. Tobit 1:2 notes this Aramaic sage was second in authority only to the king himself. Thus Nehemiah perhaps would have been a counselor who possessed significant official authority. In seeking the king's permission to undertake the mission to Jerusalem to rebuild its fortifications (Neh. 2:5), Nehemiah demonstrated proper reverence in the royal presence (2:2). Having received royal authorization, he came to Jerusalem as governor in the twentieth year of the reign of Artaxerxes II (ca. 384 BCE) to erect fortifications by rebuilding walls and gates (Neh. 1:3). This rebuilt city in the hill country would have provided the Persians some security in maintaining their control of the southern part of the Levant and in protecting against any future Egyptian rebellion. Should revolt occur and the city be taken by Egyptians aligned with Jewish cohorts, it could function as a place of defense against invading Persian forces. The Egyptians eventually succeeded in driving out the Persians for a short period (404 BCE to 343 BCE) and the strengthening of Jerusalem's fortifications would have provided the Persians a place of additional defense. There is no record of Jewish participation in this revolt.

The rebuilding of Jerusalem's fortifications also provided defense against local enemies, including the Samaritans and the 'people of the land' who had not participated in the Babylonian exile and had been relegated to insignificance politically and religiously by the Achaemenid rulers. Other enemies included Tobias of Ammon, Geshem, an Arab sheik from southern Judea or the Negev, and a Jewish landowner east of the Jordan river (Neh. 3:33–4:17; 6:1-19).

A Jewish Metanarrative and Divine Legitimation

There is significant evidence for cultural hermeneutics at work among different groups during this period of Judaism centered in Judah. The appropriate texts for examination were composed by social groups who were the offspring of parents, grandparents, and great grandparents who had been subject to forced removal during the period of captivity in Babylon. In addition, Jewish families consisted of those who remained in Judah during the exile and those who lived a largely marginal existence in the diaspora during the sixth through most of the fourth centuries BCE. Finally, Jewish families who remained in Babylonia after the return also left some indication of their presence, as noted, for example, in the Murashû papyri. This Murashû family rose to prominence in the banking business.

Jewish groups who were descendants of exiles developed various means of survival with their culture intact. Literature with different expressions of prophetic proclamations, ritual resistance in cultic celebrations, and hymns point to some mimicry comprising the desire to rule their own destiny. Mimicry is also evident in the expression of hopes for a future, universal king.

A more accommodating approach, in which living with the empire was the primary option, became important in texts written by reactionaries like Ezra and Nehemiah or their narrators. The particular elements of the cultural and religious metanarrative and divine legitimation of the temple city of Jerusalem, the temple itself, and the Torah were emphasized in particular by Zadokite priests, their scribes, and some, though not all, of the local sages. However, there are still indications of mimicry as a subversive force in the literature of the reactionaries. This is indicated by the Chronistic sources that chaff at Persian hegemony and point to a revisionist history of David as a foreword to the re-establishment of the Jewish monarchy and self-rule.

The Jewish metanarrative of the period, incorporated in the Chronist, narrates the imperial commissioning of the priestly scribe Ezra to travel to Jerusalem to instigate a wide-ranging social and religious reform.[12] He was followed shortly thereafter by Nehemiah, who was given the imperial responsibility to rebuild the city walls and to provide a military installation to withstand Egyptian and Philistine incursions into the area.

According to the book of Ezra, the scribe and priest bearing this name was commissioned by Artaxerxes II in the seventh year of his rule, ca. 398 BCE, to travel to Jerusalem and to lead a reform of Judaism especially in the city of Jerusalem (Ezra 7:7). Given extensive powers over all Jews living in Abar Nahara, Ezra was sent to establish and codify the laws of the Torah and to see that they were instituted in Jewish social and religious life. The narrative presents him as a religious and social conservative who sought to remove foreign influence on Jewish life by ordering the divorce of Jewish men married to non-Jewish women and to prohibit worship of other gods. Ezra prohibited marriages to non-Jewish women and required divorce from foreign women, since he determined they polluted the 'holy seed' (Ezra 9:1-2; Neh. 9:2). Daniel Smith-Christopher sees Ezra–Nehemiah as examples of cultural resistance and Ezra 1–7 as a statement of deference masking more subtle forms of subversive resistance.[13] Brett adds that these texts reflect not just resistance to the empire, but also conflict between children of exile and everyone else who did not go into captivity, including Jews who mixed with outside peoples, Moabites, Egyptians, and Samaritans.[14] For these books of Ezra and Nehemiah, only the exiles and their descendants are identified with the true heirs of Israel. While the exclusivist hermeneutics of Ezra and Nehemiah may have had their origins in cultural resistance adopted by certain Jewish groups against the empire in order to survive as an ethnic group, this religious faith could be co-opted for other political purposes, including the rejection and dispossession of non-Jewish minorities residing in Judah. Social ordinances or religious practices not legitimated by the Priestly document and Ezra's own understanding of Torah were to be eliminated. The objectives of Ezra's reform, which included the restoration of the temple cultus, the codification of the law,

<hr>

12. For the development of the Ezra tradition, see Kratz, 'Ezra-Priest and Scribe'.

13. Smith-Christopher, *A Biblical Theology of Exile*, 45.

14. Brett, *Decolonizing God*.

and the assumption of power by former exilic families, were designed by the Persians to squelch internal conflict, to achieve internal stability, and provide a people easily ruled. Stability was important due to Judah's strategic location along the major highways from Egypt to Mesopotamia. This situation compares to the reform ordered by the Persian authorities that was carried out by the Egyptian scribe and priest Udjahorresnet, commissioned by Darius I. This Egyptian official oversaw the restoration of the cult at Sais and the codification of Egyptian law into the spoken and read languages of Aramaic and Demotic.[15]

One of the ways that the Chronistic literature sets forth the ideology of resistance was the recording of public transcripts in the form of edicts of Persian rulers (Cyrus II, Darius I, and Artaxerxes II). These related to the return, the rebuilding of the temple, and the Persian financial support of both the construction and the sacrificial court. The first decree is attributed to Cyrus II and is written in Hebrew (Ezra 1:2-4):

> Thus says King Cyrus of Persia; YHWH, the God of heaven, has given me all the kingdoms of the earth, and he has commanded me to build him a house at Jerusalem in Yehud. Any among those of you who are of his people, may their God be with them!— are allowed to go up to Jerusalem in Yehud and rebuild the house of the Lord, the God of Israel, who is the God in Jerusalem; and let all survivors, in whatever place they dwell, be assisted by the people of their place with silver and gold, with goods and with animals, besides freewill offerings for the house of God in Jerusalem.

This edict, supposedly dictated, translated, and then quoted by Ezra to the Jewish public, presents the Great King as acknowledging YHWH as the God of Heaven. It compares to other decrees and inscriptions of Persian rulers assuming the role of devotees to foreign gods (cf. the Behistun Stone and the Cyrus Cylinder discussed above). This policy, if historical, would have been intentional propaganda to establish order through the divine legitimation of the gods of nations conquered and ruled, in this case YHWH. Hence, while it is possibly a fictional account, there is no need to conclude that this proclamation is necessarily false. Rather it is possibly a public transcript made available for an audience who knew not only Aramaic but also a limited amount of Hebrew, which still remained the sacred language.

A similar edict is attributed to Cyrus by Darius II in Ezra 6:3-5 and is written in Aramaic, although it lacks the ideological recognition of YHWH as the God of Heaven. While there is no reference in this decree to the return or to the Persian financial support of the sacrificial cult,

15. Blenkinsopp, 'The Mission of Udjahorresnet and Those of Ezra and Nehemiah'.

details of the plans concerning the size of the temple are given, along with directions to send back to this temple the vessels taken by Nebuchadnezzar II.

Finally an edict of Artaxerxes II in Aramaic is mentioned in 7:12-26 that gives Ezra the authority to lead another group of Persian Jews who so desired to return to Jerusalem and to take with them the silver and gold of Babylonia. In this text the king has authorized free will offerings to the temple of 'their God' that may be used to purchase items of sacrifice and offerings. Ezra is also given the authority to tax the Jews in the satrapy, Abar Nahara, for the temple. If historically accurate, this Persian legitimation would enhance local stability by the establishment of one authentic state religion.

Prophetic Resistance to Persian Imperialism and Public Transcripts: Haggai and Zechariah

During the initial ascension to the throne of Darius I (550–546 BCE), the fourth Achaemenid king, there was significant opposition to his rule at its onset and even later on. Most scholars assert that he was challenged by Bardiya, who laid claim to his being the younger son of Cyrus the Great and brother of Cambyses II (530–522 BCE, succeeding his father Cyrus as king).[16] Various nations opposed his reign, but these were quickly subdued.

Haggai is one of the Twelve Minor Prophets, active eighteen years after Cyrus allowed Jewish captives to return to their homeland. During this period, Zerubbabel had been appointed governor of Judah and Jehoahaz served in the role of High Priest (1:14).

The metanarrative of Haggai had at its center the rebuilding of the temple, the magnificence of which would surpass even the first one, and God's 'shaking of the heavens', suggesting revolution throughout the empire. Shezbazzar, who led the first captives home, following Cyrus' decree of liberation, may well have led them to begin to rebuild the temple (Ezra 5:14-15), but by the time of Haggai's oracles, this effort

---

16. The death of Cambyses, following his conquest of Egypt, and failed attempts to move south to take Cush and west to defeat Libya, is disputed. Based on accounts of Greek historians including Ctesias and particularly Herodotus, he returned to Persia to put down a coup by his brother Bardiya, appointed satrap by his father Cyrus as of some of the far-eastern provinces, he committed suicide, due to despondence, or accident. A minor view by Greek historians was According to many ancient historians, the man who led the coup resulting in his temporary enthronement was an imposter, pretending to be Bardiya, was likely a magus, perhaps a Zoroastrian priest named, Gaumata.

had ceased. In Haggai's metanarrative, drought had led to economic devastation. The conclusion of this drought, likely drawing on past tradition (cf. Elijah, 1 Kgs 17:1-7), so the prophet asserts, will occur only with the rebuilding of the temple.

The second feature of the metanarrative is a new Davidic ruler, in Haggai's case Zerubbabel, literally 'branch of God'. A descendant of David who enjoyed the appointment of the Persian court to serve as governor of Judah, Zerubbabel was singled out as the servant of YHWH, a common royal title, and as God's 'signet ring' (Hag. 2:23). The signet ring pointed to God's ring worn on his right hand. Thus the king benefited from YHWH's approval. Due to the uprisings in the empire that YHWH would precipitate, the Persian Empire would fall. In the prophet's judgment, God would make Zerubbabel the new Davidic ruler.

The last element of Haggai's metanarrative concerns the high priest, in his case Joshua, the son of Jehozadak. This points to a diarchic structure of leadership that endures until the Greek kingdoms. The high priest was in charge of the temple, its worship, and its maintenance. The pilgrimage festivals, the collection of the tithes and gifts from Jews in the diaspora, the sacrifices and gifts of Jews in Judea, the serving as a bank for local wealth, and the maintenance of the facilities made the temple and its priests of upper echelon status quite affluent.

IV.

Conclusion:
Unity and Diversity in Judaism
in the Persian Empire

Judaism in the Persian period was heterogeneous. Jewish communities, separated by geography and culture, were found throughout the ancient Near East during the period of Persian hegemony. In addition to Judah, those Jews living in Babylon, Egypt, and Samaria had substantial communities, but it is questionable how much religious loyalty to Jerusalem and its temple would have existed. The relationship of diasporan communities to Judaism in Judah was often only tangential. Efforts at unity were made by scribes under the oversight of the Zadokite priests to shape a canon of authoritative literature that placed emphasis especially on the Torah, the temple, the city of Jerusalem, and monotheism. Obviously, not everyone viewed these elements in exactly the same way: they were important to some Jews but not to others. For example, monotheism was clearly affirmed in the literature of the period and yet did not lead to the ending of tolerance for, much less the eradication of, the polytheism of other religions. Even the religion of YHWH was not monolithic in location and ritual practice. For example, the solar shrine at Lachish, a YHWH sanctuary, was erected during the Persian period. The devotion to the temple in Jerusalem did not eliminate either the construction or operation of other temples in Samaria, Leontopolis, Elephantine, and during the late Ptolemaic period the one built by Qasr el-Abd of Hyrcanus, son of Joseph ben Tobiah, in Araq el-Emir in Transjordan. It is clear that there were many high places, including Dan, where the hill continued well into the Hellenistic period. Other outdoor shrines that carried on their rituals and worship into the Hellenistic period included those found in Carmel, Hermon, and Tabor. Prophecy and the development of apocalyptic literature, not always attuned to sanctuary worship and ritual, added to the cultural and political mix. It was a significant force among Jews in Judah and the various locations of the diaspora, although resistance formed among reactionaries like Ezra and Nehemiah who were prone to resist any foreign incursions into Jewish religious and cultural life.

5

Judea/Israel under the Greek Empires*

In 331–30 BCE, by military victory, the Macedonian Alexander ended the Persian Empire. He defeated the Persian king Darius at Gaugamela, advanced to a welcoming Babylon, and progressed to Persepolis where he burned Xerxes' palace supposedly in retaliation for Persia's invasions of Greece some 150 years previously (Diodorus 17.72.1-6). Thus one empire gave way to another by a different name. So began the Greek empires that dominated Judea/Israel for the next two hundred or so years, the focus of this chapter.

Is a postcolonial discussion of these empires possible and what might it highlight? Considerable difficulties stand in the way. One is the weight of conventional analyses and disciplinary practices which have framed the discourse with emphases on the various roles of the great men, the ruling state, military battles, and Greek settlers, and have paid relatively little regard to the dynamics of imperial power from the perspectives of native inhabitants, the impact on peasants and land, and poverty among non-elites, let alone any reciprocal impact between colonizers and colonized. Such approaches can be readily defended (and will necessarily be evident in this chapter in places) with the recognition of the scarcity and nature of the sources.[1] Such a dearth makes the task of assessing Judea/Israel's negotiation of life as a province of these Greek empires difficult. Where sources do exist they are largely 'top-down' from elite powerful males. It is hard enough to hear the subaltern speak even when there are non-elite sources, as Gayatri Spivak has emphasized, let alone when such

---

*   My appreciation to Dr. Ariel Feldman for his helpful responses to an earlier draft of this chapter.

1.   See, for example, Walbank, 'Sources for the Period', 1-2; Grabbe, *A History of the Jews*, 23-24; Bar-Kochva, *The Image of the Jews*. Paying particular attention to archaeological sources, Berlin, 'Between Large Forces'. Berlin identifies 'two forces' more powerful than battles, namely 'commercial opportunities and religious affiliation' (3).

sources do not exist.[2] The surviving historical sources, then, are patchy, sporadic, and largely unconcerned with non-elites and their circumstances.

We might also wonder, as Roger Bagnall does in a helpful article, whether terms such as 'colonial' or postcolonial are even commensurate with these Ptolemaic and Seleucid empires.[3] Bagnall tests several definitions, similarities, and differences, before deciding that ultimately it is the imposition and inequalities of imperial power that matter for a postcolonial investigation.[4] Such impositions and inequalities of power are certainly in play for these Greek empires though engagement with Fanon, Bhabha, and other postcolonial theorists might direct our attention more to the reciprocal, hybrid, and ambivalent nature of those interactions. But how such an investigation might be conducted is not obvious. Bagnall engages the suggestion of Edouard Will to use anthropological and sociological approaches developed from the contemporary studies of colonization and decolonization. Will suggests creating a comparative model (with appropriate modifications for context) and then testing the Ptolemaic (and Seleucid) data against it.[5] Such a task is beyond the scope of this chapter, even if an all-embracing yet nuanced model was possible and adequate ancient data were accessible. Yet while a model and the requisite data are not available, postcolonial discussions offer insights into the dynamics of power operative in contexts of (de)colonization. While it is certainly true that by far the dominant concern of postcolonial work has been with *contemporary* expressions of imperialism-colonization, there are insights of relevance for the Greek imperialisms under consideration in this chapter.

More reasonable, then, within the space limits here is the use of what Fernando Segovia has called a 'postcolonial optic', a 'way of looking' at the complexities of imperial–colonial experiences (including dynamics of power, gender, class, race/ethnicity, and sexual orientations), and at the visions of societal interactions and humanity operative in these situations.[6] The opening chapter of this volume has identified some of the key dynamics concerning the exercise of power in imperial–colonial contexts

2. Spivak, 'Can the Subaltern Speak?'
3. Bagnall, 'Decolonizing Ptolemaic Egypt'.
4. Bagnall, 'Decolonizing Ptolemaic Egypt', 229-33. The classic distinction comes from Edward Said (*Culture and Imperialism*, 9) in which imperialism refers to the practice, theory, and attitudes of a dominating center over distant territory, while colonialism refers to the center establishing settlements in the distant territory.
5. Bagnall, 'Decolonizing Ptolemaic Egypt', 225, 235-36; Will, 'Pour une "anthrpologie colonial"'.
6. Segovia, 'Mapping'.

that a postcolonial optic foregrounds: the inequalities of power, a focus on the colonized and their agencies and voices, and situations marked by ambivalence, mimicry, and consensual-conflictive hybridity. Segovia appropriately wants to privilege the periphery over the center and the diverse colonized over the imperial—though the binaries are unstable— but given the lack of sources, a top-down perspective, at least in part, cannot be avoided in a postcolonially oriented historical discussion of these Greek empires.[7] There is no escaping, for example, the fact that the sources give most attention to military actions and the ideology of ruling power that informed them and little to how local common people engaged them. Postcolonial concerns and dynamics, while emerging unevenly, direct our attention to the reciprocal relations being enacted between imperializer and colonized, the ambivalences created, and the often invisible powerless who are implicated in contexts that are simultaneously consensual and conflictual, accommodative and disruptive. A postcolonial optic is a means of opening up an imaginative vista to identify likely ambivalences not explicit in the surviving historical data.

It might be helpful to recall the discussion of three key terms from Chapter 1. *Ambivalence* denotes the ambiguity, the instability of the imperial–colonized situation, especially the dynamic of both attraction toward and resistance of the imperializing power.[8] Fanon captures this ambivalence in his statement that 'the colonized subject is a persecuted man [*sic*] who is forever dreaming of becoming the persecutor'.[9] A key part of this conflictual-complicit dynamic is, as Bhabha emphasizes,[10] that of *mimicry* wherein the subordinated repeats and appropriates the imperializer's language, culture, structures etc., and thereby confuses the 'simple' dynamic of imperial 'power over'. Mimicry occurs in the colonized's cultural context but the presence of this invasive 'other' disrupts local culture, creating an emerging *hybridity* and new space. In turn, though, mimicry can never be an exact re-presentation; it is, rather in Bhabha's famous phrase, similar, 'almost the same but not quite',[11] an imperfect copy. It has the potential for parody, menace, instability; it often leads to mockery thereby challenging and decentering imperial

---

7. Segovia ('Mapping', 70-74) notes that much postcolonial discussion has focused on 'imperial–colonial formations' in 'the eighteenth through to the twentieth centuries' while the empires from which the biblical texts emerge and which Judea/Israel negotiated have received relatively little attention. It is this lack of attention that this chapter and volume seek to redress.

8. Bhabha, *The Location*, 85ff, 102ff.

9. Fanon, *The Wretched*, 16.

10. Bhabha, *The Location*, 90-92.

11. Bhabha, *The Location*, 86.

authority. For Bhabha, the imperial–colonial interaction is reciprocal in impacting all parties. The mixing or hybridity of languages and cultures identifies a crucial interdependence of, or reciprocity between, imperial power and the colonized, constituting what Bhabha calls an 'in-between' or interstitial or third space marked by contest and hybridity, constructed and deconstructed identities, negotiated traditions, and diverse cultural differences.[12]

One dynamic not given significant attention in Chapter 1 above will come to the fore in this chapter. This dynamic concerns the phenomenon of horizontal violence whereby fractures, including violent fractures, occur among those under power especially as vertical power is exerted on them. Frantz Fanon, in his study of imperial power dynamics in the French colony of Algeria, examines the creation and role of horizontal violence as vertical imperial power is asserted.

> The native is a being hemmed in... The first thing which the native learns is to stay in his place, and not to go beyond certain limits. This is why the dreams of the native are always of muscular prowess; his dreams are of action and aggression... The colonized man will first manifest this aggression which has been deposited in his bones against his own people. This is the period when the natives beat each other up, and the police and magistrates do not know which way to turn when faced with the astonishing waves of crime... The settler keeps alive in the native an anger which he deprives of an outlet; the native is trapped in the tight links of the chains of colonialism. But we have seen that inwardly the settler can only achieve a pseudo petrification. The native's muscular tension finds outlet regularly in bloodthirsty explosions—in tribal warfare, in feuds between septs, and in quarrels between individuals.[13]

In Fanon's analysis, horizontal struggles—whether tribal or individual, physical or verbal—are multi-faceted. They result in part from subjugated people being hemmed in and contained by imperial controls and from restriction without outlet. Antagonisms and fractures also exist 'between the colonized excluded from the benefits of colonialism and their counterparts who manage to turn the colonial system to their advantage'.[14] And fractures attest to considerable imperial (vertical) pressures. Fanon observes that 'violence among the colonized will spread in proportion to the violence exerted by the colonial regime'.[15]

---

12.   Bhabha, *The Location*, 1-5, 37; on the period as an 'intensely difficult, volatile, and creative time' involving the redefinition of Judea as 'competing versions of tradition negotiated with competing imperial powers', see Kurtz, 'The Social Construction'.

13.   Fanon, *Wretched*, 1963 edn, 52-54; 2004 edn, 15-16.

14.   Fanon, *Wretched*, 2004 edn, 67.

15.   Fanon, *Wretched*, 2004 edn, 46-47.

In addition to containment, horizontal struggles develop because the oppressed mimic, as Bhabha also emphasizes, the competitiveness and violent domination that mark the imperial situation. Violent domination 'has been deposited in his own bones'. The subjugated yearn for power while simultaneously and angrily resisting the assertion of it over them. Yet as Fanon also argues, horizontal violence is a means of avoiding direct confrontation with the oppressor since the oppressed know that they cannot win such struggles. Rather, they turn on each other with attacks that substitute for attacks on the oppressor. Assuming imitation of the oppressor, and noting the ambivalence and simultaneity of displacement of yet identification with the oppressor, Paulo Freire observes in relation to Latin American struggles, 'Because the oppressor exists within their oppressed comrades, when they attack those comrades they are indirectly attacking the oppressor as well'.[16] That is, horizontal violence occurs as oppressed groups in negotiating imperial power self-protectively substitute attacks on other oppressed groups for direct confrontation with the imperializer whose power seems too great. Lashing out against similarly oppressed groups deflects open and direct attacks on the too-powerful oppressor even as it mimics their power. Horizontal violence thus attests the ambivalences of the imperial–colonial situation, simultaneously the restricting pressure of overwhelming imperial power, its imitation or mimicry as both an expression of desire and a strategy of resistance, and its engagement by avoidance and attacks on substitute groups.[17]

My argument is that a postcolonial reading of this period illumines some of the ambivalent dynamics that comprise Judea/Israel's continual yet shifting negotiation of the imperial power of the Greek empires. The plural term 'empires' signals a significant way in which this chapter differs from the preceding and following ones. While those chapters focus on a single power ruling Judea/Israel—Assyria, Babylonia, Persia,

16. Freire, *Pedagogy of the Oppressed*, 44.

17. For example, Josephus attests increasing fractures in Judea/Israel and Jerusalem during the 66–70 war as imperial pressure intensifies (e.g. *J.W.* 4.377-97, 503, 544-84; 5.1-38; Eleazar, John, Simon). See Chapter 6. Carter argues for the phenomenon in relation to Matthew's Gospel ('Matthew: Empire, Synagogues') 285-308, esp. 303-308. For a discussion of recent European empires, see Abernethy, *The Dynamics*. Abernethy notes horizontal violence between Hindus and Muslims in India and between competing groups in Kenya and Malaya under British imperialism, in Vietnam under French control, and among groups in the former Belgium Congo. For black-on-black violence in South Africa during the 1980's and 1990's struggle with apartheid and white power, see Hamber, 'Who Pays for Peace?' 238-41.

Rome—this chapter focuses on multiple Greek empires with divergent metropoles:[18] Alexander the Macedonian, the Ptolemies of Egypt, the Seleucids of Syria, and the Hasmoneans of Judea/Israel. The continuity among the first three entities exists in that Ptolemy and Seleucus—after whom both dynasties were named—were companions of Alexander.

I begin in Section I with the power asserted by the Macedonian king Alexander ('the Great' so-called) and his successors (the *Diadochi*) who after his death in 323 BCE fought one another for his spoils of wealth, land, power, and legacy (ca. 323–ca. 280 BCE). Then in Section II, I discuss the Ptolemaic dynasty based in Alexandria (ca. 280–200 BCE). Third, in Section III, after the battle at Paneion, the center of power over Judea/Israel moves to the Seleucid dynasty based in Antioch in Syria (ca. 200 BCE). At first, it was 'business-as-usual' in imperial ways (200–175 BCE), but then, in Section IV, arises the perplexing terror of Antiochus IV Epiphanes (175–164 BCE). Section V considers its aftermath, including Israel's independence in ca. 142 BCE until, the Roman takeover in 63 BCE. I observe the not surprising dynamic of mimicry that emerges as Israel, now independent from empire yet marinated in it, undertakes its own imperial expansion until it loses its independence to the Romans in 63 BCE. In each context I identify ways in which power was asserted and justified, and, where possible, the ambivalent ways in which power was experienced and negotiated.

The diaspora will not be in focus in this discussion, nor will interactions with the Samaritans. Limits of space often prescribe a generalized more than a detailed consideration of numerous complex issues.

Finally, the matter of nomenclature needs consideration. In imperial contexts, naming imposes power and determines significance as Josephus, an interstitial, colonized, elite, Jewish, Flavian client, understood very well. Commenting on the changing names of nations, Josephus observes somewhat polemically that 'it is the Greeks who are responsible for this change of nomenclature, for when in after-ages they rose to power, they appropriated even the glories of the past, embellishing the nations with names which they could understand and imposing on them forms of government as though they were descended from themselves' (*Ant.* 1.121). Claiming the past, renaming and rewriting it, and inserting oneself where it is advantageous to do so and humiliating for the subjugated are common imperial strategies. In the same process of naming, colonized peoples assert their own identities, recreating (a version of) their past, language, and identity, and constructing a third space and face.

18. Bagnall ('Decolonizing Ptolemaic Egypt', 231) disputes the language of 'metropole'.

What, then, to call the land and people in focus in this study? A wide range of terms exists among scholars, with perhaps Palestine being a favorite. According to Arrian (*Anab.* 7.9.8), the conqueror Alexander asserts his claim of ownership in identifying three areas, Coele-Syria, Palestine, and Mesopotamia. Appian (*Syr.* 8.50) identifies areas of Syria, Coele-Syria, Phoenicia, and Palestine. Dio Cassius subsequently endorses a threefold division of Coele-Syria, Phoenicia, and Cilicia (Dio Cassius, 53.12.7). The Ptolemies seemed to continue the Persian use of the official name Judah[19] within the larger territory of what they called the province of Syria and Phoenicia.[20]

When local peoples name themselves, naming can also be act of resistance, contesting attempts to 'own' land, traditions, and peoples, and negating the defining power of the colonizer. The name 'Israel' pervades the Pentateuchal tradition, writings that have significant import throughout this period as the following discussion will attest. Under the Hasmoneans, the name 'Judea' emerges into prominence. In turn, the term 'Israel' has some prominence in several second-century texts (Judith, 32×) including one of the accounts of the Maccabean struggles (over 50 times in 1 Maccabees) and on the coinage of the rebels of 66–70 CE and 132–35 CE.[21] Perhaps Israel was the nomenclature of preference among some under the power of these Greek empires at least in the third and second centuries. Given this uncertainty yet recognizing the importance of the issue and a possible preference of its subjugated peoples, I will use the hybrid form Judea/Israel throughout as a symbol of imperial–colonial contest.

I.

Alexander the Macedonian (336–323), his Conquests, and Successors (*Diadochi*)

Alexander was the sort of man about whom legends quickly developed, making historical discussion difficult.[22] When he died in 323 BCE at the

19.   Kindler, 'Silver Coins'.

20.   Hölbl, *A History*, 23. On variations in name and geography for the area commonly referred to by scholars as Coele-Syria, see Bosworth, 'The Government of Syria', 48-50.

21.   Goodblatt, 'From Judea to Israel'. See also the discussion below in Chapter 6.

22.   The bibliography on Alexander is extensive. Helpful discussions include Galinsky, *Classical and Modern Interactions*, esp. 'Multiculturalism in Greece and Rome', 116-53; Bosworth, *Alexander and the East*; Stoneman, *Alexander the Great*;

age of thirty-three, he had as king, general, and warrior, conquered the world's major super power Persia, and created an empire stretching from Greece in the west to India and Afghanistan in the east and to Egypt in the south. Here follows a brief, selective, and 'top-down' account (no doubt a mix of fact and fiction) of his accomplishments.

In 336 BCE, after his father king Philip II of Macedonia was murdered, the twenty-year old Alexander became king. Immediately in 336–335, he secured his position as head of the Greek states and harshly subdued and enslaved non-submissive Celtic tribes in Thrace and the city of Thebes. The severity of the action sent a clear message to the other Greek states who readily recognized that compliance was the best course for survival.

By 334 BCE, Alexander, well-schooled in an ideology of kingship that valued military performance, launched his action against the Achemenid or Persian Empire, crossing the Dardanelles into Asia at the head of some 30,000 foot-soldiers (including archers and javelin throwers) and 5,000 cavalry. This action, inherited it seems from his father and perhaps intended initially to free Greek cities from Persian control in Asia Minor, lasted for the rest of his life and ultimately consumed him. He did not return to Macedonia. He engaged Persian forces in battle, initially winning victories at the Granicus river in northwest Asia Minor in 334 and at Issus, the crossroads of Asia Minor and northern Syria, in 333 BCE. The Persian king Darius III escaped, though Alexander captured Darius' mother, wife, and children.

Alexander headed south to protect his southern flank, taking control of Syria, Judea/Israel, and Egypt (without a battle) in 332–331. In Egypt he was proclaimed Pharaoh and son of the Egyptian god Osiris, founded the city of Alexandria, visited the famous oracle of Zeus-Ammon at Siwah Oasis, and then marched his army northeast crossing the Tigris and Euphrates rivers into the heart of the Persian Empire. At Gaugamela he again defeated Darius in October 331 but again Darius escaped as he had done at Issus. Alexander entered Babylon and Perseopolis, the Persian capital, which Alexander looted and burned, gaining vast wealth. He pursued the fleeing Darius to Ecbatana and beyond. By mid-330, however, Darius had been murdered by Bessus, one of his own satraps. Alexander honored Darius with burial in the tombs of the Persian kings and in 329 captured and executed the murderer Bessus.

Roisman, *Brill's Companion*; Worthington, *Alexander the Great*; Lane Fox, *The Classical World*, 221-32; Green, *The Hellenistic Age*; Heckel and Tritle, *Alexander the Great*; Anson, *Alexander the Great*.

Alexander was not just the victor over Darius; he established himself as king of Persia on the basis of his military victory. For the next three years (330–327), he continued to pacify the eastern Persian Empire (modern day eastern Iran) and invaded India. In 326 he defeated king Porus of the Punjab in western India at the Hydaspes river. Weary of the never-ending campaign, his army revolted and he turned back. At Susa in 324 he organized a five-day, Persian-style, wedding in which he married two women, one of whom was Stateira, eldest daughter of the defeated Darius. Women and arranged marriages secure imperial power. Some ninety of his officers married Persian women. A further army revolt took place when Alexander tried to include Persian troops in his army. Alexander's response was to execute some leaders and increase army pay.

His attention, apparently, turned to the southwest and he formulated plans to extend his power into Arabia. But at Babylon he became ill—malaria? poison?—and died in 323 at Babylon at the age of thirty-three. In an astute quest for legitimacy as his successor, Ptolemy took Alexander's body from Damascus ca. 322/1 to Memphis in Egypt (Diodorus 18.28.3-6).

First Maccabees, looking back on Alexander's deeds from the perspective of those under power, summarizes some of the means by which he imposed his power and subjugated native peoples.

> He fought many battles, conquered strongholds, and put to death the kings of the earth. He advanced to the ends of the earth, and plundered many nations. When the earth became quiet before him, he was exalted, and his heart was lifted up. He gathered a very strong army and ruled over countries, nations, and princes, and they became tributary to him. After this he fell sick and perceived that he was dying. (1 Macc. 1:2-5)

Military power, victory over opponents, execution of kings, acquisition of much territory, plunder of the lands and the inhabitants of defeated territory, the extraction of tribute, the establishment of unchallengeable power, and much pride in his enormous accomplishments of domination constitute Alexander's profile as king according to 1 Maccabees. What is not made explicit is the enormous cost to human lives and communities.

Despite his numerous wives, Alexander left no adult heir. Power struggles broke out among his generals who strove to be his successor, continue his legacy, gain his spoils, and establish their own kingship and economic gain on the basis of military power.[23] The *Diadochi* (successors) battled each other for some forty or so years through a series of

---

23. Austin, 'Hellenistic Kings', 455-57.

military campaigns and varying fortunes.[24] By around 280 BCE a three-fold division of ruling spheres emerged. Antigonus Gonatas established the Antigonid dynasty of kings in Macedonia that lasted until its defeat by Rome in 168 BCE. Seleucus established the Seleucid dynasty based in Syria and stretching across western Turkey to Afghanistan. Over the next few centuries it gradually lost territory and was conquered by the Roman, Pompey Magnus, in 64 BCE. The third area was based in Egypt under Ptolemy Soter I who established the Ptolemaic dynasty which lasted until Cleopatra's death in 31 BCE, when it was defeated by the Roman Octavian, the future emperor Augustus, at the battle of Actium.

Alexander's Metanarrative

What was Alexander trying to accomplish through his extraordinary activity and accomplishments? Historians have wrestled with this question and offered explanations emphasizing variously cultural, economic, religious, and political metanarratives. Older analyses emphasized motives of cultural evangelism, of civilizing 'barbarians' with superior Greek culture, and establishing a cosmopolitan world with a 'fusion' of Western and Eastern cultures, the unity of humankind, and the common fatherhood of Zeus.[25] Others have seen political motives, in which as a pragmatist he sought to use the expertise and skills of local people to enhance his own (Macedonian) interests and rule.[26] Others have posited economic interests derived from control of the land and wealth of the Persian Empire first through booty and plunder, then by taxes and levies, and subsequently through new economic interactions from settlements, trade, and access to resources.[27] Others have suggested that he was, as leader of all the Greek states, set on military revenge against Persia for age-old violations against Greek states inheriting an anti-Persian mission from his father Philip whom he sought to exceed.[28]

Alexander, clearly, was a complex character, the sources are diverse, and simple explanations fail in the face of personal and circumstantial complexities. Some of these options, though, are immediately less compelling than others. The proposals that center on grand all-embracing

24. Fox, *Classical World*, 233-44.

25. Tarn, 'Alexander the Great', 123-66; rejected by Badian, 'Alexander the Great', 425-44; Bosworth, 'Alexander and the Iranians'; Todd, 'W. W. Tarn and the Alexander Ideal'; for a modified reassertion, see Thomas, 'Alexander the Great'.

26. Bosworth, 'Alexander and the Iranians'.

27. Austin, 'Hellenistic Kings'. See further below.

28. Brunt, 'The Aims of Alexander'; Fredricksmeyer, 'On the Final Aims of Philip II'.

motivations such as civilizing barbarians, fusing cultures, creating economic order, and imposing political visions seem less convincing. Better explanations run along the various lines of Alexander's performance as a king and warrior in securing power and wealth, the satisfactions of contest and conquest, getting access to riches and resources from territory, taxes, tribute, and trade, and attending to the pragmatic necessities of dealing with unfolding circumstances and negotiating competing and complex demands. Among these various and complex factors, I highlight three important aspects of his metanarrative.

One central dimension concerns an ideology of kingship articulated 'by political and philosophical speculation on kingship' in the fourth century, a tradition that included the work of Isocrates, Xenophon, Plato, and Aristotle among others. This ideology was embodied to a significant extent in the reign of Alexander's father, Philip II, and was embraced by Alexander's successors over the following centuries.[29] In this ideal formulation, the king was 'supreme commander, dispenser of justice [and] god's representative on earth'.[30] The role of warrior was crucialand shaped by several realities. One was the tradition of the Homeric cult of heroic personality embodied by the successful warrior-king, particularly by Alexander's ancestor Achilles, as well as by his father Philip.[31] A second influence shaping the warrior-king role was the pragmatic realities of political power. Hellenistic kings had to create an 'aura of military success and strength' to exercise their power.[32] Military victory meant not only the display of the warrior-king's bravery and courage, but also the acquiring of territory—what Diodorus called 'spear-won territory' (18.43.1, δορίκτητον)—'a demonstrable proof of merit and an uncontrovertable claim on the loyalty of troops and subjects'.[33] Conquest or victory allowed the king to be known as protector of the people, their savior and benefactor. The latter role involved the dispensing of great benefactions or sums of wealth to troops, cities, and 'friends'. Kings were expected to be wealthy but they were to use their wealth in generous benefactions.[34] Doing so of course required further victory and

29. Walbank, 'Monarchy and Monarchic Ideas', 75-84; see also Austin, 'Hellenistic Kings'; Murray, 'Philosophy and Monarchy'.

30. Walbank, 'Monarchy and Monarchic Ideas', 79.

31. Fredricksmeyer, 'Alexander and Philip', 304-6.

32. Austin, 'Hellenistic Kings', 459.

33. Walbank, 'Monarchy and Monarchic Ideas', 66, 82.

34. See Bringmann, 'The King as Benefactor', who identifies public benefactions comprising various buildings including temples, festivals especially for gods, daily supplies and food for cities, and relief after disasters (war, famine, earthquakes), all of which secured the indebtedness of gratitude and loyalty.

much loot and booty from war in order to ensure gratitude and maintain loyalty, secure mercenary troops, and augment one's aura of military success and strength.[35] An ideology that understood kingship to be performative, both to gain and to maintain power, provides a helpful context in which to understand Alexander's activity as warrior-king and that of his successors over the next two or so centuries.

Military might was, then, fundamental to Alexander's empire-building, as with the empires of his successors. He battled and sieged his way to domination over the land, resources, and inhabitants of his empire. His military skill, strategy, demand for loyalty from his officers, courage, physical power, and magnanimous rewards were legendary. So too was his black stallion Bucephalas, who died either of wounds in the battle of Hydaspes or of old age (Plutarch, *Alexander* 6, 61; Arrian, *Anab.* 5.19.4-6) after whom he named a city Bucephala.[36] Alexander's sieges of Tyre and Gaza on his way south to Egypt in 332 BCE cannot but have left a terrifying impression on territories such as Judea/Israel, an intimidating display of Macedonian superiority in the tactics and execution of war.

Further, armies cannot exist without extracting supplies of food, equipment, and men from local communities. Alexander's actions also expressed dominance as they inflicted material hardship on local communities by these means. Military victories, though, not only subdue territory, people, and resources; they are coded with messages of the victor's cultural superiority, political and economic opportunity, and religious privilege and favoritism, while the defeated are consigned to inferiority, socio-economic exploitation, and divine abandonment and disfavor.

A second aspect of Alexander's metanarrative emerges from the ideology of warrior-kingship. While some have seen his military mission fuelled at least in part by a desire for revenge on Persia for previous humiliations (Diodorus 16.89.1-2; 17.4.9),[37] Austin argues that from Alexander on through his successors the connection between Hellenistic kings and the acquisition of wealth through conquest is an important factor that has been much neglected in scholarship.[38] The two motivations of course are not mutually exclusive; the latter in fact is closely

35. Walbank, 'Monarchy and Monarchic Ideas', 68-74, 81-84; Austin, 'Hellenistic Kings', 459.

36. Anderson, 'Bucephalas and his Legend', 10-12.

37. Fredricksmeyer, 'Alexander's Religion and Divinity', 260-61.

38. Austin, 'Hellenistic Kings', 454-55.

linked to the former. Acquiring land was often foundational for wealth and 'possession by force of arms was the surest and best' (Polybius 28.1.4). Land brought booty and loot, agricultural production for tax, people for labor and tribute, resources and opportunities for trade, and territory to reward allies. Plutarch indicates that Alexander set out with very limited funds, 'no more than seventy talents' (*Alexander* 15.1-2; *Mor.* 327d-e, 342d), yet he gains huge wealth in his conquests. Austin styles Alexander's move across the Hellespont into Asia and subsequently to Persia as a quest for wealth, both expressing power and funding increases in power:[39]

> The Macedonian conquest under Alexander can be described as two things rolled into one, a booty raid on an epic scale and the permanent conquest of vast tracts of territory together with the dependent, tributary peoples. On both counts the expedition surpasses or at least equals any other single war in the whole of ancient history. The sources quote fabulous figures for the captured Persian treasures, 50000 talents of silver from Susa, 120000 from Persepolis… And that of course was what the expedition was all about… If the Macedonian invasion of Asia was possibly the largest plundering and conquering expedition of its kind in ancient history, then the Age of the Successors can also be seen as another record, as the most bitter and prolonged dispute over sharing out the spoils of victory between the conquerors, a struggle that went on for a generation or more and affected virtually the entire Greek and Asiatic world of the time… Individual leaders fought wars, made and unmade treaties with and against each other, over who was going to get what.

Austin's contribution is to show the interconnections among notions of kingship, conquest, and the valency and necessity of wealth in gaining, maintaining, and enhancing imperial power not only in Alexander's rule but in those of the Hellenistic kings that succeed him. The kingly ideal of a generous king-patron could only exist on the foundation of a successful warrior-king: 'a king was expected to deliver the goods, above all to his followers. Hence the economic rapacity of the kings, consumers of wealth on an unending scale.'[40]

In addition to a performative and conquesting vision of military kingship, and the key role of the procurement of wealth necessary for that vision's enactment, a third factor in the metanarrative of Alexander and his successors comprises his religious identity and aspirations, especially the much-debated issue of his quest for deification. Scholars regularly rehearse a predictable progression of Alexander's growing

39. Austin, 'Hellenistic Kings', 454-55.
40. Austin, 'Hellenistic Kings', 463; Plutarch, *Alexander* 15.2-3.

determination to be recognized as more than 'like a god' and to be recognized as a god. It starts with Alexander's typical kingly claim to have divine patronage and protection for his rule, thereby setting himself in a cosmic context and aligning himself with the purposes of the gods, especially Zeus.[41] His father Philip does not seem to have been deified but gained some elevated status in cultic honoring.[42] Bosworth notes that Alexander was not content with being a 'distant descendant of Zeus through his heroic ancestors' (maternal: Aecus and Achilles; paternal: Heracles with Perseus descended from Zeus) but comes to claim that 'he was the direct son of the god', Zeus-Ammon (Arrian, *Anab.* 3.3.2-3; Plutarch, *Alexander* 27.5-6). His visit to the shrine at Sewah Oasis where he was hailed as son of Zeus-Ammon seems to have been very significant. His subsequent promotion of the paternity of Zeus-Ammon (often at the expense of the paternity of Philip) and insistence on *proskynesis*, an act of homage practiced in the Persian court toward his enemy king Darius, caused considerable disquiet, since the former was dishonoring and Greeks associated the latter action with honoring the gods. The act was ambiguous in that it established a unified court procedure, elevated Alexander with Darius, yet also, for some including Alexander himself, rendered Alexander not just the son of a god but a god manifested among humans.[43]

Many cities in Asia Minor established cults to honor Alexander. They associated him with the predictable epithets of God, savior and benefactor, pointing to the emergence of the cults in acts of gratitude for specific benefits of power such as deliverance from and/or victory over an enemy or for preserving or granting freedom or for gifts and acts that alleviated some hardship. Usually gratitude was directed to the gods for such powerful and beneficial actions, but when Alexander the powerful king performed them, he was deemed to act like a god and gratitude was directed to him. 'The honors go to the king because he does what the god is expected to do—and often does it more effectively' (cf. Plutarch, *Alexander* 64.4).[44] Bosworth comments that after his death 'the fiction soon developed that he had been translated to heaven like Heracles' (cf. Diodorus 18.56.2).[45]

41.   Fredricksmeyer, 'Alexander's Religion and Divinity', 260-62, 270-78.

42.   Badian, 'Alexander the Great', 13-15.

43.   Bosworth, 'Alexander the Great Part 2'.

44.   Walbank, 'Monarchy and Monarchic Ideas', 94.

45.   Bosworth, 'Alexander the Great Part 2', 875.

How might we account for this drive for deification and of what significance is it? Fredricksmeyer argues that this drive derived from Alexander's troubled relationship with his father.[46] Alexander's initial admiration for Philip as brilliant military leader and kingly ruler gave way to rivalry, dislike, and resentment. Fearing that Philip would 'leave no great or brilliant achievements to be displayed to the world' for Alexander to accomplish (so Plutarch, *Alexander* 5.1-3), Alexander pursues three ambitions that he in fact inherited from Philip, but he did so in order to surpass him: to conquer Persia, to gain absolute monarchy, and to be deified.[47] Ian Worthington argues similarly that Alexander's 'attempts to be recognized as a god', along with his megalomania, 'are the key to so many of' Alexander's actions, as he spends his life trying to outdo his father.[48] On this reading, Alexander's drive for deification forms part of the metanarrative expressed in and making sense of his incessant godlike—powerful, ruling, benevolent—activity.

While Alexander pursued his goal of deification, he was not, it should be noted, a religious evangelist intolerant of other religious expressions. Alexander sought to adapt to and utilize local cultural and religious expressions. This posture is one that a postcolonial optic recognizes as a reciprocal relationship between colonizer and colonized. In Persia he introduced Persians into his command structure despite the opposition of some of his Macedonian officers. He embraced some ambivalence and hybridity in adopting Persian clothing, marrying Persian women, and encouraging often resistant Macedonian officers to do the same. As noted, he adopted the custom of *proskynēsis* whereby inferiors bow to superiors, a custom some of his Macedonian officers also resisted. He did not seek to wipe out local religious observances. Rather, he found in local religious expressions the opportunity to further his own religious sanction, identity, and goals. Thus he sought to sacrifice in the temple of Hercules/Melqart in Tyre. In 331 BCE, he traveled to the shrine of Ammon at the Siwah oasis where, so it is claimed, he was identified as the son of Zeus-Ammon (Plutarch, *Alexander* 27.5-6). He allied this claim to be descended from Zeus with the Egyptian notion that the Pharaoh was a son of Re, the sun god. This link established him as divine, and an agent or representative of the gods, and doing their work.

46. Fredricksmeyer, 'Alexander and Philip'.
47. Fredricksmeyer, 'Alexander and Philip', 308-9.
48. Worthington, 'Alexander, Philip', 94.

Spreading Hellenistic Economic and Cultural Influence

Alexander was not, then, a cultural evangelist promoting a vision of a unified Hellenistic world. But that does not mean his actions did not have profound consequences in creating cultural instabilities in the intersections of imperial and local power. One such effect concerns the cultural forces that Alexander's military conquests stimulated in the ancient world, forces that reverberated across thousands of miles and hundreds of years. Military conquest is never just about military victory and defeat; it is also about cultural influence and interaction. Whatever his intentions—and the evidence suggests that neither he nor his Ptolemaic and Seleucid successors set out solely with cultural imperialist intentions to Hellenize local peoples and spread Greek language, architecture, religion, etc.—nevertheless it happened to varying degrees across the territories they conquered and ruled. Alexander's campaigns and armies, with their large supporting entourage, stimulated the spread of Hellenistic culture throughout the territory he claimed, setting up cultural reciprocities, ambivalences, and hybridities. He, of course, was not the first to do so. Greek traders and travellers had preceded him but his activities and personnel provided much momentum.

As an expression of these hybridities and ambivalences, Alexander and his successors made alliances with local peoples. He educated young men in Greek ways. He incorporated Persian elites in administering parts of his empire, utilizing their local knowledge and skills while also bringing them within the sphere of Greek culture. He included Persians and other local people in his army. He encouraged intermarriage.

Whatever the intention, establishing cities was a further important means of cultural and economic impact.[49] Alexander established numerous cities, some as military outposts, some as Greek colonies, some settled by veterans. Cities opened up areas that were relatively undeveloped, for economic activity through trade and the exploitation of resources and local populations. The military outposts were means of signifying Greek power and maintaining control through terror and intimidation by their very presence, as well as invitational spaces for cultural reciprocity. Cities included Greek institutions like the agora, theater, and gymnasium, all means of spreading Greek language, moral and philosophical ideas, literature, and providing training for elite males in rhetoric. Urban centers encouraged economic and commercial activity, including collection of taxes and spread of technologies.[50]

49. Fox, *Classical World*, 245-55.
50. Fox, *Classical World*, 256-65.

Contesting interpretations that consider only the cultural impact 'of Alexander on native peoples', a postcolonial optic emphasizes that the spread of cultural and economic influence by a conqueror and imperialist is never one way. Local religions, languages, and institutions were not instantly exterminated. Instead such interactions created hybrid cultural spaces in areas of conquest that were both appreciative and disruptive and that required assimilation and accommodation as well as contest and rejection.

Alexander and Judea/Israel

How did Judea/Israel and Jerusalem fare in these intrusions of Macedonian power? Judea/Israel was a 'small province' with Jerusalem its only sizeable settlement with a population of 'between 1,000 and 1,250 people'.[51] How does it negotiate this new victor and these dynamics of colonizing power?

Alexander, it seems, had little to do with the territory of Judea/Israel. After his victory at Issus in 333 BCE, he headed south down the Mediterranean coast through Phoenicia to Egypt. He took Damascus and thereby acquired Darius' war-chest. Tyre refused to surrender or allow him to sacrifice in the temple of Hercules/Melqart and after a seven-month siege was overrun. Gaza suffered a similar fate involving a two-month siege. Egypt, not surprisingly, thereafter surrendered without a fight. Alexander showed no interest in the areas away from the coast.

We have little evidence for any contemporary Judean/Israelite meta-narrative concerning Alexander. Tcherikover states the common scholarly view that the silence of Diodorus, Arrian, and Curtius on any activity by Alexander in Judea/Israel 'reflects historical reality…and it is doubtful whether the king even remembered the country'. Nevertheless, 'legend filled the vacuum'.[52]

Josephus narrates one such legendary incident in which Alexander visits Jerusalem, and in an act of reciprocity prostrates himself before the high priest, and submits to Judea/Israel's God (*Ant.* 11.304-45). In Josephus' scene, Alexander, in the act of besieging Tyre, requested the Jewish high priest Jaddus to send provisions for his army as well as the tribute money normally paid to Darius. Such a 'request' for supplies meant 'choosing the friendship of the Macedonians' (*Ant.* 11.317). The language of 'friendship' masks and mystifies the reality of submission to Macedonian power that included the coerced gathering of supplies from

---

51. Lipschits, 'Jerusalem', 163, 174.
52. Tcherikover, *Hellenistic Civilization*, 41-42.

the minimal surplus of peasant farmers. Jaddus refuses, choosing loyalty
to the Persian Darius. For such defiance, Alexander vows revenge on
Jerusalem and subsequently approaches the city presumably to destroy
it. In a vision from God, the anxious Jaddus is reassured to welcome
Alexander. Surprisingly, Alexander prostrates himself before the high
priest and God declaring that he had previously received encouragement
in a vision from this God in his quest to become 'master of Asia' and
victor over 'the empire of Perisa' (*Ant.* 11.333-34). He enters the temple
and, instructed by the priests, sacrifices to God, learns that the book of
Daniel 8:21 indicated his victory over the Persians, grants continued
observance of the law in Jerusalem, suspends tribute every seventh year,
permits Jews in Babylon to observe the law, and invites anyone to join
his army (*Ant.* 11.336-39).

Most scholars find the account to be fictional and apologetic, even
while it exhibits some dynamics typical of the imposition of imperial
control on a province. Scholarly consensus is that the incident has
no historical value.[53] The silence of the Greek historians is telling.
Alexander visited other holy places as the accounts recognize. He wants
to sacrifice in the temple of Hercules/Melqart in Tyre. He travels to the
shrine of Ammon at the Siwah oasis where, so it is claimed, he is identified as the son of Zeus-Amun and increasingly considers himself divine
thereby claiming sanction for his actions. The omission of a similar trip
to the Jerusalem temple is unusual if it in fact had happened.

Likewise the scene's evident linking of Jerusalem and Alexander
by means of important themes, including the (likely anachronistic) citing of Daniel 8, points to a legend rather than an historical account.
Literarily, the scene comprises an *adventus* story (the highly prescribed
welcome ceremony for a powerful male in a city that acknowledges and
submits to his power) and an epiphany story in which the Jerusalem's
deity manifests himself to protect the city/temple from the conqueror's
power.[54] The scene has in a postcolonial optic the qualities of a fantasy
topos in which the overwhelming power of a victorious general is
negotiated by imagining him paying tribute to the deities of the territory
and people he has conquered and by respecting their worship practices.

In this respect, the episode is resonant with Josephus' themes, desired
strategies, and ambivalent location under empire. His Alexander scene

53.   For a discussion, see Tcherikover, *Hellenistic Civilization*, 42-50; Stoneman,
Alexander the Great, 36-37; Grabbe, *A History of the Jews*, 274-78. For an assertion
of its historical accuracy (though with 'some legendary motifs' [142]), see Kaiser,
'Further Revised Thoughts'.

54.   Cohen, 'Alexander the Great', 44-55.

can be read as reflecting his own hybrid status and ambivalence as a captured Jewish client of Rome's ruling Flavians, writing an account of Judea/Israel's history in the decades after the 66–70 CE war. Josephus' preferences seem to be expressed in the Alexander story thus:

- Jews are protected in their specialness by their God;
- the powerful imperial ruler recognizes Judah/Israel's God, and
- tolerates the distinctive worship practices of both the temple in Jerusalem, and of Jews in the diaspora;
- the scriptures reveal the divine will for the nations in the form of a sanctioning oracle for Alexander's power;
- imperial power is benign to which the Jews readily submit.

In Josephus' vision, reflective of his liminal position, metropoles and provinces exist in happy and mutually beneficial interaction—despite the fact that Judea/Israel had a long history and recent experience of submission to various imperial powers. For Josephus, imperial powers like Rome are God's agents. Yet his vision exists in the context of the realities of Rome's power, a recognition that identifies some hidden and disguised criticism. Titus did not behave as (the fictional) Alexander had done in entering Jerusalem. Far from acknowledging Judea/Israel's God and granting continued worship practices in the temple, he had devastated Jerusalem, burned its temple, and ended worship there

In reality, we have no evidence for the scene Josephus constructs of Alexander the loyal servant of Israel's God and benign patron of Judea/Israel. Judea/Israel's ready submission was the most likely historical scenario, perhaps signified by an embassy to the conquering king, but so expected and insignificant that silence is its only remaining witness. Arrian hints at as much: 'the rest of Syrian-Palestine (as it is called) had already come over to him', except for the city of Gaza (Arrian, *Anab.* 2.25.4). If Jerusalem had allied with Tyre and/or Gaza against Alexander, its resistance—and subsequent subjugation—would have most likely been noted.

II.
Ptolemaic Rule and Judea/Israel

After Alexander's death in 323 BCE and through the third century, the Egyptian-based Ptolemaic dynasty ruled Judea/Israel. In 301 BCE, after the battle of Ipsus, the council of victors assigned Judea/Israel to Seleucus but Ptolemy refused to concede it. Seleucus, in Ptolemy's debt for assistance in helping Seleucus retake Babylon from Antigonus in 312 BCE, did not force the issue (Diodorus 21.5; Polybius 5.67). Accordingly, Judea/Israel remained in Ptolemaic hands until 200 BCE when Antiochus III gained control of it after winning the battle at Paneas near Mt. Hermon in Galilee. The Ptolemaic dynasty (until 180 BCE) comprised Ptolemy I Soter (323–282 BCE), Ptolemy II Philadelphus (282–246 BCE), Ptolemy III Euergetes I (246–221 BCE), and Ptolemy IV Philopater (221–204 BCE) whom Polybius (14.11-12) considered to live a life of dissipation. Ptolemy V Theos Epiphanes ruled from 204 until 180 BCE but the six-year old king lost control of southern Syria and Judea/Israel in 200 BCE in the Fifth Syrian War to Antiochus III.[55]

The Ptolemaic rule through the third century was marked by five so-called Syrian wars (274–271 BCE; 260–253; 246–241; 219–217; 202–199) as the Ptolemies and Seleucids struggled against each other for control of various territories, including that of disputed Judea/Israel.[56] Seleucus' successors considered Judea/Israel theirs and a useful buffer zone. They did not hesitate to press for it, finally gaining control in 200 BCE. Certainly much of the fighting in the five Syrian Wars was not in Judea/Israel though armies regularly marched through the land. As outlined above, control of territory meant, among other things, not only a display of the king's prowess in battle but also the gaining of a source of income which ensured payment of troops, their gratitude and loyalty to the king, and revenue for kingly patronal benevolence.[57]

A postcolonial optic highlights the pervasive ambivalence of the challenges and vulnerabilities facing Ptolemy I and his successors in securing their new power in Egypt.[58] In the language of Jane Rowlandson, the Ptolemies were 'upstarts' who relied fundamentally on military strength for their power both externally in maintaining control and internally in suppressing rebellions. Deterrence from the presence of military garrisons (including local Egyptians) and from the threat of military intervention as well as from actual force itself effected at least the appearance of submission.[59] Without ever abandoning the military power that provided some deterrent against jealous rivals who had been displaced, the Ptolemaic kings also moved to provide a broader rationale

---

55. For discussion, see Hölbl, *History of the Ptolemaic Empire*, 20-159; Green, *Alexander to Actium*; Turner, 'Ptolemaic Egypt'.

56. Heinen, 'The Syrian-Egyptian Wars'.

57. Austin, 'Hellenistic Kings'; Walbank, 'Monarchy and Monarchic Ideas'; Gera, *Judaea*, 4-9.

58. Rowlandson, 'The Character of Ptolemaic Aristocracy'.

59. Bagnall, 'Decolonizing Ptolemaic Egypt', 235-36.

and framework for their rule. These moves comprised a 'symbolic association with Alexander the Great, projection of their own divinity, and implanting themselves into the indigenous monarchic traditions of their new power'.[60]

One means of displaying (and requiring) royal power and wealth—combining strategies of awe and terror—involved public festivals and processions such as the one Ptolemy II Philadelphus held in Alexandria in 279/8 BCE in honor of his parents Ptolemy I Soter and Berenice: gold and silver, military might, exotic animals, entertainments, and feasting expressed Ptolemaic power over people, material resources, and animals in terms of military power and wealthy ostentation[61] The audience comprised not only native Egyptians, new Greek residents, and guests from the inhabited world, but the Ptolemies themselves. James Scott locates such spectacles in the context of the performance of imperial domination and subordination. Spectacles not only intimidate and impress subordinates into some sort of public compliance; they also have self-legitimating power for the performers themselves. As Scott describes, 'Elites are also consumers of their own performance'. They construct a public and 'collective theater' that 'becomes part of their self-definition'; such spectacles are 'a kind of self-hypnosis within ruling groups to buck up their courage, improve their cohesion, display their power, and convince themselves anew of their high moral purpose'.[62]

Moreover, Rowlandson continues, the Ptolemies faced the challenge of securing the loyalties and services of aristocratic families, both native and imported, by honoring traditional sources of power such as priesthoods as well as including them in the new power through material benefactions, access, or gifts of office. She argues that Greco-Macedonian elites, often lacking roots in land and intermarriage, found themselves in difficult ambivalent circumstances with their loyalties to the king tested by personal interests and orientations elsewhere. Another hybridity involved the ongoing challenge of the interactions between Graeco-Macedonian and Egyptian elites with struggles between attempts at fusion and a natural tendency to favor Graeco-Macedonian personnel and structures.[63]

60. Rowlandson, 'Character of Ptolemaic Aristocracy', 29.

61. Thompson, 'The Infrastructure of Splendour', 242; Rice, *The Grand Procession* discussing the account of Kallixeinos.

62. Scott, *Domination*, 49-50, 66-69.

63. Samuel ('The Ptolemies', 169) identifies three accomplishments of Ptolemy II: creating a Greek-speaking bureaucracy, regulating economic life, and accommodating Egyptian religious and legal life.

The Ptolemies and Judea/Israel

Ptolemaic power in Judea/Israel was marked by the ambivalence of an imperial–colonized situation. It was centralized and exercised from the top down, yet it existed in relationship to cooperative-submissive local power structures. It left local leadership in place while also employing its own local officials especially for the collection of taxes. Taxes expressed the reciprocity of the imperializer–colonized situation. They asserted imperializing power over the colonized even as they rendered the imperializer dependent on the colonized. The Ptolemies also relied on some military presence but the assertion of power was not militarily aggressive.

Grabbe argues that the Ptolemies continued some form of the Pharaonic system of top-down governance in Egypt, which enabled considerable control of populations at local levels.[64] In simplified form, it comprised four levels, with the first two consisting of the king and key ministers or administrators such as the finance minister (διοικητής), administrator of the countryside (ἐπιστρατηγος), recorder (ὑπομνηματογράφος), and registrar (ἐπιστολογράφος). Beyond this centralized structure, the third level comprised the forty or so nomes into which the territory was divided, each ruled by a nomarch, and a financial officer and royal scribe. The fourth level comprised villages with a village leader and scribe. Taxes on various entities—people, land, salt, animals—injected power into local contexts and effected local oversight through records and extraction of wealth.[65] Taxes were collected by tax-farming, some in kind (land) and some with money (salt-tax), with contracted amounts to be raised from each district.

Whether this simplified description tells us anything about the initial Ptolemaic administration of Judea/Israel is not clear. Basic information is lacking and what is available suggests no standard form of rule throughout Ptolemaic-controlled territory. Did Judea/Israel exist as an Egyptian nome or, as part of 'Coele-Syria' or 'Syria and Phoenicia' without distinction? Did it have a governor or *strategos* with civil and military powers including a garrison,[66] or was administration left largely in the hands of the local elite headed by the chief priest based in the Jerusalem temple with Egyptian or Greek officials especially charged with tax collection and local oversight? Josephus identifies the 'chief priest'

64. Grabbe, 'Hyparchs', 71.

65. Thompson, 'Infrastructure of Splendour'.

66. So Heinen ('Syrian-Egyptian Wars', 440-41) who makes no mention of the priestly elite but sees local elites responsible for collecting taxes.

Onias as having the 'rulership, leadership, supreme command, governor-ship' (προστασία) of the people, though other than affirming that the province was a hierocracy, exactly what this designation involves he does not elaborate (Josephus, *Ant.* 12.160-61). Imposition of Egyptian will, in whatever form, had to recognize the dynamic of accommodative and disruptive negotiation of power that required efforts to gain coopera-tion and not to provoke open and violent opposition to exertions of power. Several sources provide some information about life under the Ptolemies in the third century BCE but a larger coherent picture is not clear.

Some evidence exists for distressed circumstances in Judea/Israel under Alexander's successor Ptolemy I. During the struggles of the *Diadochi* after Alexander's death in 323–ca. 280 BCE, socio-economic conditions probably deteriorated significantly. The cause was not cultural influence but military power and its attendant socio-economic disruption and exploitation. Hengel observes that during this period, Judea/Israel 'was crossed or occupied seven or eight times by armies'.[67] Grabbe argues that 'Palestine was fought in and over many times'; he catalogues nine instances.[68] In the absence of any records, a postcolonial optic alerts us to the probable disruption of trade and barter, the material damage for poor peasant farmers and their households in the looting of crops and animals that caused hunger and lack, physical attacks on persons (includ-ing rape) as native peoples sought to defend property and persons, the likely practice of enslavement, and the humiliating indignities of being treated as a subordinate unworthy of any respect. Even as the imperial-izer asserts power, it must depend on the production and labor of the subjugated. From such indignities often emerge ambivalent expressions of consent and conflict, counter-practices and counter-narratives that contest and negate the dominant version of reality, fantasize about revenge on the oppressor, and imagine different worlds.[69]

Moreover, according to Josephus, citing the second-century historian Agatharchides of Cnidus, Ptolemy I (d. 283 BCE) took advantage of Jewish customs to attack Jerusalem on a Sabbath, perhaps around 312 BCE, when its inhabitants 'neither bear arms nor take any agricul-tural operations in hand nor engage in any other form of public service' and so 'the country was thus given over to a cruel master' (*C.Ap.* 1.209-11; a 'hard master', *Ant.* 12.6). The account stops at this point in *Contra Apion* with contrasting reflections on observance of the law: 'ridiculous'

<hr>

67. Hengel, *Judaism and Hellenism*, 14.
68. Grabbe, *History of the Jews*, 278-81, 286-87.
69. Scott, *Domination*, 7, *passim*.

as far as Agatharchides is concerned but 'grand and highly meritorious'
for Josephus since it placed faithfulness to God before all else.

In the version in *Antiquities*, however, Josephus goes on to narrate the
consequences of this defeat. Ptolemy takes captives (read slaves) from
Jerusalem and the surrounding area to Egypt and because he thinks
highly of their loyalty (!), he settles them in garrisons and in Alexandria
gives them 'equal civic rights with the Macedonians' (*Ant.* 12.8).
Ptolemy's 'liberality' (φιλοτιμίας) attracted other Jews to Egypt though
they conflicted there with Samaritans over which temple to honor.
Ptolemy's defeat of Jerusalem receives a very brief reference in Appian
(*Syr.* 8.50) and a longer reference in the *Letter of Aristeas* (12-14) that
says nothing about an attack on the Sabbath but does mention the taking
of captive Jews to Egypt (an exaggerated 'more than one hundred
thousand') and Ptolemy's arming and settling of some of these in
garrisons ('thirty thousand'!).

These scenes possibly suggest something of Judea/Israel's metanarrative through the time of Alexander and the *Diadochi*. If Josephus,
quoting Agatharchides, is to be believed, his account indicates that
despite submitting to Alexander, through the time of Alexander and the
Diadochi, the temple had an important role in Jerusalem along with the
law, including Sabbath observance. Ptolemy creates an ambivalent
situation of exercising political-economic domination while allowing
religious observance. In fact, his own embracing of Pharonic political
and Egyptian religious-cultural traditions suggests that any such intolerance would have been most unlikely. That is, in these initial decades of
the assertion of Macedonian and Ptolemaic military and political power,
Jerusalem's worship is not disrupted and the Judean/Israelite metanarrative of covenant identity and Israel's God as God of the nations
remains in place, at least some Jerusalemites. Throughout the rest of the
land, a growing and diverse range of ethnic groups and religious observances is to be found.[70] Andrea Berlin lists twenty known religious
expressions in 'Hellenistic Palestine' involving Phoenician, Egyptian,
Greek, 'local', Jewish, Samaritan, and Ituraean deities and cult sites.

The longstanding focus on and independence of the temple in the
midst of the imperial–colonized ambivalence is confirmed by Hecataeus
of Abdera's writings on the Jews (Diodorus 40.3.1-7). Hecataeus attests
Judea/Israel's administrative autonomy based on the temple and its
priests and expressed in the law.[71] Hecataeus declares that the inhabitants
of Judea/Israel were driven out of Egypt and were led by a man called

---

70. Berlin, 'Between Large Forces', 42.
71. Grabbe, *History of the Jews*, 283-86; Grabbe, 'Hyparchs', 75-77.

Moses who founded several cities including Jerusalem. More important, Hecataeus emphasizes that Moses founded the temple as a central institution and established its aniconic worship and ritual, along with instituting the law and political institutions. Hecataeus attests the absence of a king and identifies the priests as leaders of the nation who not only oversee temple worship, but are leaders in other aspects of society including warfare, dividing land for settlers, raising children, judging disputes, and as keepers of the laws and customs. The chief priest has supreme authority as messenger of God's commandments, making a king obsolete. Moses was also a military leader, defeating surrounding tribes, taking land, and reallocating it to citizens and to priests. The Jews have a written law and practice circumcision (Diodorus 1.55.5).

The implication of the record of Agatharchides and Hecataeus' idealized account is that the assertion of Macedonian and Ptolemaic power and military presence in the fifty or so year window of ca. 330–280 BCE had not overturned native religious, cultural, and political structures in Judea/Israel, though Hecataeus does indicate, realistically in a postcolonial optic, that when Judea/Israel became 'subject to foreign rule', namely the Persians and the Macedonians, 'many of their traditional practices were disturbed' (Diodorus 40.3.8). Diodorus alludes to the likely Ptolemaic creation of an ambivalent third space that left local structures in place, used them for their own advantage, and introduced their own system.

Two decrees from Ptolemy II dating to around 260 BCE and addressed to 'Syria and Phoenicia' provide some insight into these evolving administrative structures, tax collection, slaves, and war-wives in Judea/Israel.[72]

The papyri identify administrative structures somewhat similar to those of Egypt. The papyri attest districts identifying them not as nomes but hyparchies—perhaps based on the Persian districts—as the basic administrative structure. There was a chief finance officer (διοικητής); each hyparchy had an *oikonomos* as the chief financial officer responsible for the pervasive imperial strategy of taxation. Taxation involved 'taxable and tax-free' livestock. Failure to declare livestock for tax purposes to the *oikonomos* meant loss of livestock and other penalties. There was also a 'pasture tax and crown tax'. Villages were important not only for the registration of livestock but also for the collection of taxes. 'Those holding the tax contracts for the villages and the komarchs (leaders?) shall register...livestock in the villages'. Registration of livestock was annual and with penalties for failure to pay the associated

72. Text from Bagnall and Derow, *The Hellenistic Period*, 111-13.

taxes. Informers on non-payment were welcome and rewarded. That is, the papyri exhibit the reciprocity of the imperializer–colonized situation, attesting the intrusive reach of Ptolemaic taxing power into the villages and daily lives of peasant farmers, as well as its dependence on local labor and production.

Slaves seem to play a significant part in the economy. Free persons were not to be enslaved and slaves were to be registered. Slaves were procured through royal auction or from those awaiting execution. Failure to register slaves meant a fine and further punishment. Informers were again rewarded.

Soldiers also had a significant presence, both those on active duty and those who had settled land. Both groups expressed Greek presence and were symbols of superior Greek military power and of the subjugated identity of the locals. The decree recognized a particular form of inter-action between soldiers and natives in which women were not only captured (and raped?) in war but forced to marry their captors.[73] 'Soldiers on active duty and the other military settlers…living with native wives whom they have captured need not declare them'. That is, while registra-tion of slaves at least provided some monitoring of enslavement (for whatever reason), marriage to local women, either captured in battle or living in occupied areas, was apparently of no concern. As Scott notes, in addition to economic domination, personal indignities and humiliations exist in many forms in the interactions of colonizer and colonized.[74]

From about the same time (ca. 260 BCE) come letters from the Zenon papyri discovered during the First World War in Egypt.[75] Zenon was a representative of the finance minister (*dioikotes*) Apollonius of Ptolemy II (282–246 BCE). Zenon travelled in Judea/Israel and southern Syria in ca. 259–258 BCE. In relation to his travels, his archive records various letters and accounts of supplies.

The papyri indicate significant trade activities and the importance of Greek language for those in power. Greek signifies the superiority of the ruling group and highlights the desirability of a Greek education for any who wanted to participate in the exercise of power. The learning and use of the Greek language, an act of mimicry, creates Bhabha's 'third space' of similarity that is not quite the same.[76] Hybridity marks the experience of local elite Egyptian and Jewish figures wherein this foreign language

<hr>

73.   The classic discussion is Brownmiller, *Against Our Will*, 31-113.

74.   Scott, *Domination*, 198.

75.   Grabbe, *History of the Jews*, 283-86; Grabbe, 'Hyparchs', 52-53.

76.   Bhabha, *The Location*, 86. See Perdue's discussion of Bhabha's notion of mimicry and the role of language in it in Chapter 1 above.

distances them from their native language and traditions even while it intertwines them in Greek language and culture. Other references in the papyri to figures called Tobias and Jeddous identify them as Jews exercising some power, whether on behalf of the provincial administration in Jerusalem or the centralized Ptolemaic administration. Tobias seems quite at home in the Ptolemaic-Hellenistic world. In addition to being fluent in the Greek language, he seems quite tolerant of Greek culture. In a letter from Tobias to Apollonius, Tobias addresses him with a polytheistic greeting: 'If you and all your affairs are flourishing and everything else is as you wish it, many thanks to the gods' (πολλὴ χαρὶς τοῖς θεοίς).[77] Jews, at least at this more elite provincial level, thus appear to occupy the hybrid location typical of other ethnic groups under imperial power, comparatively neither privileged nor disadvantaged, at home in the Ptolemaic-administered world yet members of a distinctive tradition and practices.

Josephus offers an account of two males from two elite Palestinian families, the Tobiads and the Oniads, that provides some confirmation of this hybridity (*Ant.* 12.154-236). The genre, date, provenance, and agenda of the story have been extensively debated; we will return to some of these questions shortly but understand the story to concern the third century BCE.[78]

Hybridity is immediately evident as the story begins with the high priest Onias refusing to pay tribute to King Ptolemy thereby siding with the Seleucids against Ptolemy. Ptolemy replies with threats of taking land from Judea/Israel and settling soldiers there. Joseph Tobias (son of the Tobias named in the Zenon papyri), and nephew of Onias (his mother was Onias' sister) rebukes Onias for endangering Judea/Israel's cooperative/submissive relationship with the Ptolemies. Joseph then travels to Egypt to plead for the nation to King Ptolemy. Ptolemy welcomes him. Simultaneously, 'the chief men and magistrates of the cities' appeared before Ptolemy to buy the rights to collect taxes from their cities. Joseph outbids them promising Ptolemy a higher return from Judea/Israel. Employing his two thousand soldiers, Ptolemy makes an example of Ascalon with aggressive and violent collection including

77. Tcherikover and Fuks, *Corpus Papyrorum Judaicarum*, 1.4.

78. For example, Gideon Fuks affirms the conventional position of the 'second half of the third century BCE' as its historical context; so 'Josephus' Tobiads Again'. Schwartz argued against this more conventional position proposing that the story's historical context comprises the early second century; so 'Josephus' Tobiads: Back'. Gera, *Judaea*, 36-58, also dates 'this piece of propaganda...in the second or first century' (58); Grabbe, *History of the Jews*, 75-78, 185-92, 222-23, 293-97.

executing twenty of the principal men, an act that intimidates other cities. He continues in this tax-collection role for twenty-two years gaining much power and wealth and building connections with Ptolemy.

With the daughter of his brother, Joseph fathered a son Hyrcanus who had exceptional ability. Hyrcanus, though, becomes entangled in a dispute with his father's steward in Alexandria but manages to gain honor before Ptolemy. His jealous brothers attack him, he defends himself, withdraws to the Transjordan, but after the death of his father Joseph, engages in continuing war with his brothers and ongoing collection of taxes until—surprisingly—he commits suicide when Antiochus IV Epiphanes comes to the throne.

Josephus' story cannot be taken at historical face-value. The story is set at the beginning of the reign of Ptolemy V Epiphanes (204–180) but a fundamental problem with the chronology rules out this possibility. The Ptolemies lost control of Judea/Israel in 200 BCE to the Seleucids, making the scenario of Joseph collecting taxes for the Ptolemies in his Seleucid-controlled territory for some twenty years or so simply implausible. That his son Hyrcanus continues his father's tax-collecting activity thereafter renders such a setting even more implausible.

One solution is to redate the story to the time of Ptolemy III during the third Syrian War (246–241 BCE), in which Onias sides with the Seleucids against Ptolemy. A comparable option is Grabbe's solution which, recognizing the lack of markers linking the scene to a specific king, posits a general setting in the third century.[79] If this latter setting is adopted along with a recognition of romance elements in the story (as well as biblical intertextualities with another Joseph story concerning Egypt and jealous brothers), the story perhaps offers some possible historical data, or more likely, at least considerable verisimilitude for the ambivalence that marks imperial–colonial, metropole–province negotiations of power.

One such datum concerns the existence of some local Jewish elites—in this case the Tobiad and Oniad families linked by marriage—who make their way successfully and powerfully in Ptolemaic Judea/Israel by cooperation and minimal or no confrontation with the ruling power. A second concerns the contestive relationship with occupying power illustrated by the chief priest Onias' refusal to pay the tribute. The local chief priest, as a political, societal, and religious leader and representative of his peoples' traditions and practices, yet sanctioned by Ptolemaic power, occupies a hybrid identity and location. He challenges Ptolemaic power, perhaps strengthened by traditions concerning divine sovereignty,

79. Grabbe, *History of the Jews*, 77.

covenant, and land. Third, the story also illustrates agonistic and conflictual relationships among local elites under pressure from the dominant power and in fractured disagreement about how the rival imperial powers (Ptolemaic; Seleucid) should be engaged. Onias' actions that contest Ptolemaic power arouse considerable concern from other citizens for the country's safety, including Joseph Tobiad. That is, Ptolemaic power was not negotiated in a monolithic manner among elites; diversity exists on the periphery of the empire's power. Fourth, Joseph and his son Hyrcanus demonstrate a different expression of hybridity in the aggressive self-benefitting collusion with the ruling power at the expense of their own people. In the story, Joseph doubles the tax amount collected from his own people. He uses violence against the predominantly Gentile Ascalon/Ashkelon, including killing some of its elites. In so doing, he clearly sides with the Ptolemies in mimicking common means of asserting power in the form of violence and tax-collection, but does so for his own self-enriching and empowering ends. His use of violence against other subjects of the Ptolemies—Fanon's horizontal violence—attests the downward imperial pressure exerted in the dynamic of gaining and maintaining imperial favor and in supplying tax revenues.[80] These means of course benefit the ruling Ptolemies and reflect the reciprocity and ambivalence of the imperializer–colonized situation. Fifth, Josephus accurately depicts the 'principal men' from various Palestinian cities competing against one another for the favor of their colonial Ptolemaic overlords in being granted tax-farming rights in the province. Sixth, collection of taxes expresses the ambivalence of the imperializer–colonized relationship. They denote subjugation but they also exhibit dependence, especially the dependency of local elites on imperial favor for promoting their own self-benefitting yet derived power and interests, as well as the dependency of the Ptolemies on Judean/Israelite production. And seventh, Josephus' account attests the ambivalence and hybridity of local elites not only fluent in their own traditions and language but also evidencing facility with Greek, considerable ease with Greek culture, and the ready acceptance of provincials in the king's court even while the Tobiads and Oniads maintained the role and traditions of the chief priest and temple. The cultures of the colonizer and the colonized coexist in an often reciprocal and hybrid space.

Finally, several traditions attest a visit of Ptolemy IV Philopater to Jerusalem (221–204 BCE).[81] Third Maccabees 1:6-13 sets the scene after the fourth Syrian war (219–217 BCE) in which Ptolemy gains a

---

80. Fanon, *The Wretched*, 52-54; see Introduction and nn. 13-17 above.
81. On 3 Maccabees, see Gera, *Judaea*, 12-20; Croy, *3 Maccabees*, 37-57.

temporary victory over the Seleucid Antiochus III in the battle of Raphia (Polybius 5.79-87; 3 Macc. 1:1-7).[82] After the victory, Ptolemy, like Alexander before him,[83] visited various towns and temples in his newly acquired territory of Syria.[84] According to 3 Maccabees 1:6-13, the Jews sent representatives from 'their council[85] and elders' to Ptolemy with gifts and congratulations. In response, he visited Jerusalem, 'offered sacrifices to the supreme God', and inspected the temple.

Up to this point all is well from a Jewish perspective and similarities with Josephus' account of Alexander's fictional visit are evident. But then things go wrong. Ptolemy IV Philopater insists on moving beyond the temple precinct to enter the sanctuary despite being informed that only the high priest could enter there once a year (1:11-12; cf. Exod. 30:10; Lev. 16:2-34; Josephus, *J.W.* 1.152; Philo, *Leg. Ad Gaium* 306-307).[86] A popular outcry follows (3 Macc. 1:16-29), and the high priest Simon prays for divine protection from this 'audacious and profane man' (2:1-20). The narrative continues by claiming that Ptolemy is punished by God with temporary paralysis for his 'insolence and audacity' (3 Macc. 2:21-24). He subsequently takes revenge on the Jews in Alexandria before experiencing a change of heart (3 Macc. 6:22-41).

Much of this narrative is historically unsubstantiated and unlikely. Polybius, however, confirms Ptolemy's three-month visit to towns in Syria and Phoenicia (5.86.8-11; 87.5-7) but does not mention Jerusalem. The action against the Jerusalem temple in 3 Maccabees is quite contrary to Ptolemaic respectful policy and actions concerning local temples. Polybius also makes the observation that the people of Coele-Syria 'have always been more attached to that house (the Ptolemies) than to the Seleucids' though he goes on to attribute this loyalty to the expediency of supporting the victorious king rather than seeming to be resistant or hostile (Polybius 5.86.8-10). Yet the scene is significant in reflecting an awareness by some of misunderstandings of and threat to Jerusalem's distinctive commitments and identity in the face of foreign rulers. It imagines an almost 'worst-case' scenario and its tragic circumstances,

82.   Bar-Kochva, *The Seleucid Army*, 128-41.

83.   As noted above, Alexander visited the oasis of Siwa and the temple of Zeus-Ammon in 331, and Josephus has him visiting Jerusalem.

84.   Confirmed by the Pithom stele; see Modrzejewski, *The Jews of Egypt*, 148.

85.   Josephus (*Ant.* 12.138) notes this 'council' or *genousia* offering support to Antiochus III.

86.   Compare threats to the temple from Antiochus IV Epiphanes, 169 BCE (1 Macc. 1:20-24; 2 Macc. 5:5, 11-21; Josephus, *Ant.* 12.246); Pompey Magnus, 63 BCE (Josephus, *Ant.* 14.67-72; *J.W.* 1.145-51); Gaius Caligula, 40 CE (Josephus, *Ant.* 18.257-309; Philo, *Leg. Ad Gaium* 207-21, *passim.*

yet also fantasizes about the revenge of Israel's powerful and protective God on such violations of Jewish identity and practice. That is, as much as 3 Maccabees is written in Greek, it imagines boundaries on divinely sanctioned hybrid identity and practice in the Hellenistic world. There is a literal line, constituted by liturgical practice and centered on the holy place of the temple, which cannot be crossed.

From these various sources, some tentative generalizations about Judea/Israel's interaction with Ptolemaic rule can be drawn. One conclusion is that Ptolemaic power did not interfere with, let alone overturn, native Judean/Israelite religious, cultural, and political structures. Priests associated with the Jerusalem temple and local elite families like the Tobiads know the hybridity of gaining Ptolemaic favor even while they represent Judean/Israelite traditions and identity. From this hybrid place, they represent alien and native interests in exercising societal leadership. Second, Ptolemaic rule imposed officials as administrators at local village levels throughout Judea/Israel, thereby exercising grassroots control. Third, a primary role of these administrative structures and personnel involved collection of taxation. They were the means of the extraction and acquisition of wealth that the Hellenistic ideology of kingship, practiced by Alexander and his successors, foregrounded and on which the Ptolemies depended in the reciprocal imperializing–colonized dynamic. Extracted wealth was foundational for paying troops, exercising benefactions, securing gratitude, and rewarding loyalty, displaying the power and status of victory.[87]

Exploitative Economy in Judea/Israel

The Judean/Israelite economy was based in agriculture before the arrival of the Greeks and it continued to be long after power passed into Roman hands.[88] Throughout it remained a source of income for the imperial power claiming control of the territory. Under the Prolemies, Andrea Berlin observes heavy taxation on commerce, tax farming, and royal ownership of land especially in the north in Galilee, the Jezreel and Beth-Shean valleys, and the Golan.[89] She also observes from archaeological remains thriving economic activity in urban places in coastal Judea/Israel

87. Grabbe, 'Hyparchs'. See also Section I above.
88. Manning, *Land and Power*; Grabbe, *History of the Jews*, 208-24; van der Steen, 'Empires and Farmers'.
89. Berlin, 'Between Large Forces', 4, 12-14; that land in the vicinity of Beth-Shean was royal land is confirmed by the Zenon papyri (P.Cairo Zen. 59004) and the Hefzibah inscription. On the latter, see Section III below.

(Ashkelon, Ashdod) and in the south. Mareshah, for example, had two major industries—olive oil and breeding doves. If Qohelet/Ecclesiastes originates in third-century Jerusalem (and there is debate), it attests an elite with some prosperity from large estates worked by slaves (Eccl. 2:4-8). On the other hand, the excavated site of a village such as Tel Anafa in the north near the Panion sanctuary shows a 'small poor community... unsophisticated, insular, and self-sufficient', dependent on agriculture, especially cattle and goats, and producing its own cloth.[90]

The decrees from Ptolemy II, the Zenon papyri, and Josephus' account of the Tobiad family indicate the importance of the extractive practice of the collection of tribute and taxes for the wealth and power of the Ptolemaic kings. Josephus attests payment of an annual 'tribute of twenty talents of silver' collected by the high priest of the Jerusalem temple (Josephus, *Ant.* 12.158). The decrees identify regions (hyparchies), tax officials (*oikonomoi*), and focus on villages, suggesting extensive intrusion into local life and serve as a reminder at the local level of the identity of these people as, in part, a subjugated people. Annual registration of livestock and of slaves for taxation is required. The decrees provide rewards for those who inform on tax evaders, and name a range of taxes, as noted above. We might imagine similar taxation on crop production such as grain, vines, and olives. Josephus' narrative about the Tobiads, whatever the proportion of historical and imaginative elements, indicates a tax-collection system of competitive bidding that no doubt increased returns for both the ruling Ptolemies and their provincial allies. This reciprocal interaction created an ambivalent identity for local elites by allying them with Ptolemaic power even as it sanctioned their self-enriching and empowering practice at the expense of fellow citizens.

Josephus attests a (later or stereotypical?) perception of harsh levels of taxation and cynical elite attitudes towards the exploitative practice in his inclusion of a scene involving Hyrcanus at a feast with the Ptolemaic king. In the scene, Ptolemy's jester Tryphon mocks Hyrcanus. Pointing to the bones from the meat Hyrcanus has eaten, Tryphon declares, 'My lord, do you see the bones lying before Hyrcanus? From this you may guess that his father has stripped all Syria in the same way as Hyrcanus has left these bones bare of meat' (Josephus, *Ant.* 12.212). Berlin offers some confirmation for harsh levies on commercial activity. She points to the building of customs houses and to one of the Zenon papyri (P.Cairo Zen. 59.012) that records taxes on goods imported into Egypt from the

---

90. Berlin, 'Between Large Forces', 5-9, 14. Berlin notes that Tel Anafa undergoes significant resettlement in the 140s–120s BCE by some wealthy inhabitants from Phoenicia (26-27).

wider area of Syria.[91] Items taxed at fifty percent include grape syrup, filtered and ordinary wine, and white oil; at 33 1/3 percent wine and figs; at 25 percent cheese, fish, and wild-boar and goat meat, Samian earth, nuts, pomegranate seeds, sponges, and honey.

Trade in olive oil and wine, and less so in grain due to transportation challenges, was significant. More than 500 imported (Rhodian) stamped handles of amphorae have been found in Jerusalem, most of which date to 260–150 BCE.[92] Their use is uncertain but numerous possibilities point to significant trading activities in Jerusalem whether in the form of importing food supplies or exporting products. It is also possible they were used to ship taxes paid in kind (oil, wine, wheat). Another export, according to the Zenon papyri, comprised the export of slaves, notably young boys and girls for the household service of their owners.[93] The colonizer's power meant disruption of households as well as sexual exploitation and submission. It also meant, for some, active participation in the imperial economy and economic prosperity.

Grabbe in fact notes increase in prosperity for some throughout the third century. Figures for tribute payment reflect considerable growth. For the earlier third century, Josephus says that 20 talents of tribute were paid annually. When Antiochus IV becomes king in 175 BCE, Jason offers a total of 440 talents (2 Macc. 4:8). If the figures are accurate and realistic reflections of economic capacity more than of individual ambition and competition for favor among provincial leaders (compare Joseph Tobiad's brazen doubling of the amount of tax to be collected—Josephus, *Ant.* 12.175-76), some economic growth has occurred. Grabbe attributes this growth to several factors. One involves Jewish participation in the Ptolemaic military (Josephus, *Ant.* 11.339; 12.8; *C.Ap.* 1.192-93, 200-204). This involvement may have reduced the need for further subdivision of family land, provided fresh landholdings to veterans in Egypt, and perhaps increased some cash flow, with money sent back to Judea/Israel. And second, Josephus' account of the Tobiads, if it contains any valid historical data that can be generalized to other elite households, indicates that some local elites accumulated considerable amounts of wealth. Such families required goods and services, benefitted clients, and presumably conducted some euergetistic activities, all with economic benefits to others. And third, the increase may reflect a greater role for Jerusalem in trade activity.

<hr>

91. Berlin, 'Between Large Forces', 4-5. The text is in Austin, *The Hellenistic World*, 531-34.

92. Ariel, 'Imported Stamped Amphora Handles'.

93. Grabbe, *History of the Jews*, 216-17.

Ptolemaic Metanarrative

Viewed in a postcolonial optic, Ptolemaic kingship embraces the hybridity of interactions between Greek and Egyptian traditions. One influential tradition comprised the ideology of kingship exhibited by Alexander,[94] in which the king was 'supreme commander, dispenser of justice [and] god's representative on earth'.[95] Kingly power was performative in that military success demonstrated the king's personal bravery and courage. Repeated demonstrations in battle renewed and augmented kingly power. The first four Ptolemaic kings led their troops in battle and accomplished the glory of victory.[96] Victory was the means of acquiring territory. Territory was not only the badge of success but also the source of wealth that rewarded troops, financed further military action, and provided benefactions for friends, subjects, and allies. The Ptolemies advertised their roles and accomplishments with appellations such as Soter (savior), Euergetes (benefactor), and Theos Epiphanes (god manifest).

Austin offers an example of the wealth gained by Ptolemy III in the third Syrian war (246–245 BCE) to the tune of 40,000 talents of booty.[97] As a context, he notes that Ptolemy II took 15,000 talents as annual revenue from Egypt (minus the corn dues). In a small episode during the same war, Ptolemy III gains a Seleucid war chest from a city amounting to 1500 talents. In addition to this wealth, he took many as captives, thereby adding bodies to his workforce and military resources. Military power also had a deterrent effect as the Ptolemies sought to secure their position against possible rivals. Appeals to the legacy of Alexander along with alignment with native monarchic traditions bolstered power and marked Ptolemaic hybridity.

Also crucial for the Ptolemaic metanarrative was the use of multiple religious traditions to assert their divinity and place in the cosmos. Again hybridity is to the fore. Ptolemy I and his successors employed claims of divine sanction, both Egyptian and Greek, for their rule. Samuel cites Theocritus' seventeenth idyll, which praises Ptolemy II in terms of longstanding Greek traditions embraced by Alexander. This ideology of monarchy embraced 'divine descent, warrior prowess, reverence toward

94. Walbank, 'Monarchy and Monarchic Ideas', 75-84; see also Austin, 'Hellenistic Kings'; Murray, 'Philosophy and Monarchy'.
95. Walbank, 'Monarchy and Monarchic Ideas', 79.
96. Austin, 'Hellenistic Kings', 458.
97. Austin, 'Hellenistic Kings', 465.

the gods and generosity toward men from his great wealth'. The divinity of the king was recognized through oaths and observances of the Ptolemaic dynastic cult, often initiated by locals.[98]

Günther Hölbl attends to further dimensions of their hybrid existence, a particular challenge facing the Ptolemies as they negotiated the interaction between Greeks and Macedonians on one hand and native Egyptian elites on the other (priests, warriors, landowners). Concerning the latter, the Ptolemies needed to secure the sanction of 'the ancient Egyptian ideology of the king…as the earthly manifestation of Horus and as "the son of Re"' along with the support of the powerful Egyptian priestly establishment.[99] They sought to accomplish the latter by synthesizing Greek kingship with the role of the Egyptian Pharaoh. The former had developed, as noted, an understanding of 'charismatic invincibility, which was upheld by the gods' but needed ongoing performance in war to establish an identity as 'savior, liberator (especially of Greek cities), protector and begetter and guarantor of fertility and affluence' and to gain the subjects' recognition.[100] The Pharaoh's invincibility was grounded in 'his role as the victorious Horus', the leading god associated variously with the sky, with war, and with hunting. The king was thus defined primarily in religious terms as the one who by means of his cultic activities maintained the world order and by associating with the gods mediated between humans and gods.[101] Hölbl argues that kingship provided 'the only element of unity in all areas of culture and religion', which elevated the kingship, a status sustained by both Egyptian and Greek (Dionysos; Aphrodite) cults of the gods connected to kingship.[102]

The options secured by this hybridity meant that Ptolemy did not seek to impose his Greek tradition and eliminate Egyptian culture, language, or judicial systems. Rather, he combined the two traditions, not only thereby linking Greek and Egyptian traditions, but also using the hybrid traditions to assert strongly the multiple claims of divine sanction for Ptolemaic rule. The dynasty was deified, as was the deceased Alexander, and a priesthood was established to honor him.[103] Further sanction was gained by giving prominence to honoring particular divinities such as

98. Samuel, 'The Ptolemies', 180-83.

99. Hölbl, *History*, 1-5, 77-123, esp. 78. He identifies another challenge, namely distancing themselves from Persian rule by presenting themselves as liberators.

100. Hölbl, *History*, 91.

101. Hölbl, *History*, 1-2.

102. Hölbl, *History*, 111-12.

103. Walbank, 'Monarchies and Monarchic Ideas', 97-98.

Zeus-Ammon, who had sanctuaries in Egypt and Macedonia, as well as Serapis, connected to both Isis and Osiris, the mother and father of Horus. Hölbl comments that Isis and Serapis were seen as both Hellenistic and Egyptian deities.[104] Beyond honoring, Walbank notes the Ptolemaic convention of 'assimilating kings to particular gods' such as Dionysus, Aollo-Helios, Eros, Heracles, Hermes, Poseidon and Zeus.[105] Further, the Ptolemies instituted an annual gathering of Egyptian priests to express loyalty to the king and to engage cultic and economic matters, the latter being important to fund the succession of wars throughout the third century.

The Ptolemies' explicit positioning of themselves in Egypt in terms of these cultural hybridities contrasts with their self-presentation in Judea/Israel. In the early third century, in the decade or so after 301 BCE, the mint in Jerusalem issued silver coins with the head of Ptolemy 1 wearing a diadem on the obverse.[106] The coins signify on the reverse Zeus' divine sanction for Ptolemy's rule as the power behind the throne by means of an eagle with wings spread and standing on a *fulmen* or lightning bolt. These coins, the last ones issued by the mint before being closed ca. 270 BCE, have a legend in paleo-Hebrew (not Aramaic, the *lingua franca* of the Persian rule) that reads *Yhdh* and signifies not only the coins' local character but locates Judea/Israel as a part of Zeus-sanctioned Ptolemaic rule. There are similarities between the features of these coins and those issued by the Persians, namely the head of the Persian ruler, the falcon with wings spread, and the inscription of *Yhdh*. The differences, however—the head of Ptolemy I, Zeus' eagle and lightning, the inscription *Yhdh*—indicate a new empire under a new and victorious god. It should also be noted that while in Egypt Ptolemy's hybrid location comprised combining Hellenistic and Egyptian divine sanction, these Judean/Israelite coins utilize only Hellenistic traditions.

Dan Barag identifies other coin types, notably the 'divine' (ΘΕΩΝ) 'brother-and-sister' (ΑΔΕΛΦΩΝ) series presenting Ptolemy I, his wife and half-sister Berenice I, and possibly the co-regency with Ptolemy II and his sister and wife Arsinoe II, introduced most probably from the mid-280s to the mid-260s BCE.[107] The coins represented the trans-generational Ptolemaic rulers to their Judean/Israelite subjects even as they provided coinage for some financial transactions. Barag argues that the presence of such coins from the Jerusalem mint that operated

104.   Hölbl, *History*, 100-101.
105.   Walbank, 'Monarchies and Monarchic Ideas', 86.
106.   I am following Kindler, 'Silver Coins'.
107.   Barag, 'The Coinage', 30.

between 300 and 274/269 BCE 'certainly displays direct control from the centre of government', Alexandria, but with the closing of the Jerusalem mint, 'Judea was integrated in the current monetary system'.[108] Barag recognizes, though, that the presence of Paleo-Hebrew on the coins and the existence of a mint in Jerusalem during this quarter century or so raise unanswerable questions about the status of Judea/Israel.

We should note, though, that this hybrid metanarrative that announced the divine sanction of Hellenistic and Egyptian deities for Ptolemaic kingship did not garner universal support in the Ptolemaic world, or at least not everyone was happy all the time. As postcolonial studies have shown, whenever power is asserted, dissent is inevitable albeit expressed in various forms and often coexisting with accommodation and apparent (public) compliance. One form of protest comprised outbreaks of revolt and violence in the 250s–240s BCE in Egypt under Philadelphus (282–246 BCE) and Ptolemy III Euergetes I (246–221 BCE), spurred by poor harvests, economic disruption, and increasing demands for war supplies and manpower.[109]

Another form of protest is expressed sometime around the mid-third century or so, in the 'Demotic Chronicle'. This collection of oracles sought to decolonize subjugated minds and bodies by announcing that only compliance with the divine will, especially Isis and Harsaphes, brings harmony and successful long reigns for kings. It opposes foreign rule, notably the invasions of the Persians (IV.22-23; V.15-18) and also of the Greeks (VI.19-21), who are called 'the dogs' with Alexander probably referred to as the 'great Dog'.[110] Employing a classic strategy of fantasizing a different future based on reclaiming and redefining the past, it creates a third space that looks for a day of military rebellion. This rebellion comprises the expulsion of the Greek monarchy, the restoration of a native Egyptian ruler 'after the Greeks', the establishment of an idealized Egyptian state and monarchy based on past Pharaonic ideals

108.   Barag, 'The Coinage', 37.
109.   Turner, 'Ptolemaic Egypt', 157-59.
110.   Johnson ('Is the Demotic Chronicle?', 123) argues that this reference draws on the image of the dog of Horus, and may present Alexander as a hunting hound driving out the Persians, and the Greeks 'in a positive light'. Lloyd ('Nationalist Propaganda', 45 n. 38) reads it negatively and cites a stele of the Regnal Year of Amasis in support. The immediate context of this image in the document (VI.21) refers to young men in a gesture of mourning, suggesting the image seems to point to a negative reception of the Greeks. The other explicit reference to Greeks (II.25; III.1) expressly names a time 'after the Greeks' and exhorts rejoicing (twice) at the coming of a new ruler in Herakleopolis. It is difficult to follow Johnson's attempt to claim this as a neutral reference (Johnson, 'Is the Demotic Chronicle?', 122).

and centered on Herakleopolis (II.25; III.1), and the implementation of
the divine will or 'law' (III.15-16; IV.1, 6, 7, 10, 12).[111] Societal analysis,
a turning to the past and to the future, and an idealized fantasy combine
to present a different vision. Johnson's argument that the text is not anti-
Greek because elite Egyptian priests, its supposed source of origins, were
often loyal to the Ptolemies, fails to convince.[112] Johnson does not
recognize the complexities of the ambivalent imperializer–colonized
situation that interpret the present through the interaction of a glorified
past and ideal future, and that involve hybridities and ambivalences,
public and anonymous/private, compliant, and resistant interactions
between natives and foreign ruling powers.

The Judea/Israel Metanarratives

The above analyses of administrative and economic structures, partial as
they are, indicate diverse responses to or multivalent elite negotiations of
Ptolemaic power. Whether it has any historical validity or not, Josephus'
scene concerning Onias and Joseph Tobiad is full of the ambivalences of
the imperializer–colonized situation. Josephus can imagine the Jerusalem
chief priest Onias in a hybridized location of dependence yet autonomy
refusing to pay the tribute which he owes. The scene of course assumes
the reciprocal relationship of imperializer and colonized in that Onias
benefts from Ptolemaic favor and the Ptolemies benefit from Judea/
Israelite submission signified by tax payment. Likewise, Josephus can
imagine other elites becoming very worried by Onias' act of defiance
towards Hellenistic power, whether they be active pro-Ptolemaic supporters or readily accommodated inhabitants who know cooperation with
whoever is in power is the best means of survival. Moreover, Josephus
can imagine a member of the chief priest's own family rebuking the
priest for his refusal to pay. Fanon recognizes that the relationships
among colonials fracture under the pressure of colonial power, becoming
contestive and even violently (verbally and/or physically) competitive.[113]
The 'native under colonial power', Joseph Tobiad, travels to Alexandria

111.　I follow Lloyd, 'Nationalist Propaganda', 41-45. Johnson ('The Demotic
Chronicle as a Statement', 65-66; and Johnson, 'Is the Demotic Chronicle?') argues
that the work is certainly anti-Persian but 'not so clearly anti-Greek'. She argues that
the text presents a vision of legitimate kingship by presenting good and bad kings.
Lloyd had argued similarly in explaining the text's translation into Greek, that it
made the Macedonian rulers aware of Egyptian ideals of a good king ('Nationalist
Propaganda', 48 n. 48).

112.　Johnson, 'Is the Demotic Chronicle?', 114-24.

113.　Fanon, *The Wretched*, 52-54; see the Introduction and nn. 13-17 above.

not only to ensure peaceful relations in the face of Ptolemy's threats of retaliation, but also to compete with other elites for self-benefiting tax-collection rights, outbidding them and thereby doubling the tax return from his own people while enhancing his own wealth and favor with the king. Tobiad's expansion of his own power and wealth at the expense of his own people provokes their opposition—which he overcomes with the imperially imitative means of military violence, death, and general intimidation. The Tobiad narrative, of dubious historical worth, nevertheless captures a range of well-attested imperializer–colonized dynamics comprising hybridity and ambivalence.

Josephus' account recognizes the central place of the chief priest and of the temple. This emphasis coheres with that of Agatharchides of Cnidus (cited by Josephus, *C.Ap.* 1.209-11; *Ant.* 12.1-9) and of Hecataeus of Abdera (cited by Diodorus 40.3) discussed above. Jerusalem, priests, temple, and Mosaic law feature in their accounts. We might tentatively conclude from this cluster of emphases that they comprised the meta-narrative for at least Onias and his circle. That metanarrative would embrace traditions about Moses as deliverer of the people from Egyptian slavery, traditions that surely troubled ready accommodation with Ptolemaic power exerted from Egypt. Moses was also the maker of a covenant and revealer of the law in which God blesses the obedient and punishes the disobedient. These same traditions affirmed the importance of the land as God's gift, and the significance of the Jerusalem temple, its priests, and worship of God.[114] Such a metanarrative, as long as it was left untouched by the Ptolemies, could sustain compliant and accommodating relationships with Ptolemaic power, just as it could fuel acts of dissent, such as Onias' threatened refusal to pay tribute.

But there is perhaps some evidence that it is not the only metanarrative in town.[115] If so, again fractures under imperial power and diversities on the periphery are evident. Some have read *1 Enoch* 1–36, the Book of the Watchers, as expressing, in the view of Wes Howard-Brooks, 'a sustained protest, in the Name of YHWH, against Judea/Israel's priestly,

114.   The diasporan text *Letter of Aristeas* sets its action in the reign of Ptolemy II Philadelphus (285–247 BCE), though it was perhaps written in the second century (ca. 150 BCE). The document includes an extensive section about the temple, worship, priests, and Jerusalem (83-120). The significance is that the writer of the *Letter* has no problem recognizing the centrality of the temple and the law in the reign of Ptolomy II.

115.   *1 Enoch* 72–82, the earliest section of the Enoch collection to be written and dating perhaps from the fourth or third century, commonly called the Astronomical Book, advocates, as did some other texts, a solar calendar rather than the temple's lunar calendar.

royal, and scribal elites for their collaboration with foreign empires'.[116] Richard Horsley argues that *1 Enoch* 1–36 addresses 'the imperial political situation of Judea/Israelite under the Hellenistic empires, and looks for the "removal" of imperial rule'.[117] George Nickelsburg sees the book struggling with a human situation marked by 'violence, lies, disappointment, and lack of meaning…pulled in opposite directions by hope and despair'.[118] In this approach, if it is persuasive, chapters 1–36 provide for a contrapuntal reading strategy in explaining the origins of the violence and destruction that the Hellenistic imperial rulers create, and in providing assurance that God, the King of kings, has contained them and rules the cosmos. *1 Enoch* 1–36 provides a site for decolonizing the colonized mind.

The book of *1 Enoch* opens with a description of God's appearance to judge the world and divide the elect from the 'hardhearted' wicked who have 'transgressed and spoken slanderously grave and harsh words… against his greatness' (*1 En.* 5:4-5). Elaborating Gen. 6:1-4's account of the giants or 'sons of God', chapters 6–16 narrate the evil activities of fallen watchers led by Shemyaz and Azazel. Among other things, the watchers impregnate women who give birth to giants—figures of overwhelming power perhaps like the Ptolemies—who consume the people's food and become detested by them (7:3). Azazel teaches people how to make weapons of war and skills of beautification (8:1) along with sources of knowledge involving incantations and astrology (8:2-3). They shed 'much blood upon the earth' and bring about 'all the oppression' (9:1; also 9:6, 9-10).

What are we to make of this scenario? Choosing to read it in and against the historical context of the *Diadochi*, Nickelsburg interprets this description as referring to the *Diadochi* and their continual 'war, bloodshed, and assassination'. Claims of the *Diadochi*'s divine origins are parodied with the verdict that 'they were not gods but demons—angels who rebelled against the authority of God'.[119] Horsley chooses a much wider referent for the material in stating that it refers 'generally to the effects of Hellenistic rule on the people of Judea' including, through the third century, 'these recurrent imperial wars for the control of subject peoples'.[120] People cry out to God in terms that mimic but excel the kings in relation to power and rule (similar but not quite the same); God is 'the

116.   Howard-Brooks, 'Come out My People!' 302.
117.   Horsley, *Revolt of the Scribes*, 51.
118.   Nickelsburg, *1 Enoch 1*, 1.
119.   Nickelsburg, *1 Enoch 1*, 170.
120.   Horsley, *Revolt of the Scribes*, 56.

Lord of the potentates… Lord of lords…God of gods…King of kings' (9:4) who has authority over everything. God imitates the rulers but out-powers them. God orders the binding of Azazel and declares imminent judgment.

Subsequently, in chapters 12–16, Enoch, charged with announcing judgment on Azazel and the watchers, has a vision of the divine throne room in which he is given a message for the watchers. Their bodies are destroyed but as disembodied 'evil spirits' they roam the earth and 'oppress…and cause sorrow…against the people' (15:11-12). Horsley sees this section as providing an explanation for Judean/Israelite sufferings under Ptolemaic rule. Through 'repeatedly fought wars…, economic exploitation…seducing Judean aristocracy to compromise the traditional Judean way of life…[and the] debilitating effects on Judean socio-economic and personal life, the evil spirits of the giants were causing destructive violence and exploitation' by means of the Hellenistic imperial kings just as in Enoch's time.[121] The section explains the Ptolemaic rule as evil because it is expressive of the evil spirits of the giants who had rebelled against God's order. This explanation that accounts for oppressive Hellenistic rule in terms of controlling evil spirits counters and rejects another possible explanation for this rule derived from the Mosaic covenant traditions, namely the Deuteronomic scheme that the people are being punished by God for their own sins. There is diversity and contest among the provincials on the periphery of Ptolemaic rule.

In *1 Enoch* 17–36, Enoch experiences two visionary journeys. In the first (17–19), he sees, for example, a 'pit' beyond the heavens and the earth where the spirits of the watchers are confined (18:11–19:3). The section provides reassurance that the watchers who sought to impose their own rule are subject to God's cosmic rule. That is, in resisting the 'evil spirits' of the watchers, the section offers a fantasy[122] of their submission and the submission of the Ptolemaic kings to God's rule, a vision that ironically mimics the imperial domination that 1 Enoch simultaneously resists.

In the second journey (*1 Enoch* 21–36), Enoch sees the same pit again where the evil spirits 'are detained here forever' (21:10). He learns that the souls of the dead are separated according to the wicked and the righteous (22:12). He sees the mountain that is 'the throne of God…the Eternal King' (25:3, 5), the place 'for the righteous people' (25:7).

---

121.   Horsley, *Revolt of the Scribes*, 58-59.
122.   The term 'fantasy' is used here to describe the imaginative content of the material, not to evaluate its content nor to comment on claims of its possible origin.

Outside Jerusalem, there is the 'accursed valley for those accursed…
those who speak…unbecoming words against the Lord' (27:2), perhaps a
reference to those in Jerusalem who sided with the imperial powers and,
in the eyes of the author/s, betrayed God with their words.

If the Book of the Watchers is read in relation to post-Alexandrian
Hellenistic rule such as that of the Ptolemies, such assertions of the
continuing power of the evil spirits of the watchers at work in imperial
powers, and the scenes of reward and punishment that take place beyond
death and outside history, provide an alternative to the dominant Mosaic
Deuteronomistic schema. In this Deuteronomistic schema, God's working is seen in history through blessing and curse, the former accompanying faithful obedience to Mosaic Torah and the latter accompanying
disobedience. For *1 Enoch*, the current disordered state of the world does
not originate in the people's faithlessness and result from divine punishment. Rather, it originates in the actions of imperial rulers inspired by
evil spirits and will have cosmic consequences of punishment for those
rulers and a new world for the righteous.

Howard-Brooks argues that Qohelet—perhaps originating from
Jerusalem scribal circles around 250 BCE or so—offers a third perspective. It challenges both patriarchal and covenant traditions, contesting
the latter's Torah piety as well as the perspective of the Book of the
Watchers.[123] It does not engage them directly nor any vision of salvation.
It rejects dreams and revelations such as the heavenly tours of *1 Enoch*
21–36. 'For dreams come with many cares, and a fool's voice with many
words' (Eccl. 5:3). The writer also rejects the notion of post-mortem
judgment.

> For the fate of humans and the fate of animals is the same; as one dies, so dies
> the other. They all have the same breath, and humans have no advantage over the
> animals; for all is vanity. All go to one place; all are from the dust, and all turn to
> dust again. Who knows whether the human spirit goes upward and the spirit of
> animals goes downward to the earth? So I saw that there is nothing better than
> that all should enjoy their work, for that is their lot; who can bring them to see
> what will be after them? (Eccl. 3:19-22 NRSV)

The writer counsels a pragmatic approach to kingly power. He refuses to
correlate imperial order with God's order just as he refuses to acknowledge it as an instrument of God's punitive purposes nor condemn it as
demonic. Rather, he observes the unaccountability and self-serving
nature of royal power and the need to obey, not because it means doing
God's will, but because it ensures survival:

123.   Following Howard-Brooks, 'Come Out My People!', 309-12.

> Keep the king's command because of your sacred oath. Do not be terrified; go from his presence, do not delay when the matter is unpleasant, for he does whatever he pleases. For the word of the king is powerful, and who can say to him, 'What are you doing?' Whoever obeys a command will meet no harm, and the wise mind will know the time and way. (Eccl. 8:2-5 NRSV)

Consistently he urges caution and discretion:

> Do not curse the king, even in your thoughts, or curse the rich, even in your bedroom; for a bird of the air may carry your voice, or some winged creature tell the matter. (Eccl. 10:20 NRSV)

The writer also rejects the dualism of the Deuteronomic reward and punishment system as well as the Book of Watchers' post-mortem division of the righteous and wicked. Instead he advocates a third way between righteousness and wickedness:

> In my vain life I have seen everything; there are righteous people who perish in their righteousness, and there are wicked people who prolong their life in their evildoing. Do not be too righteous, and do not act too wise; why should you destroy yourself? Do not be too wicked, and do not be a fool; why should you die before your time? It is good that you should take hold of the one, without letting go of the other; for the one who fears God shall succeed with both. Wisdom gives strength to the wise more than ten rulers that are in a city. Surely there is no one on earth so righteous as to do good without ever sinning. (Eccl. 7:15-20 NRSV)

Howard-Brooks locates such sentiments among some Jewish elites who observed 'injustice and poverty around [them] but neither involve [themselves] nor offer a vision of a solution'.[124] The writer of Qohelet urges enjoyment of life but seems to be oblivious to those such as over-taxed peasant farmers who are struggling to survive. Such elites are accommodative and protective of their own interests.

These various texts indicate fractures and diversities among the native Judean/Israelite population under the pressures of Ptolemaic power.[125] The experience of Ptolemaic power is evaluated in quite different ways as punitive, demonic, and accommodative. 1 Enoch negates Ptolemaic rule with a revelation of its demonic nature, a catalogue of its violent and destructive ways, and a mimicking fantasy of its judgment by the more powerful and victorious God who also secures victory for God's faithful—a classic instance of Bhabha's mimicry that is similar but not quite the same. The Deuteronomic option majors on ambivalence, framing the people as complicit in their own suffering and domination,

---

124. Howard-Brooks, 'Come Out My People!', 311.
125. So Fanon, *The Wretched*; see Introduction above.

sanctioned by God, in appointing Ptolemaic power as the agent of God's punitive purposes. But along with complicity and consent, repentance would mean the end of Ptolemaic punitive power. Qohelet affirms the hybridity of the status quo that requires accommodative and pragmatic practices as the way of surviving in the imperial world.

III.
Seleucid Rule of Judea/Israel
200–175 BCE

The Seleucid claim to rule Judea/Israel—asserted since the 301 BCE council of victors assigned Syro-Judea/Israel to Seleucus though Ptolemy refused to concede it—finally became a reality in 200 BCE. In the Fifth Syrian War (202–199 BCE), Antiochus III realized his ambition, regaining control of southern Syria and Judea/Israel from the very young (6 years old) Ptolemy V Theos Epiphanes and his intrigue-ridden and discordant regents.[126] Although details are sketchy largely because Polybius' account is fragmentary, Antiochus invaded Syro-Judea/Israel in 202 BCE, most of which readily submitted. One major exception was Gaza which remained loyal to the Ptolemies and was besieged before it submitted (Polybius 16.22a). The Ptolemies led by the general Scopas counter-attacked and reclaimed much of the territory conquered by Antiochus. The decisive battle was fought in the vicinity of the shrine at Paneas near Mt. Hermon in the Galilee. Scopas was defeated and pursued before being captured in 199 BCE.[127] The remaining action of the war concerned the defeat of Ptolemaic garrisons stationed throughout the reclaimed territory, including one in Jerusalem.

The Seleucid Metanarrative

The Seleucid kings exemplify and develop an ideology of kingship similar to that of Alexander, the *Diadochi*, and the Ptolemies.[128] Like them, the Seleucid king was also 'supreme commander, dispenser of

126.   Gera, *Judaea*, 18-35. On Antiochus III, see Sherwin-White and Kuhrt, *From Samarkhand to Sardis*, 201-2.

127.   I am following Grabbe, *History of the Jews*, 321-22, who quotes Porphyry; also Bar-Kochva, *The Seleucid Army*, 146-57.

128.   Gruen, 'Seleucid Royal Ideology'; Gruen identifies such means of sanction as links with Alexander, coins, honoring Apollo, ruler cults, generosity in benefactions, sensitivity to local customs, and colonization.

justice [and] god's representative on earth'.[129] Susan Sherwin-White and Amélie Kuhrt underscore the military force that lies at the heart of this ideology of imperial power and kingship and of the task of extracting wealth from conquered land and peoples. The Seleucid empire, they argue, originates in and is maintained 'by military constraint (armies, colonies, military expeditions, garrisons) which permits the levy of tribute and service from the subjugated peoples'.[130] The Seleucids promoted this royal ideology through the standard means used by empires: titles (Seleucus I was called 'Nikator' or Victor because of his victories [Appian, *Syr.* 9.57]); appeals to predecessors (Alexander), establishing a local civic ruler cult in cities through coins, architecture, statues, and texts; and of course the practices of war, enlistment, acquisition of booty, tribute, and patronage wherein kingly power was renewed by exertion and performance and maintained in gratitude and loyalty, thereby creating a reciprocal interaction between imperializer and colonized.[131]

After his death, Seleucus Nikator was deified as an incarnation of Zeus with cities establishing a ruler cult for him that not only lauded the image of the victorious warrior-king but expressed divine contextualization for the Seleucid line. Not surprisingly, Seleucus' coinage emphasized these qualities of power and successful military conqueror. He chose, for example, appropriate divine figures that sanctioned his military power: the divinized Alexander (prototype and patron), winged or wreathed Nike (goddess of victory), Athena goddess of war, Apollo the oracle who prophesied his kingship, and Zeus the most powerful.[132] Jan Zahle observes that such presentations were 'political and ideological and everything served to convey a message to the subjects. The names of the kings, their portraits and their Greek gods on the coins of the state all advertise the firm control or claim of the king in question.'[133] Hadley sketches a wider significance in arguing that not only were such displays of divine sanction necessary for Seleucus I as he sought to legitimize his power, they were also significant for 'the longevity of the dynasty... transcending the life-span of the individual upon whom they were originally conferred'.[134] Later, Antiochus III initiated a 'centralised

129.   Walbank, 'Monarchy and Monarchic Ideas', 79.
130.   Sherwin-White and Kuhrt, *From Samarkhand to Sardis*, 40, 53-59.
131.   Sherwin-White and Kuhrt, *From Samarkhand to Sardis*, 114-40.
132.   Hadley, 'The Royal Propaganda'.
133.   Zahle, 'Religious Motifs', 127.
134.   Hadley, 'Royal Propaganda', 64.

"state" cult of himself and his *progonoi*, and a "state" cult of his queen and wife, Laodice'.[135]

Another example of Seleucid activity expresses propaganda claims that include both military domination and a societal vision. Amélie Kuhrt and Susan Sherwin-White discuss the Borsippa Cylinder that evidences the temple-patronage of Antiochus I. He (re-)builds the temple of the Babylonian god Nabu (Ezida) at Borsippa, the foundation of which was laid in 268 BCE.[136] Among other thing, this interesting cylinder shows Antiochus not only concerned with Babylonian matters but also with cultural continuities as he manipulates traditional Babylonian forms to identify himself as

> Antiochus, the great king, the mighty/legitimate king, king of the world, king of Babylon, king of lands, caretaker of Esagila and Ezida, first son of Seleucus, the king the Macedonian, king of Babylon, am I.

Antiochus goes on to pray that Nabu, son of Marduk, would accomplish for him as a gift

> [t]he overthrow of the countries of my enemies, the achievement of my battle-wishes against my enemies, permanent victories, just kingship, a happy reign, years of joy, children in satiety...

This prayer sets out 'the ideal picture of the king's socio-political functions: the conquest of enemies and enduring superiority, and the establishment of justice, peace, a long reign, and a stable succession'.[137] Kuhrt and Sherwin-White observe, though, that this patronage is not one-way traffic; it reflects the reciprocity and ambivalence of the imperializer–colonized situation. His prayer offers 'a set of expectations of how a good king should rule' and in so doing it provides for his subjects, or at least the more powerful ones, 'a basis for the exercise of pressures on the king'.[138] While the vision attempts to frame Seleucid power in terms that highlight its societal benefits, the emphasis on the king (his well-being, great power, many children) and his military might cannot be disguised.

---

135.   Sherwin-White and Kuhrt, *From Samarkhand to Sardis*, 202-10.
136.   Kuhrt and Sherwin-White, 'Aspects of Seleucid Royal Ideology'.
137.   Kuhrt and Sherwin-White, 'Aspects of Seleucid Royal Ideology', 76-78. Further prayer requests long days and years, 'my throne firm', long reign, victory in battle, and tribute to be offered to Nabu.
138.   Kuhrt and Sherwin-White, 'Aspects of Seleucid Royal Ideology', 85-86.

Antiochus III and Judea/Israel

The Fifth Syrian War (202–199 BCE), by which Antiochus III gained control of Judea, had significant impact on the people and land. Josephus notes that during the reign of Antiochus III

> it was the lot of the Jews to undergo great hardships through the devastation of their land, as did also the inhabitants of Coele-Syria…whether he (Antiochus) was victorious or defeated they experienced the same fate; so that they were in no way different from a storm-tossed ship which is beset on either side…crushed between the success of Antiochus and the adverse turn of his fortunes. (*Ant.* 12.129-30)

We are left to elaborate Josephus' gaps in terms of socio-economic hardship with the taking of crops and animals to supply and billet troops moving across the land, resultant hunger and poor nutrition, disruption of trade, damage to property and buildings, the personal indignities suffered at the hands of the colonizer, divisions among Jews over (self-protective) loyalties to contesting super-powers, and the inevitable departure of local young men who joined the armies.

Porphyry attests the divisions among the local population: 'Judea… was rent into contrary factions, the one group favoring Antiochus and the other favoring Ptolemy'.[139] This fracturing, leading to horizontal violence involving colonized against colonized, occurs, as noted in the Introduction above,[140] in situations where vertical pressure and violence are exerted. The colonized are unable to retaliate directly whether because of the power imbalance or, more likely in this context, because of uncertainty as to which superpower would prevail. Accordingly, they substitute other natives for the colonizer in expressions of violent desire to conquer a conqueror.

Evidence that pro-Seleucid support was stronger than the pro-Ptolemaic forces emerges from Porphyry's comment that 'the aristocrats of Ptolemy's party [went] back to Egypt',[141] and from Josephus' claim that Jews assisted Antiochus, and his unnuanced statement that 'the Jews went over to' Antiochus (*Ant.* 12.131-32, 138).

Josephus provides some glimpse into the economic cost for Judean/ Israelites of allying with Antiochus in the experience of the ambivalence of favor and subordination. Josephus says that 'the Jews went over to him (Antiochus) and admitted him to their city (Jerusalem) and made

---

139.   Grabbe, *History of the Jews*, 323 quoting Porphyry; Gera, *Judean and Mediterranean Politics*, 25-28.

140.   Fanon, *Wretched of the Earth*; Freire, *Pedagogy*.

141.   Grabbe, *History of the Jews*, 321 quoting Porphyry.

abundant provision for his entire army and his elephants; and they readily joined his forces in besieging the garrison which had been left by Scopas in the citadel of Jerusalem' (Josephus, *Ant.* 12.132-33, 138). Again we have to make explicit what Josephus conceals, namely the human desperation and deprivation for peasant farmers that lie beneath Josephus' smooth assertion that Jews made 'abundant provision for this entire army and elephants'.

For instance, Antiochus' elephants numbered one hundred and fifty (Polybius 11.34.10-11). According to Portier-Young, one elephant eats five per cent of its body weight on a daily basis which translates to between 330 to 550 pounds of vegetation daily per elephant, a huge demand on local food provisions normally destined for people and local livestock.[142] Such provision came from peasant surplus and necessity levied (not donated) for the conquering military force, consigning numerous peasant households to food insecurity.

Hengel points to letters published around 200–195 BCE on the Hefzibah stele between the *strategos*, the military governor and chief priest of Syria and Phoenicia, and King Antiochus III. These letters concern the protection of the rights of villagers, forbidding the billeting of troops and forbidding troops and officials to force locals from their homes (Letter IV), as well as a request that civilian officials and personnel be stopped from doing (unspecified) 'violence' and 'injustice' as they travel through villages (Letter V). The exchange of letters thereby functions as a means of 'countering the acts of violence which had been perpetrated by his troops' and officials.[143]

Further provisions were demanded when Antiochus sealed an alliance with Ptolemy by marrying his daughter, Cleopatra, to Ptolemy (Arrian, *Syr.* 1.5). Josephus claims that her dowry comprised tribute collected by 'the prominent men' from the provinces of 'Coele-Syria, Samaria, Judea, and Phoenicia', though the exact details of the collection (amount? regularity?) are not clear (Josephus, *Ant.* 12.154). Accompanying the hardships caused by material extraction is the toll exacted by the loss of dignity in being coerced and disrespected.

Further, there was significant material damage to Jerusalem in the fighting, though it is unclear whether or how much it resulted from horizontal Jew-on-Jew violence in the city and/or from the alliance of

---

142. Portier-Young, *Apocalypse Against Empire*, 65-66, who cites Caniotis, *War in the Hellenistic World*, 121-29, 140-41; Thorne, 'Warfare and Agriculture'.

143. Hengel, *Judaism and Hellenism*, 9; on the Hefzibah stele, see Landau, 'A Greek inscription Found Near Hefzibah', esp. Letter IV; Grabbe, *History of the Jews*, 326-27.

Antiochus and local Jews against the Ptolemaic garrison in Jerusalem. Josephus records a decree from Antiochus, generally regarded as authentic,[144] addressed to Ptolemy the governor of Coele-Syria and Phoenicia, in which Antiochus expresses appreciation for the Jewish welcome to Jerusalem, for supplies for his army, and for assistance in expelling the Ptolemaic garrison (*Ant.* 12.138-44). Reflecting and reinforcing his alliance with the Jerusalem temple-based leaders, he goes on to commit supplies for sacrifices in the Jerusalem temple and for rebuilding the temple that would not be subject to a toll in entering the city (*Ant.* 12.141). He allows the Jews to govern themselves 'in accordance with the laws of their country', provides some tax relief for three years for the Jerusalem temple-based governing elite (poll, crown, and salt taxes; *Ant.* 12.142-43), and reduces tribute by one third. He stimulates resettlement with this temporary and localized tax and tribute relief, and declares that 'those who were carried off from the city and are slaves' are free and their property restored (*Ant.* 12.144). He does not specify in what circumstances slaves were taken (by Scopas? by Antiochus?) but the reference to them attests further damaging impact on the people of Judea. In addition to bolstering the loyalty and appreciation of the Jerusalem leadership who were the main beneficiaries of the decree, G. Aperghis notes the ambivalent economic impact of these measures whereby tax relief and speedy repairs to the temple, central to the province's economy, stimulated some local economic recovery even while it expanded the contribution of Judea to the Seleucid rulers as part of the tax base.[145] But there is no relief from taxes and tribute for towns and villages outside Jerusalem on which Antiochus was dependent, and certainly nothing for peasant farmers in relation to their animals and land production. There is also some evidence for increased settlement in the central hill country during this time, perhaps by ex-Seleucid military figures.[146]

Generally these provisions for local temples and some tax relief especially for elites are consistent with Seleucid policy that served their revenue-raising interests and do not suggest Jewish exceptionalism in treatment. These factors point to the historical reliability of Josephus' material. A reference in 2 Macc. 4:11 ('the existing royal concessions to the Jews') confirms the granting of concessions, and Sirach 50:1-4

144.   Marcus, 'Appendix D', 481-91; Hengel, *Judaism and Hellenism*, 10, 271; Grabbe, *History of the Jews*, 324-26; Bickerman, *Studies in Jewish and Christian History*, 2.24-43, 315-56, 357-75.
145.   Aperghis, *The Seleukid Royal Economy*, 166-68.
146.   Berlin, 'Between Large Forces', 15-16.

praises the chief priest, Simon II (the son of Onias II), who died in 198 BCE, for work in rebuilding the temple and guarding Jerusalem. In Sirach 50:1-4, Simon seems to function as the nation's leader in carrying out the work that Antiochus funds, repairing and fortifying the temple, building protective walls, providing a water cistern, and 'saving his people from ruin and fortify[ing] the city against siege'. The provisions indicate a willingness on Antiochus' part to form alliances with provincial elites, once submission was established, involving compensation for damage in the war and respect for local leadership, customs, and religious institutions.[147]

Josephus follows Antiochus' letter or decree with a brief proclamation from Antiochus issued 'throughout the entire kingdom' upholding temple practices (*Ant.* 12.145-46). Its authenticity is disputed.[148] While its upholding of temple practice is consistent with Antiochus' decree to Ptolemy, the details of its concerns—forbidding foreigners in the temple precincts as well as certain animals—seem unusual. The forbidden animals were not sacrificial animals. And the prohibition on bringing the skins of various animals (horses, leopards, foxes, hares, etc.) into Jerusalem assumed a forbidden practice for which there is no evidence, and overlooked the transportation roles of several animals in the city. Portier-Young argues that these two latter provisions guard both the temple's and city's purity and prevent 'new' or 'foreign' worship practices being inaugurated which would exchange divine favor for disaster. She also suggests that the provisions may 'encode a subtle act of resistance in the face of Seleucid occupation' whereby Seleucid military presence (horses, other supply animals, and supplies) could not be resisted militarily but their presence in the city could be resisted on cultic grounds.[149]

147.   What financial return did Judea/Israel provide for the Seleucids? Under Antiochus IV, Onias the chief priest had the rights for tax collection but was outbid by Jason who committed to 360 talents plus 80 more (2 Macc. 4:8). In turn he is outbid by Menelaus (172 BCE) who almost doubled the amount by 300 talents (2 Macc. 4:24) but he does not pay (2 Macc. 4:27). Whether his nonpayment was an act of defiance and independence or because he had exceeded Judea/Israel's financial capacity is not clear.

148.   Marcus, 'Appendix D', 491-94. Josephus also includes a letter attesting 'our piety and loyalty' sent to Zeuxis, the governor of Phrygia and Lydia. Antiochus outlines his plans to help subdue revolts in these areas by settling 'two thousand Jewish families there from Babylon as military colonists because they will be a compliant and loyal presence'. Given the settlement of Jews as military colonists in Egypt for example, the scenario is not unlikely. Marcus, 'Appendix D', 494-96.

149.   For discussion, Portier-Young, *Apocalypse against Empire*, 57-62. Gera, *Judaea*, 34 n. 109, notes several studies establishing that the bans on these impure animals occur in Halachic Qumran texts (4QMMT). Sefer, 'The Priestly' (Hebrew).

Perhaps a genuine decree upholding temple sanctity and Jewish ancestral sacrifices was elaborated somewhere in the transmission process along these lines.

One further account should be considered. Two Maccabees 3 narrates the story of a high-ranking Seleucid official Heliodorus in Jerusalem. Heliodorus, sent from the court of Seleucus IV Philopator (187–75 BCE), is to rob the Jerusalem temple of some two hundred talents of gold and four hundred talents of silver (2 Macc. 3:7-40). The scene is set up with an apparently perfect situation of piety under the pious high priest Onias III that is disrupted by a falling out between Onias and an official of considerable standing, the captain (προστάτης)[150] of the temple, Simon, concerning administration of the market. Simon takes revenge by reporting the great wealth in the temple through the governor of Coele-Syria to the king who, in the rapacious ways sanctioned by Hellenistic kingship, sends Heliodorus to attain it. The high priest Onias resists, drawing a line against the reach of his imperial overlord. He is supported by the priests, crowds, women, and young girls who beseech God to intervene to protect the sanctity of the temple (2 Macc. 3:13-21). As Heliodorus goes to the treasury to take the money, he and 'his great retinue and all his bodyguard' are overcome by a vision or epiphany of a great horse and angelic beings who attack and beat them. These expressions of divine presence function to protect the temple funds (3:22-30). After sacrifices from Onias, Heliodorus returns to the king bearing witness to God's great power and advising the king not to act against the temple again.

The incident seems to be significantly at odds with the practices of both Ptolemies and Seleucids to honor local religious practices and sites.[151] Both Ptolemies (Josephus, *Ant.* 12.50, 58, Ptolemy Philadelphus) and Seleucids (Josephus, *Ant.* 12.138-44, Antiochus III) had made provisions for the Jerusalem temple and its sacrificial worship. Yet several observations suggest the account of 2 Maccabees 3 is not completely fictional but credibly reflects, at least, some features of exploitative colonial politics, particularly the reciprocal relationship between imperializer and colonized..

150. In 2 Chr. 24:11 this captain or administrator of the high priest collects taxes for temple repairs.

151. There are some exceptions. Antiochus III plunders gold and silver to the tune of 4,000 talents from the temple of Aine at Ekbatana (Polybius 10.27.10-13). He also attempted to plunder the temple of Zeus-Bel in Elam (Diodorus 28.3; 29.15) and Antiochus IV attempts to plunder the temple of Artemis in Elymas (Polybius 31:9.1-2). Aperghis, *Seleucid Royal Economy*, 173-74.

First, as Cotton and Wörrle note, an inscription attests that Heliodorus was a leading official in the court of Seleucus with some role akin to that described in this incident.[152] The Heliodorus stele indicates that in 178 BCE Seleucus, under the guise of a well-intentioned euergetistic act motivated by concern for his subjects, appointed Heliodorus to have oversight of sanctuaries in Coele-Syria and Phoenicia in the same way as sanctuaries in the other satrapies. Moreover, the Seleucids had economic reasons to benefit from the temple finances. The Seleucids were restricted by the terms of the treaty of Apamea (188 BCE) concluded after Rome had defeated Antiochus III at the battle of Magnesia in 190 BCE.[153] The treaty imposed limits on the Seleucid military, restricted its geographical reach, removed cities and territory to Roman control, and imposed harsh reparations. Dov Gera notes the intention of the reparations in creating a permanent shortage of money that curtailed Seleucid assertions of power.[154] They challenged Antiochus III, and his successors Seleucus IV and Antiochus IV, to find new sources of income from their empire.

Following Cotton and Wörrle, the stele's concern with 'taking care of these sanctuaries' seems to be a euphemism that masks the task of 'exercising close control, in the interests of the royal administration, over the assets, revenues and liabilities of the sanctuaries...' Scott notes that euphemisms are part of the imperial repertoire to conceal acts of aggressive power. They 'serve cosmetically to beautify aspects of power that cannot be denied'.[155] Exactly what was involved in this 'taking care' of temples to be exercised by the official Heliodorus is not explicit, though economic return is to the fore as Antiochus finds opportunity in dependence on the Jerusalem temple. But anything that interfered with Jerusalem temple practices and finances, including additional 'payments' from the temple treasury to the Seleucids, heightens a sense of local vulnerability and the emergence of an explosive and conflictual situation. The issue, of course, does not fall neatly along a religious–economic axis, but involves cultural and political power as Seleucid control over Jerusalem's central institution and basis for political power, the temple and its priesthood, is asserted. Given that the temple was the basis of power for the Jerusalem ruling elite, these actions placed them in a

152.   Cotton and Wörrle, 'Seleukos IV to Heliodorus'.
153.   On the battle, see Bar-Kochva, *Seleucid Army*, 163-73.
154.   Gera, *Judaea*, 92-93.
155.   Scott, *Domination*, 52.

position of considerable ambivalence as allies of Seleucid power yet as victims of its rapaciousness. Nor is it difficult to imagine a narrative such as that of 2 Maccabees 3 emerging that frames the actions as an affront to the temple that requires its God to demonstrate protective power.

Given these factors outlined above, and the recognition of postcolonial approaches that imperial–colonial situations of disparities of power are marked by ambivalence, mimicry, hybridity, and reciprocity, it seems unconvincing to claim that the years ca. 200–c. 170 BCE were 'three decades of cordial collaboration between the Seleucid regime and the Jewish nation', even a time of 'serenity'.[156] Such an analysis needs considerable complexifying. The situation of non-elites facing the aftermath of war and considerable economic burdens was by no means cordial and collaboration seems too generous a euphemism for oppressive military interventions. And the Jerusalem elite itself was adjusting to political change, in a context of reciprocity in which imperial favor was to be returned with gratitude and loyalty, under some pressure in relation to the temple, and experiencing internal divisions.

Ambivalence rather than monolithic 'cordial collaboration' seems also to be evident in the writing of Ben Sirah. Noting the influence of Greek ideas and language in the work, Leo Perdue locates Ben Sirah among Jerusalem's more elite and wealthy residents, teaching in a Jewish school (51:23; 33:16-19) 'in a period in which Hellenistic culture permeated the urban sites of Eretz Israel'.[157] Perdue dates the work to between 200 and 175 BCE, particularly in the reign of Seleucus IV. He argues that Ben Sirah was a teacher who 'educated leaders and scribes for various roles in Judea/Israel as a Seleucid colony' in the arenas of the 'government, temple, and private houses' (38:24–39:11).[158] In the absence of any hostilities to Jewish life and religious practice in Judea, Ben Sirah affirms the Torah as authoritative for Jewish life (24:23; 41:8), 'Israel's sacred history, the theocratic character of postexilic Judaism most clearly expressed in the temple and its worship, and loyalty to the office of the high priest'.[159] Yet without surrendering his Jewish identity, Sirah is also open to Hellenistic culture such as Stoicism,[160] Greek language, literature, and philosophy. He does not share the reactionary response

156.   Gruen, 'Hellenism and Persecution', 240.
157.   Perdue, The Sword and the Stylus, 257, 272-74.
158.   Perdue, *The Sword and the Stylus*, 259-60, 282.
159.   Perdue, The Sword and the Stylus, 265.
160.   Any direct influence from the Stoics is denied by Mattila, 'Ben Sira and the Stoics'.

of withdrawal attested by Onias IV and the temple at Leontopolis in Egypt,[161] and the Dead Sea community at Qumran opposed to the Zadokite priesthood.

Yet to describe Ben Sirah only as accommodationist is to miss the ambivalence that Bhabha identifies as constitutive of the identity of the hybridized native.[162] Sirah holds together openness to Hellenistic culture with loyalties to Jewish traditions (Israel as God's possession, 17:17) to create an identity that is hybrid, purely neither Jew nor Hellenistic, a third face. Such ambivalence is also evident in Sirah's positioning of kings in the space between power and powerlessness. He recognizes that kings have great power for good (making a city 'fit to live in', 10:3b) as well as for ruin (10:3a). Rulers with princes and judges are to be honored (10:24a). But kings do not have absolute power whatever their delusions. They are subject to Israel's God, the 'King of kings' (51:12).[163] Israel's God raises them up (10:4b), destroys them along with nations (10:14-15; 48:6), overthrows their lands (10:16), uses them as God's agent to inflict retribution (48:8). In God's hands, not kingly hands, is 'the government of the earth' (10:4a). Kings who fail to recognize the kingly hand exhibit pride and arrogance (10:6-18). Kings exist between power and power-lessness.[164] Ben Sirah expresses here the hybridity of an elite native under power who represents local traditions in a context of imperial power.

161.   Hayward ('The Jewish Temple at Lentopolis') argues that the temple rejected the Jerusalem temple and priests; Gruen ('The Origins and Objectives') argues the Onias IV withdrew as a rejection of Menelaus and the Seleucid empire, not of the temple itself, and his Egyptian temple is not a rival to Jerusalem but a reinforcement.

162.   Bhabha, *The Location*.

163.   Wright, 'Ben Sira', 84-85; Sira 9:17–10:18 'contains the essentials of Ben Sira's thoughts about kings and kingship'. Also, Wright, 'Put the Nations'.

164.   Aitken ('Judaic National Identity', 40-41) points out that Sirah offers some insight into socio-economic conditions. Aitken recognizes, for example, the activity of merchants and tradesmen in gaining wealth though he emphasizes their common sinful activity (26:29–27:2). He is also aware of a significant societal divide between the rich and poor in which the rich have the upper hand and the poor (including orphans) have great need (4:1-10). The latter are consigned to constant toil to avoid need (31:4). He recognizes that the rich exploit the poor (13:4-7) and that there is considerable animosity and conflict between them (13:18-19). But he also knows the usefulness of an 'influential person' for a person of lower status as long as the superior is treated with appropriate deference (13:9-11). The rich person has social influence (13:21-23) though alms-giving is an expected and self-benefitting behavior (29:8-13). In this context, Sirah's scribal group emerges with considerable social influence and wealth, unlike peasants, laborers, or craftsmen (e.g. smiths; potters; 38:24-34; jeweler, 45:11).

How might these comments participate in a context of Ptolemaic and Seleucid kingship?[165] Such statements echo both Israel's traditions and Hellenistic ideologies of kingship. This consonance with familiar material could render the assertions commonplace, with a proverbial quality that suggests the familiar content is harmless. Yet the possibility exists that this same quality of the harmless familiar functions to deliver criticism in a way that protects Ben Sirah, masking it, while also enabling it, by articulating the criticism under the guise of the commonplace. For example, is 10:8—'Sovereignty passes from nation to nation on account of injustice and insolence and wealth'—a familiar generic observation? Or is it a commentary on the passing of the control of Judea/Israel from the Ptolemies to the Seleucids in 200 BCE veiled by a commonplace? If the latter, it announces divine judgment on Ptolemaic injustice, insolence, and wealth, while simultaneously offering a warning to the Seleucids that such could be their fate. The Ptolemies, then, would be the thrones overthrown by the Lord (10:14; cf. 48:6) while the Seleucids are those whom God raises up, perhaps anointed 'to inflict retribution' (10:4; cf 48:8). But how is an audience to know whether it is proverbial or scathing criticism? Bhabha's attention to the role of ambivalence in the situations of colonized peoples suggests we have to recognize that it is both.[166]

Yet there is a further dimension beyond ambivalence. Immediately following the section on kingship, chapter 10 introduces another section concerning persons deserving honor (10:19-24). The section ends: 'the prince and the judge and the ruler are honored, but none of them is greater than the one who fears the Lord' (10:24). The verse inscribes familiar ambivalence. Honor for rulers is upheld but that honoring coexists with and is contextualized by another and greater honor: 'the one who fears the Lord'. That fear of the Lord is embodied supremely in the scribe, the sage, one like Ben Sirah who has had 'the opportunity of leisure' to devote 'to the study of the law of the Most High (38:24a, 34b). As Bhabha noted, with ambivalence so often comes mimicry as the colonized sage Ben Sirah mimics the kingly obsession with honor, aspiring to a greater honor than the king who rules his country. He does so by asserting his own native wisdom tradition (the fear of the Lord) as the means by which a colonized provincial can be an adviser to and thus out-honor an empire's king (39:4). 'Many will praise his understand-

165.   Wright ('Ben Sira') raises the question, suggests some possible contact (83), but ultimately decides that taking on the Ptolemaic and Seleucid monarchs was not Sirah's primary aim (88). Aitken ('Judaic National Identity', 40-43) sees a link with the beginning of the Seleucid monarchy (43).

166.   Bhabha, *The Location, passim*.

ing...his memory will not disappear...his name will live through all generations, nations will speak of his wisdom...he will leave a name greater than a thousand...it is enough for him' (39:9-11). The mimicry is similar to imperial structures but not quite the same.[167]

The material cited above from Josephus and Porphyry as well as Bhabha's emphasis on ambivalence troubles any analysis that claims the decades between ca. 200 and ca. 170 BCE were serene and marked by 'cordial collaboration'.[168] More likely in a colonized context is a situation marked by ambiguity, considerable imperial pressure, horizontal violence, and hardship. John Ma, for example, notes that the effect of Antiochus' so-called benefactions/commands to the Jerusalem elite was to *permit* local Judean/Israelite customs centered on the temple but now by placing them on a different basis. No longer is the existence and customs of the colonized sufficient. The Seleucid decrees have performative power in substituting royal Seleucid 'efficacy for theirs', thereby ensuring 'the supremacy and ubiquity of royal form and authority over local sources of legitimacy. This maneuver is typical of the way "empires of domination" function: tolerating local autonomy by redefining it in terms of central authority, through administrative speech-acts.'[169] The effect is, in other words, to render local autonomy and 'cordial collaboration' an illusion and delusion as past and established traditions intersect with new and present assertions of imperial power to create a third space of hybridity.

Anathea Portier-Young more accurately describes this hybridity and ambivalence in terms of major stressors and 'multiple sites of internal division' in these decades, noting a 'lack of political autonomy, imperial exploitation, military occupation, rapid political change, the ravages of war, personal and economic hardship, internal division, and unequal distribution of privilege'.[170]

IV.
Antiochus IV Epiphanes (175–164 BCE)

At the death of Seleucus IV in 175 BCE, murdered by the aforementioned official Heliodorus (Appian, *Syr.* 45), his brother Antiochus seized power ahead of Seleucus' son.[171] The rule of Antiochus IV Epiphanes

167.   Bhabha, *The Location*, 86.
168.   Gruen, 'Hellenism and Persecution', 240.
169.   Ma, 'Seleukids and Speech-Acts', 87, 89.
170.   Portier-Young, *Apocalypse against Empire*, 73.
171.   Habricht, 'The Seleucids and their Rivals', 338-53.

marks a profoundly significant period in the interaction between Israel and the empires involving, among other things, an ending of the policy of tolerance for local religious observance practiced by father Antiochus III, open military revolt, and eventually the establishing of Judea/Israel's independence. Simplistically (mis)understood, this violent revolt has been generalized as a paradigm of Israel's perpetually contestive cultural and/or religious interaction with empires. The above discussion, as well as that which follows, reveals the lie of such a claim. More accurately understood, the events exhibit multiple and complex ways in which Jews simultaneously negotiated assertions of imperial power.

Reconstructions of and motivations for the events are difficult to establish as a long line of distinguished scholarship attests. The events are complex, the timeline of events is not agreed, the literary sources—primarily 1 and 2 Maccabees—are somewhat at odds with one another, with some different perspectives, and are clearly not neutral in attributing blame and adulating heroes.[172] Here our discussion largely pursues an outline based on 2 Maccabees, but we are less interested in establishing exactly what happened (an impossible quest) and more concerned with identifying some of the main dynamics of the imperializer–colonized situation, particularly how Jews negotiated this assertion of imperial power and terror.

Chief Priestly Competition

One starting point for the crisis involves not an overtly aggressive act by Antiochus IV, though he has a significant role in the whole situation, but the ongoing agonistic interactions between local Jerusalem factions led by the chief priest Onias III and Simon according to 2 Maccabees 4:1-6. Since, somehow, Onias had prevented Heliodorus' attempted robbery of the temple, Simon stirred up accusations against Onias that he, Onias, had been behind Heliodorus' actions. Onias appealed to King Seleucus, but the king died and Antiochus IV became king (175 BCE). Fractures in local interactions are common, as we have noted, in contexts of significant vertical imperial pressure.

Onias' brother Jason took advantage of the situation to secure the priesthood for himself (ca. 174 BCE), while also introducing a new and divisive factor into the mix, a move to adopt 'the Greek way of life'

---

172. Weitzman, 'Plotting Antiochus's Persecution'; Doran, 'Independent or Co-Existence'. In addition to the literature cited here, there are numerous discussions including Hayes and Mandell, *The Jewish People*, 47-100; Gera, *Judaea*, 109-254.

(2 Macc. 4:10). In the ambivalent location of an elite under power yet needing the king's favor, Jason seeks the king's favor, offering Antiochus 440 silver talents for the priesthood and, for an additional 150 talents, permission to establish Jerusalem as a Greek city with a gymnasium, training for young men (an *ephebate*), and enrolling Jerusalemites as citizens of Antioch ('Antiochenes of Jerusalem'; 2 Macc. 4:7-10). With permission granted, Jason and his supporters set about establishing these privileges, actions that brought both support and opposition.[173] He also introduced the Greek hat associated with the god Hermes who was especially identified with contests and the gymnasium, allowed the priests to neglect somewhat the duty of offering sacrifices, and welcomed Antiochus to Jerusalem (so 2 Macc. 4:11-17, 22). This initiative to promote 'the Greek way of life' comes not from Antiochus but from the new chief priest Jason and his supporters. Both 1 Maccabees 1:11-15 and 2 Maccabees 4:10 attest this initiative, an attribution of responsibility that has likely historical accuracy since it runs counter to both sources' vilification of Antiochus.

After Jason has been chief priest for three years, Simon's brother, Menelaus, outbids him for the chief priesthood by three hundred silver talents. The author of 2 Maccabees describes Menelaus as having 'no qualification for the priesthood, but having the hot temper of a cruel tyrant and the rage of a savage wild beast' (2 Macc. 4:25). In addition to being a man who cannot master himself, he is impious in stealing and selling gold vessels from the temple. Onias (whose piety was praised in 3:1-2) exposes Menelaus but Menelaus resorts to violence and has him murdered (2 Macc. 4:33-34). Menelaus' brother, Lysimachus, the deputy chief priest, is complicit in the thefts. Violence breaks out as crowds gather against him, Lysimachus attacks them with 'three thousand men', the crowd counter-attacks, and Lysimachus is killed (2 Macc. 4:39-42). What Bickerman calls civil war among these factions is the horizontal violence typical of imperial–colonial situations where vertical pressure is exerted.[174] Three men from the Jerusalem *gerousia* appear before Antiochus with charges against the chief priest, Menelaus. Menelaus, however, bribes the king, has the three men killed, and remains in office (4:43-50).[175]

173. Bickerman, *Studies in Jewish and Christian History*, 2:1072-76.
174. Bickerman, *Studies in Jewish and Christian History*, 2:1125.
175. For a different and confused account, Josephus, *J.W.* 1.33, including Onias' flight to Egypt and establishment of a temple at Leontopolis.

This conflict over the chief priesthood exposes several dynamics of the complex and multivalent colonizer–colonized interactions. First, it confirms Seleucid tolerance of local customs and religious practices. There is no Seleucid attempt as a matter of regular policy to close down local practices. But given the ambivalences of colonial situations, the Seleucids do not leave the local practices alone. Instead, in selling the chief priesthood, they replace traditional sanctions with their own sanction and control over them as Ma has noted.

Second, Seleucid patronage and benefaction are clearly on display in the purchasings of the chief priesthood and in the granting of the privileges concerning the gymnasium, *ephebate*, and citizenship. Jerusalem's priestly leadership knows a very ambivalent location as leaders of Jerusalem's temple and sacred traditions and practices, yet as deeply embedded in and dependent on this patronage and benefaction.

Third, the competition among Jerusalem figures expressed in the bidding wars for the position indicates the desire among Jerusalem elites for Seleucid favor and their imitation of Seleucid power, even while they represent and have oversight of temple practices and the worship of Israel's God. The situation exhibits, as Fanon has observed, the ambivalence of the native's lust for the power and prestige gained by cooperation with the occupying power, the very things that he both rejects yet desires.[176] Bhabha has similarly highlighted the role of mimicry in the negotiation of power between colonizer and colonized. Jason's increased investment in Greek education and culture, and downplaying of traditional Jerusalem custom and practice, heightens the hybridity of the colonial situation with two quite disparate traditions and identities in play, especially among Jerusalem elites, training in Greek culture and in the Torah.

Fourth, the violence among the competing Jerusalem parties attests the phenomenon of horizontal violence in this colonial situation. According to Fanon, horizontal violence among locals erupts in situations where considerable vertical pressure is exerted by the colonizing/ruling power. Violent resistance to the agents of the colonizing power is deemed to be futile because of the overwhelming power dynamic, so the violence is deflected, redirected toward competing groups who are seen to take on characteristics of the governing power. Horizontal violence thus attests not just a situation of individual ambition or desire for power, but the experience or perception of considerable pressures being exerted by the occupying force whose favor is desired/needed. Such recognitions

---

176. Fanon, *The Wretched*, 52-54; see Introduction and notes 13-17 above.

indicate that attempts to understand these interactions and the following crisis in terms only of cultural entities ('Hellenism' versus 'Judaism'), while ignoring the colonizer–colonized power dynamics, are misdirected.[177]

And fifth, the Seleucids' economic dependence on their colonized territory is evident in the sale of the chief priesthood. The imperializer–colnized dynamic does not only comprise 'power over' but also the reciprocity of the imperializer's dependence on the colonized.

First Maccabees tells a story similar in broad outline to that of 2 Maccabees but different in detail. It identifies Antiochus as a 'sinful root' and locates him in a line from Alexander. It narrates that 'certain renegades came out from Israel and misled many' (1 Macc. 1:11) though it does not locate the center of their actions in the contenders for the chief priesthood nor name Jason, Menelaus, or Lysimachus specifically. At the heart of the action of the so-called renegades, though, are actions akin to Jason's in 2 Maccabees: 'joining with the Gentiles' by building a gymnasium, reversing circumcision, and abandoning 'the holy covenant', though no specifics are given (1 Macc. 1:11-15). Reversing circumcision—the procedure is described by Celsus (7.25.1)—could signify a renouncing of the covenant and a means of removing a mark that distinguished Jewish males from Gentiles.[178]

Antiochus Attacks Jerusalem

The next major development is Antiochus' attack on Jerusalem. Both First and Second Maccabees have Antiochus waging war in Egypt as the context for his military action against Jerusalem, though they differ on the number of wars he waged in Egypt (one, 1 Macc. 1:16-22; two, 2 Macc. 5:1[179]). Second Maccabees continues to develop the dispute over the chief priesthood. Jason, displaced and outbid by Menelaus, attacks Jerusalem to regain power, slaughters many, but is driven off. Antiochus IV hears of the battle and, thinking Jerusalem is in revolt, attacks the city, killing many and enslaving others (2 Macc. 5:11-21). Verse 14 notes that 'within the total of three days eighty thousand were destroyed, forty thousand in hand-to-hand fighting, and as many were sold into slavery as were killed'.

177. Fanon, *The Wretched*, 52-54.
178. Hall, 'Epispasm'. Grabbe (*Judaism from Cyrus*, 276-77) argues against the claim that exercise in the gymnasium was done in the nude and that this provided the reason for the reversal of circumcision.
179. So also Polybius, *History* 28.18-23; 29.26-27.

Even allowing for significant exaggeration in the figures, such ethnic cleansing is a brutally effective tactic of colonizing control. It reduces the population physically, it psychologically humiliates survivors as members of a people hardly worthy of existence, it allows for resettlement of one's own (superior) people, and it sends a frightening message of intimidation and submission to survivors and other peoples. Antiochus then enters the temple with Menelaus, loots its 'holy vessels' and 'eighteen hundred talents', leaves Menelaus as chief priest, and appoints two governors. Subsequently (the time span is unspecified, perhaps 168–167 BCE), he sends Apollonius with 'twenty-two thousand' troops on a subsequent ethnic-cleansing and terrorizing attack to deplete and humiliate the population further and to enslave others (2 Macc. 5:11-26; cf. 1 Macc. 1:20-40; Josephus, *Ant.* 12.248).[180] Victory was secured with the building of a citadel (Akra) in Jerusalem in which were stationed Seleucid troops along with one of the city's faction, some Jews (the 'Antiochenes' enrolled by Jason as citizens of the *polis*), as well as some foreign settlers (Dan. 11:39). The occupied citadel would remain there for the next quarter of a century or so.

Antiochus Bans Jewish Religious Practice (167 BCE)

First and Second Maccabees offer different scenarios for the subsequent banning of Jewish religious practices. In 2 Maccabees 6:1, 'not long after' the second attack from Apollonius, Antiochus sends Geron, an Athenian senator, with orders to dismantle Jewish religion. He forbids observance of the law, renames the temple the temple of Olympian Zeus, and introduces prostitutes and 'things unfit for sacrifice' into the temple where intercourse takes place. Forbidden offerings cover the altar, sabbath and festival observances are forbidden, as is claiming Jewish

---

180. First Maccabees lacks both an account of the disputes over the chief priesthood and an explicit alternative explanation for Antiochus' action against Jerusalem, beyond labeling him 'arrogant' (1 Macc. 1:21, 24). It stipulates a time period of two years between Antiochus' attack and the second one, and attributes the second attack not to Apollonius but to an unnamed collector of tribute who not only destroys and enslaves, but also establishes a citadel or *akra* in Jerusalem involving both Greek and Jewish ('sinful people...renegades') troops (1 Macc. 1:29-40). Josephus similarly offers no reason for Antiochus' initial attack on Jerusalem after his Egyptian campaign, but notes he was welcomed by 'those who were of his party' but opposed by any others (*Ant.* 12.246-47). Like First Maccabees he identifies a two-year gap before the second attack which he attributes specifically to Antiochus. The greedy Antiochus (*Ant.* 12.249) in person plunders the temple and bans Jewish religious observance (*Ant.* 12.251-56).

identity. Jews are forced to participate in sacrifices for the king's birthday and in the festival of Dionysus. The penalty for refusing to participate is death (2 Macc. 6:1-11), exemplified in several martyrdom stories (2 Macc. 6:12–7:42).

First Maccabees' version of this dismantling of Jewish religion ends in the same place but by a different means. After the second attack by the collector of tribute, Antiochus issues (unlikely) general decrees requiring his whole kingdom to abandon local customs and to adopt his religion.[181] For Israel this meant the end of observance of the law including offerings and sacrifices, Sabbath and festival observances, and circumcision. It also meant defilement of the sanctuary and priests, the presence of altars and idols, sacrifices of swine and other unclean animals, and the erection of 'a desolating sacrilege on the altar of burnt offering' in the temple. Antiochus sent officials to enforce the non-observance of Torah and the observance of the king's practices. Refusal to comply resulted in death (1 Macc. 1:41-64). Ma comments that Antiochus' performative decree 'clashed with another set of performatives: the Mosaic law, and its definitions of the licit and the illicit. The conflict [was] between two authorized discourses'.[182]

As is clear, the sources are not in agreement on the number of attacks on Jerusalem and/or the temple, the personnel involved, the motivations, and the circumstances in which Jewish religious observance was banned. Given the numbers for those supposedly killed or enslaved in these various attacks and acts of ethnic cleansing—especially in 2 Macc. 5:12-14, 26—it is somewhat surprising there was anyone left to observe anything! Nevertheless the accounts have some degree of consonance, at least in their broad sweep, centered on Antiochus' vigorous ending of Jewish religious practice centered on the temple and law.

Antiochus IV's Metanarrative?

What was the metanarrative informing Antiochus' action, both his attack on Jerusalem and his deconstruction of Jewish religion? Predictably the second question has received most attention though it must be recognized that in the ancient world religious and political matters are tightly intertwined and so the two questions are interrelated. Any answer runs into problems of sources—their scarcity, patchiness, and pro-Hasmonean bias—as well as the very nature of Antiochus' act. As Lester Grabbe remarks, 'The real puzzle is why a short time later Antiochus sent Geron

---

181.   Gruen ('Hellenism and Persecution') argues such a decree is very unlikely.
182.   Ma, 'Seleukids and Speech-Acts', 91.

to crush the Jewish religion… This religious suppression was unique in antiquity. Religious intolerance has historically been a practice of monotheistic religions…polytheism is tolerant by its very nature.'[183] The Seleucids were certainly tolerant and even promoters of local religious traditions.[184] Given these realities, any claims about Antiochus' meta-narrative can be tentative at best; the following discussion will emphasize the humiliating and terrifying nature of the assertions of power by Antiochus in the colonizer–colonized context.[185]

In accounting for Antiochus' action, some ancient sources locate the metanarrative in Antiochus' character. The emphases on Antiochus' deformed character include Polybius' *epimanes*, 'the mad man' (26.1),[186] and 1 Maccabees' 'a sinful root' and the adverb 'arrogantly' (1 Macc. 1:10, 21, 24). While character descriptors offer some insight into how these writers evaluated him, much larger circumstances must be taken into account. We will return to First Maccabees below.

Tacitus offers a possible metanarrative and one that has been developed in some modern analyses. Tacitus sees Antiochus as a cultural evangelist seeking in relation to Judeans/Israelites 'the meanest of their subjects', to 'abolish Jewish superstition and to introduce Greek civilization' (Tacitus, *Hist.* 5.8). Parts of First Maccabees 1 can be read along similar lines. After two military attacks on Jerusalem and the temple (1:20-28, 29-40), Antiochus issues a decree 'that all should be one people', banning any local or 'particular customs', and adopting the king's religion (1 Macc. 1:41-50).

What, then, is the king's religion that Antiochus imposes (1 Macc. 1:43)? Antiochus' reputation 'as a devotee of Zeus Olympius' is well-attested.[187] Second Maccabees 6:2 says the Jerusalem temple is dedicated

183.   Grabbe, *Judaism from Cyrus to Hadrian*, 1:284. For a collection of similar sentiments, see Portier-Young, *Apocalypse against Empire*, 176-77, citing Collins, Bickerman, and Gruen.

184.   Kuhrt and Sherwin-White, 'Aspects of Seleucid Royal Ideology'.

185.   Influential in the discussion that follows is the classic contribution of Tcherikover, *Hellenistic Civilization*, 175-203. He evaluates as unacceptable four explanations that foreground Antiochus' character: his Hellenizing zeal, his attempts to unify his kingdom, attempts to assert his political power, and Bickermann's argument that Menelaus and his supporters, not Antiochus, were responsible for the abolition of Jewish 'particular' religious practices in favor of more acceptable 'universalism'. Tcherikover advocates an explanation based on 2 Maccabees 5 whereby Antiochus understood the civil war in Jerusalem to be a dangerous revolt against Syrian rule and in support of Egypt (188).

186.   In 28:18 Polybius describes him as 'energetic, daring…and worthy of royal dignity…'

187.   Rigsby, 'Seleucid Notes', 233-38.

to Olympian Zeus. He 'resumed construction of the temple of Zeus Olympios' at Athens (Polybius 26.1.11; Pausanius 5.12.4),[188] and he renamed, in a parallel action that changed cult practice for the Samaritans, the temple in Gerizim as 'Zeus-the-Friend-of-Strangers' (2 Macc. 6:2). Zahle notes Antiochus replaced images of the seated Apollo with an enthroned Zeus Nikeohorus.[189] And Antiochus did, as Mørkholm argues, take 'a special interest in the cult of Zeus, according him a place of preference on his coinage, donating freely to his sanctuaries, and promoting his cult within his kingdom'.[190] Mørkholm, though, insists that he had no missionary zeal,[191] a verdict with which Rigsby agrees.[192] Rigsby presses the question as to why, then, Zeus Olympius was so special to Antiochus. He argues that Zeus Antiochus was 'the god of his fathers...the patron of his native place and first city of his dynasty...an emblem of Seleucidness'.[193]

In contrast to seeing Antiochus' religious practices as centered on the Greek God Zeus, Bickerman argued for a polytheistic cult practice involving Syrian deities.[194] Common practice was to give Greek names to local deities, and the high Syrian god Baal Shamen ('Lord of Heaven') was often called 'Zeus'.[195] The phrase 'abomination of desolation' (Dan. 11:31; 12:11) points to some cultural hybridity in that it is a play in Aramaic on Baal Shamen ('the lord of heaven'). It seems that a similar phenomenon occurs with the reference to Dionysus worship (2 Macc. 6:7) whereby the Greek name refers to a Syro-Canaanite deity, perhaps Dusares. In this view, the king's religion, then, was not Greek but centers on a native Syrian cult with its various deities known by Greek names.

Deciding between the two options is difficult given the limited information. Helpful is Doran's observation that 2 Maccabees 4–6 is devoid of Syrian soldiers.[196] In 4:29 Cypriot soldiers are in Jerusalem. In 5:24 Mysian soldiers garrison the city. In 6:1 Geron, an Athenian, carries out Antiochus' will. Perhaps supporting this conclusion is Dan Barag's argument that Antiochus established a mint in the citadel (*akra*) in

<hr>

188.   Doran, *2 Maccabees*, 134.
189.   Zahle, 'Religious Motifs', 130.
190.   Mørkholm, *Antiochus IV of Syria*, 131.
191.   Mørkholm, *Antiochus*, 133.
192.   Rigsby, 'Seleucid Notes', 235.
193.   Rigsby, 'Seleucid Notes', 237-38.
194.   Bickerman, *Studies in Jewish and Christian History*, 2:1107-9.
195.   For links between Ba'al Samem, Oden cites Hiram of Tyre building a temple for Zeus Olympios, behind whom stands Ba'al Samem; Josephus, *C.Ap.* 1.113, 118; *Ant.* 8.145, 147; Oden, 'Ba'al Šāmēm and 'El', 460, 463-64, 466.
196.   Doran, *2 Maccabees*, 135-36.

Jerusalem between 167 and 164 BCE intended to assist in payment of taxes and tribute as well promote Seluecid propaganda.[197] The coins present a portrait of Antiochus with a radiate head reflecting the Greek sun-god Helios and serving Antiochus' claim to be *theos epiphanes* ('god-manifest'). The reverse includes a seated female character who holds a statue of the Greek goddess of victory, *Nike*, holding a victory wreath. These observations, along with a longstanding Seleucid tradition of honoring Zeus' (above) and Antiochus' own commitment to Zeus, point to a cult practice perhaps centered on Zeus rather than on a particularly Syrian expression.

Yet given the multi-cultural nature of a colonizer–colonized situation, some hybridity is to be expected since Greek and Syrian traditions are clearly not mutually exclusive options. And however the issue of the identity of the deity/deities is adjudicated, pertinent to the discussion here is the observation that identifying Antiochus as a devotee of either Zeus or Baal Shamen does not, in and of itself, establish the motivation and identity as a cultural or religious evangelist, intolerant of Jerusalem's God or as a persecutor of Jewish religious practices as an impassioned advocate of Greek culture and religion. As Erich Gruen demonstrates, Antiochus 'did not inherit any ideology of Seleucid rule that propagated the spread of Hellenism'.[198]

If religious and cultural zeal does not provide Antiochus' meta-narrative, perhaps it is to be found in his assertions of imperial power and his pragmatic and astute political ability for keeping or recreating power (for a price) and reordering provincial alliances. One dimension of his pragmatic approach lies in his use of local alliances in exercising his power. His willingness to sell the chief priesthood to the highest bidder can be seen not only as an expression of political dependence and economic pragmatism in the quest for further sources of funds, or as an expression of greed (the verdict of 2 Macc. 4:50), but as a means of allying with the wealthiest and most powerful in the province in order to secure local loyalties and gratitude.

In this context of reciprocity with and dependence on local elites, Antiochus' decree against the Torah might result from local Jerusalem pressure on him to effect such a measure. In making this argument that some local Jerusalemite elites were responsible for Antiochus' action, Bickerman points to several texts that explicitly identify Menelaus as 'the man to blame for all the trouble' (Dan. 11:30-31; 2 Macc. 13:4;

197.   Barag, 'The Mint of Antiochus IV'.
198.   Gruen, 'Seleucid Royal Ideology', 44.

Josephus, *Ant.* 12.384).[199] Bickerman goes on to wrestle with 'the paradox of the high priestly shepherd who wants to lead his own herd to apostasy', arguing that its explanation lies in Jason and Menelaus' reforming rejection of Jewish traditions of particularism (Torah, temple, festivals) and a return to a tolerant primal age not marked by separation from the nations.[200] Bickerman attends astutely to forces of intellectual assimilation fuelled by a line of Greek thinkers, but his explanation is too monolithic, failing to take account, amongst other things, of the complexities, the ambivalences, and the hybridities, noted in postcolonial studies of imperial–colonial situations, wherein the Jerusalem leaders are *both* representatives of a sacred tradition yet dependent on the favor of their imperial master.

Jonathan Goldstein has identified another factor that contributes toward a pragmatic scenario for Antiochus' attack. Goldstein noted that while Antiochus was a hostage in Rome, he witnessed in circumstances of civic disorder Rome's suppression and expulsion of various cults such as that of Dionysus/Bacchus and attacks on various philosophers, including Pythagoreans and Epicureans.[201] That is, Antiochus observed that religious and philosophical movements could be subversive and, from the various parallels between Roman actions and Antiochus' actions against Jewish practice, Goldstein argues that Antiochus also learned various methods by which to constrain such movements.

Goldstein's argument is that this experience in Rome may well have provided a framework for Antiochus' action in Jerusalem. He knew that religion was a key factor in the provincial unrest and struggles in Jerusalem since he had twice sold the priesthood for varying rates, so now with apparent revolt, he concluded, the problematic religion needed to be suppressed and replaced. Whether Second Maccabees provides an accurate account in every detail or not (1 Maccabees does not offer a reason for Antiochus' action), its narrative establishes ongoing unrest around the chief priesthood comprising actions of supporters and opponents, even while it shows the king enriching himself through these struggles for power.[202]

<hr>

199.   Bickerman, *Studies in Jewish and Christian History*, 'The God of the Maccabees', 2:1117.

200.   Bickerman, *Studies in Jewish and Christian History*, 'The God of the Maccabees', 2:1118-22.

201.   Goldstein, *1 Maccabees*, 104-60.

202.   So, for example, Second Maccabees first introduces Antiochus in 4:7a. Immediately in 4:7b-8 it has Jason outbidding his brother Onias for the chief priesthood to the tune of 440 silver talents plus 150 silver talents more for Antiochus'

Such a scenario, though, does not account for all the dynamics of the imperial situation in the acknowledge. A crucial piece, underrated in both Bickermann's and Tcherikover's scenarios, concerns the valences, indeed the ambivalences, of revolt in an imperialized–colonized situation. On one hand, it represented the efforts of the colonized to gain independence, On the other, 'revolt' presented an important opportunity for kings in the context of the ideology of Hellenistic kingship. F. W. Walbank underlines the importance of control of territory for a king's 'status and renown'. He cites Polybius' comment that Antiochus IV regarded that 'possession by force of arms was the surest and best' (Polybius 28.1.4).[203] Extending this insight, Vincent Gabrielsen argues that conquest meant for Hellenistic kings the creation of an empire.[204] Empires could therefore be re-created and power asserted afresh by reconquest of a land and people. Revolt offered an excellent opportunity to reassert power and re-establish subjugation of the local population, thereby increasing local dependency and augmenting the gains of power, wealth, and prestige.

Portier-Young helpfully places Antiochus' actions against Jerusalem in this context of revolt, opportunity, and re-creation of empire. She argues that Antiochus shatters 'the people's sense of autonomy and will to resist' so that any future freedoms would derive only from his

support in introducing a gymnasium into Jerusalem and enrolling residents as citizens of Antioch. Second Maccabees indicates dis-ease by some over Jason's administration of the temple (2 Macc. 4:13-15). Three years later Menelaus outbids Jason with payment of even more money though subsequently he fails to hand over revenue that was due and is summoned to appear before Antiochus (2 Macc. 4:23-25, 27-29). Thereafter he has Onias murdered and Jews appeal to Antiochus for justice (2 Macc. 4:36). After further violence in Jerusalem involving Menelaus' brother Lysimachus and his pillaging from the temple, three men from Jerusalem charge Menelaus before Antiochus but again money talks more loudly and Menelaus bribes his way out of trouble. His alliance with Antiochus seems truth-proof. Second Maccabees 4:50 comments, employing the *topos* of the greedy ruler, 'But Menelaus, because of the greed of those in power, remained in office...' Then considerable violence breaks out between the deposed Jason and Menelaus (2 Macc. 5:5-10). Antiochus, so Second Maccabees claims, 'took it to mean that Judea was in revolt' and attacked Jerusalem to establish order and secure the position of his ally Menelaus while he helped himself to temple funds as a source of ever-needed income (2 Macc. 5:11b). Having (re-)established order by subduing and ethnically cleansing Jerusalem (2 Macc. 5:11-27), he then removed the cause of this provincial unrest, the observance of the law and temple worship, replacing it with worship of Zeus/Baal Shamen (2 Macc. 6:1-11).

203. Walbank, 'Monarchies and Monarchic Ideas', VII.1.66.
204. Gabrielsen, 'Provincial Challenges', 23-28.

person.[205] She goes on to argue that Antiochus relied not just on 'simple force but state terror' to dismantle the order and security of Judea/Israel. State terror, she argues, impacts both individuals and communities, destroying the world of the subjugated, overwhelming local sources of power, crushing any will to resist, and imposing another order. She identifies Antiochus' tactics of state terror, of reconquest, from 2 Maccabees 5:11-26 (noted above), as massacre, murder in the home, abduction (for slaves), plundering the temple, shaming Jerusalem, Apollonius' further conquering mission and parade of killing power, and the unmaking and remaking of Jerusalem's religious world and identity through Antiochus' edict banning Judaism.[206] In this context, Antiochus' actions make sense as an act of reimposing order on a territory he thinks is in revolt by dis-ordering it through (re)conquest, terror, dismantling its important socio-political-religious world, and the imposition of his own order.

Such a scenario does not require Second Maccabees to be historically accurate or comprehensive in every detail. It does, though, require it to offer a persuasive scenario of (re-) imperializing action. And it is evident that Second Maccabees' scenario provides a classic experience of imperial–colonial dynamics.

First are the agonistic relationships among leading provincials for the favor of the imperial overlord. Onias, Jason, Menelaus, and Lysimachus compete for Antiochus' favor and sanction to occupy Jerusalem's most powerful provincial post, that of chief priest. Such competition is a given in imperial contexts as provincial elites seek to benefit from the colonial situation but can only do so by gaining imperial favor. At heart is the dynamic of mimicry in which provincial elites mimic the quest and rewards of power that their overlord exemplifies. In Fanon's terms, they want to be like him—as much as he permits, or more accurately in this situation, as much as they can afford to spend and to exercise power over rivals.

Another key dynamic emerges, that of horizontal violence. As top-down pressure is exerted—in terms of the costs and benefits of pleasing the colonizer—so violence among provincial competitors for those rewards and favor increases. Mimicry and horizontal violence do not mean that provincial leaders do not care about local traditions and practices. Colonial pressure places them in a liminal space of ambivalence in between the colonizers' favor and local customs, traditions, and institutions that they represent.

205.   Portier-Young, *Apocalypse against Empire*, 136-39.
206.   Portier-Young, *Apocalypse against Empire*, 140-216.

Third, not only do provincials benefit and lose in these agonistic and conflictual trials. The imperial overlord also benefits through dependency. Antiochus, cash-strapped by the treaty of Apamea with Rome, benefits financially from a regular stream of bids and bribes for favor, as well as politically from the indebtedness of gratitude and loyalty. Jason's bid of some 600 silver talents is exceeded by the skilled opportunist Menelaus by 300 talents (2 Macc. 4:8-10, 24). Reciprocity marks the interactions of imperializer and colonized. Antiochus also wins in terms of displays of loyalty and gratitude for favors granted. Given such competition, displays of disloyalty are calculated risks and can be severely punished. Menelaus makes a mistake in not paying the revenue he promised the king, and Jerusalem subsequently pays a harsh price. Moreover, the horizontal violence hands Antiochus the gift of construing it as revolt and the opportunity to employ state terror to re-conquer Judea, dismantle its order, and recreate the territory by imposing his own order.

Fourth, the imposition of new religious practices as fundamental aspects of the recreated order, those of the conqueror, makes sense not only in a context of revolt, but also where there is a struggle for control and where religion is understood to be a significant factor in the social-political unrest. Such a move may well be fuelled by the in-between space in which local leaders are located, whereby the holders of the chief priestly office have not shown themselves to be sufficiently passionate defenders of their own traditions and practices. Jason is regarded by some as slack in his oversight of priestly duties, while Menelaus loots the temple for personal gain. Antiochus' act of re-conquest and re-creation of order makes sense as an act of political expediency. He treads the well-worn path, noted above, of Seleucid civic ruler cults, including a 'state' cult instigated by Antiochus III, for worship of the king.[207] In something of a local vacuum, Antiochus seeks to secure social order and provincial compliance.

Fifth, 2 Maccabees 5:24-26 narrates the terrorizing and subjugating actions of Apollonius whom Antiochus sent to Jerusalem. Apollonius feigns peaceable intent, orders his troops to 'parade under arms' on the Sabbath, then attacks those who 'came out to see him', and killed many in the city. In considering Ptolemaic power above, I noted Scott's attention to the self-dramatizing and self-hypnotizing use of parades by dominating elites to display the permanence of their ruling power and to awe and intimidate the dominated into compliance.[208] Scott also notes

207. Sherwin-White and Kuhrt, *From Samarkhand to Sardis*, 202-10.
208. Scott, *Domination*, 58-69.

that rulers fear the unauthorized gatherings of the ruled because such gatherings can be, by force of numbers and anonymity, an 'incitement to boldness by subordinates'. Holidays or no-working days, such as a Sabbath, especially hold fear because they provide the opportunity for unsanctioned gatherings.[209] A parade, however, authorizes a gathering of spectators but seeks to manage the risk of incitement by a display of powerful deterrence that promotes compliance. Apollonius' action both employs and breaks these conventions. He seeks to manage a Sabbath and its risks of unsanctioned gatherings with a parade. Yet he not only parades power but actively exerts it. He turns the spectators into the attacked and the viewing of awe-full power into the actual experience of its terror. This act is a cynical display of intimidating power that terrorizes the local population into compliance.

Violent Resistance and the Hasmoneans

When power is asserted in imperial–colonial contexts to effect material appropriation, status and ideological subordination, and personal humiliations through public injury to dignity,[210] various dynamics follow in the ambivalent and hybridized situation that results, as the above discussion indicates, in: agonistic conflict; willing cooperation and accommodation; horizontal violence; defiance; and non-violent resistance. Violence also emerges in the intersection of imperial and local power, mimicking the forcible assertions of the imperializer's terror and order in a struggle to defend, reassert, or reestablish native order, dignity, and world view.[211]

The accounts are agreed that out of Antiochus' assertion of Seleucid power over Jerusalem and its religious practices comes violent revolt (1 Maccabees 2–9; 2 Maccabees 8–15; Josephus, *Ant.* 12.265-434; *J.W.* 1.36-47). This revolt is centered, at least in First Maccabees, in the Hasmonean family, the father Mattathias a priest, and his five sons, who lived at Modein, some seventeen miles northwest of Jerusalem. In 1 Maccabees 2, it is Mattathias who leads the initial action, refusing to offer sacrifice as Antiochus had commanded, killing a Jew willing to sacrifice as well as the king's enforcement officer, and withdrawing to the hill country. There he allies with the Hasideans, refusing Antiochus' orders, attacking 'renegades' who comply with Antiochus, and observing

---

209.   Scott, *Domination*, 64-65.

210.   The categories are from Scott, *Domination*, 111-12, 191.

211.   Scott, *Domination*, 109, uses reactance theory which 'begins with the premise that there is a human desire for freedom and autonomy that, when threatened by the use of force, leads to a reaction of opposition'.

the law as much as possible until Mattathias' death, when he appoints Judas Maccabeus as commander of the army to defeat Antiochus, and eventually, to achieve independence (1 Macc. 2:1-70).

Second Maccabees passes over any role for Mattathias and moves immediately to Judas Maccabeus' command of military action. According to 1 Maccabees, Judas wins initial victories over Apollonius and then Seron (1 Macc. 3:10-26). He gains a more decisive victory over a Syrian army led by Nicanor and Gorgias at Emmaus, gaining weapons and considerable money (1 Macc. 3:27–4:25; 2 Macc. 8:8-36). Lysias, who had been entrusted by Antiochus IV with the task of subduing Judas, launches an attack and is forced to withdraw (1 Macc. 4:26-35). Building on this victory, along with the death of Antiochus IV (2 Maccabees 9), Judas enters Jerusalem and restores and rededicates the temple in 164 BCE, while keeping guard over the Syrian troops in the citadel (1 Macc. 4:36-61; 2 Macc. 10:1-9). Second Maccabees 11 seems to deal with this same situation, though it relocates Lysias' military action to after the rededication of the temple. It also narrates that Lysias (now governor of Coele-Syria, 2 Macc. 10:11) and Judas (and other representatives?) agreed to a settlement in which Antiochus' religious demands were revoked and Jewish religious observance permitted (2 Macc. 11:13-38).

Judean/Israelite Metanarratives

While violent revolt played a key role in effecting the rededication of the temple, Judeans/Israelites negotiated Antiochus in other ways, including through the formation of multiple metanarratives.

As is evident in the above discussion, hybridity marks the engagement of some Jerusalem elites such as Jason, Menelaus, and their supporters, who adopted Greek institutions and ways of living even while some at least also continued to observe temple practices. Unfortunately we do not have records from those who negotiated Antiochus in this way that elaborate their position. While 1 Maccabees 1:11 condemns them as 'wicked men' (KJV) or 'traitorous Jews who had no regard for the law' (TEV) or 'renegades' (NRSV; JB), or 'breakers of the law' (NAB; παράνομοι) who 'abandoned the holy covenant' (1 Macc. 1:15), it is more likely that their adopting of Greek customs expresses the ambivalence of negotiating both local and imperial traditions.

First Maccabees attests a quite different response, the terrible suffering and deaths of those who 'stood firm' and refused to comply with Antiochus' edict (1:41-63). The account presents these deaths as resulting from a refusal to 'profane the holy covenant' (1:63). Herein lies a metanarrative—at least according to First Maccabees—of loyalty even to death to a covenant identity as God's people expressed in faithfulness to the Torah (1:57) and in practices such as circumcision, festival and Sabbath observance, the refusal to worship another God, and temple sacrifice.

While some died rather than comply, First Maccabees notes a further response, that of those who fled but were hunted down and killed (1 Macc. 2:29-38). This group so valued obedience to the law that they refused to fight on the Sabbath (2:34, 38). Consequently they are attacked on the Sabbath, refuse to fight, and die. By contrast, Mattathias and his sons, especially Judas Maccabeus, led a military response—to which we will return below in consideration of First and Second Maccabees.

Other metanarratives emerge from the midst of the crisis particularly concerned with decolonizing minds. Rejecting claims that apocalyptic writings are apolitical and signify retreat, Portier-Young argues that three apocalyptic writings, written during Antiochus IV's reign and drawing on various scriptural traditions, express resistance to his strategy of terror, conquest, and re-creation. Each offers a 'counter-discourse' that centers on YHWH's sovereignty and demand for exclusive allegiance, while 'each text calls its audience to take up resistance—effective action—against the empire and its ordering of the world'.[212]

This work of negation, as Scott calls it, is a social product not just in its address but in its origin. It typically requires physical locations that are autonomous, unauthorized by and protected from power, 'locations in which the unspoken riposte, stifled anger, and bitten tongues created by relations of domination find a vehement, full-throated expression'.[213] It also requires particular agents, typically the socially marginal who are leaders of subordinated groups and carriers of traditions. From these locations and agents emerge hidden transcripts that are 'the privileged site for…contrapuntal, dissident, subversive, discourse'.[214]

Daniel

The first of three such works that Portier-Young discusses is the book of Daniel. It negotiates Antiochus' terror by urging faithfulness through the example of Daniel and his associates, and waiting for God to act in

---

212.   Portier-Young, *Apocalypse against Empire*, 217-18; also Horsley, *Revolt of the Scribes*, 33-104.

213.   Scott, *Domination*, 108-35, esp. 108.

214.   Scott, *Domination*, 25. I omit Scott's adjective 'nonhegemonic' because such discourse frequently mimics the hegemonic quality of dominant discourse in asserting an alternative power over the imperializing power.

bringing about a yet-future overcoming of Antiochus. It emerges between 167 and 164 BCE from, and is addressed to, a circle of wise teachers or scribal class (*maskilim*, Dan. 11:32-35; 12:3, 10), who in turn teach and make righteous a much wider secondary audience comprising the people of Judea/Israel.[215] Its various non-violent strategies include:[216]

- The use of both Hebrew and Aramaic that functions to move the audience from accommodation and collaboration to complete rejection of Seleucid domination and defiance of Antiochus' decrees.[217]

- Teaching and making wise the people so that they receive the revealed knowledge about God's sovereignty and covenant commitments that enables the learner to be strong in resistance to Antiochus' edict and persistent in obedience to the Torah (11:32);

- Prayer, fasting, and penitence as expressed in the prayer of Dan. 9:4-19 that employs the Deuteronomistic theological recognition that the 'calamity…against Jerusalem' was punishmentfor sin for which it seeks forgiveness. Liturgical prayer was communal and expressive of community commitments, history, and future;

- Stories and examples of faithfulness against coercive royal power even to death. Daniel and his friends Shadrak, Meshak, and Abednego display such faithfulness in maintaining a distinctive Jewish identity in a context that threatens it. They insist on food purity (Daniel 1), refuse to bow down to the golden image (Daniel 3), and refuse to pray to the king (Daniel 6). Such faithfulness in the midst of persecution required a willingness to die that in turn provided an example to strengthen others and a means of purification for Israel's sin;

- Waiting for the end revealed in Daniel's visions in which in God's timing God will demonstrate God's power and justice against and over Antiochus;

- Reading scripture and, as Antiochus' soldiers burned Israel's scriptures and sought to destroy Israelite memory, writing it afresh. So Daniel reinterprets the prophecy of seventy years in Jer. 25:11-12, 29:10 (Dan. 9:20-27), a historical review that not

---

215.   Portier-Young, *Apocalypse against Empire*, 227-34, 254-58.

216.   I follow Portier-Young, *Apocalypse against Empire*, 235-79; Horsley, *Revolt of the Scribes*, 33-45, 81-104.

217.   Portier-Young, *Apocalypse against Empire*, 227.

only assures with an assertion of God's control of history but destroys the new cultic time that Antiochus' edict imposed. A reinterpreted Isaiah's suffering servant (Isaiah 52–53) constructs the identity of the *maskilim* as suffering servants. This writing concerning the past and the future and involving prayer, story, vision, and revelations places Antiochus' actions within God's plan for history. It negates Antiochus' power and creates an alternative reality that is both counter-discourse and active nonviolent resistance.

- The narrative commissions the reader to continue Daniel's work in trusting God for salvation, teaching God's plan and practices of nonviolent resistance, and making righteous.[218]

While Portier-Young's discussion is insightful and its emphasis on Daniel as literature resisting Antiochus' edict is well placed, the analysis suffers from a significant flaw in failing to recognize that Daniel's meta-narrative is not monolithic in an oppositional stance vis-a-vis Antiochus' terror. Evident in these strategies of resistance are unnoticed elements of imitation or mimicry of Antiochus' imperializing work and the imposed practices that they simultaneously resist. Daniel mimics Antiochus in making total demands—similar but not quite the same, to echo Bhabha.[219] The scribal teaching for the people is as much about control of their identity—mind and body, thought and action, loyalty and commitments, past and future—as is Antiochus' program. The religious practices that Daniel asserts are as much about communal solidarity and identity as are Antiochus' imposed practices that allow for no exception. Daniel's evoking and reinterpreting of liturgical and scriptural traditions likewise resist and imitate Antiochus' manipulation of traditions and liturgy. A vision of the completion of God's purposes and eternal, cosmic, victorious, and coercive empire (Daniel 7) mimics the overpowering nature of Antiochus' empire and edicts but out-empires Antiochus in asserting the over-riding dominance of God's reign and sovereignty. It is similar but not quite the same. This vision is what Scott calls a daring 'world-upside-down' fantasy that reverses the status quo and fantasizes

---

218.   Flusser ('Apocalyptic Elements in the War Scroll') argues that the opening column of the War Scroll takes the unfulfilled prophecy of Dan. 11:40 and following as its point of departure, prophesying war against 'the Kittim of Assyria' (1:2) which Flusser concedes could refer to Rome but more probably, given the prediction of the Kittim's defeat in 1:6, it refers to the Syrian Greeks and a Seleucid ruler (pre-83 BCE).

219.   Bhabha, *The Location*, 86.

God's victory over the oppressor.[220] Such fantasies are ambivalent in function, providing a means of venting frustrating and thereby assisting compliance, even while they dream of a different domination. This recognition of the co-existence of mimicry and difference in the intersection of imperial, local, and cosmic powers highlights both the complexity of Daniel's metanarrative as well as the discursive strategies it shares with, even as it contests, Antiochus' program. Portier-Young's discussion misses these dynamics highlighted by postcolonial approaches.

*The Apocalypse of Weeks (*1 **Enoch** *93:1-10; 91:11-17)*

This short, seventeen-verse vision in the Enoch tradition offers another metanarrative to resist Antiochus' efforts and decolonize colonized minds.[221] Portier-Young dates it to 167 BCE, after Antiochus' edict but just before the Maccabean revolt breaks out. She locates its author among a community, the righteous, planning armed resistance against the wicked Antiochus, his forces, and supporters.

The work 'reveals' two opposing forces active in history through contrasting ethical behaviors and human communities. Enoch addresses 'the children of righteousness', also described as 'the elect' (93:2) and 'the plant of the righteous judgment' (93:5), who are contrasted with and opposed to the wicked who are subsequently identified with oppression, violence, and sin (91:11). Enoch's revelation for the righteous derives from his seeing a heavenly vision, hearing the holy angels, and reading the heavenly tablets (*1 En.* 93:2). Such multiple heavenly and divine authorizations for his revelation, the identity it constitutes, and the practices it authorizes, exceed anything Antiochus' edict could muster, and provide the basis for a revelation that will shape the resistant just or righteous practice of its human audience.

The revelation or apocalypse divides history into ten numbered weeks and some unnumbered weeks. Using the technique of *vaticinia ex eventu* (presenting past events as prophesied future events), the first six weeks turn to the past to identify and interpret monumental identity-forming events from Israel's scriptures such as Enoch's birth, Noah, the call of Abraham, Sinai and the giving of the law, Solomon's temple, and the destruction of the temple and exile (93:3-8). Week seven addresses the present audience with an interpretation and strategies for resistance

220.   Scott, *Domination*, 166-72.

221.   I follow Portier-Young, *Apocalypse against Empire*, 313-45, and assume her discussion of 'Enochic Authority', 280-312; see also Collins, *The Apocalyptic Imagination*, 33-67; Nickelsburg, *1 Enoch 1*; Horsley, *Revolt of the Scribes*, 73-76.

(93:9-10; 91:11), and the remaining weeks envision a future of judgment, righteousness on earth, and a new heaven (91:11-17).

Within this framework, the righteous have three roles in their current situation. The description of the seventh week elaborates the difficult circumstances in which they live and which they must resist by witnessing, cutting off or uprooting, and effecting justice (93:10; 91:11).[222] Having been given 'sevenfold wisdom and knowledge', they witness to truth and righteousness concerning God's ordering of earthly events (93:2, 10). They have an active commitment to lived justice or righteousness which derives from their faithfulness to YHWH. They uproot or cut off the roots of oppression or 'the foundations of violence and structure of deceit' (93:5; 91:11) that mark the present under Antiochus' edict. And, third, they will exercise YHWH's righteous judgment on earth in an eschatological role mimicking but exceeding the judgment that Antiochus has effected in his actions (93:5; 91:11). In the eighth week God gives the righteous the sword to execute judgment on the oppressors and sinners, suggesting military action against the oppressors (91:12). Once this is accomplished, the righteous acquire possessions and build a temple, the foundations of 'a new economy of justice and right social relations'.

The mapping of history, the fantasy of victory, and the vision of a different future function to decolonize subjugated minds, shape a different identity, and craft a third space.

The Book of Dreams (1 Enoch 83–90)

This third text, originating during the Maccabean revolt in the years 165–160 BCE and, like the Apocalypse of Weeks, drawing on the Enoch tradition, presents another metanarrative operative in the midst of Antiochus' actions of terror and re-creation.[223] It presents its metanarrative in two visions, both of which also employ the past as visions of the future. The first vision (*1 Enoch* 83–84) comprises the destruction of the world (83:5, 9) with the images of the trees being thrown down, evoking the downfall of the Egyptian and Assyrian Empires, and by extension Antiochus' empire, all subject to the sovereignty of God whose will determines 'all the things upon the earth' (83:9). Enoch's response is

---

222.   There are significant variants among translations of 93:10 and 91:11. I follow Portier-Young, *Apocalypse against Empire*, 329: 'The chosen will be chosen as witnesses of righteousness from the eternal plant of righteousness, to whom will be given sevenfold wisdom and knowledge. And they will uproot the foundations of violence and the structure of deceit in it, in order to effect justice.'

223.   I continue to follow Portier-Young, *Apocalypse against Empire*, 346-81; Horsley, *Revolt of the Scribes*, 65-73.

to lament (83:6) this vision of the 'sins of the whole world' (83:7) and to pray to the 'Lord of judgment' (83:11). Enoch's prayer (84:2-6) sets out an alternative yet in numerous ways an imitative cosmology, blessing God in expansive terms of authority that identify God's sovereign, creating ('you have created all'), ruling ('O Great King'; 'King of kings'), and all-knowing ('Everything you know, you see, you hear') roles that embrace the heavens and the earth ('Lord of all the creation of heaven'; 'God of the whole world'), the political order ('all things you rule'), and the past and future ('your authority and kingdom abide forever and ever and your dominion throughout all the generations of generations'). Enoch recognizes that 'the angels of your heavens' are sinning and that God's wrath is provoked, and he prays that God will destroy the sinners but save and sustain a righteous and upright generation (84:5-6). The petitioning prayer functions to recontextualize and thereby diminish the power of Antiochus' edict in God's sovereign purposes and power, to recall traditions of divine creation and sovereignty, to reassure with the recognition of God's all-knowing gaze, and to strengthen resistance to Antiochus' edict.

The second vision, the so-called Animal Apocalypse of *1 Enoch* 85–90, adds to the resistance practice of prayer two further strategies, prophetic witness and armed revolt. The vision uses allegory and animal symbolism to re-present Israel's history from Adam (85:3) through to the Hellenistic period, Maccabean revolt, and its aftermath (90:6-39). Using a familiar symbol from the tradition, it portrays Israel as sheep under attack from wild animals and birds with the sheep blinded and their eyes pecked out, a symbol of Israel gone astray (89:35, 54). The Deuteronomistic sequence of sin, oppression as punishment, crying out to God, and deliverance is evident. The use of animal symbolism functions as a form of disguise for this subversive discourse, protecting its audience from retaliation, while simultaneously employing a symbol of the sheep that had deep resonance in native Judea/Israelite traditions asserting covenant identity and divine protection (e.g. Psalm 23).[224]

In this context, Antiochus' persecution has blinded the sheep (90:2). But a new group of lambs—the group the writing particularly addresses—is able to see. With proper insight they cry out to the rest of the sheep, prophetically calling them to the right action of lived faithfulness (90:2-6). In so doing they emulate Moses who spoke against Egyptian power (89:17-18) and Elijah who similarly 'cried out' to the sheep in calling them from accommodating false worship and in urging obedience to the

---

224.   Scott, *Domination*, 136-56.

covenant (89:51-53). Enoch's vision is thus to function as a means of recognizing the true nature of the imperial attack and to call the audience to resist accommodation and to embrace faithful resistance.

After one of the lambs, perhaps the chief priest Onias III, is killed (90:8), a great horn grows on one of the sheep (Judas Maccabeus) who opens the eyes of the sheep, helping them see the true nature of the situation and a faithful way of living, and 'cries aloud' to the sheep (90:9b-10). He fights the wild birds (90:9-17) until God ensures military victory and exercises judgment (90:18-27). Thereafter follows a vision of a transformed world with a new house/temple, all the nations submitting to the Jews, resurrection, pervasive gentleness and the abandoning of the sword, and all have open eyes.

Again Portier-Young's discussion is insightful in identifying the metanarrative of the Animal Apocalypse that asserts God's longstanding sovereign power and purposes in the midst of attacks on Israel's sheep. Similarly she helpfully identifies strategies of resistance: prayer, understanding, prophetic witness, and military violence. Yet as with the discussion of Daniel, the relationship to Antiochus' terror remains monolithic in terms of resistance. She fails to notice two dynamics highlighted by postcolonial discussions, namely the presence of horizontal violence in the context of imperial pressure with the attack on the sheep who see, and that the Apocalypse's vision of the establishment of God's reign includes not only an alternative vision of gentleness and peace but also mimicry of features of imperial scenarios. Thus Judas employs military violence just as Antiochus did, God exercises punitive and subjugating judgment similar to Antiochus' actions, and the nations are imagined to submit to the Jews just as Antiochus imposed Jewish submission. These mimicked features are similar to, but not quite the same as, Antiochus' strategies.

First and Second Maccabees

Though written later than the three apocalypses just discussed, and perhaps dating to around 100 BCE, First and Second Maccabees offer significant information about and perspectives on the crisis. On this basis, they may offer further instances of Judean/Israelite metanarratives.

First Maccabees' main emphasis falls on a response of military resistance funded by loyalty to covenant and Torah. Unlike the group that refuses to fight and dies, this resistance is pervaded by ambivalence. Pragmatically and ironically, it decides that defense of the law, including Sabbath observance, requires contravening Sabbath observance in order to ensure survival (1 Macc. 2:39-41). This military response is led by a priestly family of Mattathias and his five sons (2:1). Mattathias laments the Gentile profanation of Jerusalem and its temple with language that resembles Lamentations 2:11 and 3:48. This intertextuality, again evoking the past to interpret the present, links Babylon's destruction of Jerusalem and the temple and exiling of Judea's leaders in 587 BCE with Antiochus' actions against Jerusalem and religious observance. Mattathias refuses to sacrifice as Antiochus requires because of his faithfulness to the covenant and law (2:20-21). When he saw a Jew come forward to make the required sacrifice, Mattathias 'burned with zeal' and in a classic instance of horizontal violence exerted in a context of increased vertical colonizer pressure, he killed the Jew and the king's officer overseeing the sacrifice.

First Maccabees 2:26 interprets his 'zeal for the law' by again turning to the past to evoke the actions of Aaron's grandson: 'just as Phinehas did against Zimri, son of Salu'. The reference is to an incident in which Israelite men had sex with Midianite women and worshipped the god Baal of Peor (Num. 25:1-13) in violation of the prohibition of worshipping foreign gods (Exod. 34:12-16). God's judgment took the form of a plague that killed twenty-four thousand (Num. 25:9). The plague ended when the priest Phinehas killed an Israelite man named Zimri and a Midianite woman named Cozbi with his spear, piercing 'the two of them…through the belly' (Num. 25:8, 14-15). God commends Phinehas twice for exhibiting zeal on God's behalf (Num. 25:11, 13). God thus sanctions the use of violence and killing—contravening a provision of the law—in the cause of maintaining observance of the law. Mattathias urges the people to show 'zeal for the law' (2 Macc. 2:50) and cites Phinehas 'our ancestor' (1 Macc. 2:54), among others (Abraham, Joseph, Joshua, Caleb, David, Elijah, Hannaniah, Azariah, Mishael, and Daniel) who trusted in God and did not lack for strength (1 Macc. 2:49-70).

This zeal is expressed in the Maccabean-led military revolt against Antiochus and, after the rededication of the temple, in the quest for Judean/Israelite independence accomplished under Simon (1 Macc. 13:41). The narrative focuses on military conflicts as the means of deliverance and exalts the military accomplishments of the Hasmonean brothers, Judas in 3:3-9; 9:19-21, and Simon in 14:4-15. The ambivalence of the imperial–colonial situation is again evident as the resistance mimics a fundamental strategy of the Hellenistic kingship that it resists, namely the use of military force. A further mimicry occurs in that this military resistance is divinely sanctioned. First Maccabees presents their military accomplishments as not existing apart from God's assistance. Judas announces that God 'will crush them before us' (3:22), a reference not to human passivity and miraculous divine intervention but to human military action in which, so it is understood, God is also active in helping

(3:53). Thus throughout there is a recognition of divine favor (often referenced as 'Heaven') in granting military success. This divine favor in crushing 'this army before us today' expresses God's faithfulness in remembering 'his covenant with our ancestors...to redeem and save Israel' (4:10-11). In seeking and acknowledging this divine help, prayer, thanksgiving, scrupulous observance of the law, and sacrifices punctuate the narrative.[225]

Second Maccabees participates in the same mimicry of the strategies of Hellenistic kingship in narrating the Hasmonean military successes in restoring the temple and expelling the profaning Gentiles. The account clearly reverences the temple and the festival celebrating its cleansing and rededication after Antiochus IV's defeat (2 Macc. 2:19-22; 3:12; 5:15-21; 10:1-8; 14:33–15:36). But in its midst, three important theological emphases emerge to form its metanarrative. One is the recognition of God's miraculous and powerful intervention at crucial moments, whether to protect the temple from Heliodorus intent on looting it and 'doing it injury' (3:24-40), or to protect Jerusalem (5:2-3), or to ensure victory in battle through the appearance of five angelic beings (10:24-38, esp. 29-31) or a glorious horse and rider (11:8), or even of God himself (12:22; 15:27). against any further violation of the temple. Appropriate acts of piety also punctuate the narrative.

Second, the narrative is framed by Deuteronomic piety (also evident in the prayer of Daniel 9) in which God blesses the obedient, Torah-observant, covenant-keeping people and their leaders (notably the chief priest Onias, 2 Macc. 4:2) with protection and safety (3:1–4:6). Yet God also punishes the people for unfaithfulness. Antiochus Epiphanes' attack on Jerusalem and the temple succeeds—unlike that of Heliodorus (2 Macc. 5:18)—because of 'the sins of those who lived in the city' (presumably the accommodating chief priests and their supporters, Jason, Menelaus, and Lysimachus, 4:19, 39); thus the Lord 'was disregarding the holy place' (5:17, 20a). Second Maccabees explains the calamitous events as a temporary punishment for these sins (6:12, 17; 7:32-33), disciplining the people though without ever forsaking them (6:16).

The narrative particularly attends to the specific displays of divine punishments and judgment on these leading figures—Andronicus where he had killed the righteous chief priest Onias (4:38), Antiochus with much suffering in his bowels just as he had tortured others (9:5-6), Menelaus in ashes just as he had violated the fire and ashes of the temple

---

225. See for example 1 Macc. 3:18-19, 44, 47 (fasting, sackcloth and ashes), 50-54; 4:10-11, 24 (thanksgiving for victory), 30-35 (prayer), 40, 55-56 (thanksgiving); 5:31, 54 (sacrifice); 7:36-38; 9:44-46; 12:15; 16:3.

altar (13:4-8), and Nicanor with the tongue and hand displayed that had blasphemed God (15:32-35). Yet, Second Maccabees emphasizes, the responsibility is not theirs alone. After the temple is cleansed and rededicated, the people 'implored the Lord that they might never again fall into such misfortunes but that, if they should ever sin, they might be disciplined by [God] with forbearance and not be handed over to blasphemous and barbarous nations' (10:4). That is, this text that strongly resists Antiochus reflects ambivalence in colluding with him, seeing the people's suffering at his bloodied hands as justified and his actions as divinely sanctioned in order to carry out God's punitive will. The king's identity is constructed simultaneously as the one who is resisted and the one who is God's agent.

And what turns God's wrath to mercy, bringing the punishment to an end and ensuring Judas' military success (8:5)? Second Maccabees' third theological emphasis of its metanarrative concerns the critical role of martyrs. Chapters 6 and 7 narrate the martyrdoms of Eleazar (6:18-31) and of seven sons/brothers (7:1-42). Eleazar is presented as a model of faithfulness (6:19-20, 28, 31). The seven brothers declare variously that death is better than sin (7:2), that God will raise up the faithful righteous (7:9, 23), and that God will restore their broken bodies (7:9, 11, 14) and their familial relationships (7:29). Conversely, God will punish the tyrant Antiochus and his descendants (7:17, 19, 31, 34-35). Most of these arguments for voluntary death in the service of faithfulness to the ancestral laws (7:9, 23, 30) were well known among educated Greeks familiar with the notion of voluntary or noble death, another reflection of the ambivalence and mimicry involved in negotiating Antiochus' power. It is similar but not quite the same. A key distinctive here concerns the declaration of the youngest brother. He acknowledges that the people's suffering is 'because of our own sins' but that it is temporary (7:32-33). The deaths of himself and his six brothers, he argues, are an appeal to God to show mercy and to end God's wrath for the nation (7:38). That is, the martyrdoms do not have atoning efficacy (compare *4 Macc.* 6:28-30; 17:21-22) but seem to function to move God from wrath to mercy. That they have this effect is signaled by the fact that immediately after the martyrdoms, the account of the military actions led by Judas Maccabeus begins with a notice that 'the Gentiles could not withstand him, for the wrath of the Lord had turned to mercy' (8:5).

As the discussion of these five texts indicates, Judean/Israelite metanarratives expressed under the assertion of Antiochus' tyranny, were not only diverse but reflected the ambivalences, instability, and mimicry that pervade imperial–colonial situations. Assertions of resistance are simultaneously assertions of (counter-)power in which the resistant counter-narratives mimic the imperializing strategies—totalizing scenarios, liturgy, military force, violence, justified suffering, cosmic divine victory over the enemy—evidenced by Antiochus and his allies.

V.
Post-164 BCE Rededication
of the Temple and Independence

Following the reversal of Antiochus' edict and restoration of the temple, the Seleucids leave Judea/Israel in relative, though partial, peace (2 Macc. 12:1). The Hasmoneans turn their campaign against Antiochus' edict into a campaign for independence. But, as we would expect in an imperial–colonial context, Judea/Israel reinscribes and mimics the imperial ways against which it had struggled but from which it had also learned much.

In blatant mimicry of the imperial ways to which Judea/Israel has been subject and in which it has marinated for centuries, Judas Maccabeus pursues military action against neighbors in Idumea, Galilee, and Transjordan to secure and enlarge Judean/Israelite territory. He also sieges the citadel in Jerusalem provoking Antiochus V Eupator to order Lysias to attack Jerusalem again (Josephus, *Ant.* 12.362-66). Lysias has greater military strength and sieges Jerusalem, only to abandon the siege at news of a coup in Antioch and to make peace with the Jews agreeing 'to let them live by their laws as they did before' (1 Macc. 6:18-63; 2 Macc. 13:22-24; Josephus, *Ant.* 12.379-83). According to Josephus, as Lysias heads to Antioch, he executes the chief priest Menelaus, ending his ten years in power, because he was 'the cause of the mischief by persuading the king's father to compel the Jews to abandon their fathers' religion', and appoints Alcimus chief priest in his place (*Ant.* 12.384-85).

Further internal struggles for power developed in the Seleucid empire and play a significant factor in the subsequent course of events.[226] Demetrius, the son of Seleucus IV Philopator (187–175 BCE), has Antiochus V and Lysias killed and seizes power (ca. 162–150 BCE). The Jerusalem chief priest Alcimus and his supporters approach the king wanting to maintain their position and favor. They report Judas Maccabeus' continued opposition despite the restoration of temple practice. Demetrius sends troops south under Bachides. A group of Hasidim seek peace but for reasons that are not clear. Bachides kills sixty of them and alienates would-be supporters (1 Macc. 7:12-18). He returns to Antioch,

226.   Sherwin-White and Kuhrt, *From Samarkhand to Sardis*, 217-29.

leaving Alcimus in power with both significant local support (1 Macc. 7:20-22) as well as opposition from Judas (7:23-24). That is, some (what percentage?) were willing to support Alcimus and accept Syrian rule in return for the freedom to observe traditional religious practices. Others, led by the Hasmoneans, sought a larger goal of independence from the Syrians. Ambivalence marks the colonized space as do fractures among colonized peoples.

Alcimus appealed again to King Demetrius for assistance against Judas (1 Macc. 7:25; 2 Macc. 14:3-15). The king sent troops under Nicanor, the governor of Judea/Israel (2 Macc. 14:12), who seems to have negotiated a truce with Judas (1 Macc. 7:26-38; 2 Macc. 12:18-25) but it did not last and Judas defeated Nicanor who dies in the battle (1 Macc. 7:39-50; 2 Macc. 14:26–15:37). In 161 BCE, King Demetrius sent troops under Bachides and they defeated Judas' army and killed Judas (1 Macc. 9:1-22). Bachides predictably installed pro-Syrian leaders ('wrongdoers' and 'the godless' according to 2 Macc. 9:23-27).

Jonathan followed his brother as leader (161–143 BCE). Bachides unsuccessfully sought Jonathan, but fortified cities in Judea and stationed troops throughout before returning to Antioch at the time of the death of Alcimus (ca. 160; 1 Macc. 9:32-57). Jonathan took advantage of the next two years or so to build support and he extended Judea's territory (as did Simon after him for example at Beth-Zur; Josephus, *Ant.* 13.156) by capturing Gentile sites, expelling their residents, and populating the sites with Jewish settlers.[227] His power increased so much that allies of Bachides persuaded Bachides to return to fight Jonathan. Bachides lost, concluded a peace agreement with Jonathan including a return of captives, and withdrew to Antioch (ca. 157 BCE; Josephus, *Ant.* 13.28-33). The absence of Syrian military presence ('the sword ceased from Israel') left Jonathan largely in control. Again imitating the imperial practices in which he had marinated—ambivalently resisting and admiring—he employs violence to destroy his opponents ('destroy the godless out of Israel', 1 Macc. 9:57-73; Josephus, *Ant.* 13.34).

About five years later (ca. 153–152 BCE), a new crisis arises in Seleucid politics that creates an opportunity for the Hasmonean quest for independence. Alexander I Epiphanes (Alexander Balas) claimed to be the son of Antiochus IV Epiphanes and challenged Demetrios I for the throne (Polybius 33.18; 1 Macc. 10:1; Josephus, *Ant.* 13.35-36). Demetrios sought the benefit of an alliance with Jonathan, permitting him to raise troops and release the Jewish hostages in the citadel. With

---

227. Berlin, 'Between Large Forces', 28.

this sanction, Jonathan established his headquarters in Jerusalem (to the alarm of some, 1 Macc. 10:8). He gained further sanction when Alexander sent a competing offer of friendship including appointing Jonathan chief priest, the first of a line of Hasmonean chief priests (1 Macc. 10:18-21). The struggle for loyalty ended in ca. 151–50 BCE when Alexander defeated and killed Demetrius in battle (1 Macc. 10:46-50). Alexander publically honored Jonathan in Ptolemais as a 'friend' and refused to listen to allegations from 'renegades' (1 Macc. 10:59-66). Jonathan's authority is thus further secured and he seems to gain public standing and support from Seleucid patronage. But he remains, ambivalently, a chief priest appointed by and dependent on the Syrian king and Judea remains a province under administration from Antioch with Syrian troops still garrisoned in the citadel in Jerusalem.

Jonathan maintains his leadership position against the threat of another Seleucid claimant Demetrius II and his agent Apollonius, defeating them in battle and, imitating the way of imperial powers, gaining control of further territory (Joppa, Ascalon, Ekron: 1 Macc. 10:67-89). Further struggles resulted in Demetrius II defeating Alexander to become king (145–140 BCE). Jonathan took advantage of this unrest to lay siege to the citadel (*akra*) in Syrian hands in Jerusalem, building the city walls higher and erecting a barrier between the city and the citadel so as to prevent it from buying or selling (1 Macc. 12:35-36). In the now familiar pattern of fragmentation and agonistic interaction in which one faction of Jews ('renegade') seek the favor of a new Seleucid king (cf. 1:11; 6:21-27; 7:5-7; 10:61), opponents of Jonathan reported his action to king Demetrius. Jonathan had a successful meeting with the king, having his chief priesthood confirmed and gaining freedom for Judea from tribute, though gaining no concessions on the citadel (1 Macc. 11:20-37). Subsequently Demetrius promises to remove the troops in return for Jonathan's help in putting down a revolt. Jonathan keeps his word but the king does not (1 Macc. 11:38-53).

Another coup sees Demetrius overthrown by Antiochus VI. In an act that both asserts power over and relies on Judea/Israel for support, Antiochus confirms Jonathan's chief priesthood and extensive power as military commander of Coele-Syria (1 Macc. 11:60). Subsequent intrigue, however, sees Trypho, a key advisor to Antiochus, seek to overthrow the king and make himself king. Fearing Jonathan's power, Trypho deceives Jonathan and takes him prisoner. He attempts to take Jerusalem but cannot succeed against Simon's troops. He kills Jonathan and withdraws (ca. 143–142; 1 Macc. 12:39-53; 13:12-24). In an expression of the hybrid 'third space' and ambivalence that marks their struggle, 1 Maccabees describes the way that Simon imitates the emerging Hellenistic practice of 'ostentatious *exterior* funerary architecture' in constructing an elaborate tomb at Modein for Jonathan and his family comprising pyramids, columns, suits of armor, and carved ships (13:27-29).[228]

A third Hasmonean brother, Simon, now leads the movement toward independence from Syrian rule as military commander and chief priest. Trypho killed Antiochus VI (ca. 142–139) and took the throne. Simon made alliance with Demetrios II who had aspirations to regain the throne and built up the defenses in Judea and stored up food. He gains significant concessions from Demetrius including tribute and tax relief. The writer of 1 Maccabees declares: 'In the one hundred seventieth year, the yoke of the Gentiles was removed from Israel' (1 Macc. 13:41; cf Josephus, *Ant.* 13.213), though the declaration seems premature since the Syrian garrison remained in the citadel. Simon accomplishes its removal shortly thereafter (ca. 142 BCE) having starved them into submission, expelling the troops from the citadel and purifying it. Their military presence had been the last obvious sign of Seleucid control, lasting some twenty years after rededicating the temple (1 Macc. 13:49-53). Since Tiglath-pileser in the eighth century, Judea had been under the control of an empire. It was now an independent state with its own small but growing empire, well-schooled in imperial ways. It would remain so until Roman control was asserted in 63 BCE.

Judean/Israelite Metanarratives?

First Maccabees extravagantly lauds Simon's rule as a time of peace, fertility, and faithful display of Jewish identity in adherence to the law and temple (1 Macc. 14:4-15). The reality was not quite so idyllic. He continues to extend Judea/Israel's territory in an imperializing process called 'Judaization',[229] in which he moved against Joppa and Gezer, driving out Gentile residents and settling it with Jews (1 Macc. 14:33-34). The archaeological evidence attests *miqvaot* in houses there indicating the residents' religious observance, but it also reflects their economic independence. Pottery remains, for example, are locally produced and there are no signs of the fancy tableware known as Phoenician Eastern Sigillata A pottery or semi-fine vessels, nor of 'Aegean wine amphoras, Hellenistic decorated wares such as West Slope-style plates and cups, Alexandrian white-painted pagynoi, nor southern Italian table wares and wine amphoras' so common elsewhere.[230]

228. Berlin, 'Between Large Forces', 32.
229. For a description, Berlin, 'Between Two Forces', 28-29.
230. Berlin, 'Between Two Forces', 28-30.

Simon himself comes to a murderous end at the hands of his son-in-law Ptolemy. Mimicking decades of murderous Seleucid political strategies, Ptolemy attempts to gain power through a coup, murdering Simon and two of his sons (1 Macc. 16:11-17). And Syrian imperial ambition has not ended. Simon's successor, John Hyrcanus (135–104 BCE), has to fight off the further assertion of Syrian power in the form of an attack and siege of Jerusalem from Antiochus VII Sidetes (ca. 134–132 BCE). He manages to survive the siege and negotiate its end, agreeing to pay some tribute, refusing a garrison in Jerusalem, forming a friendly alliance, and joining in Antiochus VII's military action against the Parthians (Josephus, *Ant.* 13.236-49).[231] Thereafter continued dynastic infighting among Syrian rivals largely meant Hyrcanus and Judea/Israel were left alone (Josephus, *Ant.* 13.267-72). Josephus comments that Hyrcanus 'revolted from the Macedonians, and no longer furnished them any aid either as subject or as a friend' (Josephus, *Ant.* 13.273). He also renews the treaty with the Roman senate (Josephus, *Ant.* 13.259-66), and sets about constructing a large and ostentatious palace at Jericho, imitating the Hellenistic practice of extravagantly displaying wealth.[232]

The brief rule of Aristobulus I (104–103 BCE) is significant for his 'transforming the government into a kingdom'. In further imitation of Greek practices, he makes himself king, the first Jewish king since 587 BCE (Josephus, *Ant.* 13.301). After Aristobulus' early death, his successor, Alexander Jannaeus (103–76 BCE), also a king and chief priest, continues the imitation of imperial ways by expanding his territory northeast of the Sea of Galilee and fighting with internal opponents, especially Pharisees. He has to fend off incursions from both Ptolemy Lathyrus of Egypt, the ruler of Cyprus, and attacks by the Seleucid Demetrius III (94–88; Josephus, *Ant.* 13.377-86)[233] and Antiochus XII Dionysus who was killed (ca. 86–84 BCE; Josephus, *Ant.* 13.387-92). Alexandra Salome (76–67 BCE) maintains Judea's independence, though the same cannot be said for her successors who became enmeshed in in-fighting (just like the Seleucids).

231. Tessa Rajak ('Roman Intervention') suggests Roman assistance with material aid in compliance with a treaty made with Simon may also have been a significant factor.

232. Berlin, 'Between Two Forces', 34-35.

233. Berrin (*The Pesher Nahum Scroll*, 88-130) identifies the Demetrius in Pericope 2, Pesher Units 6-10, who comes to Jerusalem 'at the counsel of Seekers-after-Smooth-Things' as Demetrius III. According to Berrin, 'Antiochus' is Antiochus IV, the Seekers are the Pharisees, the 'Kittim' are the Romans, and 'the Young Lion of Wrath' is Alexander Jannaeus.

Hyrcanus succeeds her in 67 BCE but immediately his younger brother Aristobulus attacks him. A settlement is reached in which Aristobulus becomes king. Interference in this arrangement comes from Antipater, whose father Alexander Jannaeus had appointed governor of Idumaea. The younger Antipater stirred up opposition to Aristobulus and persuaded Hyrcanus to obtain help from the Arab king Aretas. Aretas and Hyrcanus led an army against Aristobulus and besieged him in Jerusalem. Aretas is forced by Scaurus, an envoy of the Roman general Pompey, to lift the siege and withdraw. Aristobulus attacked Aretas and Hyrcanus. Both Aristobulus and Hyrcanus sent envoys to Pompey at Damascus seeking his favor and patronage. Pompey bound both parties to peace and to wait for his arrival in Jerusalem. But further strife develops and Pompey advances on Jerusalem. The city was divided in support between Aristobulus and Hyrcanus because, according to Josephus, the people rejected kingly rule and wanted rule by priests (*Ant.* 14.41). Aristobulus's supporters withdrew to the temple while Hyrcanus' supporters welcomed Pompey into the city. A three-month siege of the temple followed with many Jews, including Aristobulus' supporters, killed by Hyrcanus' supporters. Pompey entered the temple but did not damage it. He established order with Hyrcanus as chief priest, took Aristobulus captive, executed others involved in the war, levied tribute, set free cities, and placed them under his own governor as part of the Roman province of Syria (Josephus, *Ant.* 14.74-76).[234]

Josephus declares:

> For this misfortune which befell Jerusalem Hyrcanus and Aristobulus were responsible, because of their dissension. For we lost our freedom and became subject to the Romans, and the territory which we had gained by our arms and taken from the Syrians we were compelled to give back to them, and in addition the Romans exacted of us in a short space of time more than ten thousand talents; and the royal power which had formerly been bestowed on those who were high priests by birth became the privilege of commoners. (Josephus, *Ant.* 14.77-78)

234.   Flusser, 'The Roman Empire'.

6

Judea/Israel under the Roman Empire

What might a postcolonial optic highlight in the interactions between Rome and Judea/Israel in the centuries between 63 BCE when Pompey asserts Roman control, and 135 CE when the Bar Kokhba-led revolt is crushed?[1] The question gains some pointedness with the general abandonment of the old stereotype of Judea/Israel as a seething cauldron of rebellious anger that finally boils over in the 66–70 CE war.

Martin Goodman has largely argued the opposite view in proposing a double thesis: the lack of anti-Roman resentment and an accidental war. 'The travails of Judea up to 66', he writes, 'do not suggest a society on the brink of rebellion for sixty years'. Rather, the tensions of the 50s CE comprised 'terrorism within Jewish society rather than revolt against Rome… [They were]…internal to Jewish society rather than symptoms of widespread resentment of Roman rule.' The reason for the lack of 'blatantly revolutionary behavior to support [Josephus'] picture of a decline into war was that no such revolutionary behavior occurred'. Josephus makes 'little mention of any consistent anti-Roman ideology'.[2] The destruction of Jerusalem was the

> product of no long-term policy on either side. It had come about through a combination of accidents, most of them unrelated in origin to the conflict: the death of Nero, leading to Vespasian's bid for power in Rome and Titus' quest for the propaganda coup of a rapid conquest of Jerusalem, and the devastating effect in the summer heat of a firebrand thrown by a soldier into the Temple of God.[3]

Goodman concludes there was no widespread resentment against Rome and that the war of 66–70 CE was accidental.

Seth Schwartz offers a different evaluation of the interaction between Rome and Judea/Israel. He argues that 'the impact of different types of

---

1. Segovia, 'Mapping the Postcolonial Optic'.
2. Goodman, *Rome and Jerusalem*, 389-95.
3. Goodman, *Rome and Jerusalem*, 423.

foreign domination on the inner structure of ancient Jewish society primarily in Palestine' was, at least initially, galvanizing and integrating. Recognizing that 'the effects of domination were complex, pervasive, and varied' and emphasizing the generative and galvanizing impact of imperialism, notably Rome's strategy of autonomous provinces and empowered local elite leadership, Schwartz argues that a significant homogeneity in Jewish society resulted. 'A loosely centralized, ideologically complex society came into existence by the second century BCE [and then] collapsed in the wake of the destruction and the imposition of direct Roman rule after 70 CE'.[4] The heart of this homogeneity comprised God, Temple, and Torah.[5] 'I argue', writes Schwartz, 'that imperial support for the central national institutions of the Jews, the Jerusalem temple and the Pentateuch, helps explain why these eventually became the chief symbols of Jewish corporate identity. The history of the Second Temple period is one of integration, in which more and more Jews came to define themselves around these symbols.'[6] In emphasizing Judaism as 'the integrating ideology of the society', he recognizes that Judaism was 'complex, capacious, and rather frayed at the edges... [though] I reject the characterization of Judaism as multiple'.[7] Discussion of sectarianism does not disappear from his work and he argues for significant numbers of elite (male) adherents at least for various sects, and for their mainstream location.[8] After 70 and the revolt of 132–135, the impact of imperialism was quite different. In a word or two, 'Judaism shattered' or fragmented.[9]

How are we to describe the interaction between Rome and Judea/Israel? A seething cauldron of resentment? Relatively benign interactions with little anti-Roman resentment and an accidental war? An initial and protracted galvanizing and integrating impact followed by a shattering and destructive impact (though the last chapter suggested considerable fragmentation from the outset)? What might a postcolonial optic offer in the consideration of this well-rehearsed but contentious material?[10]

4. Schwartz, *Imperialism*. He concludes (291) that imperial domination and the imperial empowerment of Jewish leaders produced 'the complex loosely centralized but still basically unitary Jewish society'.

5. Schwartz, *Imperialism*, 49.

6. Schwartz, *Imperialism*, 14.

7. Schwartz, *Imperialism*, 9, 98.

8. Schwartz, *Imperialism*, 91-98.

9. Schwartz, *Imperialism*, 15.

10. In addition to Chapters 1 and 5 above, useful introductions to postcolonial discussion include Williams and Chrisman, *Colonial Discourse;* Ashcroft, Griffiths, and Tiffin, *The Post-Colonial Studies Reader*; Gandhi, *Postcolonial Theory*; Young,

While nearly everything about postcolonial studies is disputed, the discourse at its center concerns the assertions and representations of unequal and multi-dimensional power relations of domination (the imperializing center) and subordination (the receiving margins) that comprise complex imperial–colonial experiences marked by ambivalence, hybridity, and mimicry.[11] The extent of such discussion is enormous. This chapter will focus on the imperial–colonial interactions involving Rome and Judea/Israel in the period from 67 BCE–135 CE.

One danger of such an exploration is to regard all colonial interaction with the center in homogenized perspective. Studies alert us to multiple forms of negotiation employed by both provincial elites and powerless or subaltern groups. Our focus will concern the various dynamics in play when colonials of various statuses negotiate imperial power with varying, simultaneous, and sometimes violent strategies.

Some previous discussions that cast this interaction in terms of dualisms such as resistance or compliance, peaceful coexistence or violent rebellion, foreign imperializer and local rebel are simplistic and distorting. I emphasized in the last chapter the reciprocal interaction between imperializer and colonized and the ambivalent situation or 'third space' that is created. As James C. Scott argues, in-between poles of cooperation and disruption are the ambivalent spaces (the third spaces), where much actual negotiation of superior power takes place.[12] Some locals, especially elites but not exclusively so, openly and fully cooperate because it serves their needs to do so. Others do so in varying degrees, whether for reasons of self-interest or of pragmatic survival. The powerless also often use apparent compliance to disguise and mask dissent as well as to ensure survival. What seems to be cooperation can hide acts of resistance or of distancing from the imperializer's agenda. Anonymity masks defiance, and careful and self-protective calculation accompanies its expression. Compliance and resistance exist simultaneously; ambiguity is common; ambiguity and hybridity the norm. Violence is by no means the only expression of opposition and physical confrontation is not the only form of violence. To equate opposition with violence is to miss much imperial–colonial negotiation. In fact, powerless subalterns are often reluctant to employ public physical violence because they know that the rupturing of the social fabric of apparent

Postcolonialism: An Historical Introduction; Young, *Postcolonialism: A Very Short Introduction*; also standard works, Bhabha, *The Location*; Spivak, *A Critique*; Mbembe, *On the Postcolony*.

11. Segovia, 'Mapping the Postcolonial Optic', 66-67.

12. Scott, *Domination*, 136.

compliance is very dangerous and, more likely than not given the power dynamics, will result in their own demise. Scott argues that the powerless nurture a hidden transcript, an alternative version of reality, in spaces away from the imperializer's gaze. Local traditions and practices form the basis of this hidden transcript that contests the public transcript, or the imperializer's 'official' way of ordering the world and narrating its story. As I will note in the subsequent discussion, equating the lack of violence with a lack of opposition or resentment, equating relative public 'peace' with compliance, seems to mar much of Goodman's analysis.

In relation to violence, another dynamic of imperial–colonial interactions must be noted. As discussed in the previous chapter, horizontal disputes in the form of inter-group conflict, verbal polemic, and physical violence are common where vertical imperial pressure is exerted on a society. Various imperial situations, ancient and modern, attest this dynamic. Josephus indicates increasing divisions and inter-faction conflict in Judea/Israel and Jerusalem during the 66–70 war as imperial pressure intensifies on rebel groups: for example, Eleazar against Menachem (*J.W.* 2.442-48), John of Gischala against Josephus (*J.W.* 2.592-94), Idumeans against Ananus (*J.W.* 4.300-325), Zealots against John (*J.W.* 4.377-97), Simon bar Gioras (*J.W.* 4.503-44), and Eleazar, John, and Simon (*J.W.* 5.1-20) to name but some factional conflicts.[13] In discussing the situations created by the exertions of power by recent European empires, David Abernethy notes increasing horizontal violence between Hindus and Muslims in India and between competing groups in Kenya and Malaya under British imperialism, in Vietnam under French control, and among groups in the former Belgium Congo.[14] We could add black-on-black violence in South Africa in the 1980s' and the 1990s' struggle with apartheid and white power.[15]

As noted in the previous chapter, the postcolonial pioneer Frantz Fanon, in his study of imperial power dynamics in the French colony of Algeria, examines the creation and role of horizontal violence as vertical imperial power is asserted.

> The native is a being hemmed in... The first thing which the native learns is to stay in his place, and not to go beyond certain limits. This is why the dreams of the native are always of muscular prowess; his dreams are of action and aggression... The colonized man will first manifest this aggression which has

---

13.   E.g. 'στάσις', Josephus, *J.W.* 4.133, 388, 395, 545; 5.98, 105, 255, 257, 441; 6.40.

14.   Abernethy, *The Dynamics of Global Dominance*, 147-61.

15.   Hamber, 'Who Pays for Peace', 238-41.

been deposited in his bones against his own people. This is the period when the natives beat each other up, and the police and magistrates do not know which way to turn when faced with the astonishing waves of crime... The settler keeps alive in the native an anger which he deprives of an outlet; the native is trapped in the tight links of the chains of colonialism. But we have seen that inwardly the settler can only achieve a pseudo petrification. The native's muscular tension finds outlet regularly in bloodthirsty explosions—in tribal warfare, in feuds between septs, and in quarrels between individuals.[16]

In Fanon's analysis, horizontal conflicts—whether tribal or individual, physical or verbal—are multi-faceted. They result in part from subjugated people being hemmed in and contained by imperial controls and from restriction without outlet. They indicate considerable imperial (vertical) pressure. In addition to containment, horizontal struggles also develop because the oppressed mimic, as Fanon and Homi Bhabha note, the competitiveness and violent domination that mark the imperial situation. Violent domination 'has been deposited in his own bones'. The subjugated yearn for power while simultaneously and angrily resisting the imperial power exercised over them. Such horizontal violence is a means whereby subjugated groups compete with each other for power. In so doing they assert various identities that subvert the imperialists' attempts to control them by homogenizing them as 'the colonized'.

Yet as Fanon also argues, horizontal violence is a means of avoiding direct confrontation with the oppressor, since the oppressed know that they cannot win such struggles. Rather, they turn on each other with attacks that substitute for attacks on the oppressor. Assuming imitation of the oppressor, and noting that displacement of, yet identification with, the oppressor go hand in hand, Paulo Freire observes in relation to Latin American struggles, 'Because the oppressor exists within their oppressed comrades, when they attack those comrades they are indirectly attacking the oppressor as well'.[17] That is, horizontal violence occurs as oppressed groups in negotiating imperial power substitute attacks on other oppressed groups for direct confrontation with the oppressor. Lashing out against similarly oppressed groups is a safer option. Horizontal violence thus attests the restricting pressure of overwhelming imperial power, its imitation, and its engagement by avoidance and attacks on substitute groups.

I will return to this dynamic of horizontal violence in our subsequent discussion. But the recognition of it likely renders false Goodman's claim that inter-faction violence among Judeans/Israelites has nothing to

16. Fanon, *The Wretched*, 52-54.
17. Freire, *Pedagogy*, 44.

do with resentment toward Roman power. A postcolonial optic establishes Goodman's claim as comprising a false alternative that misses a vital connection. Following Fanon, factional violence among Judeans/ Israelites has everything to do with Roman imperial pressure and its negotiation by Judeans/Israelites. It attests the expression and management of considerable anti-Roman sentiment and a context in which war is not surprising. Moreover, recognition of this dynamic of horizontal violence similarly calls into question Schwartz's insistence on the initial, predominantly integrating impact of Roman power on Judean/Israelite society. This dynamic indicates that we might expect conflictual fragmentation and some integration to occur simultaneously, not sequentially, as in Schwartz's analysis.

My argument will be that a postcolonial analysis alerts us to the complexities and ambivalences of imperial–colonizer interactions in Judea/Israel in ways that conventional analyses of relatively benign interaction without much resentment, accidental war, and ready integration have not been able to identify. Because of space constraints, the discussion must be limited, partial, and perspectival. I will employ as a partial framework the three spheres that Scott identifies as arenas in which imperial rule is exerted and encountered by the colonized.[18] After an introduction in Section I, I begin in Sections II and III with *ideological domination* that utilized a set of convictions and/or a metanarrative that justified and expressed elite oppression, privilege, self-benefiting rule, and societal inequality. The elite's political, economic, societal, and cultural hierarchical order and exploitative practices were sanctioned as the will of the gods, as the metanarrative shows. This stable, 'natural', and immutable societal and cosmic order awed, impressed, and cowered the subordinated, while bolstering the elite.[19] This metanarrative and the spheres of domination it sanctioned comprised the 'Great Tradition', the official version of reality. In Sections 4-9 I consider two further forms of domination. Roman elites and their provincial allies also exercised *material domination*, using political and military power to exact agricultural production through taxation, services, and labor. Land ownership, the hard manual work of non-elites, including slave labor, and coerced extractions of production sustained the elite's extravagant and elegant lifestyle which was marked by conspicuous consumption. Further, elite alliances also enacted *status domination*, comprising societal and economic practices, social interactions, and punishments

18.   Scott, *Domination*, 198.
19.   Scott, *Domination*, 2.

that damaged the personal well-being of the subjugated non-elites and deprived people of dignity through humiliation, insults, degradation, and forced deference, exacting a personal toll of anger, resentment, and learned inferiority.[20] I will argue throughout that previous analyses have not paid sufficient attention to the indignities and psychological terror of the imperial–colonial situation. Goodman's attention to open conflicts, for example, pays little attention to such daily experiences and underestimates the conflict-contributing legacy of such treatment over decades of imperializer–colonized interactions. The discussion assumes the outline of postcolonial theory in Chapter 1, and the discussion and approach of Chapter 5. Because of space consideration, I will not repeat those here.

I.
Historical Introduction

By way of orientation to Rome's interaction with Judea/Israel, I begin with a brief and standard sketch of some major moments and players across this nearly two-hundred-year period. The subsequent discussion selectively, but not comprehensively, elaborates aspects of this sketch with a postcolonial optic.

In 63 BCE, the Roman general Pompey Magnus (Pompey the Great) takes control of Judea/Israel. Pompey's intervention came about partly because of Roman imperialist expansion (in 64 BCE Pompey had taken control of the Seleucid's territory of Syria) and partly because of civil strife in Jerusalem.

Queen Salome Alexandra, widow of Alexander Jannaeus who had ruled Judea/Israel as king and chief priest from 103–76 BCE, died in 67 BCE. A power struggle and civil war developed between her two sons, Hyrcanus II and Aristobulus II. After several military battles, both brothers appealed to Pompey. Followers of Aristobulus established themselves in Jerusalem. Pompey attacked the city and after three months defeated it and sacrilegiously entered the temple in 63 BCE. The Jewish historian Josephus reports that 12,000 died in the fighting (*J.W.* 1.150). He laments the loss of independence, the end of the one-hundred-or-so-year reign of the Hasmoneans over a Judea/Israel independent of foreign control, and the establishment of Roman rule:

20.   Scott, *Domination*, 111-15; see 198 for a summary chart.

> Now the occasions of this misery which came upon Jerusalem were Hyrcanus and Aristobulus, by raising a sedition one against the other; for now we lost our liberty, and became subject to the Romans, and were deprived of that country which we had gained by our arms from the Syrians, and were compelled to restore it to the Syrians. (*Ant.* 14.77).

The next twenty or so years after 63 BCE, predictably in a context of the assertion of imperial power, are marked by horizontal conflicts among various factions competing with each other for Rome's favor. Power struggles among factions of the Hasmoneans continue. In the mix also was the powerful Antipater from Idumea to the south whom Julius Caesar appointed governor of Judea/Israel in the 40s BCE. In turn, Antipater appointed his son Phasael governor of Jerusalem, and his younger son, Herod, governor of Galilee. By the year 40 BCE, there were further complications with the Parthians setting up a Hasmonean king in Judea/Israel while Rome supported the seemingly more stable and less nationalistically ambitious Herod. By 37 BCE Herod had won the military struggle with the support of several Roman legions to emerge as Rome's client-king (Josephus, *Ant.* 14.381-93).

Herod ruled until his death in 4 BCE. His reputation has been of a cruel and ruthless ruler who even put his own sons and other family members to death. He has never lived down the comment that Macrobius attributes to the emperor Augustus in saying that he would rather be Herod's pig than his son (*Saturnalia* 2.4.11)! One historian comments, 'Through a combination of political cunning, good luck, and an occasional murder, King Herod retained his Roman support, his throne, and his life!'[21]

Recent scholarly work, however, has significantly modified the wholly negative evaluations of Herod with an appreciation for his astute and practical adaptation to the increasingly Roman world, and for his effective handling of the numerous challenges he faced.[22] His reign was marked by constant challenges from Hasmoneans, a lack of popular support, a need to keep his Roman patrons happy through changing political alliances, numerous strategic building projects including the Jerusalem temple, and a high level of paranoia concerning possible rebellious family members and officials.

Herod's death in 4 BCE led to an unstable succession. His succession plan divided his kingdom among three sons with one son, Archelaus, becoming ruler of Idumea, Judea, and Samaria. The plan needed Rome's

---

21. Levine, 'Visions of Kingdoms', 356.
22. For a summary, see McCane, 'Simply Irresistible'.

approval but public opinion was divided. A series of civic disturbances broke out requiring the Roman governor of Syria, Varus, to intervene by sending a legion into Jerusalem. Further unrest resulted from the harsh actions of the legion's commander Sabinus. More disturbances in Galilee and Perea led to Varus returning to put down the rebellion and to crucify several thousand locals. In 6 CE the emperor Augustus removed Archelaus and exiled him to Gaul.

Augustus added Judea/Israel and Samaria to the province of Syria, and (with the exception of 41–44 CE) they were ruled by Roman governors until the war of 66 CE. This period of rule combines both calm and conflict; I shall return to it below. Certainly the Jewish historian Josephus sees in the inability of the governors, especially in the 50s and 60s, to maintain order and to refrain from self-enriching greed a contributing factor to the war that breaks out in 66 CE.

The outbreak of the war, as with its continuation, was marked by constant internal conflicts among Jewish groups. It seemed to promise initial Judean/Israelite success when the governor of Syria, Cestius Gallus, having marched troops south from Antioch, withdrew from Jerusalem before securing control, his troops being decimated in the retreat. By 70 CE, though, Roman forces under the command of Titus, son of the new emperor Vespasian (69–79 CE) and himself to be emperor in 79–81 CE, captured the city after a siege and burned the temple.

Emperors Vespasian and Titus and their successors used the war to enhance their prestige and to vilify Jews as Rome's enemies. Rome did not permit the temple to be rebuilt. In 130 CE, the emperor Hadrian refounded Jerusalem as a Roman colony, naming it Aelia Capitolina and dedicating a new temple to Jupiter Capitolinus. Such an act was extremely provocative and in 132 CE another revolt broke out. Led by Shimon bar Kokhba, it asserted, as did the war of 66–70 CE, Israel's independence from Roman rule. But as with the 66–70 CE war, this assertion was crushed after fierce fighting in 135 CE.

This brief outline of some of the main events between 63 BCE and 135 CE is standard fare. It is a 'top-down' approach that focuses on the powerful, on key moments of the assertion of military power, on Roman success. A discussion shaped by a postcolonial optic seeks to trouble such a benign account, to expose the strategies and violating misuse of imperial power, to identify the ambivalences, mimicry, and hybridities that arise in imperialized–colonized interactions, to recognize its psychological terror, and to identify the agency whereby local peoples (who were not destroyed by it) negotiated this power with multivalent and simultaneous strategies along a spectrum bounded by opposition and acceptance. This postcolonial optic is interested in foregrounding the complex dynamics of the unequal power relations of imperial–colonial interactions. It seeks to understand the emergence and consequences of such an assertion, its self-representation as superior to the subjugated 'Other', and its reframing by local people. And this optic questions the ongoing effects of historical representations that have more often admired than questioned Roman power, more often lauded its benefits than evaluated its cost, more often attended to its supposed benefits than noticed its ambivalences.[23]

A postcolonial optic, for example, raises again the question of nomenclature. Naming, of course, is an act of power, an assertion of control, a means of defining, an expression of perspective. So what name do we employ for the territory and people over which Rome asserts its power? Noting the slogans on the coins issued by Jewish 'rebels' (or are they 'freedom fighters?') in the 66–70 CE war, Martin Goodman points out the significance of the act of naming. With slogans such as 'Jerusalem is holy', 'Freedom of Zion', and 'Shekel of Israel', these rebels/freedom-fighters explicitly avoid the term 'Judah' which 'was too close to *Judaea* (the Roman name for the province)'.[24] They refuse Rome's naming of them and contest it by turning to the past (a common strategy of colonized peoples as postcolonial studies have noted) to retrieve terms that presented their independent state as 'Zion' and 'Israel'. These terms freshly asserted old and central traditions of Israel's covenant and royal identities with YHWH as God. In 130 CE, Hadrian, also knowing the power of naming, removes the name Jerusalem from the city, renaming the newly established Roman colony Aelia Capitolina. The province also receives a new name, Syria Palaestina, 'resurrecting an ancient Greek designation of the region, which referred not to the Jews but to their ancient enemies, the Philistines'.[25] During the 132–35 CE revolt, the rebels/freedom fighters again draw from their own 'native' traditions and past to employ slogans on coins that present their identity as an independent people with the nomenclature of 'Israel' and 'Jerusalem' ('for the freedom of Jerusalem') as counter assertions to Roman naming.

Goodman helpfully raises the question of nomenclature but the title of his book, *Rome and Jerusalem*, offers an unhelpful solution even if we regard his nomenclature as a synecdoche. While it creates a 'tale of two cities', the title also creates a false pairing and a perspective that focuses on the powerful elite, to the neglect of poor non-elites. Roman power

23. Morley, *The Roman Empire*.
24. Goodman, *Rome and Jerusalem*, 14-15; Goodman, 'Coinage and Identity'.
25. Goodman, *Rome and Jerusalem*, 471; also Eck, 'The Bar Kokhba Revolt'.

was by no means restricted to Jerusalem, extending as it did over the province of 'Judea', what the resistance of 66–70 CE and 132–35 CE called 'Israel', and whose power was negotiated by non-elites as well as elites. Throughout this chapter, I will again use the hybrid form 'Judea/Israel' to denote the contested nature of the subjects of this discussion.

II.
The Metanarrative of the Roman Empire

In the reciprocal relationship between imperializer and colonized, Rome's self-presentation legitimates its subjugation of peoples with divine sanction even as Rome depends on these subjugated peoples to confirm and authenticate its metanarrative.

Virgil's *Aeneid* and Horace's *Carmen Seculare*

The Augustan poet Virgil presents Rome as chosen by the gods to exercise 'rule without end' (*Aeneid* 1.279) and as inaugurating a golden age of superior cultural blessing. Peter Brunt observes that 'What was most novel in the Roman attitude to their empire was the belief that it was universal and willed by the gods'.[26] At the heart of this imperializing identity is 'a myth of supernatural character…beyond military, economic, and socio-political bases of power',[27] even as it includes and sanctions such bases. John Dominic Crossan styles this metanarrative as Religion which leads to War which leads to Victory which leads to Peace.[28] The cultural blessing of peace, a linguistic euphemism for subjugation, comes about through the assertion—often militaristic but not always so—of divinely sanctioned, Roman supremacy and victory. I survey several literary and visual/material examples.[29]

Virgil's epic poem *The Aeneid* emerges after the torturous decades of the 40s–20s BCE, which saw the end of the republic, civil wars, economic struggle, and apparent religious and social decline. With the emergence after the battle of Actium in 31 BCE of Octavian (named Augustus by 27 BCE) as supreme leader, a significant reversal of fortune followed for Rome consisting of civic peace, prosperity for some elites,

26. Brunt, 'Laus Imperii', 291.
27. Fears, 'The Cult of Jupiter', 5-7.
28. Crossan, 'Roman Imperial Theology'.
29. Crossan, 'Roman Imperial Theology', highlights the *Aeneid*, Octavian's Tent Site Inscription, the Actium Coinage, the *Gemma Augustea* Cameo, the Prima Porta Statue, the Altar of Augustan Peace, and the *Sebasteion* at Aphrodisias.

renewed religious piety with Augustus' rebuilding of temples and reconstituting of rites, and an emphasis on responsible social and civic participation. Reflecting this optimism, Horace, at the occasion of Augustus' Saeculum games in 17 BCE, happily sang of a Golden Age in his *Carmen saeculare*, performed by twenty-seven boys and girls, the very personification of the domestic fertility and civic order that were the mark of Augustus' golden age. Horace celebrates

- Morality: 'Rear up our youth, O goddess, and bless the Fathers' edicts concerning wedlock and the marriage-law, destined, we pray, to be prolific in new offspring' (17-20);

- Fertility: 'Bountiful in crops and cattle, may Mother Earth deck Ceres [goddess of agriculture, corn, and harvest] with a crown of corn; and may Jove's wholesome rains and breezes give increase to the harvest' (29-32);

- Social Conformity and Harmony: 'O gods, make teachable our youth and grant them virtuous ways; to the aged give tranquil peace' (45-46);

- Blessing on Rome: 'If Rome be your handiwork…[give] to the race of Romulus, riches and offspring and every glory' (47-48);

- Military Victory and Alliances with the Submissive: 'And what [Augustus]… entreats of you, that may he obtain, triumphant o'er the warring foe, but generous to the fallen!' (49-52);

- Renewed Social Morality: 'Now Faith and Peace and Honour and old-time Modesty and neglected Virtue have courage to come back, and blessed Plenty with her full horn is seen' (57-60);

- Eternal Empire: may Apollo 'prolong the Roman power and Latium's prosperity to cycles ever new and ages ever better' (66-68).

The poet Virgil was at work through the 20s BCE on the *Aeneid* and reflects this optimism in his work. Just how he reflects that optimism is debated. Some see the poem as ambivalent about Augustus' power, somewhat appreciative yet also subversive of and pessimistic about Augustus' achievements, while others see it much more as a celebration of his accomplishments.[30] Whatever the final verdict, the epic with its appeal to the past certainly articulates key emphases in Rome's imperial self-presentation, notably Rome's divinely sanctioned right to empire. It

---

30. See the brief discussion (and cited literature) in Bonz, *The Past as Legacy*, 195-202.

tells the story of the Trojan Aeneas who, along with other Trojan survivors, leaves the ruins of Troy and guided (Jupiter) and thwarted (Juno) by gods undertakes a mission to travel to Italy to establish a city. Detoured through Carthage and the underworld, his party arrives in Italy and through battles takes control of Latium from which Rome emerges.[31]

In Book 1, Jupiter delivers a prophecy that outlines a version of Rome's certain and magnificent future (1.254-96). It sets out the divinely destined events of Aeneas' military success in founding Latium, the royal line of Alba Longa from which emerge Romulus and Remus and Rome's founding, the success of Julius Caesar, and of Augustus in closing 'the gates of war', in restraining 'impious Rage', and establishing peace. Jupiter describes Rome's identity and mission:

> For these I set no bounds in space and time; but have given empire without end… Romans, lords of the world and the nation of the toga. Thus it is decreed (1.278-83).

With Jupiter's words, Rome is presented as divinely commissioned to rule without any temporal or geographical limits. As 'lords of the world', global domain is in view. As 'the nation of the toga', Roman males are to attend actively to the task of bringing peace and 'civilizing' other nations.[32] Whether nations and peoples want Roman civilizing is not an issue.

A second prophecy about Rome's future comes in Book 6 as Aeneas journeys into the underworld to meet his father Anchises. Beside the River Lethe, Aeneas sees a parade of the future 'great ones', including Romulus whose 'blessed' Rome has worldwide empire (6.781-84), and 'Augustus Caesar, son of a god' (Julius Caesar) who will 'establish a golden age [and] advance his empire' (6.788-807). The parade conveys a sense of inevitability, that Rome's domination is predestined, unstoppable, natural, and divinely sanctioned. Subsequently, Anchises exhorts and commissions his son: 'you, Roman, be sure to rule the world…to crown peace with justice, to spare the vanquished and to crush the proud' (6.851-53). Romans are to rule, but in refusing to recognize any ambivalence, reciprocity, and hybridity, and thereby removing any agency from the subjugated, Roman rule is to be worthy rule in imparting the benefits not only of peace but also of justice and mercy.

31.　For discussion, see Galinsky, *Aeneas*; Bonz, *Past as Legacy*, 31-65; Kamudzandu, *Abraham*, 59-86.

32.　The toga has ideological significance signifying a national identity of 'peaceful, civilized, male', which mandates for Roman (elite) males active attention to such a civilizing mission. Vout, 'The Myth of the Toga', 214.

The presentation, of course, envisages a benign and noble Rome engaged in a 'civilizing' mission for the benefit of all, but it cannot disguise the fact that this 'rule' consists of coercive domination over nations and that it requires 'vanquishing' and 'crushing' any who stand in Rome's way. At heart is a presumed military superiority and a cultural arrogance derived from divine sanction that assumes and asserts Rome's way as superior and desirable. Of little concern are any reciprocities between conquerors and conquered and any sense of the disruptive and destabilizing impact of the assertion of empire.

There is plenty of written and visual evidence that attests the seriousness with which Rome and its elite provincial allies promoted this self-representation as a divinely sanctioned empire with superior military power and a civilizing mission. Augustus displayed the Aeneas myth in his *forum Augusti* in Rome particularly in the temple of Mars Ultor (Mars the avenger) where both Aeneas and Romulus feature. On the Ara Pacis (the Altar of Peace), both are again displayed but in ways that highlight, according to Paul Zanker, 'divine providence that governed Roman history from the beginning'.[33] Aeneas, for instance, is depicted arriving in Latium under an oak tree where the prophesied pig and piglets are found (cf. *Aeneid* 3.390; 8.84).

Res Gestae

Augustus' work, *Res Gestae*, displayed on his mausoleum in Rome as well as in the provinces (copies have been found in Galatia at Ancyra, Apollonia, and Antioch), outlines his numerous accomplishments and benefactions as 'father of the fatherland' (*pater patriae*). Augustus' opening boast in presenting himself is that he ensured Rome's security and extended 'the power of the Roman people' over 'the entire world' (1). He did so by filling political offices at the behest of the senate (1, 7), by waging many battles 'throughout the whole world' and extending mercy where appropriate (3), by subduing and administering Spain and Gaul (12), by 'securing peace on land and on sea…by victories throughout the whole empire of the Roman people' (13), by taking 'control of the sea from pirates', by returning rebellious slaves to their owners, by securing with oaths of loyalty the allegiance of 'all of Italy' and 'the provinces of Gaul, Spain, Africa, Sicily, and Sardinia' (25), by enlarging 'the territory of all provinces of the Roman people', pacifying Gaul, Spain, Germany, the Alps, and Arabia and Ethiopia, where 'great forces of both peoples were cut down in battle and many towns captured'

33. Zanker, *The Power*, 201-10, esp. 203.

(26), by adding Egypt, subduing Armenia, and recovering the provinces from the Adriatic to the east (27), by recovering military standards lost in battle in Spain, Gaul, Dalmatia, and Parthia (29), by extending the 'authority of the Roman people' over Pannonia, Illyricum, and Dacia (30), and by friendships and alliances with various Eastern (client) kings (31-33). As ruler of the world—land, sea, people—he extended the empire 'where the ocean encloses it' (26).

Augustus calls this benefaction the rare situation of peace, effected through submission to Roman will and rule. 'The doorway of (the temple of) Janus Quirinus' had been shut—to signify 'peace on land and on sea'—only twice 'from the time of the city's foundation until before my birth'. During Augustus' time 'the senate ordered it shut three times' (13). The *Res Gestae* presents Augustus' ordering of the world, at times by military might, at times by negotiation and alliance. It portrays a hierarchical dichotomy between Rome and the rest of the nations.[34] Augustus' 'matter-of-fact' tone in summarizing his deeds cloaks his actions with a sense of the natural and inevitable. He maintains this sense by omitting detailed or humanizing description of the impact on local peoples of his actions. There are no casualty lists, no public opinion polls, no catalogues of personal or collective indignities and resentments and no recognition of the psychological terror inflicted by Roman rule, no voice for subalterns, and no recognition of any acceptable 'push back' against Roman power.

The Sebasteion at Aphrodisias

From the mid-first century CE, from the city of Aphrodisias in Asia Minor, comes a graphic display of Rome's divinely sanctioned mission.[35] Worshippers approached its Sebasteion, dedicated to Aphrodite and the emperors, Augustus, Tiberius (14-37 CE), Claudius (41-54 CE), and Nero (54-68 CE), through a large paved area or processional way, eighty meters long (about 250-300 feet) and fourteen meters wide (about 45 feet). This large paved or processional way was flanked on both its north and south sides by porticoes or three-story high walls that provided, by one estimate, some one hundred and eighty spaces for panels and statues.

The panels and statues order the Roman world in particular ways, only some of which can be discussed here.[36] As worshippers approached the temple, they were not just reminded of, but were enabled to experience,

34. Lopez, *Apostle to the Conquered*, 86-113.
35. Erim, *Aphrodisias*, 106-23; Smith, 'The Imperial Reliefs'; Smith, 'Sacra Gentium'.
36. Carter, *John and Empire*, 99-101.

the divinely sanctioned and overwhelming power of Rome. Statues personified peoples and provinces that had been conquered by Rome, including Cretans, Cypriots, Sicilians, Egyptians, Judeans, Arabs, Bosporans, Bessi, Dacians, Dardanians, Iapodes, Andizeti, Pirousti, Rhaeti, Trumpilini, and Callaeci. The statues, displayed in the approach to an imperial temple, represent a peaceful/submissive empire gained by military conquest under religious sanction. Moreover, significantly, these subjugated people are presented as female figures. Roman power is gendered as manly power; defeated people are womanly and weak. Roman power is also sexualized as sexually violent power. One panel depicts a divinely nude and macho emperor Claudius with a spear or sword standing over and holding down a defeated and semi-nude female figure Britannia who raises her right hand either in defense or to beg for mercy. The scene personifies Claudius' invasion and annexation of Britain (43–47 CE) as a sexual conquest in which the rapist Claudius prepares to penetrate the defeated people. A similar panel presents the divinely nude and heroic emperor Nero subduing a slumping, kneeling, mostly nude, female figure who represents Armenia. Military conquest is rape. By penetration, the 'Father of the Fatherland' produces more children/subjects/slaves for his empire-wide household. Rome's self-presentation of its imperial military power is gendered and sexual.[37]

And who was responsible for such a visual/material and dramatic display of the empire's metanarrative? It would be tempting to think that this was a 'top-down', centrally coordinated message sent out to the provinces from Rome. But while emperors and their agents did plenty of that, these displays in provincial Aphrodisias did not originate in Rome. They express the hybrid identity of colonized elites celebrating their place in the hierarchy of Roman power. Members of two very wealthy Aphrodisian families were responsible for funding these impressive structures. Two brothers, Menander and Eusebes, funded the northern wall, and another two brothers, Diogenes and Attalus, funded the southern wall. The porticoes were not forced on Aphrodiasians by Rome. They were 'home-grown', the voluntary actions of two very wealthy Aphrodisian families experiencing the ambivalence of being elite provincials under power and intent on honoring Rome's 'accomplishments' as well as displaying and enhancing their own wealth, power, and prestige as loyal participants in the empire. There are many such examples of provincial elites grasping opportunities to express their place in and loyalty to the empire.

37. Lopez, *Apostle to the Conquered*, 42-48.

Tacitus

Tacitus' biography of his father-in-law Agricola, written in the 90s CE, attests to this Roman self-presentation as conquering and civilizing power in the province of Britain. Agricola was governor of Britain from 77–84 CE, an agent and beneficiary of Roman power, just as Tacitus himself is. Tacitus presents Agricola's service as comprising his role as Rome's agent, notably as military commander and administrator 'who first thoroughly subdued' Britain (*Agricola* 10). Tacitus celebrates elite virtues, holding up for admiration and imitation Agricola's conventional male roles as warrior (*Agricola* 18, 22-25, 35-38), ruler and administrator (19), judge (19, 21.1), and priest (9). Agricola collects taxes and tributes (13, 19), and imposes and upholds Roman order. He spreads Roman 'culture' among the British by constructing temples, market-places, and houses, by educating sons of chieftains, and by advocating the use of Latin and wearing the toga (21).

Tacitus' commentary on this civilizing mission is, nevertheless, biting just as it is culturally arrogant in its assumed superiority: 'and little by little the Britons went astray into alluring vices: to the promenade, the bath, the well-appointed dinner table. The simple natives gave the name of "culture" to this factor of their slavery' (*Agricola* 21.2). Elsewhere Tacitus returns to this theme and has Civilis, a Batavian military commander, warn his people against Roman culture: 'Away with those pleasures which give the Romans more power over their subjects than their arms bestow' (*Histories* 4.64.3).

Whatever Tacitus' ambivalent presentation of the colonized under imperial power, he is unhesitating in presenting Agricola's greatest accomplishment as military conquest. About a quarter of the biography is concerned with the year 84 CE, including a description of the bloody battle of Mount Graupius in which Agricola slaughtered the united British tribes (29-39). Tacitus gives voice to anti-Roman sentiment by attributing a speech to Calgacus, the leader of the British forces (30-32).[38] Ironically, Tacitus supplies Calgacus with words of protest; the constructed speech includes some terse critique. Tacitus' Calgacus offers a very different construction of Roman identity from below: 'robbers of the world…to plunder, butcher, steal, these things they misname empire; they make a desolation and they call it peace' (30). Tacitus has Agricola describe his own rule as 'armed occupation' and he boasts from his Romocentric perspective without any regard for the locals' history in the land that he has 'discovered and subdued Britain' (33.3). Interestingly,

---

38.   See James, 'The Language of Dissent', 279-89.

Tacitus says he writes this account in part to show that 'great men can live even under bad rulers' (42.4). He, of course, is not referring to the British tribes under Roman rule but to Roman elites having to negotiate the emperor Domitian and his (for Tacitus) tyrannical ways. Ironically, Agricola provides a fine exemplar of the metanarrative that is, in Tacitus' view, larger than and betrayed by the emperor.

Josephus

This same metanarrative appears in the speech that the elite Jewish writer Josephus (client of the Flavians Vespasian and Titus) gives to the general, later to be emperor, Titus (79–81 CE). In Josephus' account, Titus addresses his troops in the Galilee as they prepare to battle Jewish troops outside Tarichaeae on the shores of the Sea of Galilee during the war of 66–70 CE. He begins by appealing to their identity as Romans:

> Romans—it is well at the outset of my address to remind you of the name of your race, that you may bear in mind who you are and whom we have to fight. Our hands to this hour no nation in the habitable world has succeeded in escaping. (*J.W.* 3.472-73)

His immediate construction of Romanness consists of undefeated military power. Titus goes on to present Romans as superior to Jews in military discipline (3.475), preparation (3.475-76) armour and leadership (3.477) courage (3.478-79), and cause:

> You will contend for a higher cause than the Jews; for though they face war for liberty and country in jeopardy, what higher motive could there be for us than glory and determination, after having dominated the world, not to let the Jews be regarded as a match for ourselves? (*J.W.* 3.480)

Titus pits Jewish liberty and defense of country against Roman glory which comprises the maintenance of Rome's domination of the world. The latter has, for Josephus' Titus, the greater value. At the heart of the antithesis is Rome's unrivaled domination over all peoples expressed in and secured by military supremacy. Jewish concerns simply recede before this value. And what underwrites it? Titus declares:

> Do you then not fail me, have confidence that God is on my side and supports my ardour. (3.484)

Divine sanction for Rome's empire means the battle is inevitable as is victory which creates a situation of subjugation that Rome calls peace. For the record, Titus prevails, and Vespasian dispatches the conquered under military supervision to nearby Tiberias. There he executes (accepting that Josephus' numbers are exaggerated) twelve hundred of the 'old and unserviceable', sends six thousand youths to Corinth to work on Nero's canal, and the remaining thirty thousand he sells into slavery (*J.W.* 3.532-42). Whatever the accuracy of the numbers, the ripples of the indignities, resentment, and psychological terror of military defeat throughout families and villages were far-reaching and permanent.

Rome's 'myth of supernatural character', its divine sanction for *imperium sine fine* ('empire/rule without end') foregrounds what Michael Mann calls Rome's ideological power or control of meaning-making and interpretation. This power existed along with military (violence and concentrated coercive power), economic (control of labor and production) and political (territorially centralized control of organization and institution) power, to which we will return below.[39] Scott observes that such metanarratives or 'great traditions' exist primarily for the benefit of elites. They empower and embolden elites in the exercise of their power, legitimating and confirming their privileged place in the social order and self-benefitting rule, rendering such structures 'natural' and 'god-given'. In Scott's words 'elites are also consumers of their own performance'.[40] That is indeed true, but it cannot be overlooked that the metanarrative was not the preserve of elites. Its public and multimedia declaration in literary texts and inscriptions, on coins and statues, by images and buildings, with altars and ritual, ensured non-elites were exposed to it also, and, to varying degrees, found it variously persuasive, convenient, and/or unconvincing in making meaning of their world.

The assertion of such a metanarrative in the midst of provincial subjects interacts with local traditions, practices, and power structures to create ambivalence and hybrid identities that hold together Roman dominance with dependence on subjugated Judea/Israel to confirm and authenticate the former's metanarrative.

III.
Rome and Judea:
Roman Religious Acts and Imperial Cult Observance

While claiming religious sanction for its empire, Rome—with a few exceptions—did not impose its polytheistic religions on subjugated provinces and it did not prohibit local religious practices. This is true for Judea/Israel for much of the period from 37 BCE–66 CE. For much of this time, with two notable exceptions (Gaius Caligula and Hadrian), Rome did not attempt to shut down worship in the Jerusalem temple or

39. Mann, *Sources of Social Power*, esp. 11, 22-28, 250-300.
40. Scott, *Domination*, 49.

forbid obedience to the Torah, as the Seleucid ruler Antiochus IV Epiphanes had attempted to do in the 160s BCE. With the destruction of the temple in 70 CE, however, Rome steadfastly prevented any temple rebuilding until Hadrian's humiliating action of 130 CE.

Since religious claims and practices were simultaneously self-presentations of political claims and identities, as the previous section makes clear, it is not surprising that the hybridity that marked Judea/Israel under Roman rule featured a considerable strand of religious-political tensions and indignities. For example, this period is marked by a series of 'incidents' concerning the temple that created tensions and resentments. Among the more prominent are the following:

- In 63 BCE supporters of Aristobulus took refuge in the temple (Josephus, *J.W.* 1.143). Pompey's troops captured the temple, and killed both supporters and priests 'in the act of pouring libations and burning incense'. In contradictory manner Josephus first says that the Romans 'butchered' many; but then he blames the factions of Aristobulus and Hyrcanus for killing each other (in total, twelve thousand; *J.W.* 1.150-51). Josephus also notes Pompey's entry into the temple and comments that 'of all the calamities of that time none so deeply affected the nation as the exposure to alien eyes of the Holy Place, hitherto screened from view' (*J.W.* 1.152). The effect no doubt included horror, outrage, resentment, and hope for revenge. By his own words, Josephus notes this truly offensive act on Pompey's part. But Josephus, living the hybrid identity of Jewish apologist for and client of the Roman Flavian emperor, sets about minimalizing any Roman offense by presenting Pompey, the 'able general', as a respectful sightseer in the temple who did no damage and 'conciliated the people' (1.153).

- In 54–53 BCE, Crassus, the governor of Syria, funded a war against Parthia by stripping 'the temple at Jerusalem of all its gold, his plunder including the two thousand talents left untouched by Pompey' (*J.W.* 1.179). Josephus continues to minimalize the impact of such an act by ignoring any local response and invisibilizing any local agency. Again we are left to imagine the indignity and resentment of it.

- Herod, Rome's client-king, placed a golden eagle over the great gate of the temple (*J.W.* 1.650). This act not only set a forbidden image on the temple, but as 'a symbol of empire' (Josephus, *J.W.* 3.123), the eagle proclaimed Judea/Israel's submission and

Herod's loyalty to Rome. Two legal scholars encouraged students to 'avenge God's honor', which they did by cutting down the eagle. Herod avenged Rome's honor by burning alive the scholars and students, and executing the other forty or so who had been arrested (*J.W.* 1.648-55). The subsequent violence attests the depth of the insult sustained by the subjugated body politic.

- Pilate, governor from 26–37 CE, continued these provocations. He brought images of Caesar attached to military standards into Jerusalem. Offended by these images in the city, and exerting considerable agency in countering Roman violation of their local traditions, Jews followed Pilate to Caesarea to protest their presence. Sustained and non-violent demonstrations of a willingness to die persuaded Pilate to remove the images (Josephus, *J.W.* 2.169-74). Pilate also took money from the temple treasury for construction of an aqueduct; the resultant angry protest saw 'large numbers' of Jews killed, creating further ripples of resentment and indignity throughout households and towns (*J.W.* 2.175-77).

- Governor Florus (64–66 CE) removed seventeen talents from the temple treasury. The resultant protest that pushed back against this indignity that violated both national identity and sacred space provoked Florus to march troops into Jerusalem (*J.W.* 2.293-300).

The hybrid space of interactions between Rome and Judea/Israel also involved observances of the imperial cult. In a context of monotheistic and aniconic Judaism, claims of Roman superiority and divine sanction were asserted in the cult, thereby contributing to tensions with the local population. Some have argued that Jews had formal exemption from the cult, but there is no evidence for such a view since observance of the imperial cult was not compulsory throughout the empire.[41] Jews in Judea/Israel did, though, have to negotiate its presence even though it was not a centrally imposed phenomenon, nor was observance required. Frequently in Rome's empire, elite citizens in local cities and provinces were the driving force for its celebration, embracing it as a way of negotiating and honoring Roman power and advancing their own interests. The surviving evidence from the hybridized situation of Judea/Israel certainly confirms the key roles of local elites in its promotion, notably Herodian rulers and Roman governors.

41. So correctly, Bernett, 'Roman Imperial Cult', 340-41.

James McLaren argues that while it might seem that 'a clash of world-views was bound to happen' over this practice in Judea/Israel, such a (violent and open) clash was avoided because Herod negotiated the ambivalent situation by establishing a basic strategy of 'separate but parallel sacred space'. This strategy accommodated the cult, and kept his Roman masters happy without offending Jews.[42] While rebuilding the Jerusalem temple, for example, Herod also built three temples for the worship of Rome and its emperor in Sebaste (Josephus, *J.W.* 1.403), Banias (*J.W.* 1.404), and Caesarea Maritima (*J.W.* 1.414). McLaren points out that Herod chose towns of mixed population with perhaps Jewish populations in the minority in Sebaste and Banias. Nor is there evidence for a Jewish abandonment of Caesarea Maritima, suggesting that Jewish inhabitants could accommodate the presence of an imperial temple and were not pressured to participate. Perhaps some chose to, though Josephus does not describe any such reactions. McLaren also notes that Herod, not surprisingly, did not try to establish an Augusteum in Jerusalem, thereby securing 'separate but parallel sacred space'.

McLaren's observation is astute, but the separation of space, Herod's assumed sensitivities to local religious concerns, and a lack of local offence may not be quite as clearly delineated as he suggests. As both 'king of the Jews' and 'friend of the Romans', to use Peter Richardson's phrase, Herod walked the difficult path of hybridity, leading his subjects into the Romanization of the new world while also maintaining faithful Jewish practices.[43] As a result, observance of imperial honoring (perhaps without cultic and iconic dimensions?) was by no means restricted to the sites of Caesarea Maritima, Sebaste, and Banias as McLaren's argument suggests. Herod introduced games in honor of Augustus in Jerusalem, which, according to Josephus' multiple references, clearly troubled many, who feared this violation of their customs and introduction of foreign practices 'would be the beginning of great evils' (*Ant.* 15.267, 280-81). Herod also covered the theater with 'inscriptions concerning Caesar and trophies of the nations which he won in war'. These trophies 'irked' native Judeans/Israelites who, thinking of them as forbidden images, 'were exceedingly angry' (*Ant.* 15.272-76). Herod was unable to placate this anger and removed the images (15.277-79). According to Josephus, the construction of the temple for Augustus at Paneion also seems to have caused considerable resentment and fear concerning 'the dissolution of their religion and the disappearance of their customs', so much so that Herod tries to buy favor by remitting taxes by a third. To

42. McLaren, 'Jews and the Imperial Cult', 257, 276.
43. Richardson, *Herod*; McCane, 'Simply Irresistible', 726-27.

establish control, he initiates a rule of terror by forbidding gatherings, setting up surveillance with spies, using the death penalty for dissenters, and requiring an oath of allegiance and commitment to a 'friendly attitude to his rule' (Josephus, *Ant.* 15.363-69). Subsequently, embracing his hybrid location and identity, he required an oath of allegiance to himself and to Augustus, though Josephus does not describe the range of strategies local people employed to negotiate that act (*Ant.* 17.42). In addition, priests in the Jerusalem temple embraced their hybrid location by offering sacrifices of lambs and a bull twice daily in the temple *for* (but not *to*) the emperor and the Roman people until lower-ranked priests refused to do so in 66 CE, an action that also blurred the notion of the separated space claimed by McLaren (Josephus, *J.W.* 2.197, 409-10; *C.Ap.* 2.77; Philo, *Leg. ad Gaium* 157, 317).

Moreover, Herod's sons continued to emphasize imperial honoring. Monika Bernett argues that when Antipas founded and named the city Tiberias after the emperor Tiberius as the capital of Galilee (19–20 CE), he formed a very Hellenistic city in structure and facilities. Antipas, though, avoided conflict over the imperial cult by promoting imperial games that probably lacked cultic and iconic dimensions. Antipas' successor in ruling Galilee and Judea/Israel from 41–44 CE, Agrippa, however, seems to have been a more active proponent of the cult. His coins of 42–44 CE present himself, a sacrificial act, and the emperor Claudius.[44] While honoring the emperor Claudius in 44 CE, he himself receives address as a god, only to be struck down with intense pain and to die, a death interpreted both in Josephus (*Ant.* 19.343-50) and Acts 12:19-23 as divine punishment for overstepping human limits. Bernett finds evidence from coins issued between 44 and 66 CE by Agrippa II that the presence of 'the imperial cult in Judea-Palestine (including Galilee)' was 'strong'. She argues that the cult's expression of foreign rule in the land of the God of Israel contributed to increasing tensions between locals and Rome leading up to the war of 66–70 CE. It must also be recognized, though, that if its presence was 'strong', significant numbers participated perhaps without major doubts or concerns about its disruptive impact.

Bernett's argument for a strong presence of the imperial cult gains some support from Joan Taylor's examination of governor Pilate's activity.[45] She examines numismatic and epigraphic material to argue that governor Pilate promoted the imperial cult, including a Tiberium in Caesarea Maritima. Literary evidence (Philo's account of Pilate, *Leg. ad*

44. Bernett, 'Roman Imperial Cult', 349.
45. Taylor, 'Pontius Pilate'.

Gaium 299-305) confirms his encouragement of appropriate imperial honoring. Taylor does not regard these attempts as an attack on Jewish sensibilities, but they reflect the duty of a Roman governor to advance the Roman imperial cult in Judaea. While these actions are not open attacks on Jewish sensibilities, they give impetus to the presence of imperial honoring. If Taylor's analysis is correct, it would follow that all the governors through the first century undertook a similar responsibility to varying degrees, creating an ambivalent location that comprises a range of responses from willing compliance to feigned cooperation to outright avoidance and to resentment.

The most direct confrontation over the imperial cult pre-70 takes place in 39–40 CE when the emperor Gaius Caligula ordered a statue of himself as Zeus be set up in the Jerusalem temple, by military force if necessary.[46] If the command was carried out by Petronius, the legate of Syria, it would mean the end of Jewish practices and the introduction of the imperial cult into the Jerusalem temple. For both Philo and Josephus, the central motivation for this demand seems to be Gaius' insistence that Jews do not honor him as a god with statues as other peoples do (Philo, *Leg. ad Gaium* 198; Josephus, *Ant.* 18.257-60). All three accounts emphasize the agency of thousands of Jews, elites and non-elites, male and female, adults and children, who met Petronius at Ptolemais and Tiberias and declared that they were willing to die rather than allow the statue to be placed in the temple. The whole situation is resolved when Gaius Caligula dies in 41 CE, before the order is enacted. Gaius' actions are an aberration in terms of forcing a direct and public confrontation with the Jerusalem temple pre-70 CE. The rest of the evidence, though, suggests that, fostered by various governors, the imperial cult was actively, if somewhat sporadically, observed throughout our time period. How extensive its presence, and the various ways in which local peoples, especially subalterns, negotiated it, have largely not been remembered in the surviving record.

Nearly a century after Gaius Caligula, and sixty years after the temple was destroyed in 70 CE, the emperor Hadrian inflicted an even greater indignity in 130 CE. The temple was not rebuilt after 70, partly, as Martin Goodman argues, because portraying Jews as villains well served the self-presentation of the Flavian emperors, Vespasian, Titus, and Domitian (d. 96 CE), as legitimate rulers.[47] Frustration at this failure seems to have been a factor in the Jewish revolts of 115–117 CE. Goodman argues that in turn punishment for these revolts saw Hadrian

46. Among others, Bilde, 'The Roman Emperor Gaius'.
47. Goodman, *Rome and Jerusalem*, 428-46.

establish the colony of Aelia Capitolina with a temple for the supreme all-conquering Roman god Jupiter Capitolinus on the site of Jerusalem. This was not to be a rebuilt city for Jews with a restored temple, but a city for Gentiles that explicitly excluded Jews and their religious practices by placing the worship of Jupiter at its center.[48] Such a humiliation, such an indignity, so typical in Scott's description of the interactions between the powerful and the powerless,[49] signaled that no temple was to be rebuilt. Goodman sees the revolt led by Bar Kokhba in 132–35 CE, and provoked by Hadrian's action, as a (temporary) assertion of both deep-seated resentment and a new identity until it was crushed by Rome.[50]

IV.
Imperial and Provincial Rule

In addition to ideological/religious and military power, Rome also exercised political power, which Michael Mann defines as the control of 'centralized, institutionalized, territorial' organization and institutions.[51] Rome did not rule, though, as some other empires have done, with a huge civil service sent out from the metropole to colonies and provinces. Rather, in part it sent a small number of officials (governors) from Rome, and it worked through alliances with local elites and political institutions. In Judea/Israel, Rome ruled with Herodian client-kings (Herod, 37–24 BCE; his son Archelaus 4 BCE–6 CE; his grandson Agrippa I, 41–44 CE), governors (6–41, 44–66 CE), and alliances with local elites, notably the chief priestly families and lay, wealthy landowners.[52] While the Sanhedrin played some role, probably under high priestly leadership, it was not a fully recognized or consistently powerful local assembly equivalent, for example, to the Senate.[53]

Roman rule in alliance with the Herodians placed the latter in the difficult ambivalent third space of representing both Judean/Israelite traditions and Roman imperial interests. Herod was appointed king of Judea/Israel in 40 BCE by the Roman senate and with the support of

48. Goodman, *Rome and Jerusalem*, 457-65.

49. Scott, *Domination*, 111-15.

50. Goodman, *Rome and Jerusalem*, 465-69.

51. Mann, *Sources of Social Power*, 11.

52. Goodman, *Ruling Class*; on high priestly families, see VanderKam, *From Joshua*, 337-436.

53. On the Sanhedrin and its fluctuating influence, see Grabbe, 'Sanhedrin', 16-19.

Octavian and his patron Antony. It took three years of military action for him to secure his power from the Parthian-backed Hasmoneans. His dependence on his Roman overlords and his identity as a client or puppet king are clearly illustrated in 31 BCE when Octavian and not Antony emerged as the victor from the decisive battle of Actium. Herod persuaded Octavian/Augustus on the basis of his former loyal friendship to Antony that he (Herod) would have even greater allegiance to Octavian. Octavian confirmed his appointment as king. Josephus notes that Herod now had greater 'honour and freedom of action' and, typically, attributes his success to 'the kindness of God' (Josephus, *Ant.* 15.187-98). For Josephus, just as God's favor resided with Rome (*J.W.* 2.390; 3.351-54; 5.367), so it resides with this local imperial representative. Herod's 'greater freedom' meant little interference from Rome in Herod's reign, since Herod maintained rigid control of the societal order for his own benefit.

Roman legitimation for Herod's rule also, of course, carried the mandate for Herod to promote Roman interests in Judea/Israel. Herod walked the hybridized line between honoring Judean/Israelite religious sensitivities (with varying success as noted above), and keeping his Roman bosses happy. In the scholarly makeover of Herod in recent discussions, Herod appears very much as a 'friend of Rome'. As an 'astute reader of the times', in which republican practices gave way to a new constellation under Augustus, so Byron McCane argues, Herod and Augustus 'were able to recognize that the material and social conditions of their world had changed and that Roman administrative control was going to generate a new pattern for civilization. Augustus stepped out front to lead the parade, and Herod fell right in step behind him.'[54] McCane offers the examples of the two temples Herod built, one for Augustus in Caesarea Maritima and the temple in Jerusalem. McCane notes Herod's addition of the large Court of the Gentiles to the Jerusalem temple as a place both to welcome Gentiles from Rome's empire as well as to impress Judeans/Israelites. It facilitated hybridity in altering the Judean/Israelite impressions of the empire and the empire's impressions of Judeans/Israelites. That is, while Herod attended to and fostered Jewish traditions, he also carried out his 'responsibilities as a Roman client to socialize the Jews of Palestine to the Roman empire'.[55]

Herod's honoring of Augustus, of course, paid huge dividends. He kept his throne until his death in 4 BCE. Augustus has Herod's back, for example, when Gadarenes complain that Herod was too 'severe…and

<hr>

54. McCane, 'Simply Irresistible', 727, 735.
55. McCane, 'Simply Irresistible', 732-33.

tyrannical' (Josephus, *Ant.* 15.354-59). Such a complaint conveys an enormous depth of resentment for numerous (social, economic, political, religious, and personal) indignities, but the local concerns are dismissed. However, when things did not go well, as with discontent over Herod's son Archelaus, Rome freely intervened. 'Leading men', presumably a grouping of high priestly and elite lay families, brought charges to Augustus against Archelaus of 'cruelty and tyranny'. With the failure of the local elite ruling alliance, Augustus exiled him to Gaul in 6 CE (*Ant.* 17.342-44).

Even with Herod's death and Archelaus' exiling, members of the Herodian family continued to exercise power and influence in their ambivalent place of being both representative of their people and tradition, yet friends of Rome. Berenice, sister of Agrippa II, voicing the terror and indignation of the people, petitions the governor Florus to stop 'the carnage' of his soldiers' attacks on Jerusalem (*J.W.* 2.309). Josephus attributes to her brother Agrippa II a key speech in 66 CE, pleading with a Jerusalem crowd not to pursue war with Rome. As Tessa Rajak has observed, the speech is remarkable for what it reveals about the 'ambiguous stance of the native governing class, superficially pre-Roman ([*sic*] pro-Roman, in varying degrees), but harboring doubts and even deep resentments'.[56] Agrippa, educated in Rome and an active ally of the Flavians and supporter of their war effort in 66–70 CE, ruled territory to the north of Jerusalem in Galilee and Transjordan. He also had responsibility for oversight of the Jerusalem temple, including appointment of chief priests. The speech Josephus provides for him covers predictable, even 'Josephan', ground: for example, those in favor of war were only a vocal minority; power should be 'conciliated by flattery not irritated' (*J.W.* 2.350); bad governors do not reflect all emperors or the empire as a whole (2.352-54); fortune or God has prospered the empire (2.360, 390); it is too late to fight now—that should have happened more than one hundred years ago against Pompey (2.356-57); and the temple will be destroyed if war occurs (2.400).

Yet while Agrippa pleads for war-free acceptance of Roman rule, there are undertones of critique in 'the voice of the realists' who knew the demerits of empire but the necessity of compliance. Agrippa affirms that Rome's rule is slavery (2.356). Roman military power is so intimidating that a relatively few soldiers control and deter large populations (2.365-80). Gaul is willing to be exploited as a 'source of revenue' (2.372). Africans 'ungrudgingly devote their contributions' through 'tribute of all kinds' (2.383). Yes, God has prospered this empire

---

56. Rajak, 'Friends, Romans, Subjects', 133.

(2.390), but all apocalyptic thinkers know that God will, finally, bring down all empires, including Rome's. The critique is sharp even as it is veiled. The public message is clear in its demand for cooperation but so too is a subtext that recognizes the harsh realities of imperial rule. The ambivalence is explicit. As an agent and ally of Rome and a huge beneficiary of Roman rule, yet as a Judean/Israelite, Agrippa expresses the ambiguities of his liminal location. The provincial ruling elites cannot be understood to embrace one homogenized attitude to Roman rule.

After Archelaus' exile in 6 CE, Rome appointed governors to rule from 6 CE until 66 CE, with the exception of Agrippa I's reign (41–44 CE). Governors, with some troops, were based in Caesarea Maritima. Their duties were to be the 'face' of Rome in the province, looking out for and promoting Roman interests and those of their elite provincial allies. Top priorities for a governor involved law and order (commanding troops, hearing cases, and carrying out the death penalty; Josephus, *J.W.* 2.117), collecting revenues, and promoting public works and building projects. It was a difficult role and no doubt governors of Judea/Israel tried hard to perform their basic tasks.

Though Josephus' agenda to maintain elite privilege is front and center, he nevertheless presents the governors as largely inept, ineffective in quelling local uprisings, greedy in their accumulation of personal wealth, and generally not well-intentioned toward Judeans/Israelites. I have noted above Pilate's insensitivities concerning images and the misuse of temple funds (*J.W.* 2.169-77). While Cuspius Fadus (44–45 CE) and Tiberius Alexander (46–48 CE from an Alexandrian Jewish family) 'kept the nation at peace' (*J.W.* 2.220), Cumanus (48–52 CE) could not and was banished by the emperor Claudius after a dispute between Galileans and Samaritans (*J.W.* 2.232-46). Felix (52–60 CE) was a tough law-and-order governor: 'of the brigands whom he crucified, and of the common people who were convicted of complicity…and punished by him, the number was incalculable' (*J.W.* 2.253). Of course, the existence of brigands attests a violent form of dis-ease with Roman rule and the socio-economic challenges that resulted for local people.

Also incalculable was the residual terror, resentment, and bad will between people and governor as Rome's representative. Festus (60–62 CE) continued the attack on brigands (*J.W.* 2.271). With Albinus (62–64 CE), Josephus' tone changes: 'there was no form of villainy which he omitted to practice'. His 'villainy' included stealing private property, increasing taxes, accepting bribes, and colluding with brigands (*J.W.* 2.272-76). But Albinus was a 'paragon of virtue' compared to the last governor Gessius Florus (64–66 CE), who engaged in robbery, violence, collusion with brigands, avarice, theft from the temple, and violence against the people (*J.W.* 2.277-79, 293, 305-308). Josephus' harshest criticism is clearly reserved for the last three governors Festus, Albinus, and Forus. Running through his account is the claim that their misgovernings were significant factors in leading to the war of 66–70 CE. The claim covers a multitude of personal indignities, resentments, and desire for retaliation.

Governors exercised rule in alliance with local elites. Petronius, legate of Syria, charged with enacting Gaius Caligula's command to install a statue in the Jerusalem temple, meets with local 'aristocracy' to secure their compliance with the emperor's will (*J.W.* 2.199). Florus seeks the support of 'the chief priests and leading citizens' in securing the loyalty and compliance of Jerusalem citizens (*J.W.* 2.318). These alliances among the ruling elites were often tensive in being marked by both contest and cooperation. Both groups quested for power and sought their own advantage and interests, yet both needed the other to protect their mutual interests.

The tensive quality of these interactions is clearly seen in the Gospel accounts of Pilate's dealings with Jesus (Mark 15:1-15; Matt. 27:1-2, 11-26; Luke 23:1-25; John 18:28–19:16).[57] Pilate's allies, the Jerusalem chief priests and 'elders of the people', bring Jesus to Pilate for crucifixion. Since Jesus is of concern to his allies, he must be, in the reciprocal interaction of Roman and Judean/Israelite, of concern to Pilate because they have shared interests in maintaining public order. But it will not do for Pilate to acquiesce immediately to their request to crucify Jesus. That would make the governor subservient to the wishes of the provincials. So Pilate appears reluctant, seemingly not persuaded that Jesus is any threat. This response forces the Jerusalem leaders, along with the crowd, to beg for Jesus' crucifixion. With this display of their dependence on and subservience to Pilate's power, Pilate orders Jesus' crucifixion.

A further dynamic existed in the relationship between governor and local elites in Judea/Israel. Josephus makes clear that after the demise of Herod and Archelaus, 'the high priests were entrusted with the leadership of the nation' (*Ant.* 20.251). In the first half of the first century CE, governors appointed the chief priests. Josephus records that Pilate's predecessor, the governor Valerius Gratus (15–26 CE), appointed and deposed five chief priests. The first four seem to last a year in office at the most; the last one 'Joseph, who was called Caiaphas' was chief priest

---

57. For the following, see Carter, *Pontius Pilate*.

from 18–36 CE, through the rest of the governorship of the apparently hard-to-satisfy Gratus as well as that of Pilate. Caiaphas was clearly very adroit at the difficult and ambiguous task of representing his traditions while keeping his patron's happy (*Ant.* 18.33-35, 95). Later in the century, Agrippa II became overseer of the temple. He appointed 'six different men…from a different priestly family between 59–66' as chief priest, perhaps to prevent any one person becoming too powerful.[58]

Such priests, like Rajak's analysis of Antipas' location as a member of the native ruling class, occupied a difficult ambivalent or hybrid third space, though its lines are drawn somewhat differently. They represented a tradition that affirmed Jerusalem and its temple to be the dwelling place of Israel's God to whom the earth and its fullness belonged (Ps. 24:1). Yet they were appointed and accountable to Roman governors, agents of a metanarrative that declared Rome as sanctioned by the gods to rule the world. Betwixt-and–between, the priests occupied a liminal place.

Something of the same ambivalence is seen in Josephus' evaluation of the governors. Josephus, a Jew yet writing as a client of the Flavians in Rome, recognizes the crucial role of governors as Roman representatives. Yet, as I have noted above, he does not draw back from criticizing their misrule and identifying their role in contributing to the outbreak of war. In a surprising but somewhat 'oblique' passage, he evaluates the whole gubernatorial system as consisting of 'blood-sucking flies' (*Ant.* 18.172-76). Josephus presents the emperor Tiberius explaining that he prefers long-term gubernatorial appointments because new appointments mean new governors who bleed provincials dry. Tiberius tells a parable to explain that it works against a wounded man to shoo flies away from his wound because new flies will replace the sated ones and his life-blood will be sucked out more quickly. The parable, told by the emperor about his own governor-appointing practices, is stunningly critical in its presentation of governors as blood-sucking flies who suck the life blood out of provinces by exploitative maladministration. Josephus allows the emperor to condemn himself by his own words even as he names one of the imperial power's self-benefitting dependencies as the province of Judea/Israel. But it is also eerily prescient in its presentation of the wounded man's hybridity. The man is capable of asking a stranger not to shoo the flies away and is thereby complicit with the gubernatorial system, but he is utterly incapable of making any other request or taking any other action that might ameliorate his situation.

58. Goodman, *Rome and Jerusalem*, 363.

Conventional analyses commonly see the exercise of power in the hands of these elite functionaries, albeit with ambiguity for these provincial figures. But to look only there is to miss the powerful agency exercised by non-elites in negotiating Roman power and influencing events. Josephus frequently refers to 'crowds', 'multitudes', 'the people', and 'the Jews' (δῆμος, ὄχλος, ἔθνος, λαός). At key moments these constantly shifting and contextualized groups exercise significant agency, surrounding and intimidating Roman troops after Herod's death (*J.W.* 2.42-44), extending their necks and exposing their throats to Pilate's troops, thereby forcing him to remove images of the emperor from Jerusalem (*J.W.* 2.169-74), non-violently resisting Gaius Caligula's order to Petronius concerning the statue ca. 40 CE (*J.W.* 2.192), protesting Florus' use of violence in 66 CE that killed many Jerusalemites in the upper market (*J.W.* 2.315), and resisting Titus' breech of the city's second wall (*J.W.* 5.331-42). Such efforts—and this is but a very partial listing—exerted considerable power, reciprocating Rome's exercise of power, influencing the outcome of events, and asserting the dignity and will of local people in the face of terrifying power. Informing such agency is a long history of indignities that empower people to risk an open challenge to imperial power.

Also to be noted are numerous popular movements of social unrest that arose through the century. In a number of studies, Richard Horsley has drawn attention to this important phenomenon. Following Fanon, such movements express the splintering of society under imperial pressure in which resentment is directed more often horizontally to scapegoats rather than vertically in direct confrontation with Roman power. In some cases direct and violent challenge to Rome is also avoided by the use of speech and symbolic actions. To claim that these movements had nothing to do with Rome as Goodman does but were directed toward local Judean/Israelite rulers fails to understand the alliances between Rome and local elites and the various ways subjugated peoples negotiate the assertion of imperial power. Oracular prophetic figures emerge, for example, such as John the Baptist who attacks Herod Antipas' lifestyle (*Ant.* 18.117-19), and the temple-denouncing Jesus ben Hananiah (*J.W.* 6.300-309), and those who just before the 66 CE war exercised considerable power by promising with signs and declarations that God would assist the revolt (*J.W.* 6.285-87), while ignoring ominous signs (*J.W.* 6.288-315). These prophetic figures risk a contrary word contestive of the status quo.

Prophetic movements also emerged around leaders with sizeable groups of followers who performed some sort of symbolic action, often based on the actions of Moses and Joshua, to declare divine deliverance from Rome.[59] Josephus' elite perspective disparages such figures. He identifies prophets—whom he regards as false—as 'villains' and as 'deceivers and imposters' in leading people into the desert to receive from God 'tokens of deliverance'. These 'madmen', however, received the sword from governor Felix's troops (52–60 CE; *J.W.* 2.258-60). A similar fate befell the 'Egyptian false prophet' and the 'thirty thousand dupes' (four thousand in Acts 21:38) he led against Jerusalem and the Roman garrison (*J.W.* 2.261-63; *Ant.* 20.169-70). Earlier, under the governor Fadus (44–45 CE), 'a certain imposter named Theudas' amassed people at the Jordan river and awaited its parting, while later under governor Festus (60–62 CE) a 'charlatan' and his followers awaiting deliverance into the wilderness found Festus' cavalry instead (*Ant.* 20.188). We cannot expect Josephus to have mentioned every such instance of these prophets claiming acts of divine deliverance. Nor does he mention the ripples of terror and resentment that emanated from each harsh military response to a prophet. However unreliable Josephus' numbers, these figures clearly indicate some significant social reach by these prophetic figures. They attracted sizeable followings and were certainly perceived by governors to pose some threat requiring vicious and swift military action. The governors gambled that severe military responses would kill more such rebels than harsh socio-economic conditions would breed them, even though these responses contributed to the indignities and anguish of local peoples whose households and villages were impacted. Horsley argues that participants were common people, a mixture of urban and rural, discontented with the status quo and under increasing economic pressure, questing for 'freedom' and a change in social and political conditions.[60]

Moreover there were also popular movements led by figures who presented themselves as popular kings mimicking and desiring the imperial power they were resisting. The sources, notably Josephus, indicate that such figures emerged at two moments of social upheaval in particular. After Herod's death in 4 BCE, the rural-based Judas, Simon, and Athronges appeared with their largely peasant followers who were facing economic difficulties and seeking relief from Herodian-Roman rule (*J.W.* 2.55-65; *Ant.* 17.271-84). In the 66–70 CE war, Menachem assumes a leadership role in Jerusalem 'like a veritable king' and with armed followers (*J.W.* 2.433-48). Subsequently Simon bar Giora

---

59. Horsley, 'Like One of the Prophets of Old'; Horsley, 'Popular Prophetic Movements'.

60. Horsley, 'Popular Prophetic Movements', 12-20.

exercised leadership in 68–70 CE in Jerusalem as a king (*J.W.* 7.26-36, 153–57). Also to be included is Jesus of Nazareth who is crucified around 30 CE as 'king of the Judeans' (Mark 15:18-20, 26). Since kingship was Rome's prerogative to grant, these figures committed a treasonous act for which retaliation was again swift and severe, and the ripples of fear and resentment considerable. Horsley argues that in addition to reflecting economic hardship, these movements indicate a 'religio-political consciousness' of a society of 'just social relations' under God's sanctioned or anointed leader.[61]

Further, the widespread presence of 'bandits' or 'brigands' who violently attack people and seize or destroy property also attests both popular dis-ease with Roman administration as well as economic injustices and exploitation.[62] According to Josephus, within twenty years of Pompey's imposition of Roman rule, Herod (as governor of Galilee) takes action against a 'large horde of bandits' (*J.W.* 1.204). As king, he takes further actions (*J.W.* 1.304). The kingly (rebel) figure Simon allies with brigands after Herod's death to attack elite property and houses before being killed (*J.W.* 2.57). Brigands largely disappear from Josephus' account of the period from Archelaus to Agrippa I (d. 44 CE). But thereafter, at least according to Josephus' narrative, they play an increasing role during the governorship of Cumanus (*J.W.* 2.228-29) and explode during the governorship of Felix in the 50s as 'the imposters and brigands, banding together, incited numbers to revolt...threatening to kill any who submitted to Roman domination...[and] they looted the houses of the wealthy, murdered their owners, and set the villages on fire... throughout all Judea' (*J.W.* 2.264-65). Felix crucifies an 'incalculable' number of brigands and their local supporters (*J.W.* 2.253), as does Festus (*J.W.* 2.271). Albinus (62–64 CE), though, takes a completely different approach, being susceptible to bribes (*J.W.* 2.273-76). Florus also becomes an active partner with brigands, collecting a share of their takings (*J.W.* 2.277-79). Josephus also calls the *Sicarii* brigands. These were dagger men who emerged in the 50s under Felix to assassinate leading Jewish figures who were allies of Roman rule (*J.W.* 2.254-57). They participated actively in the revolt (*J.W.* 2.425) as did various other 'brigands' (*J.W.* 2.441, 541, 587, 593).[63] Fanon's articulation of the experience of natives hemmed in by imperial power and absorbing its violence and indignities suggests that excitement, relief, and a sense of justice and revenge accompanied every bandit figure that

61. Horsley, 'Popular Messianic Movements', 494-95.
62. Horsley, 'Ancient Jewish Banditry'; Shaw, 'Tyrants, Bandits, and Kings'.
63. Horsley, 'Ancient Jewish Banditry', 426-32.

emerged. Imitating the violence of imperial power, they redeploy it as they resist it. Every death of a bandit or follower—and they were numerous judging from Josephus' account—meant that further ripples of terror and resentment spread through Judean/Israelite villages and households.

Horsley contextualizes this phenomenon of banditry in relation to the work of Eric Hobsbawm.[64] Social banditry, Hobsbawm argues, arises in agrarian societies where peasants are exploited by landowners, are economically vulnerable to taxes, rents, and debt, face an unstable social order, and experience an inadequate administration that creates a power vacuum. They gain support from local peasants who ally with bandits over a sense of justice and 'righting of wrongs'. The existence of widespread banditry attests such socio-economic conditions in Judea/Israel across the first centuries. I will examine economic conditions more specifically below.

There is, though, a further dimension of the phenomenon of banditry. Frantz Fanon observes that in an imperial situation 'the native is an oppressed person whose permanent dream is to become the persecutor'.[65] That is, as much as there might be dynamics of distancing and disavowal or disputing the presence and impact of imperial power, there are also dynamics of imitation and mimicry, of desiring to be the beneficiary of and agent of its power. Fanon recognizes the powerful draw of wanting to escape its oppressive realities in order to reverse the exercise of power. While banditry reflects social deprivation and vacuums of power, Fanon's insight suggests it also reflects and enacts the impact of marinating in a violent and exploitative system that hems in and confines the oppressed. Some dream of using the oppressor's methods of violence to redress their situation, of competing with other figures and groups to become precisely what they resist and hate.

Goodman claims that these attacks by brigands on other Judeans/Israelites 'should not suggest that Jerusalem in these years was really a haven of peace, only that the tensions…in general turn out…to have been largely internal to Jewish society rather than symptoms of widespread resentment of Roman rule'. He continues, 'the causes of such class resentment lay less in Roman rule than in the inequitable distribution of resources within what was essentially a prosperous society'.[66] A post-colonial optic highlights several problems with this claim and points to a

---

64. Horsley, 'Ancient Jewish Banditry', *passim*, esp. 411-12, 416-22. See also the helpful summary in Hanson and Oakman, *Palestine in the Time of Jesus*, 86-91.

65. Fanon, *Wretched*, 53.

66. Goodman, *Rome and Jerusalem*, 390.

much more complex situation. First, the hybrid nature of the colonized space does not allow for the neat binary of two separated entities named 'Jewish society' and 'Roman rule'. The two are entangled, hybridized, reciprocal. Second, the discussion above of Fanon's and Freire's notion of horizontal violence in imperial–colonial contexts exposes the limits of the claim that unrest is 'internal' with no connection to Roman rule. The presence of such violence has everything to do with Roman rule. It expresses, as Hobsbawm's analysis highlights, economic hardship resulting from the imperial economic system in which both Romans and elite Judeans/Israelites participated (see next section). The 'inequitable distribution of resources' was foundational to the imperial system and its elite provincial beneficiaries; a neat division of Jewish society from Roman rule in which 'class resentment' is expressed against the former but not the latter is simply not possible given the dynamics of imperial rule with local alliances. Moreover, banditry expresses the resentment that has been building in Fanon's native 'hemmed-in' by imperial controls, and mimics the violent domination that 'has been deposited in his own bones'. The subjugated yearn for such power while simultaneously and angrily resisting the power exercised by the imperializing power. And, fearful of direct and open confrontation with the vertical power of Rome and its local allies, the horizontal violence of banditry self-protectively avoids a direct confrontation because of the perception of the imperializer's overwhelming power advantage. Finally, in the next section I take up questions of economics. To anticipate the conclusion, claims that Judean/Israelite society was 'essentially a prosperous society' is a very misleading generalization for many in a highly stratified society.

V.

Economics

With Pompey's assertion of Roman power, Judea/Israel was incorporated in 63 BCE into the tributary economy of the empire. John Kautsky declares that 'to rule in aristocratic empires is, above all, to tax'.[67] Garnsey and Saller describe Rome's empire as comprising an 'under-developed pre-industrial economy' in which labor-intensive agriculture dominates, trade is important, and manufacturing is underinvested and technologically limited,[68] though more recent work disputes some of

67. Kautsky, *Politics of Aristocratic Empires*, 150.
68. Garnsey and Saller, *Roman Empire*, 43-103; Safrai, *Economy of Roman Palestine*.

these claims and posits the presence of a market economy.[69] Cities consume goods and food produced in surrounding areas and procured through trade. Provinces supplied Rome with funds and production especially of food. Massive disparities of wealth, power, and status were the norm.

As a primary means of effecting imperial domination, taxes and tribute extracted and moved resources from provinces to center, from non-elites to elites, from ruled to rulers, from colony to metropole. Yet in the reciprocal relationship of imperializer and colonized, taxes expressed not only Rome's domination but also Rome's dependence on provinces for supplies and wealth. Gerhard Lenski comments, 'the exercise of proprietary rights, through the collection of taxes, tribute money, rents, and services, undoubtedly provided the chief sources of income for most agrarian rulers'.[70]

The central question concerns the economic nature of this rule in Judea/Israel and the role of taxes and tribute in it. Were economic conditions in Judea/Israel from 67 BCE–135 CE harsh and oppressive?

One view rejects analyses that depict particularly harsh or oppressive economic circumstances. Fabian Udoh, for example, states that 'the arguments used to build an impression of continuous tax oppression and economic depravity in Palestine do not stand up to scrutiny. Palestine was not continually "oppressed" by three levels of ruinous taxes from 63 BCE until the Revolt of 66 CE.'[71] Richard Horsley argues, to the contrary, that

> intense economic pressure had been placed upon the Jewish peasantry for several decades by the multiple demands for tithes, taxes, and tribute... many were forced eventually to forfeit their lands. Many others came heavily onto debt... Heavy taxation compounded by the tendency of the wealthy to take advantage of marginalized peasant families and the predatory behavior of the ruling families brought intense economic pressures on the heretofore independent and free-holding peasantry.[72]

There are numerous difficulties in adjudicating this matter. Sources on economic conditions and practices are not especially prolific for the empire, and they are much more interested in elites than non-elites. The primary source for information on Judea/Israel, Josephus, is of course not disinterested in his presentation, written under the sponsorship of his Flavian patrons and with elite distance. Nevertheless we do know

69. Temin, *Roman Market Economy*.
70. Lenski, *Power and Privilege*, 217.
71. Udoh, *To Caesar*, 285.
72. Horsley, 'Popular Prophetic Movements', 19-20.

something about economic conditions from historical data and from social-science models of how agrarian empires work (such as those developed by Kautsky and Lenski).[73] Udoh complains about the relevance of social science models, but Lenski's model explicitly builds out of, among others, studies of the Roman Empire.[74] Models provide a helpful framework within which various data can be understood as part of a larger system. For example, imperial structures such as Rome's empire were very hierarchical, with a small percentage of the population both in the center and in the provinces exercising power and making decisions for their own benefit and largely at the expense of the rest, whose value largely consists of their contribution to the wealth, power, and status of elites. It is in the context of this system of power that economic questions must be addressed.

Most 'maps of wealth' for the empire recognize considerable disparities in levels of wealth with a very sizeable group of people who were poor. Steven Friesen suggests a seven-category scale in which those 'near', 'at', and 'below' subsistence levels comprise ninety percent of the population.[75] Peter Garnsey, to whose work on food access I will return below, remarks that in the Roman Empire 'for most people, life was a perpetual struggle for survival'.[76] Such studies suggest that a significant percentage of the population lived near or just above subsistence levels, with the likelihood that at some time through any given year they might spend some period of time under subsistence level.

Given this reality—which Udoh does not take seriously in his impressive and often insightful discussion of taxes and tribute—any levying of taxes and tribute, on which the whole imperial structure depended, will be experienced as harsh or oppressive because much of the population has little surplus and economic conditions are difficult even without taxes. In these circumstances, the levying of taxes and tribute adds to the indignities and resentments of the imperial–colonial experience.

The following discussion delineates some of the tax pressures experienced in Judea/Israel under Roman rule, and then recognizes several other factors contributing to an economically harsh environment for many in Judea/Israel across the two centuries of Roman control.

73. Kautsky, *Politics of Aristocratic Empires*; Lenski, *Power and Privilege*.

74. Udoh, *To Caesar*, 284.

75. Friesen, 'Poverty on Pauline Studies', 347; Scheidel and Friesen, 'Size of the Economy'. Also Whittaker, 'The Poor'; Atkins and Osborne, *Poverty in the Roman World*.

76. Garnsey, *Food and Society*, xi.

Judea/Israel became part of the Roman tributary system in 63 BCE when, according to Josephus, Pompey places 'the country and Jerusalem…under tribute' (*J.W.* 1.154; *Ant.* 14.74, 77-78, 202). Josephus is not clear about the amount of the tribute; the reference in *Ant.* 14.78 to 'ten thousand talents' is difficult to interpret.[77] In 47–44 BCE, Julius Caesar reorganized what seems to have been a somewhat chaotic situation. He continued the tribute for Judea/Israel and for Joppa, as well as the payment of tithes to priests (*Ant.* 14.202-6; 14.196). In 43 BCE, with the changing fortunes of power among Rome's elite 'great men', Cassius demanded seven hundred talents and took punitive action on towns and officials that were slow to pay (*J.W.* 1.220-22; *Ant.* 14.275-76). Such demands of course fall largely, though not exclusively, on small peasant farmers and their yields, causing hardship for villages and households.

The circumstances under the Herodians have been a particularly contentious issue as I have noted above. Three arguments are commonly made to suggest that Herod was an oppressive and destructive ruler, namely (1) the large size of Herod's 'annual total royal income' (960 talents according to *Ant.* 17.318-21 or 760 talents in *J.W.* 2.95-99); (2) the extensive nature of his building projects; and (3) Josephus' emphasis on negative responses to Herod including his having too much to do with Gentile cities and practices at the expense of Judean/Israelite cities. Udoh rejects all three arguments, arguing that determinations of Herod's income are fraught with difficulties, that he paid for much of his building activity out of his own funds, and that scholars have not taken sufficient account of Josephus' negative spin on Herod.[78]

While Udoh often argues convincingly and brings a commendable concern for what the sources do or do not tell us that functions as a necessary corrective to some excessive claims, the picture is not quite as rosy as he suggests. When he declares that 'Herod's kingdom was prosperous', he does not ask with a clear sense of the massive social inequities in the province where elites benefitted at the expense of non-elites, prosperous for whom? His assumption of trickle-down benefits needs to be demonstrated.[79] Goodman makes the same claim of an 'essentially prosperous society' but undercuts his claim by identifying in the very next sentence increasing debt among the poor![80] Friesen reminds us that 'the poor' comprise some ninety percent of the population, in

77.   Udoh, *To Caesar*, 27.
78.   Udoh , *To Caesar*, 180-206.
79.   Udoh, *To Caesar*, 286.
80.   Goodman, *Rome and Jerusalem*, 390.

varying gradations. When Udoh claims that Herod's 'extensive building program' and other projects are evidence of that prosperity, he forgets his own argument that Herod funded much of his building activity from his own fortune and that non-elites contributed to that fortune. The projects may provide evidence for Herod's wealth, but they do not attest a general prosperity. When Udoh argues that reports of complaints about Herod's taxation must be separated from claims that they attest 'excessive' taxation, he is correct—until one recognizes the general level of poverty that was the lot of most peasant farmers for which any demand was more than taxing. When he claims that Herod was not an economically harsh ruler because he twice reduced taxes—in the 20s BCE by a third (Josephus, *Ant.* 15.304) and again around the year 9 BCE by a quarter (*Ant.* 16.64-65)—he overlooks the thirty-one years (close to an average lifetime for some non-elites) in which there was no such relief and throughout which a peasant economy remained in place.

Udoh, though, is correct that the data about Herodian taxation are limited, not impartial, and not always clear.[81] Josephus, the leading source, is clearly no friend of Herod's and his emphasis on the burden of taxation needs to be construed, at least in part, in the context of that agenda (*Ant.* 17.191-92; 19.328-31). Arguments and conclusions about taxation remain somewhat tentative and need to be brought into conversation with other economic indicators as I will do below.

With Herod's kingship underway in 40/37 BCE, an annual tribute paid directly to Rome was removed—only to be replaced by annual tribute to Herod. The delegation to Augustus after Herod's death complains about the tribute, including the bribes that had to be paid to Herod's slaves who collected it (*Ant.* 17.308-309). Appian's reference has inaccuracies and vagueness, though it could well suggest some payment of tribute to Rome for some limited period of time (Appian, *Bell. Civ.* 5.75). Nevertheless, Herod was deeply indebted to his Roman masters for his power. He made numerous gifts of gratitude and payments that had to be paid for either from his extensive personal wealth[82] and/or by raising revenue from his subjects.[83] In addition, his extensive building projects

81. Udoh, *To Caesar*, 116, 200-204, notes that Josephus' bias is against Herod and the data cannot be accepted uncritically.

82. Udoh, *To Caesar*, 190-206 identifies four sources of Herod's personal wealth: family inheritance, Hasmonean estates, areas of his kingdom he exploited for his own gain, and money-lending ventures.

83. For example, Crassus had demanded 700 talents in 43 BCE, one hundred of which Herod raised from Galilee (*J.W.* 1.220-22). There was the bribe to be appointed king (*Ant.* 14.381), and the gift of 'a great sum of silver and gold' to Antony (which he acquired by despoiling the well-to-do) when Herod had secured

both within his territory and beyond it in numerous cities required funding (*Ant.* 16.136-49; *J.W.* 1.400-428).[84]

Where did he get the money? Not surprisingly, Josephus says several times that Herod runs out of money because of, for example, 'the lavish construction of cities' in the 20s and poor tax returns because of drought-induced low agricultural yields (*Ant.* 15.304). During the famine, he cuts up gold and silver ornaments to pay for grain for both his subjects and foreign cities (*Ant.* 15.306-16). He runs out again in 9 BCE but instead of increasing taxes he raids the tomb of David and takes gold and other valuable ornaments (*Ant.* 17.179-80).

Herod's tax base comprised agricultural products and land (*Ant.* 15.109). During the drought and famine of 25–24 BCE, Josephus comments that Herod was 'deprived of the revenue which he received from the products of the earth' (*Ant.* 15.303). So too, of course, was the population of Judea/Israel who had nowhere near the levels of protection Herod enjoyed. Josephus does not say, though, at what rate Herod taxed land production. He also gained revenue from indirect taxes (tolls and duties) on the production of cities like Jericho (exported balsam and dates) and on the abundant goods that moved along the trade-routes and through the ports of Gaza and Caesarea Maritima which he built in part to compensate for the inadequacies of Joppa's and Dora's ports (*Ant.* 16.331-34). He also applied a sales tax on his own subjects who, after his death, complained of its harshness and demanded Archelaus remove it, along with a reduction in other taxes (*Ant.* 17.204-205). The subsequent delegation to Augustus also complains about another source of revenue, namely forced 'lavish contributions' to Herod and his friends (*Ant.* 17.308-309). Josephus sounds this theme of the burdensome nature of Herod's taxes several times (*Ant.* 15.365 after poor crop yields; 17.308), including in his own evaluation of Herod's 'warring tendencies' and love for honor which 'caused him to be a source of harm to those from whom he took this money' (*Ant.* 16.154-56). The delegation to Augustus sums up the negative impact of Herod's 'spend-and-tax' ways: 'while he

control of Jerusalem in 37 BCE (*Ant.* 15.5; *J.W.* 1.358-59). Herod subsequently paid tribute to Cleopatra (*Ant.* 15.106). There were supplies of money and grain (*Ant.* 15.189) for Antony's war efforts at Actium, as well as auxiliary troops and corn (*J.W.* 1.388). Likewise, after Octavian's victory at Actium and confirmation of Herod as king, there were gifts and lodging for Octavian and his friends, gifts and provisions (especially wine and water) for his army, and a cash gift to Octavian of 800 talents (*Ant.* 15.196-200). He makes a later cash gift to Augustus of 300 talents (*Ant.* 16.128).

84. Roller, *The Building Program*; Richardson, *Herod*, 191-96; Rocca, *Herod's Judea*, 323-47.

crippled the towns in his own dominion, he embellished those of other nations, lavishing the life blood of Judea on foreign communities. In place of their ancient prosperity and ancestral laws, he had sunk the nation to poverty and the last degree of iniquity' (*J.W.* 2.85-86). Josephus similarly condemns Agrippa II for taking revenue from his subjects to use on foreign cities (*Ant.* 20.211-12). Udoh rightly points out the tendentious nature of Josephus' critique, but that recognition of Josephus' spin cannot hide the discontent over economic conditions that Josephus feels the need to spin, nor the fact that the handing over of products was a constant source of indignity and subjugation.

With the removal of Archelaus and the establishment of rule by governors came some changes in taxation. Now Judea/Israel paid tribute directly to Rome. The newly appointed governor of Syria, Quirinius, was sent to assess property in Judea/Israel as the basis for the tribute (*Ant.* 17.355; 18.1-2). The move of course was controversial. Opponents argued, at least according to Josephus, along more ideological than economic lines. They oppose it as 'slavery' (*Ant.* 18.4) and/or 'tolerating mortal masters, after having God for their lord' (*J.W.* 2.118). Josephus suggests that this rebellion 'made serious progress'. It would be foolhardy to think every supporter had only ideological and never economic concerns in mind. The high priest Joazar, an elite living a hybrid identity representing Judea/Israel's traditions while in cooperation with and dependent on Rome, intervened on the side of his imperial bosses to quell the unrest and persuade cooperation.

The tribute was levied on property though it is not clear whether both land and yield are in view, and whether it was levied on persons. In 40 CE, in the struggle with Gaius Caligula's command to put a statue in the Jerusalem temple, Jewish leaders tell Petronius (the legate of Syria) that 'since the land was unsown there would be a harvest of banditry, because the requirement of tribute could not be met' (*Ant.* 18.273-75). Will the tribute not be met because it comprises a percentage of crop yield, or because the sale of some yield means enough income to pay a cash tribute on land, or a combination of both? Tribute on at least production seems clear and is perhaps confirmed by Josephus' reference to 'stores of imperial corn' in Galilee (*Vita* 71). It has been commonly assumed that tribute also included a tax per person. But while there is clear evidence for a registration of property, Udoh argues well that it does not seem that tribute was levied per person until after 70 CE.[85] The collection of the tribute seems to have been the responsibility of the Jerusalem ruling elite as agents of Roman power (*J.W.* 2.404-407).

85. Udoh, *To Caesar*, 190-206, 208-18.

It is likely that Roman governors continued Herod's lucrative collection of indirect taxation comprising various tolls and duties. We get glimpses of a couple of such indirect taxes when Vitellius, governor of Syria, in 37 CE remitted taxes on sale of agricultural products in Jerusalem (*Ant.* 18.90), and Agrippa I in 39 CE remits tax on real estate in Jerusalem which had been levied by the Roman governor (*Ant.* 19.299). Such remittances, like Herod's reduction in taxation percentages, were probably temporary. How many other such taxes were in use and at what rate are not known.

After the fall of Jerusalem and its temple in 70 CE, all land in Judea/Israel came under Vespasian's ownership, who settled some veterans in a colony at Emmaus near the destroyed Jerusalem. The land was subject to tribute and presumably rent (*J.W.* 7.216-17). People were also now subject to tribute. Vespasian added to the tribute on property the punitive tax of two drachma on all Jews (*J.W.* 7.218; Dio Cassius 65.7.2; Matt. 17:24-27[86]). This tax coopted the former temple tax and made it payable to the temple of Jupiter Capitolinus in Rome. The tax had remunerative, punitive, and propaganda value in constructing Judean/Israelite identity as defeated, subjugated, and subject to the divinely sanctioned power of Rome's empire. The tax that had previously honored the Jewish God now provided a rebuilt temple in Rome for the triumphant Jupiter, patron of the Flavians. Subsequently, Domitian exempts Josephus' property in Judea/Israel from taxation (*Vita* 429 also 422, 425); most of course were not so well-connected. The depth of the indignity of this tax and its construction of Judean/Israelite identity as subjugated to the all-powerful Jupiter and the divinely sanctioned Roman troops are clear.

Another layer of taxation needs to be noted. Not only were taxes due to Herodians and Romans, but tithes and offerings were also paid, with Rome's permission, to the temple and priests pre-70 CE (Josephus, *J.W.* 6.335). A tax for the functioning of the temple was also paid by Jews in the diaspora and in Judea/Israel until 70 CE. Augustus' protection and legitimation for the tax suggests significant amounts sent to Jerusalem (Josephus, *Ant.* 16.162-65, 167-70; Philo, *Leg. ad Gaium* 156-57).

The Jerusalem temple and the priesthood were supported in part by tithes from the people. For example, Tobit 1:6-8 describes three tithes— the first for priests in Jerusalem comprising 'the first of the crops…the flock…the cattle, and the shearings of the sheep', and a tenth of 'the grain, wine, olive oil, pomegranates, figs, and the rest of the fruits to the sons of Levi' in Jerusalem; a second tenth for offerings and sacrifices in

86. Carter, *Matthew and Empire*, 130-44; Carter, 'Paying the Tax'.

the Jerusalem temple; and a third tenth for orphans, widows and converts. The first two tenths were paid annually; the third every three years. Josephus largely concurs with Tobit, describing a tithe for priests and levites, one for expenditures on feasts and sacrifices in Jerusalem (both paid annually for each of six years), and a third tithe every third year for widows and orphans (*Ant.* 4.4.68, 205, 240). The high priest oversaw the collection and storage of tithes for the needs of temple personnel. According to both Tobit and Josephus, farmers were paying twenty to thirty percent of yield to the Jerusalem temple and priests.

In terms of collection, it seems dubious that every person acted like Tobit and took their produce to Jerusalem each year. Such a journey would simply be beyond the economic and physical means of many peasant farmers. Certainly some centralized collection in Jerusalem for tithes was necessary to maintain the temple and the priests on duty (also Philo, *Spec.* 1.152). But since numerous priests were not on duty in Jerusalem, the local collection of tithes from their immediate vicinity makes sense. Josephus provides support for this notion, first in his comment that the priests Joazar and Judas (his fellow commanders in Galilee) gained much wealth 'from the tithes they accepted as their priestly due' (*Vita* 63), and second from his declaration that in Galilee he declined the tithes offered to him (*Vita* 80).

The mode of collection raises the interesting question of levels of participation in the payment of tithes. If some collection was local, local priests were no doubt active in their oversight. Concerning Jerusalem, Josephus indicates that around the time of the transition from governors Felix to Festus (ca. 59–60 CE), high priests shamelessly and brazenly sent slaves 'to the threshing floors to receive the tithes that were due to the priests with the result that the poorer priests starved to death' (*Ant.* 20.181, 206-207). Josephus seems concerned to highlight high priestly greed rather than the reluctance of people to pay tithes.

Our information on taxes and tributes is by no means complete. But the above material indicates a pervasive, though somewhat shifting, constellation of taxes, tributes, and tithes paid by inhabitants of Judea/Israel across the first centuries. Did these taxes constitute an oppressive situation of 'economic depravity' (to use Udoh's phrase)? Attempts to answer in terms of particular percentages (is fifteen percent fair whereas twenty-five to fifty percent is harsh?[87]) or in comparison to (limited) data from elsewhere in the empire (were practices relatively commensurable?)

---

87. Lenski, *Power and Privilege*, 228, for example, argues that governing classes received 25–50% of income in an agrarian empire.

miss a more fundamental point, namely that for many inhabitants of Judea/Israel, especially rural peasant farmers living near subsistence levels and struggling to maintain a sustainable level of food production and surplus for trade, any taxes were to some extent burdensome and oppressive. In addition, as James Scott highlights, taxes and tributes were one of the basic forms of indignities to which subjugated peoples were subjected, a very tangible display of their vulnerability to the damaging power of the empire and its local allies.

Other factors in addition to taxes suggest economic hardship for many. Martin Goodman has pointed to an increase in indebtedness among urban and rural non-elites.[88] He argues that Jerusalem elites (supporters of and allied with Rome) became increasingly wealthy as Jerusalem and its pilgrimage traffic expanded.[89] Those with wealth (priests, those with monopolies on supplying the temple, and those in service industries) displayed it in magnificent houses,[90] stored it in the temple (Josephus, *J.W.* 6.282), bought land, or made loans to urban and rural non-elites. Land was a central avenue of investment with most elites being large landowners whose estates were farmed by tenants. In addition they loaned cash, a practice made more lucrative with the introduction at least by the 50s CE of the *prosbul* that enabled repayment of the debt by the poor beyond the seven-year cycle. Goodman cites evidence for twenty percent interest rates after the fixed period of time for the loan.[91] One can imagine the growing resentment among the poor at this indignity as well as their economic losses and hardship.

Urban and rural non-elites borrowed for various reasons such as to buy increasingly expensive plots of land (because of limited supply) in order to make small farms viable, to buy seed or livestock, to pay rent and taxes when there was insufficient surplus, or for urban elites to sustain households during unemployment or underemployment, and to pay rent and taxes. If loans were not repaid, misery and economic hardship increased for peasants and artisans while elites gained more wealth. Property, especially land, was forfeited, and debtors and/or their family members became slaves if the loan was guaranteed by their person. Default on loans increased the number of landless peasants and day laborers congregating in a city like Jerusalem to look for work, as well as the indignities and shame of being forced from the land, and the insecurities of day laboring (cf. Matt. 20:1-16).

88.   Goodman, 'The First Jewish Revolt'.
89.   Goodman, *Ruling Class*, 51-75.
90.   Goodman, *Ruling Class*, 55.
91.   Goodman, 'The First Jewish Revolt', 421-23.

How much of a problem was indebtedness? Goodman notes that when urban non-elites (Josephus says eighteen thousand) became unemployed after temple construction was completed in 64 CE, there was considerable social tension. Agrippa undertook a paving project to provide some work (*Ant.* 20.220-22). In 66 CE as the war gets underway, non-elites attacked elite houses (the chief priest's house and the palace of Agrippa and Bernice) and burned the debt recording agency, according to Josephus, 'to prevent the recovery of debts, in order to win over a host of grateful debtors and to cause a rising of the poor against the rich' (*J.W.* 2.427-28). Goodman also posits a link between rural indebtedness and banditry with attacks against the wealthy (*J.W.* 2.264-65). This link between banditry and economic hardship is confirmed not only by the fact that Josephus makes the connection (*Ant.* 18.274), but also, as I observed above, by social-science models of banditry that recognize the key role of increased socio-economic pressures on peasants from ecological (drought, famine) and political-economic factors like indebtedness, taxation, and land confiscation.

Peter Garnsey's work on food access in the Roman Empire provides a further indication of the likely economic and social difficulties experienced by non-elites in Judea/Israel. While there is limited specific information for Judea/Israel, the work of Garnsey and others across the empire provides some general indicators of likely conditions.

Garnsey remarks that in the Roman Empire 'for most people, life was a perpetual struggle for survival'.[92] Economic activity based on land produced much of the empire's food, but its production, distribution, and consumption were shaped by and expressive of the fundamental values and inequities of the elite-controlled, hierarchical, exploitative political-economic system described above. Philostratus (*Vit Apoll.* 1.8) narrates the incident of empty markets in Aspendus because 'the rich had shut up all the grain and were holding it for export from the country'. Food, then, was about power, hierarchy, abundance for a few, and deprivation for many. Food practices reflected the fundamental injustices of the imperial system.

The 'Mediterranean diet' is, in theory, healthful. Staples such as cereals, olives, vine products (wine), and legumes (beans) supply energy, protein, vitamins B and E, calcium, and iron.[93] Yet numerous factors reduced the diet's actual healthfulness. The quantity and quality of

92. Garnsey, *Food and Society*. I follow Garnsey extensively in the following summary. See also Wilson, *For I Was Hungry*.

93. For discussion, Foxhall and Forbes, '*Sitometreia*'; Mattingly, 'First Fruit'; Purcell, 'Wine and Wealth'.

available food was subject to various factors such as weather and soil conditions (there were famines in Judea/Israel in the 20s BCE [*Ant.* 15.299-316] and 48 CE [*Ant.* 20.51-53]), affordability, variety of food, distribution and storage limitations, and geographical location. City dwellers (about 10 percent of the empire) largely depended on what was produced in the surrounding *chora* or *territorium*. Most had minimal resources to buy food; their diets were limited by high prices, low supply, and a limited range of goods. Peasants depended on their own production while also producing some surplus to trade for what they could not produce, to store against crop failures, and to pay rents and taxes. Garnsey also discusses 'Famine Foods' that peasants acquired from cultivated crops, gathering wild plants, and eating foods not normally eaten.[94]

One impact of the actual diet was malnutrition. Garnsey details its impact in terms of diseases of both deficiency and of infection. The former were evident in eye diseases and limb deformities (rickets). The latter lowered immunity to diseases such as malaria, diarrhea, and dysentery that spread because of high population densities in cities, inadequate sewage and garbage disposal, limited sanitation with restricted water supply, inadequate water distribution, and unhygienic storage. Poor nutrition with low calorific value means a diminished capacity for work, a serious challenge to earning capacity when much work comprised manual labor.

Garnsey's insightful discussion of food supply, diet, malnutrition, and diseases of deficiency and contagion nevertheless neglects a further consequence of such conditions under imperial power, the phenomena of psychosomatic illness and demonic possession. Numerous studies have noted the link between these phenomena and contexts of oppression.[95] Fanon's study of the impact of imperial power in Algeria's struggle with France, for example, describes the physical impact of colonial domination on terrified locals: 'his glance… shrivels me up…freezes me, and his voice…turns me into stone'.[96] Fanon describes symptoms of pains, menstruation disorders, and muscular rigidity and paralysis.[97] Reporting on Serbian imperialism in Kosovo in 1999, ABC News reporter Deborah Amos observed extensive paralysis and muteness in response to the

---

94. Garnsey, *Food and Society*, 34-42.

95. For the following, Fanon, *Wretched*; Hollenbach, 'Jesus, Demoniacs, and Public Authorities'; Crossan, *The Historical Jesus*, 313-53; Carter, *Matthew and the Margins*, 123-27.

96. Fanon, *Wretched*, 45.

97. Fanon, *Wretched*, 289-93.

trauma and violence, phenomena well attested in research on the effects of trauma.[98] These responses attest the ambivalence of the imperializer–colonized context. On one hand, they represent subduing power, but they are also coping mechanisms, even self-protective protest against imperial power, through inactivity and non-compliance. Fanon notes the schizophrenic or hybridized identity that forms in oppressed peoples who despise the exploitative power, have to cooperate with it to survive, and desire to be free from it, thereby acknowledging that it is desirable. 'The native is an oppressed person whose permanent dream is to become the persecutor'.[99]

Martin Goodman argues in his 1982 study for a growing gap and social tensions between the rich and poor across first-century Judea/Israel.[100] While not pretending to name the whole of the situation—rich *and* poor Judeans/Israelites revolt against Rome—it does name an important dynamic. Josephus observes 'those in power oppressing the masses, and the masses eager to destroy the powerful. There were those bent on tyranny, those on violence and plundering the property of the wealthy' (*J.W.* 7.260-61). The above discussion of taxes, tributes, tithes, peasant and artisan indebtedness, banditry, limited food access, diseases of deficiency and contagion, and psychosomatic conditions bears out the difficult economic conditions under which many lived during Roman rule.

VI.
Judean/Israelite Religion

Peter Brunt has argued that we should look to the peculiarity of Jewish religion to account for the revolt of 66–70 CE.[101] My concern here is broader than Brunt's quest for the cause or causes of that war, but his (generally unconvincing) argument raises the question of how to assess the roles of Judean/Israelite religion in the imperial–colonized experiences of the two centuries under discussion. My argument will be that the same complex and ambivalent dynamics are at work in Judean/Israelite religion as in the other spheres under consideration.

98. Amos, 'The Littlest Victims'.
99. Fanon, *Wretched*, 53; also Bhabha, *Location*, 'Of Mimicry'.
100. Goodman, 'The First Jewish Revolt'.
101. Brunt, 'Addenda', 527-28.

As I have noted above, with the exception of Gaius Caligula's actions around 40 CE, Rome did not, prior to the 66–70 CE war, attempt to disrupt Judean/Israelite religious practices based in the Jerusalem temple. After the war and the destruction of the temple, this situation of apparent Roman cooperation and tolerance changed significantly to be marked by explicit Roman control. No action was taken to rebuild it until 130 CE when Hadrian redeveloped Jerusalem as the colony Aelia Capitolina with a new central temple dedicated to Jupiter Capitolinus.

It would be mistaken, though, to think that the apparent laissez-faire stance that dominated much of the two centuries reflected Roman disinterest, or that it indicated a division between the political and the religious spheres as though they were unrelated spheres. As I have shown above in discussing Rome's metanarrative, religion and politics were interlapping spheres, and, as this section will suggest, often marked by the ambivalence of cooperation and contest, accommodation, and instability. Rome permitted this provincial Judean/Israelite temple system to function, the priesthood to exist, and the collection of sacrifices and tithes to proceed. But by *granting* or *permitting* such favors, Rome replaced the sanction of native traditions and practices with the permission of the imperializer that exercised a means of managing them for its own purposes. When the temple no longer served the interests of maintaining the Roman status quo and Judean/Israelite compliance, it was destroyed.

Josephus gives the victorious Titus a speech addressed to defeated Jews in 70 CE that elaborates this imperially permissive stance toward subjugated provincials and their religious practices.

> we allowed you to occupy this land and set over you kings of your own blood; then we maintained the laws of your forefathers and permitted you not only among yourselves but also in your dealings with others, to live as you willed; above all we permitted you to exact tribute for God and to collect offer-ings…only that you might grow richer at our expense and make preparations with our money to attack us! (*J.W.* 6.333-35)

The language is significant in its claims of Roman superiority and benign and generous permission that 'allowed' this cultural expression of Jewish identity. Titus' tone is of favor betrayed, of trust broken, of benevolence taken advantage of, of beneficence turned to treachery.

Yet there are important resonances and intertexts with authoritative Judean/Israelite traditions from the past that disclose the ambivalence of the imperialized–colonized situation and reframe Titus' claims about imperial rule. For Judean/Israelite ears, there could be nothing more false than Titus' claim, 'we allowed you to…' The traditions represented by the temple system declared God's sovereignty, 'The earth is the Lord's and the fullness thereof' (Ps. 24:1) or in Josephus' words, 'The universe is in God's hands' (*C.Ap.* 2.190). They similarly announced a covenant tradition which presented God, not the Romans, as giving this land to Judeans/Israelites (Exod. 3:7-8). Nor could there be anything more false than Titus' claim to have permitted kingship. He is of course speaking of the Herodians, but Judean/Israelite ears hear the traditions about God's choosing of David and the divine promise of his kingship that lasts forever, a tradition that shows Herod (Rome's puppet king) and now Titus to be imposters in this land (2 Sam. 7:11-16). Similarly, Titus' hubristic claim to allow 'the laws of your forefathers' to be observed flies in the face of the very covenant identity of this people committed to God's will revealed to them by Moses (Deuteronomy 27–30). Likewise, Titus' boast to have permitted tribute and offerings for God, a key part of temple practice, mistakenly claims superiority over traditions such as Deuteronomy 14:22-29, Leviticus 27:30-33, and Numbers 18:21-32 that authorized such gifts to be offered in worship. In the setting of Titus' speech in Josephus' narrative, legitimation for all of Titus' claims derives from divinely sanctioned military supremacy expressed in a defeated and destroyed city and temple.

But in a larger context, the speech highlights the clash of cultures and traditions and the resultant hybridized situation at the heart of the Roman–Judean/Israelite interaction. Imperial permission, sanctioned by a divine purpose, meets another mandate and identity sanctioned by another deity. Pre-70 CE, the temple, its practices, and its priests occupy this difficult contested, imperialized space, representing traditions asserting the superiority of Israel's God yet subjugated by a nation that gives no legitimacy to that God and overrides their traditional claims. The Jerusalem chief priests and priestly families have the ambivalent and fractured role of representing such traditions and practices in a context that not only betrays their claims but also embodies the occupiers' superiority in permitting them to do so. Yet the context of imperial permission is not the only word. The worship being conducted and the practices of bringing tithes and offerings to priests speak of another reality. They point to another order, another way of understanding and structuring the world, another set of priorities and commitments that destabilize claims of Rome's superiority and relocate it in submission to God's purposes. Rome, of course, permits such contestive commentary.

This ambivalence seems to be the resolution embraced by the priest Josephus. On one hand, God's favor has passed to the Roman Empire (*J.W.* 2.390; 3.351-54; 5.367). It has performed its punitive mission in punishing Israel and its unclean temple with the city's destruction and the temple's burning (*Ant.* 20.166, 218; *J.W.* 4.323). These events have taken place, for Josephus, according to the divine plan prophesied by Daniel in Daniel chapter 8 concerning the kingdoms of the Medes, the Persians, the Greeks, the Seleucid Antiochus Epiphanes, and the Romans (*Ant.* 10.272-81). These other kingdoms have passed and come to nought in God's purposes. Will it be likewise for Rome?

Some of this ambivalence can be traced out in actions involving the construction, personnel, vestments, and festivals associated with the temple.

The Jerusalem temple was the center of Judean/Israelite political religion. Herod's rebuilding of it highlights the complexities and instabilities of the imperialized situation. His activity is motivated, according to Josephus, variously by a desire for eternal remembrance (*Ant.* 15.381), by an 'act of piety to make full return to God for the gift of this kingdom' (*Ant.* 15.387), or by a desire for honors (*Ant.* 16.153), no doubt especially the good opinion of his Roman masters.[102]

McCane's analysis of the significance of the expansive Court of the Gentiles can be recalled.[103] As a meeting place of empire and temple, of the nations and Judea/Israel, it is a third place that expresses the ambivalence of the imperialized–colonized experience. It asserts and enhances local religion even while it denotes an openness to the nations. Herod gains honor even while his rebuilding mimics and promotes something of the cultural integration of the cosmopolitan empire. Josephus notes subsequently that the inner sanctuary was completed within eighteen months, provoking much celebration but also an opportunity for Herod's political glory: 'And it so happened that the day on which the work of the temple was completed coincided with that of the king's accession…and because of the double occasion the festival was a very glorious one indeed' (*Ant.* 15.423). Whatever his motivations, in addition to promoting his own political advantage, Herod financed a project (at least in the initial building; Josephus, *Ant.* 15.380; 17.162) that profoundly enhanced the appeal and reputation of Jerusalem to foreigners.

It also underscored the wealth of the temple, at least for those overseeing it. Josephus describes the incredible wealth of the physical building: the building, gates, and door were covered with gold, and it

102.   Richardson (*Herod*, 192-95) identifies a multivalent rationale for Herod's building activity: gratitude and honor; self-preservation; personal comfort; family piety; economic expansion; cultural integration; imperial piety; Jewish piety; and international reputation.

103.   McCane, 'Simply Irresistible', 732-33.

was decorated with a vine and grape-clusters made of gold, 'as tall as a man' (*J.W.* 5.207-11, 222-24). He also notes the huge amounts of wealth deposited within it over a long period of time (*Ant.* 14.110-11, 185-267; Bar. 1.10-14). Goodman outlines the pilgrimage economy that Herod promoted involving international visitors to the temple who required accommodation, food, and souvenirs, who delivered offerings from diaspora communities, and who spent their second tithe in Jerusalem.[104]

The nexus of religion and politics and the ambivalence of imperial center and provincial practice are evident in the appointment of chief priests to the oversight of the temple. The power to appoint chief priests—the twenty eight who held the office from Herod's time until 70 (*Ant.* 20.250)—resided not in genealogy as Josephus observes it did originally (*Ant.* 20.225-26), but in Rome's designated rulers, Herod (who appointed 'some insignificant persons', *Ant.* 20.247), Archelaus and the Roman governors (*Ant.* 20.250), and Agrippa II whom the emperor Claudius appointed as 'curator of the temple' (*Ant.* 20.222; cf., 203, 213, 223). Yet Josephus describes the chief priests as being, after the removal of Archelaus, 'entrusted with the leadership of the nation' (*Ant.* 20.251). They were, of course, not free agents and like Herod and Agrippa II and countless other provincial elites they occupied that liminal space of constantly negotiating the interface of tradition and occupier, of representing the nation's sacred traditions and claims, yet accountable to the interests of their imperializing patrons. In the reciprocity of imperializer–colonized interactions, imperial favor in granting the office is to be met with gratitude and loyalty. The question as to whether they were either collaborators or independent operators misses this ambivalence or hybrid location comprising multiple dimensions simultaneously.[105]

How do they negotiate these interfaces? Something of the complexities and ambivalences of negotiation emerge in the following six moments:

- When unrest grows because of the census of property to be assessed for tribute to Rome in 6 CE, the chief priest Joazar sides with Rome and against those opposed to tribute (*Ant.* 18.2-3) even though that opposition led by Judas the Galilean argued theologically that resistance to 'mortal masters' [Rome] was necessary 'after having God for their lord' (*J.W.* 2.118). In the eyes of the opponents of the census, Joazar sides with Rome

104. Goodman, 'The Pilgrimage Economy'.
105. Horsley, 'High Priests'.

rather than God. Yet, whatever his motivation—perhaps for pragmatic, survivalist reasons—his alliance with the Roman ruling power does not protect him. In a demonstration of agency in which subalterns speak by their actions, he is opposed and removed from office by popular pressure (*Ant.* 18.26).

- Josephus' two accounts of the murder of the chief priest Jonathan in the mid-50s CE vary considerably. The longer account in *Antiquities* presents this murder as the result of conflict between Roman governor and Jerusalem chief priest. In this account, it was the action of the Roman governor, the ex-slave Felix, who 'bore a grudge against Jonathan the high priest because of his frequent admonition to improve the administration of the affairs of Judaea'. The frequency of these admonitions arises from Jonathan's fear and self-interest that the crowd might censure him for asking Claudius to appoint Felix as governor! But Felix resents Jonathan's critique, for 'incessant rebukes are annoying to those who choose to do wrong', moralizes Josephus. With bribes, and despite having actively attacked brigands, Felix arranges to have brigands kill Jonathan using daggers concealed beneath their clothes (*Ant.* 20.161-66). Jonathan, in this account, dies because of his advocacy of the people's welfare. In the shorter account, he dies because he was regarded by the Sicarii as too much of a collaborator with Rome (*J.W.* 2.254-57). In this latter text, another native group takes agency against him.

- The Ananias–Albinus situation demonstrates the reciprocal relationship between colonizer and colonized in the form of the dependence of the former and the gain of the latter. The high priest Ananias supplied the governor Albinus (62–64 CE) with money and 'he daily paid court with gifts to Albinus' (*Ant.* 20.205).

- In the unstable mix of religion and politics, in 66 CE, Eleazar, the son of the chief priest Ananias and himself the 'captain of the temple', persuades priests to stop offering the daily sacrifices for the emperor (cf. *J.W.* 2.197). Josephus observes that 'this action laid the foundation of the war with the Romans', a theme that will repeat through the following scenes as 'the chief priests and the notables' seek to maintain the status quo by urging them to recommence offering the sacrifices but without success. Then the chief priests meet with 'the principal citizens' and 'the most notable Pharisees' and the people. Debate results, as well as armed fighting and 'slaughter', the burning of Ananias' house, and his escape with others to the palace of Herod (*J.W.* 2.409-29). The priests are shown to be divided over how to negotiate Roman power, whether by non-violent defiance or active cooperation. The division runs through the chief priestly family, separating son and father, Eleazar and Ananias. In the context of vertical imperial power, there is division, violence, and diversity on the periphery.

- Ananus, the (ex)[106] chief priest, sides with the rebellion. He is elected, along with Joseph, 'to the supreme control of affairs in the city' including raising the height of the walls (*J.W.* 2.563). Josephus describes him as being with others of the 'leading men (τῶν δυνατῶν) who were not pro-Romans' (*J.W.* 2.648). He is also strongly opposed to the 'domestic tyrants', the Zealots (*J.W.* 4.158-93, esp. 178), engages in battle with them, and is killed by the Zealot–Idumean alliance (*J.W.* 4.314-17). These internal divisions and horizontal violence reflect, as Fanon argues, the pressure of Roman rule. Josephus identifies Ananus' death as the beginning of 'the capture of the city…and the downfall of the Jewish state dated from the day on which the Jews beheld their high priest, the captain of their salvation, butchered in the heart of Jerusalem' (*J.W.* 2.318). Josephus' subsequent praise of Ananus presents him as primarily desiring peace with Rome yet, failing that, wishing to conduct effective military resistance (*J.W.* 2.319-25). Ananus embodies the ambivalences and ambiguities of a local priestly elite negotiating Roman pressure and his own people's resistance.

- When the temple is taken in 70 CE, and before the city is destroyed, the Romans 'carried their standards into the temple court and…sacrificed to them, and with rousing acclamations hailed Titus as imperator'. Some priests in the temple begged Titus for their lives but he rejected their plea saying that 'it behoved priests to perish with their temple, and so ordered them to execution' (*J.W.* 6.316-22). Religious duty and service are political statements, as is their execution.

The ambivalence of the priests' location and temple's existence in the imperial–provincial nexus is resolved by Rome's destruction of the temple.

106.   He had been chief priest for three months in 62 CE when Agrippa II deposed him for the death of James by stoning (Josephus, *Ant.* 20.197-203).

The tensive relationship between Rome and the temple is also seen in the struggle over the high priestly garments. Josephus explains that Herod and Archelaus had kept the high priestly garments in the Antonia fortress because it was customary to do so. From 6 CE, the Romans continued to store them there, releasing them to the chief priest seven days before a festival and receiving them back immediately after the festival. That is, the control of the garments, symbolizing local leadership, traditions, and power, enacted the same dynamic of the granting of imperial 'permission' to allow a native tradition of subordinated provincials that Titus articulates at the fall of Jerusalem (*J.W.* 6.333-35). Interestingly, in response to a warm reception in Jerusalem, Vitellius, governor of Syria, arranges to restore the garments to Judean/Israelite control. That is, Vitellius is assured of the provincials' compliance so in 'return for their kindness', he meets their request in 36 CE, thereby continuing the same permissive power dynamic (*Ant.* 18.90-95; 15.403-405). Governor Fadus (42–44 CE), however, 'ordered the Jews to deposit the robe in Antonia for…the Romans ought to be masters of it, just as they had been before'. The 'oughtness' that Fadus claims again asserts control by reminding the priests that they carry out their duties in the ambivalent place between their own religious traditions and by Rome's permission and under Rome's watchful eye. The subsequent petition to the emperor Claudius for Judean/Israelite control is granted in 45 CE (*Ant.* 15.407; 20.10-14). Apparently, the provincials have shown themselves to be appropriately compliant and are rewarded with permission to supervise their own garments. As part of the hybridity of being colonized subjects yet Roman allies, the chief priests are *permitted* to carry out their roles.

Festivals centered on the Jerusalem temple reflect the same ambivalence. They offered an opportunity to draw from the past in order to assert Judean/Israelite identity in the midst of Roman control but thereby they also created the potential to disrupt imperial power. Josephus himself emphasizes the link between festivals and revolts, noting that 'it is on these festive occasions that sedition is most apt to break out' (*J.W.* 1.88). The elite person Josephus fears the gathering of unruly crowds, but it is to be noted that more than opportunities for violence, festivals were also occasions in which the traditions and memories that defined Judeans/Israelites as a people free from Roman or any imperial power were publically performed. It is not surprising, then, that festivals were also occasions for intimidating displays of Roman military power in Jerusalem (*J.W.* 5.244; also 2.224; *Ant.* 20.106). The display of troops in such a context embodies an ideology and practice of terror.

Josephus attests the following instances of open conflict at festivals. It seems reasonable to assume that if violence fractures the imperial interface in these instances, the same dynamics of power asserted, disputed, and deflected, permeated every festival observance, even when not expressed in violence. When violence was deployed, such experiences of terror, violence, death, and of collision of cultural traditions caused ripples of indignity and resentment.

- Passover, 4 BCE: violent protests against and clashes with Archelaus break out after Herod's death and the deaths of the teachers which Herod ordered; 'three thousand' are killed and Archelaus shuts down the festival (*J.W.* 2.4-13; *Ant.* 17.213-18).

- Pentecost, 4 BCE: 'indignation' against and major fighting with Sabinus the Roman military officer left by the governor of Syria to establish order in Archelaus' absence takes place (*J.W.* 2.39-75; *Ant.* 17.254-98).

- Passover, during Cumanus' governorship, 48–52 CE: a lewd gesture by a soldier provokes widespread violent unrest (*J.W.* 2.224-27; *Ant.* 20.105-12).

- An unnamed festival (Passover?) is abandoned in 51–52 CE in order to take revenge after an outbreak of horizontal violence. Some Samaritans murder some Galileans traveling to the festival. Further 'robbery, raids, and insurrections' follow as Rome tries to establish order (*J.W.* 2.232-46).

- At festivals during the 50s CE, the Sicarii assassinate key figures beginning with the high priest Jonathan (*J.W.* 2.254-57; *Ant.* 20.161-66).

- Festival of Tabernacles, 62 CE: Jesus son of Ananias begins seven years of announcing woes against Jerusalem and the temple (*J.W.* 6.300-309).

- Passover, ca. 65 CE: verbal complaints are made to Cestius Gallus, governor of Syria, against the governor Florus (*J.W.* 2.280-83).

- Festival of wood-carrying, 66 CE: Sicarii and others take over the upper city and (perhaps appropriately given the festival) burn the Record Office containing money-lenders' bonds (*J.W.* 2.425-29).

- Festival of Tabernacles, 66 CE: the festival is abandoned as the Roman governor of Syria, Cestius Gallus, threatens Jerusalem with troops (*J.W.* 2.517-22).

- Passover 66–68 CE(?): Sicarii based at Masada attack surrounding villages causing other bandit attacks throughout Judea/Israel (*J.W.* 4.398-409).
- Passover, 66–69 CE (?): the war envelops those in Jerusalem for Passover (*J.W.* 6.420-29).

Just as Judeans/Israelites saw festivals as an opportunity to contest power, Josephus notes Rome's use of festival occasions as moments to assert control. Governors stationed troops in the city and deployed them strategically in the temple area during festivals: 'for a Roman cohort was permanently quartered there (the Antonia fortress), and at the festivals took up positions in arms around the porticoes to watch the people and repress any insurrectionary movements' (*J.W.* 5.244; also 2.224; *Ant.* 20.106). That is, the stationing of troops recognizes, as much as it contributes to, a contestive situation with its impact of terrifying presence.

These fears of and precautions against insurrections belong to elite suspicions about non-elite urban and rural mobs. Josephus makes no attempt to hide his own animosity toward non-elite crowds (*Ant.* 4.37). They also express common imperial tactics to control gatherings of local subjects by military intimidation. Further, military preparations suggest a recognition that festivals were carriers of subversive traditions, little traditions, that were contestive and potentially disruptive. Festivals were occasions on which Judea/Israel's metanarrative of divine sovereignty and acts of liberation was remembered, and national identity as a covenant people was secured. For some, former divine actions were celebrated without any mandate to disrupt the present. But for others, celebrations of former acts interpreted the status quo and mandated contemporary actions intended to accomplish the same ends, namely deliverance from foreign enslavement and restoration of the land. The local people's metanarrative can be contestive and disruptive of imperial power.

Josephus declares at the outset of *Jewish War* that he will speak about festivals (1.26). He speaks in *Antiquities* of three pilgrimage festivals in Jerusalem held 'to render thanks to God for benefits received, to intercede for future mercies, and to promote…feelings of mutual affection' (4.203). All three festivals, namely Passover, Pentecost, and Sukkoth (Tabernacles/Booths), turned attention to the past to emphasize the people's identity in relation to God's purposes and covenant. The 'benefits received' focused on deliverance from Egypt (Passover, *J.W.* 4.402; cf. *Ant.* 17.213-14), the production of the land (Pentecost, *Ant.* 3.252-57), and the gift of Torah to shape the people's way of life (Tabernacles) where the reading of Torah played a prominent part

(*Ant.* 4.209-11; 8.100-105; 11.154-58). These benefits readily shape an 'intercession for future mercies' that is quite subversive of the status quo where political, economic, and cultural control lies in Rome's hands, and where at least some seek deliverance from the current slavery to Rome (so Agrippa, *J.W.* 2.356-57), the restoration of land and its production, and the embracing of covenant identity in a way of life obedient to Torah unencumbered by foreign presence and control.

Josephus indicates that other festivals also contribute to this metanarrative of covenant identity and carry the potential to inspire open attacks on the status quo or nourish hopes for divine intervention and transformation. The festival of wood-carrying (*J.W.* 2.425), understood pragmatically to ensure 'an unfailing supply of fuel for the (temple's) flames', becomes in 66 CE, for those restless with Rome's control, the occasion for burning the house of the high priest, the palaces of Agrippa and Bernice, and the Record Office, thereby destroying the money-lenders' bonds and preventing 'the recovery of debt'. Such a gesture is a significant strike against priestly elite, religio-political, and economic domination of which the temple economy was a primary instrument.

Josephus also notes that 'from that time to the present we observe this festival, which we call the festival of Lights' (Hanukah, *Ant.* 12.325). Again this festival, evoking the Maccabean victory over Antiochus Epiphanes, carries a subversive script, pointing to deliverance from a foreign power, to the re-establishment of the temple worship, and to faithfulness to the covenant stipulations. Josephus praises Judas Maccabeus for having 'freed his nation and rescued them from slavery to the Macedonians' (*Ant.* 12.434). These are subversive scripts in any context of domination for some, though not all, residents. To deter and control 'the some', Rome stationed troops in Jerusalem 'to watch the people and repress any insurrectionary movements' (*J.W.* 5.244; also 2.224; *Ant.* 20.106). The strategy assumes that Rome can contain or even destroy the Israelite/Judean metanarrative of an alternative identity and longing for liberty that the observance of festivals evokes and secures, even as Rome in this hybrid location enables them.

VII.
Material Culture

The discussion thus far has identified political, economic, social, and religious/ideological means by which Roman imperial power was asserted and engaged in Judea/Israel. In these arenas, the ambivalent situation and hybrid identities of the imperialized–colonized situation are experienced. It has also noted from both colonizers and colonized outbursts of violent confrontation, self-protective ambiguous acts, and constant sources of terror, indignities, and resentments that rippled through Judean/Israelite society. This section will briefly highlight material cultural expressions that also exhibited Rome's metanarrative, notably buildings and coins. Ramsay MacMullen has argued that Romanization worked both to push and to pull people into the orb of Roman power, compelling and attracting people by its benefits. Material benefits or culture could function as one of the means of 'pulling' people into positive interaction because benefits like baths and wine 'felt or looked good'.[107]

The extensive building program of the local, Rome-appointed king Herod has been well documented. Peter Richardson has classified Herod's material benefactions, both within and outside Judea/Israel, into five categories:[108]

- *Major Projects*: including new cities such as Caesarea Maritima and Sebaste;

- *Fortress and Palaces*: the former included Massada and the Antonia fortress, walls for Jerusalem, towers. Palaces included the Winter Palace at Jericho and at Herodium near Bethlehem.

- *Religious Buildings*: the Jerusalem temple was the center piece of his Jewish piety. But as discussed above, he also built three temples for the imperial cult of Augustus and Roma, at Caesarea Maritima, Sebaste, and Panias. Richardson comments, 'the Augustan age required 'piety' toward Augustus, and Judea must participate to attain its proper place'.[109]

- *Commercial Construction and Infrastructure*: these projects include the harbor at Caesarea Maritima, with its facilities like warehouses for trade, and several manufacturing sites, as well as roads, sewers, reservoirs, and aqueducts.

- Richardson's fifth category concerns *cultural buildings* such as theaters, hippodromes, stadia, amphitheaters, baths, and gymnasia, the common trappings of Hellenistic and Roman culture. Josephus has Herod building a theater, hippodrome, and amphitheater in Jerusalem, Herodium, Jericho, and Caesarea Maritima. Richardson notes that Herod mostly locates these

---

107.   MacMullen, *Romanization*, 134.
108.   Richardson, *Herod*, 174-202.
109.   Richardson, *Herod*, 194.

facilities away from areas where they might cause religious offense. But they also express the hybridity of Herod's commitment to 'encourage Roman culture' and foster Judea/Israel's cultural integration with the new age of Roman power.

This commitment meant that Herod included Hellenistic-Roman features in his building projects in Jerusalem as reminders of his Roman patrons and as expressions of the desire for:

> cultural integration: the Temple in Jerusalem included Roman features (the Royal Basilica, the stoas); many buildings incorporated Roman decorative elements (Corinthian and Doric columns, Pompeian interior decoration); and urban design elements reflected late Hellenistic civic patterns (Hippodamian plans, agoras). Herod minimized offensive elements, but he was a good Roman and a 'Hellenist'.[110]

Josephus refers to other material signs of Roman presence including a hippodrome at Taricheae, (*J.W.* 2.599) and hot baths at Tiberias (*J.W.* 2.614). Governor Pilate builds an aqueduct using money from the temple (*Ant.* 18.60). Josephus has Agrippa I fortifying the walls of Jerusalem though he desists when Claudius rebukes him for doing so (*Ant.* 19.326-27). Josephus extols Agrippa's generosity (more so than Herod's; *Ant.* 19.328-31) and says he 'erected many buildings in many other places' and gives examples from Berytus that include a theater, amphitheater, baths, porticoes, and entertainments (*Ant.* 19.335-37). Agrippa II also built a theater and funded entertainments in Berytus though his own subjects resented it. He also enlarged Caesarea Maritima and renamed it Neronias 'in honor of Nero' (*Ant.* 20.211-12). Such buildings express the 'pull' of Roman power functioning as visual displays of the civilizing and seductive benefits of Roman rule.

Coins also provided material presentations of the ambivalence of the imperialized–colonized interplay. On one hand, they proclaimed Roman dominance by carrying the message of Roman presence and global rule. For Judean/Israelites, there was no escaping this propaganda and reality as it pervaded daily life. The common silver denarius that was widely used in everyday life bore images of emperors such as Augustus and Tiberius.[111] As I will note momentarily, coins also provided an opportunity to display Roman generosity and sensitivity to Judean/Israelite identity. Moreover, they offered client-kings like Herod a space in which to honor his Roman patrons as well as present himself as a faithful Judean/Israelite king.

110.   Richardson, *Herod*, 194.
111.   Burrows, 'Significant Recent Finds'.

Herod's coins, issued only in bronze, reflected the ambivalence resulting from the change from what was 'an independent Jewish state to a Roman client-kingdom'.[112] He employed inscriptions in Greek, and symbols that were more international. Herod's coins, at least initially, reflected his double audience and expressed his hybrid location and identity as both Roman client-king and king of the Jews. For example,[113] among his early coins, one coin on the obverse has symbols of the worship of Apollo along with his title, 'King Herod', but on the reverse a censer from the Jerusalem temple. Another has on the obverse a winged caduceus (the staff of Hermes the messenger of the gods) yet on the reverse a Jewish symbol, the pomegranate, or a poppy head. Another shows on the obverse the curved stem of a ship, and on the reverse a palm branch associated with the feast of tabernacles. He did not, though, seem to sustain this hybridity, with Roman symbols tending to dominate subsequently: a military shield (#4902),[114] caduceus (#4903, #4910), anchor (#4908, #4910, #4911). One coin also features an eagle (#4909), which created perhaps a defiant intertextuality with the incident late in Herod's life of the tearing down of the eagle image which he had placed on the great gate to the temple.

Herod's son Archelaus continued the same Roman images: cornucopia or horns of abundance (#4912, 4914, 4915), anchor (#4912, 4913), a war galley or prow (#4914, 4915, 4916), the caduceus (#4917), and helmet (#4917). Agrippa I (ruled Judea 41–44 CE) declared his identity as Roman client-king with images of Caligula (#4973, 4976), Claudius being crowned by Agrippa (#4982), Claudius and Agrippa with a temple (#4983), and, in a show of independence, Agrippa himself (#4974, 4978, 4985). Inscriptions declared him to be 'King Agrippa' or 'The Great King Agrippa, Friend of the Emperor'. Agrippa II included images of Nero as well as of himself. Under the Flavians, his coins featured images of the emperors and a goddess like Tyche/Fortuna and Nike/Victoria. Coins issued through the century from Caesarea Maritima not surprisingly feature images of Emperors Claudius (#4858, 4859), Nero (#4860, 4861), and Domitian (#2231).[115]

112.   Kanael, 'Ancient Jewish Coins', 48; also Hendin, *Guide to Ancient Jewish Coins*; Meyshan, 'The Symbols on the Coinage'.

113.   I follow Kanael, 'Ancient Jewish Coins', 48-49.

114.   Numbers throughout this section refer to entries in the catalogue of Burnett, Amandry, and Ripollès. *Roman Provincial Coinage. Vol 1: 1-2.*; and Burnett, Amandry, and Carradice. *Roman Provincial Coinage. Vol 2: 1-2.*

115.   DeRose Evans, 'Ancient Coins'.

The coins issued by the governors generally avoided images of emperors, divine figures, or religious symbols, preferring various plant representations (ear of barley, palm tree, vines, and wreaths; #4954, 4958, 4959, 4961-64). Some included the names of emperors using variously Caesar, Tiberius, and Nero (#4958, 4960, 4962, 4964, 4972).

Some gubernatorial coins pushed a Roman agenda more aggressively. There is an instance of a caduceus (#4960). Felix struck a coin, naming Nero, with two shields and crossed spears on the obverse but, in a sign of sensitivity, without the usual legionary standard (#4971). The reverse features palm tree and fruit. Governor Pontius Pilate represented a significant departure by including Roman religious symbols such as the *lituus*, a crook shaped staff used by augers for divination (#4967), and the *simpulum*, used as a ceremonial ladle or pouring vessel (#4968, 4969).[116] His coins also explicitly named the emperor Tiberius.

The most aggressively propagandist imperial coins were the *Judea Capta* coins issued after the defeat of 70 CE.[117] These coins issued both throughout the empire and in Judea/Israel openly proclaimed the Roman, particularly Flavian, victory over the province. The coins functioned as legitimation for the Flavians as successful military exponents of Roman rule, but also as instruments of terror for local people by coercing compliance under the threat of repeat military action. They presented on the obverse the head of Vespasian or Titus (#2310-2313). On the reverse, scenes featured Victory/Nike with a foot on a helmet usually with a shield and palm tree, and, in at least one type, a captive with arms tied (#2313). The palm tree represented the exotic East in general and Judea/Israel in particular. It also carries connotations of abundance and fertility now in the service of Roman power. The people and land are represented, as in the Sebasteion panels from Aphrodisias, by a woman on her knees with hands tied. The female body presents Judea/Israel as weak, subjugated, inferior, and humiliated by manly, superior, conquering Roman power. Rome is dominant and masculine, Judea/Israel is pacified and feminized. The gendering and militarizing of the power dynamics of the imperializing–imperialized interaction is clear as is its agenda to legitimate Flavian rule and intimidate local peoples.

Of course, the propaganda game can be played two ways with coins. The colonized can mimic and adapt the techniques used by the colonizer to their own advantage. During the 66–70 CE war, Judeans/Israelites minted their own coins, thereby announcing their rejection of Roman

116.   Taylor, 'Pontius Pilate'.
117.   Zarrow, 'Imposing Romanization', with bibliography; Cody, 'Conquerors and Conquered'.

rule.[118] The minting of coins was an act of defiance in itself since Rome controlled the issue of coins. The coins themselves presented fundamental commitments of the revolt in proclaiming 'freedom', 'holiness', and asserting its traditional identity of 'Zion'. These 'freedom' coins were made in silver or bronze. The silver coins announced their weight ('shekel of Israel', half-shekel), the year numbered from 1–5 corresponding to 66–70 CE, and in Hebrew (not Greek or Latin) 'Jerusalem the Holy'. The obverse displayed a chalice, a vessel from the Jerusalem temple, and the reverse three pomegranates that reflect the priestly authority by which the coins were minted (cf. Exod. 28:33-34). Years two and three of the bronze coins declared 'Freedom of Zion' and the fourth-year coin, 'to the redemption of Zion'.

In 132–35 CE, a further revolt broke out in response to Hadrian's scheme to re-found Jerusalem as the Roman colony Aelia Capitolina with a temple dedicated to Jupiter Capitolina.[119] Led by Shimon Bar-Kokhba, the revolutionary government minted silver coins, overstriking existing Roman tetradrachms and denarii. In this instance, the colonized (over)strike back. The coins issued over three-and-a-half years starting in year one, 132 CE, show considerable variety with five denominations and diverse emblems and legends. Fundamental to their agenda was a turning to the past, in fact an idealization of the past, with a yearning to reestablish the temple. The temple is presented as an idealized form of national identity. Emblems include the Jerusalem temple, musical instruments used in temple worship such as the lyre, kithara, and trumpets, sacred vessels such as amphora, and fruit and branches (*lulav* and *etrog*) used in the festival of Sukkoth/Tabernacles. This concentration of emblems concerned with the temple, along with the name 'El'azar the priest', as well as legends such as 'of the redemption of Israel' and 'of the freedom of Israel' and 'for the freedom of Jerusalem', indicate that the restoration of the Jerusalem temple as a place of worship, as the capital of the nation of Israel, and as a symbol of independent nationhood was a foundational goal for the revolt. It was over sixty years since the temple had been burned in 70 CE, but as commonly happens in imperial–colonial interactions, the memory of the past becomes a powerful source of identity and motivation for oppressed

118.   Kanael, 'Ancient Jewish Coins', 57-59; Meshorer, *Jewish Coins*, 88-91, 154-58; Kadman, *The Coins of the Jewish War*; Goodman, 'Coinage and Identity'. For good images and some discussion, see Brenner, 'Spending Your Way', 50-51; Deutsch, 'Roman Coins'.

119.   Kanael, 'Ancient Jewish Coins', 59-62; Meshorer, *Jewish Coins*, 92-101, 159-69; Kindler, 'The Coinage of the Bar-Kokhba War'.

peoples in the present. In similar vein, the prominence of the name 'Jerusalem' or 'for the freedom of Jerusalem' on more than half the coins recalled this past of peoplehood. It also recalled slogans from the 66–70 CE revolt and reasserted independence and this remembered identity in the face of Rome's new name Aelia Capitolina which expressed subjugation and Roman denial of that past.

VIII.
Decolonizing the Mind

In this final section, I briefly discuss four texts produced across the 63 BCE–135 CE time period of Judea/Israel under Roman rule to examine their negotiation of Roman power. Seth Schwartz has correctly pointed out the limited levels of literacy during this period.[120] Schwartz is not alone in proposing a figure of under ten percent literacy. These texts clearly originate with elite authors but as locals who under imperial power 'write back' to the empire to express something of the ambivalence of the experience of the assertion of imperial power. The four texts are chosen because of their origin at different points across the two-hundred-year period under discussion. They decolonize the minds of colonized Judeans/Israelites by asserting Judean/Israelite identity informed by Judean/Israelite traditions, by fantasizing about Rome's demise, and by imagining a world without Roman power.

Psalms of Solomon

This collection of eighteen writings probably dates from around the time of the beginning of Herod's reign as Rome's client-king. *Psalms of Solomon* 1, 2, 8, and 17 especially seem to engage Pompey's assertion of Roman power in Jerusalem in 63 BCE.

- *Psalms of Solomon* 8:1-22 describes Pompey's entrance into Jerusalem unopposed and welcomed by Hyrcanus II (8:15-19). Aristobulus II's supporters barricaded themselves in the temple, to which Pompey responded with a siege for three months before entering the sanctuary and killing priests offering sacrifices (8:20). He exiled Aristobulus and his supporters to Rome where many were paraded in Pompey's triumph (*Ps. Sol.* 8:21-22).

120. Schwartz, *Imperialism*, 10-11.

- *Psalms of Solomon* 2:1-2 refers to part of Pompey's capture of Jerusalem, namely his use of a battering ram to break down walls around the temple and his entrance into the sanctuary. Verse 19 refers to the Roman ('Gentiles') capture of Jerusalem.

- *Psalms of Solomon* 2:26-30 makes celebratory reference to the death of Pompey in 48 BCE.

- *Psalms of Solomon* 17:7-12 also refers to various aspects of Pompey's attack on the temple (17:11) and his exiling of Aristobulus (17:12).

Rodney Werline notes that *Psalms of Solomon* 17 also seems to show signs of redaction with the referent moving from Pompey to Herod.[121] Verse 9b's reference to the end of the Hasmoneans more accurately reflects Herod's elimination of them, and verse 14's reference to doing in Jerusalem what Gentiles do probably fits Herod's reign better than Pompey's in expressing disapproval for Herod's receptiveness to and advocacy of Roman culture. And the reference to a famine in 17:18b-19a is also more accurate for Herod's taking of the city in 40–37 BCE than for Pompey.

These Psalms probably come from Jerusalem, perhaps from a group of scribes.[122] They engage these contemporary events from the perspective of Israel's covenant identity and relationship with God. Their analysis of Pompey's actions and their aftermath is very bleak. They are surprised and deeply perturbed by the Roman invasion and occupation of Jerusalem and the land in 63 BCE, as well as by the divisions and corruption among the Judean/Israelite leadership, presumably their verdict on accommodating and receptive alliances with the Romans. The opening of *Psalms of Solomon* 1:1-3 (as well as 8:1-6) expresses terror and surprise: 'Suddenly, the clamor of war was heard'. The Psalms strongly condemn the Romans under Pompey Magnus for desecrating the city and temple in 63 BCE:

> Gentile foreigners went up to your place of sacrifice:
> They arrogantly trampled it with their sandals...
> For the Gentiles insulted Jerusalem, trampling it down. (*Ps. Sol.* 2:2, 19a)

While 'the [Jerusalem] leaders' welcomed Pompey 'with joy' (8:16), the Psalmist recoils from his violent and arrogant ways. He wrestles with explaining why this dreadful situation came about. Why did God not

---

121. Werline, 'The *Psalms of Solomon*', 71; see also Atkinson, *I Cried to the Lord*; Horsley, *Revolt*, 143-57.
122. Werline, 'The *Psalms of Solomon*', 82; Horsley, *Revolt*, 144-47.

protect the land, city, and temple? The Psalmist's explanation is that God was punishing Israel for numerous sins. That is, it employs Deuteronomic theology whereby obedience is met by divine blessing but disobedience by divine punishment in the form of disastrous national events. The 'disobedience' or 'sins' for which they are being punished (2:7-8) focus on the actions of the Hasmoneans. They expanded militarily (1:4). They exalted themselves (1:5). They profaned the temple (1:8). 'They defiled Jerusalem and the things that had been consecrated to the name of God' (8:22; also 8:9-13 using stock polemical accusations). They are also illegitimate kings, though Herod may also be in view if the Psalms were written around the beginning of his reign. 'By force' and

> [w]ith pomp they set up a monarchy because of their arrogance
> They despoiled the throne of David with arrogant shouting. (*Ps. Sol.* 17:6)

The Psalmist looks to the past. Only a return to the ancient line of David provides legitimate kings. It is no accident or surprise that the collection is called *Psalms of Solomon* after David's son.

Because of these terrible violations of God's will, so the Psalms of Solomon insist, Pompey, 'a man alien to our race', carried out God's purposes of overthrowing and punishing their sinful actions (17:7-10). Pompey, of course, did not know he was carrying out God's purposes, and he certainly did not see himself as an agent or puppet of God's punishment! It is the perspective of these Psalms and the group from which they originate. This presentation draws on a common motif of the foreign king who is the unwitting agent of God's wrath: the king of Assyria (Isa. 10:5), king of Babylon (Isaiah 14), king of Tyre (Ezekiel 28), Pharaoh (Ezekiel 31–32), and Antiochus IV Epiphanes (Dan. 11:40-45).[123] The Psalms thus construct a hybrid identity for Pompey. He is the one who violates Jerusalem yet he is also the agent of the divine work of punishing God's people.

While the Psalmist constructs this hybrid identity, he remains deeply troubled. Pompey has overstepped the mark in constructing a situation that the Psalmist thinks is marked by illegitimate rule, greedy and unclean temple leadership, disregard for religious and civil law, and the presence of foreign invaders. So the Psalmist petitions God: 'Do not delay, O God, to repay…to declare dishonorable the arrogance of the dragon' (2:25). The biblical tradition uses the image of the dragon for several oppressive rulers (Pharaoh, Ezek. 29:3; Nebuchadnezzar, Jer. 51:34). Pompey Magnus has over-reached, declaring ' "I shall be lord of

---

123. Werline, 'The *Psalms of Solomon*', 75.

land and sea" but he did not understand that it is God who is great', who judges 'even kings and rulers'. Rome's rule is thus deemed to be both a form of punishment and inevitably subject to demise at God's timing for overreaching. Again turning to the past, the Psalmist wonders if God will be faithful to the covenant God has made with Israel to preserve Israel's existence in the face of such horror. He reminds God:

> You are God and we are the people whom you have loved… Do not take away your mercy from us, lest they set upon us. For you chose the descendants of Abraham above all the nations. (*Ps. Sol.* 9:8-9)

The Psalmist, though, does not wait long and rejoices at Pompey's death (2:26-27), declaring to the ruling elite: 'And now, officials of the earth, see the judgment of the Lord' (2:32).

Psalm 17 reruns the whole scenario but, in an example of decolonizing colonized minds, with a vision of a time beyond the death of Pompey and the establishment of God's justice on earth through another king. In contrast to the illegitimate Hasmonean (and Herodian?) kings (17:5, 9b), there will be a legitimate king from the line of David. He is God's anointed one, the Messiah or Christ (17:32). Verse 5 identifies the Hasmonean rulers as 'sinners' who 'set upon us [the Psalmist's group] and drove us out' (17:5b). As a result, all Jerusalem is bereft of 'mercy or truth' and the devout were forced to flee into the wilderness (17:15-17). The likely references to Herodian actions (17:9b, 18b-19a) suggest that this bleak scene in which 'the king was a criminal and the judge disobedient and the people sinners' continues after the end of Hasmonean rule, after Pompey's death, and into Herod's reign—as far as the Psalmist is concerned.

God's justice comes in a new time, a third space/time, 'in the time known to you, O God' by another king from the line of David (17:21). His job description of justice is to 'destroy the unrighteous rulers', remove Gentiles from Jerusalem, destroy and subdue nations, gather a holy people, distribute land according to tribal divisions, and rule justly and wisely (17:22-29). Ending Roman rule and ordering the future according to God's purposes is what he is 'anointed' to do.

How does he do it? Verse 24 says he does it 'by the word of his mouth'. Verse 30 says he glorifies God (not oversteps like Pompey). Verse 33 says he does not rely on 'horse and rider and bow', does not 'collect gold and silver (taxes) for war', and does not look to 'a day of war'. That is, he does not mimic imperial ways of waging war to drive out the Romans and their allies and to establish God's rule. While he expresses the desire both to replace Roman power and to exercise power, his mimicry does not embrace the same military means. But just exactly how 'the word of his mouth' accomplishes these purposes is mysterious. As with creation, the divine word is efficacious in bringing a new space into being. Non-violence, not violence, is his mode of effecting God's will.

Interestingly, this is one of the earliest and fullest references to an 'anointed one' or Messiah in Jewish writings. It comes out of a situation of powerlessness where divine justice seems to be denied. This presentation of the Messiah does not imagine a superhuman or divine figure. He is a Davidic king; like Pompey, he is powerful. He is an agent of God's justice who brings about God's rule. The *Psalms of Solomon* endure the shame, suffering, indignity, and offence of the present by looking to God's justice-bringing action. God will be faithful to the covenant. God's justice will be established through this figure. The Psalms function to decolonize colonized minds.

Qumran: Shock and Awe

I make no attempt here to offer a representative or wide-ranging discussion of Qumran writings or history. Instead I will restrict the discussion to one group of texts.

In an interesting article, George Brooke analyzes the use of the term 'Kittim' in the four Qumran Pesharim that use the term.[124] Arguing that the term refers to the Romans, he investigates how the Romans are presented in this body of literature. It will be impossible to summarize here the rich detail of his discussion, so I concentrate on the main contours of the presentations. The military might of the Kittim/Romans is to the fore, but the texts also highlight the economic and cultic threat they pose, as well as the psychological terror they instill and the fear with which they are regarded.

- The Nahum pesher (4QpNah; dating to around the end of the 1st century BCE) interprets Nah. 2:12b as indicating that the Kittim/Romans will enter Jerusalem and trample it (4QpNah frgs. 3-4, l. 2-4). Military power is the focus.

- The Isaiah pesher (4QpIsa[a] frgs. 7-10) interprets Isaiah 10:33-34, which refers to the Assyrian advance that Israel will halt.

- The Psalm pesher (1QpPs frg. 9) interprets Ps. 68:30-31. As a victory song, it describes an enemy that poses both a military and economic threat, the latter being concerned with taking tribute.

___

124.   Brooke, 'The Kittim'. For a wider discussion, see Horsley, *Revolt*, 123-41.

- The Habakkuk pesher (1QpHab) interprets Habakkuk 1–2 and contains numerous references to the Kittim. The Chaldeans/ Kittim are the focus of Habakkuk 1:6-11 (1QpHab 2-4) and Habakkuk 1:14-17 (1QpHab 6). Brooke discusses in detail eleven uses of the term to reconstruct 'the author's picture of the Kittim, his image of empire'.[125] One emphasis falls on their military might—'swift' and 'mighty in battle', they will exercise 'dominion' (1QpHab 2.10-16), moving across the land and plundering cities. Their terrifying impact is also to the fore. They are 'fearsome and terrible' inspiring 'fear and dread' (1QpHab 2.163.6). They are 'like an eagle', they 'trample' the land and 'devour' the people without satisfaction but with 'anger, wrath, fury, and indignation' (1QpHab 3.7-14). They 'deride, scorn, mock and scoff' at rulers and threaten the temple treasury (1QpHab 3.17-4.2). They are 'military plunderers' and 'their plunder may include the contents of the temple treasury'.[126] They gather 'wealth and loot', tribute and 'sustenance' by ravaging many lands 'year by year' in relentless taxation, an action that economically threatens annual payments for Levites (1QpHab 5.12–6.8). Sustaining all this is their merciless use of the sword (1QpHab 6.8-12), including bringing justice upon unjust priests, thereby plundering the plunderers (1QpHab 8.13-9.7). 1QpHab presents a graphic of the violence and terror of Roman military, imperializing power from the perspective of the colonized.

Brooke concludes correctly that the Romans are presented as 'militarily mighty, economically threatening, but ultimately cultically no match for the God of Israel'.[127] Yet a further dimension needs to be highlighted from the presentation of the pesharim, namely the psychological terror and fear the Romans impart on vulnerable colonized peoples.

First Enoch 37–71: **Fantasies of Revenge**

Within the Enochic traditions, the section known variously as the *Similitudes of Enoch* or the *Parables of Enoch* or *1 Enoch 37–71* originates in 'early or mid first century CE'.[128] This time-period locates the material after the end of Herodian rule and during the time of the governors, before the war of 66–70 CE. This section of *1 Enoch* offers

125. Brooke, 'Kittim', 142.
126. Brooke, 'Kittim', 148-49.
127. Brooke, 'Kittim', 159.
128. Collins, *The Apocalyptic Imagination*, 178.

insight into how this Enochic group and tradition negotiate the political, military, economic, and ideological assertions of imperial power outlined above. It sets about the task of decolonizing the subjugated mind by setting the imperial present in the context of divine purposes and fantasizing a very different future or third space marked by revenge and reversal.

1 Enoch 37–71 subdivides into three main units after the introduction of chapters 37, chapters 38–44, 45–57, and 58–69. Enoch is authorized as a prophet/revealer in chapter 37 by seeing a vision and declaring the words of the 'Holy One'. The first two units are largely concerned with revealing judgment on the unrighteous, while the third section continues this emphasis but also addresses the vindication of the righteous, thereby assuring them that their destiny is safe with the 'Lord of the Spirits', the dominant name for God in *1 Enoch* 37–71.

Chapters 38–44 present the enacting of oppression as central to the identity of the unrighteous or the sinners, and basic to the judgment enacted on them. Chapter 38 employs a perspective from below among those who are oppressed. At the judgment, the 'Righteous One', God, will reveal the sinners, those who 'denied the name of the Lord of the Spirits' (38:2). These wicked ones 'possess the earth' but at the judgment 'they will be driven from the face of the earth' (38:1). They will no longer be 'rulers nor princes' since 'at that moment, kings and rulers will perish' (38:4-6). Significant here is the definition of sinners in terms of those with land who exercise oppressive power. The scenario of the chapter reflects a typical situation in an agrarian empire like Rome's where land is the key commodity and those with power, wealth, and status own large quantities of it, while peasants struggle to have access to sufficient land (by owning or renting) to sustain their existence. This imperial 'norm' of the distribution of the land is shown in chapter 38 to be sinful and unjust, contrary to the will of the Lord of the Spirits. The wickedness on earth dominated by imperial structures is such that in chapter 42, wisdom cannot find a place to dwell among humans on earth, but she resides in heaven.

Subsequent chapters intensify this analysis and develop the fantasy of revenge in which the powerful rulers and landowners are punished. In chapters 44–57, this judgment of 'the kings and the mighty ones' is entrusted to the 'Son of Man' (46:3). In a painfully cruel image that expresses the oppressed's lust of revenge, he will 'crush the teeth of the sinners' (46:4) and will 'depose the kings from their thrones and kingdoms' (46:5). Details of the revenge are gloatingly elaborated: their faces are slapped, they are filled with gloom and shame, and beset with worms (46:6). Their sins comprised a lack of accountability to God, not 'glorifying and extolling' the Son of Man, nor obeying him as 'the source of their kingship' (46:5). They arrogantly defied heaven, which means self-serving and oppressive rule on the earth. They 'manifest all their deeds in oppression; all their deeds are oppression. Their power depends upon their wealth. And their devotion is to the gods which they have fashioned with their own hands. But they deny the name of the Lord of the Spirits' (46:7-8). Their condemnation results from a failure to honor God, oppressive social actions, misused power, accumulated wealth, and idolatry associated with foreign gods and the imperial cult. The fantasy of judgment confirms Fanon's observation that the oppressed imitate their oppressors, wanting to be like them even as they exercise destructive power over them.

Chapter 48 reruns this judgment though in abbreviated form. The Lord of the Spirits and the righteous are allied against the powerful and wealthy in that 'they have hated and despised this world of oppression… In those days the kings of the earth and the mighty landowners shall be humiliated on account of their deeds' (48:7-8). In an appropriate irony, their judgment day is described as 'the day of their misery and weariness', precisely what they have forced on peasant farmers and laborers (48:8). While they have had their way on earth, they cannot resist God. 'Oppression cannot survive his judgment' (50:4). Such visions serve to decolonize the colonized's mind.

Chapter 52 adds a further dimension to the revelation and condemnation of their unjust rule and their acquisition of land and wealth. Their oppressive rule was carried out by military might. Accordingly, their judgment involves the removal 'from the surface of the earth' of the resources necessary for war (52:9). So Enoch sees mountains of iron, copper, silver, gold, colored metal, and lead (52:2). The mountains of iron and lead indicate resources for and stockpiles of weapons. Silver and gold suggest both the funds needed for war and the booty and loot taken in war. The angel or messenger 'of peace' informs Enoch that in God's presence these mountains will disappear. They will become like melted honey—'there shall be no iron for war, nor shall anyone wear a breastplate…all these substances will be removed and destroyed from the surface of the earth' (52:6-9; 53:7).

Chapter 53 elaborates the economic exploitation that this military power sustained. Enoch sees 'a deep valley with a wide mouth', an image that suggests a huge capacity for consumption. There, the imperial tributary economy is at work. 'All who dwell upon the earth…shall bring to it gifts, presents, and tributes' (53:1). But, in an image of the incessant and never-satisfied greed of the ruling elite, 'this deep valley shall not become full'. The discussion above has identified the imperializer's dependence on the colonized through the means of taxes, tributes, tithes, and 'gifts' to seize peasant production and transfer it to the ruling elite, from the provinces to the center. Enoch also sees (ironically) chains being prepared 'for the kings and potentates of this earth in order that they may be destroyed thereby... and the righteous ones shall have rest from the oppression of sinners' (53:5-7). In a reversal motivated by hate, chapter 54 describes those kings and potentates, who had put numerous subject people in chains, themselves being fettered and punished.

The third parable (58–69) continues this concern with the punishment of the oppressive rulers but increasingly emphasizes the deliverance of the righteous who have suffered under their rule but remained faithful to the Lord of the Spirits. Chapters 62–63 present God's condemnation of 'the kings, the governors, the high officials, and the landlords...all the oppressors shall be eliminated from before his face' (62:1-3). When 'the governors and the kings who possess the land' (63:1) see the Lord of the Spirits and the Son of Man, the rulers beg for mercy but it is denied (62:9). God, the Lord of the Spirits, is blessed as 'the Lord of kings, the Lord of rulers and the Master of the rich...who rules over all kings' (63:2, 4). This power is displayed and these titles vindicated in the judgment on kings, rulers, and the wealthy. Along with these rulers, the 'fallen angels' are punished also (64–69).

The parables present various dimensions of the imperial structure of Judea/Israel as sinful and thereby contrary to the divine will: the elite's self-interested rule over the people, its control of land, its exploitative and insatiable use of taxes, tributes, gifts, and tithes, its amassing of wealth, its use of military power, and its neglect of the Lord of the Spirits and honoring of idols and other gods that sanction its rule. The parables bravely resist the paralyzing terror of this imperial world, and refuse to accept its divinely sanctioned normalcy. In the midst of such an overwhelming vision of power, *1 Enoch* 37–71 decolonizes the mind by daring to imagine a very different world, one not ruled by the alliances of local and Roman elites and one not marked by these oppressive structures. The scenes of judgment and torture express the accumulated experiences of humiliation, depravation, powerlessness, shame, terror, and envy of the oppressed for the world of the oppressors. Fuelled by the protracted experience of such indignities, *1 Enoch* 37–71 presents the fantasies of the powerless for the demise of their oppressors. Such acts of imagination de-colonize the minds of subjugated people, affirming their dignity and vindication by God, and conceiving of a very different world.

Fourth Ezra

Fourth Ezra emerges in the post-70 CE era, after the destruction of Jerusalem and the temple (10:19-24). Central to it is a wrestling with the justice of God in relation to God's action in history and the Roman destruction of Jerusalem and temple in 70 CE in particular. The initial three dialogues between Ezra and the angel Uriel (3:1–9:25) engage the theodicistic questions of Israel's ambivalence and location: elected by God yet 'abused' by the nations (3:31; 4:22-24; 6:55-56), gifted with God's law but unable to abide by it except for a few exceptional humans (3:21, 35-36), a few who are saved while the majority are damned (7:45-61), and salvation by individual merit yet membership of a covenant people, the relationship between God's mercy and God's justice (8:6-19). The angel repeats several refrains—that God's purposes are mysterious and difficult to understand yet sovereign, that God's purposes span two ages (7:50), and that Ezra should consider 'what is to come, rather than what is now present' (7:16, 26-44; 6:6, 33-34; 8:46).

In chapter 9, Ezra's stance changes. Confronted in a vision with a woman mourning her dead son, he advises her to accept 'the decree of God to be just...[and]...you will receive your son back in due time' (10:16-17). His advice to accept the providence of God and turn to the future is consonant with the angel's instruction to him in the previous chapters in terms of making meaning of the destruction of Jerusalem and its temple in 70 CE. Two further visions or dreams (11:1; 13:1) reinforce the point and outline the nature of that future, at least in general terms.

The first of the two dream visions in chapters 11–12 will be our focus here. The unit divides into three sections, the vision of the eagle (11:1-35), a judgment scene (11:36-12:3), and an interpretation (12:4-39).[129] In the vision and judgment, an eagle appears that rules the world. It has 'twelve wings and the two little wings' and three heads appear (11:22-23). A lion-like creature who speaks for the Most High condemns the eagle and destroys it. The eagle represents Roman power.

Not surprisingly, the description emphasizes the worldwide rule of the eagle/Rome. Stone interprets the eagle 'spreading his wings over all the earth' (11:2) as an expression of rule.[130] Verse 5 confirms the interpretation ('to reign over the earth and over those who dwell in it'), as does verse 6a ('all things under heaven were subjected to him'). The intimidating and fearful nature of that reign that coerces all before it is

---

129.   Stone, *Fourth Ezra*, 346-47, where Stone divides the vision into fifteen sections or stages.

130.   Stone, *Fourth Ezra*, 349.

suggested by the statement that 'no one spoke against him, not even one creature...' (11:6). It is a rule that silences all alternative voices of protest and dissent. Subsequently, its eight wings 'reign over all the earth' for a period of time; individually, 'they wielded power' one after another (11:12-21). Then the middle head of its three heads 'gained control of the whole earth, and with much oppression dominated its inhabitants and it had greater power over the world than all the wings...' (11:32). When it disappears, the remaining two heads 'also ruled over the world and its inhabitants' (11:34) before the right head devoured the left. Again the intimidating nature of its rule is emphasized, and its oppressive impact is named explicitly.

A lion-like creature appears and speaks the words of the 'Most High' to the eagle. In the context of Rome's recent destruction of Jerusalem, this nomenclature of the 'Most High' for God, employing the superlative, and the use of the imperial, masculine animal, the lion, mimic and exceed the claims of power. They frame the triumphant eagle's power as lesser and subject to greater divine power. The Most High is imagined to have power over the eagle, granting it 'to reign in my world', the fourth of four empires that lead to 'the end of my times'. The possessive pronoun 'my' underlines the Most High's control of the world and of time, setting up a significant juxtaposition with the 'reigning' language attributed to the eagle. The eagle's powerful reign is described in terms of the impact of its force ('conquered') and its extent ('over the world/earth'). It is evaluated negatively in terms of its terrifying impact on subjugated peoples, ruling 'with much terror', 'with grievous oppression' and

> with deceit. And you have judged the earth, but not with truth, for you have afflicted the meek and injured the peaceable; you have hated those who tell the truth, and have loved liars; you have destroyed the dwellings of those who brought forth fruit, and have laid low the walls of those who did you no harm. And so your insolence has come up before the Most High. (11:40-43)

The catalogue of its evil concerns the corruption of social interaction and justice with terror, injustice, violence, falsehood, and pride. Taking 'meek' to mean the powerless and humiliated who are vulnerable to the wicked powerful (so Psalm 37), the eagle's rule has 'afflicted' many. And such rule that damages social well-being is deemed to be offensive to the Most High. Accordingly, the powerful lion-like figure announces the Most High's verdict: 'you will surely disappear...so that the whole earth, freed from your violence, may be refreshed and relieved' (11:45-46). The Most High's word is efficacious and judgment on the eagle/Rome is accomplished (12:1-3). This audacious vision, spoken out of a hybrid situation in which Roman power has been asserted in the defeat of Jerusalem, mimics Roman power yet attributes it in greater measure to God.

Its mimicry, though, is not quite the same.[131] Ezra asks for an interpretation from the 'sovereign Lord', the Most High who appoints kings and kingdoms (12:7-9; 11:39-40). Evoking the past figure of Daniel, the Most High reveals the interpretation of the eagle as Rome. Daniel 2 and 7 speak of four kingdoms or empires, the last of which was Greece, but here the kingdom which is 'more terrifying than all' is identified with Rome. The twelve kings (12:14) are the emperors,[132] and the three kings (12:23) the Flavian emperors from 69–96 CE, Vespasian, Titus, and Domitian. They bring the oppressive rule to its climax since they 'rule the earth and its inhabitants more oppressively than all' (12:23-24). Their end is brought about by the lion-like creature who is the Messiah from the line of David (12:32). This Messiah 'will denounce them for their ungodliness and for their wickedness and…their contemptuous dealings' and then 'he will destroy them' (12:32-33). That is, the Messiah performs not a military role but a legal one of indicting (or rebuking) and condemning. He is also a deliverer; he will 'deliver in mercy the remnant of my people' (12:34). The vision of deliverance from Roman rule serves in decolonizing minds that regard Rome's rule as normative.

Several features of the ambivalence of Roman power emerge in this presentation. Its worldwide power is emphasized, though not elaborated specifically in terms of political, military, economic, or ideological power. Also emphasized is its terrifying impact on subjugated people. Likewise, the oppressive nature of the rule is stated several times from the perspective of the subjugated. This oppression involves at least corrupt social interaction and injustice. It is afflicting and damaging power. And by the religious traditions of the defeated, it is offensive rule, offensive to the purposes of the Most High. Hence it is constructed as accountable and contained power that is, finally, brought to an end by the will of the Most High. The writing seeks the decolonizing of colonized minds through the fantasy of subjugated peoples subjected to countless indignities imagining the end of oppressive Roman imperial power through mimicking and out-menacing it with a vision of the triumph of the God 'Most High'.

131. Bhabha, *Location*, 86.
132. For discussion, see Stone, *Fourth Ezra*, 363-65.

IX.
Conclusion

I have argued in this chapter that the Roman imperial system as it was experienced in Judea/Israel exerted ideological domination with its metanarrative of divine choice to sanction its political, military, economic, social, and cultural religious control over Judea/Israel. It also exerted material domination through the same means to exact taxation, services, and labor from the province. Further, by these means it constantly exercised status domination to inflict indignities, humiliations, and terror on subject people.

A postcolonial perspective has identified the hybrid and ambivalent situation that results from the reciprocal interaction between imperializer and colonized. The assertion of Roman power dominated Judea/Israel even as it depended on Judea/Israel for authenticating its own metanarrative and on tribute and taxes levied from the province. Judeans/ Israelites negotiated this exertion of power in diverse and simultaneous ways. The absence of violence toward Rome at times throughout the two hundred years under discussion does not signify either ready acquiescence or the absence of conflict and dissent. Factional conflict and horizontal violence attests not to local conflicts unrelated to Roman presence, as some have argued, but intimidating and terrifying power exerted by Rome and its local elite allies. A picture of ambivalence emerges comprising complex and wide-ranging, multi-layered and simultaneous negotiation by provincial elites and non-elites across the two-hundred-year period from Pompey's assertion of control in 63 BCE to the humiliating defeat of the revolt of 132–135 CE sparked by the construction of the colony of Aelia Capitolina and its temple dedicated to Jupiter Capitolinus on the site of Jerusalem.

Bibliography

Abernethy, David (2000), *The Dynamics of Global Dominance: European Overseas Empires, 1415–1980*. New Haven: Yale University Press.

Ackroyd, Peter R. (1968), *Exile and Restoration*. Old Testament Library. Philadelphia: Westminster.

Aitken, James (2011), 'Judaic National Identity'. In *Judah Between East and West*, 31-48. Edited by L. L. Grabbe and O. Lipschits. Library of Second Temple Studies 75. New York: T&T Clark International.

Albertz, Rainer (2003), *Israel in Exile: The History and Literature of the Sixth Century B.C.E.* Atlanta: Society of Biblical Literature.

Allen, Lindsay (2005), *The Persian Empire*. Chicago: University of Chicago Press.

Amos, D. (1999), 'The Littlest Victims'. *ABC News*, April 13.

Anderson, Runni (1930), 'Bucephalas and His Legend'. *American Journal of Philology* 51: 1-21.

Anson, Edward M. (2013), *Alexander the Great: Themes and Issues*. London: Bloomsbury.

Aperghis, G. G. (2004), *The Seleukid Royal Economy: The Finances and Financial Administration of the Seleukid Empire*. Cambridge: Cambridge University Press.

Ariel, Donald T. (1990), 'Imported Stamped Amphora Handles'. In *Excavations at the City of David 1978–1985*, 13-98. Edited by D. Ariel. Jerusalem: Hebrew University Press.

Ashcroft, Bill, Gareth Griffiths, and Helen Tiffin (eds) (1995), *The Post-Colonial Studies Reader*. New York: Routledge.

—(1998), *Key Concepts in Post-Colonial Studies*. London: Routledge.

Atkins, Margaret, and Robin Osborne (eds) (2006), *Poverty in the Roman World*. Cambridge: Cambridge University Press.

Atkinson, Kenneth (2004), *I Cried to the Lord: A Study of the Psalms of Solomon's Historical Background and Social Setting*. Leiden: Brill.

Austin, M. M. (1986), 'Hellenistic Kings, War, and the Economy'. *Classical Quarterly* 36: 450-66.

—(2006), *The Hellenistic World from Alexander to the Roman Conquest*. 2nd ed. Cambridge: Cambridge University Press.

Badian, E. (1958), 'Alexander the Great and the Unity of Mankind'. *Historia* 7: 425-44.

—(1996), 'Alexander the Great between Two Thrones and Heaven: Variations on an Old Theme'. In *Subject and Ruler: The Cult of the Ruling Power in Antiquity*, 11-26. Edited by A. Small. Ann Arbor: Journal of Roman Archaeology.

Bagnall, Roger (1997), 'Decolonizing Ptolemaic Egypt'. In *Hellenistic Constructs: Essays in Culture, History, and Historiography*, 225-41. Edited by P. Cartledge, P. Guernsey, and E. Gruen. Berkeley: University of California Press.

Bagnall, Roger, and Peter Derow (eds) (2004), *The Hellenistic Period: Historical Sources in Translation*. Blackwell Sourcebooks in Ancient History 1. Oxford: Blackwell.

Baker, Coleman A. (2012), 'Social Identity Theory and Biblical Interpretation'. *Biblical Theology Bulletin* 42.3: 129-38.

Baltzer, Klaus (1971), *The Covenant Formulary: In Old Testament, Jewish and Early Christian Writings*. Philadelphia: Fortress.

Bar-Kochva, Bezalel (1976), *The Seleucid Army: Organization and Tactics in the Great Campaigns*. London: Cambridge University Press.

—(2010), *The Image of the Jews in Greek Literature: The Hellenistic Period*. Berkeley: University of California Press.

Barag, Dan (1994–99), 'The Coinage of Yehud and the Ptolemies'. *Israel Numismatic Journal* 13: 27-37.

—(2002), 'The Mint of Antiochus IV in Jerusalem: Numismatic Evidence on the Prelude to the Maccabean Revolt'. *Israel Numismatic Journal* 14: 59-77.

Barnett, R. D., and W. Forman (1960), *Assyrian Palace Reliefs and their Influence on the Sculptures of Babylonia Persia*. London: Batchworth.

Barstad, H. M. (1996), *The Myth of the Empty Land: A Study in the History and Archaeology of Judah During the 'Exilic' Period*. Symbolae Osloenses Fascicle Supplement 28. Oslo: Scandinavian University.

Baumann, Gerlinde (2003), *Love and Violence: Marriage as a Metaphor for the Relationship Between YHWH and Israel in the Prophetic Books*. Translated by L. Maloney. Collegeville: Liturgical. Translation of *Liebe und Gewalt: Die Ehe als Metapher für das Verhältnis JHWH-Israel in den Prophetenbüchein*. Stuttgarter Bible Studien 185. Stuttgart: Katholisches Bibelwerk, 2000.

Behr, J. W. (1937), *The Writings of Deutero-Isaiah and the Neo-Babylonian Inscriptions*. Publications of the University of Pretoria, Series III, Arts, n. 3. Pretoria: University of Pretoria.

Berger, P.-R. (1973), *Die neubabylonischen Königinschriften*. Alter Orient und Altes Testament 4/1. Kevelaer: Butzon & Bercker.

Berlejung, Angelika (1998), *Die Theologie der Bilder: Herstellung und Einweihung von Kultbildern in Mesopotamien und die alttestamentlichen Bilderpolemik*. Orbis biblicus et orientalis 162. Göttingen: Vandenhoeck & Ruprecht.

Berlin, Andrea M. (1997), 'Between Large Forces: Palestine in the Hellenistic Period'. *Biblical Archaeologist* 60: 2-51.

Bernett, Monica (2007), 'Roman Imperial Cult in the Galilee: Structures, Functions, and Dynamics'. In *Religion, Ethnicity, and Identity in Ancient Galilee: A Region in Transition*, 337-56. Edited by J. Zangenberg, H. W. Attridge, and D. B. Martin. Tübingen: Mohr Siebeck.

Bernhardt, K.-H. (1961), *Das Problem der altorientalischen Königsideologie im Alten Testament*. Vetus Testamentum Supplements 8. Leiden: Brill.

Berrin, Shani (2004), *The Pesher Nahum Scroll from Qumran: An Exegetical Study of 4Q169*. Leiden: Brill.

Betlyon, John W. (2003), 'Neo-Babylonian Military Operations Other Than War'. In *Judah and the Judeans in the Neo-Babylonian Period*, 263-83. Edited by Oded Lipschits and Joseph Blenkinsopp. Winona Lake: Eisenbrauns.

Bhabha, Homi (1989), 'Location, Intervention, Incommensurability: A Conversation with Homi Bhabha'. *Emergences* 1: 63-88.

—(1994), *The Location of Culture.* New York: Routledge.

—(2000), 'The Vernacular Cosmopolitan'. In *Voices of the Impact of Britain on Writers from Asia, the Caribbean, and Africa,* 133-42. Edited by F. Dennis and N. Khan. London: The Serpent's Tail.

Bickerman, Elias J. (1984), 'The Babylonian Captivity'. In *The Cambridge History of Judaism.* Vol. 1. *Introduction: The Persian Period,* 342-58. Edited by W. D. Davies and L. Finkelstein. Cambridge: Cambridge University.

—(2007), *Studies in Jewish and Christian History: A New Edition in English.* 2 vols. Edited by A. Tropper. Ancient Judaism and Christianity 68/2. Leiden: Brill.

Bilde, Per (1978), 'The Roman Emperor Gaius (Caligula)'s Attempt to Erect his Statue in the Temple of Jerusalem'. *Studia Theologica* 32: 67-93.

Blenkinsopp, Joseph (1987), 'The Mission of Udjahorresnet and Those of Ezra and Nehemiah'. *Journal of Biblical Literature* 106: 409-21.

Boer, Roland (2004), *Marxist Criticism of the Bible: A Critical Introduction to Marxist Literary Theory and the Bible.* Biblical Seminar. London: T&T Clark International.

—(2008), *Last Stop Before Antarctica.* Atlanta: Society of Biblical Literature.

Bonz, Marianne Palmer (2000), *The Past as Legacy: Luke-Acts and Ancient Epic.* Minneapolis: Fortress.

Bosworth, A. B. (1974), 'The Government of Syria Under Alexander the Great'. *Classical Quarterly* 24: 46-64.

— (1980), 'Alexander and the Iranians'. *Journal of Hellenic Studies* 100: 1-21.

—(1994), 'Alexander the Great Part 2: Greece and the Conquered Territories'. In *The Cambridge Ancient History, Second Edition.* Vol. 6, *The Fourth Century B.C.,* 871-75. Edited by D. M. Lewis, J. Boardman, S. Hornblower, and M. Ostwald. Cambridge: Cambridge University Press.

—(1996), *Alexander and the East: The Tragedy of Triumph.* Oxford: Clarendon.

Boyce, Mary (1989), *History of Zoroastrianism.* Leiden: Brill.

—(2001), *Zoroastrians: Their Religious Beliefs and Practices.* London: Routledge.

Braziel, Jana Evans, and Anita Mannur (2003), 'Nation, Migration, Globalization'. In *Theorizing Diaspora,* 1-22. Edited by J. E. Braziel and A. Manner. Malden: Wiley-Blackwell.

Brenner, Sandy (2003), 'Spending Your Way Through Jewish History; Ancient Judean Coins Tell Their Story'. *Biblical Archaeological Review* 29: 46-51.

Brett, Mark G. (2008), *Decolonizing God: The Bible in the Tides of Empire.* Sheffield: Sheffield University Press.

Briant, Pierre (2002), *From Cyrus to Alexander: A History of the Persian Empire.* Winona Lake: Eisenbrauns.

Bringmann, K. (1993), 'The King as Benefactor: Some Remarks on Ideal Kingship'. In *Images and Ideologies: Self-Definition in the Hellenistic World,* 7-24. Edited by A. Bulloch, E. Gruen, A. Long, and A. Stewart. Berkeley: University of California Press.

Brinkman, Jennifer A. (1968), *A Political History of Post-Kassite Babylonia, 158–722 B.C.* Rome: Pontificium Istitutum Biblicum.

—(1973), 'Sennacherib's Babylonian Problem: An Interpretation'. *Journal of Cuneiform Studies* 25: 89-95.

—(1983), 'Through a Glass Darkly: Esarhaddon's Restrospects on the Downfall of Babylon'. *Journal of the American Oriental Society* 103: 35-42.

—(1984), *Prelude to an Empire: Babylonian Society and Politics, 747–626 B.C.* Occasional Publications of the Babylonian Fund 7. Philadelphia: Babylonian Fund of the University Museum.

—(1990), 'Political Covenants, Treaties, and Loyalty Oaths in Babylonia and Between Assyria and Babylonia'. In *I trattati nel mondo antyico. Forma, ideologia, funzione*, 81 112. Edited by L. Canfora, M. Liverani, and C. Zaccagnini. Saggi di storia antica 2. Rome: 'L'Erma' di Bretschneider.

Brooke, George J. (1991), 'The Kittim in the Qumran Persharim'. In *Images of Empire*, 135-59. Edited by L. Alexander. Journal for the Study of the Old Testament: Supplement Series 122. Sheffield: JSOT Press.

Brownmiller, Susan (1993), *Against Our Will: Men, Women, and Rape*. New York: Fawcett Columbine.

Brueggemann, Walter (2008), 'The Recovering God of Hosea'. *Horizons in Biblical Theology* 30: 5-20.

Brunt, Peter A. (1965), 'The Aims of Alexander'. *Greece and Rome* 12: 205-15.

—(1990), 'Laus Imperii'. In *Roman Imperial Themes*, 288-323. Oxford: Clarendon.

Burnett, Andrew M., Michel Amandry, and Ian Carradice (1999), *Roman Provincial Coinage*. Vol. 2.1-2, *From Vespasian to Domitian (AD 69–96)*. London: British Museum.

Burnett, Andrew M., Michel Amandry, and Pere Pau Ripollès (1992), *Roman Provincial Coinage*. Vol. 1.1-2, *From the Death of Caesar to the Death of Vitellius*. London: British Museum.

Burrows, Millar (1943), 'Significant Recent Finds of Coins in Palestine'. *The Biblical Archaeologist* 6: 37-39.

Butler, Kim D. (2001), 'Defining Diaspora, Refining a Discourse'. *Diaspora* 10: 189-219.

Caniotis, Angelos (2005), *War in the Hellenistic World*. Oxford: Blackwell.

Carter, Charles E. (1999), *The Emergence of Yehud in the Persian Period: A Social and Demographic Study*. Journal for the Study of the Old Testament: Supplement Series 297. Sheffield: Sheffield Academic Press.

Carter, Warren (1999), 'Paying the Tax to Rome as Subversive Praxis: Matthew 17:24-27'. *Journal for the Study of the New Testament* 76: 3-31.

—(2000), *Matthew and the Margins: A Sociopolitical and Religious Reading*. Maryknoll: Orbis.

—(2001), *Matthew and Empire: Initial Explorations*. Harrisburg: Trinity Press International.

—(2003), *Pontius Pilate: Portraits of a Roman Governor*. Collegeville: Liturgical.

—(2008), *John and Empire: Initial Explorations*. New York: Continuum.

—(2011), 'Matthew: Empire, Synagogues, and Horizontal Violence'. In *Mark and Matthew I*, 285-308. Edited by E. M. Becker and A. Runesson. WUNT 271. Tübingen: Mohr Siebeck.

Clements, R. E. (1989), *Jeremiah*. Interpretation, a Bible Commentary for Teaching and Preaching. Louisville: Westminster John Knox.

Cody, Jane M. (2003), 'Conquerors and Conquered on Flavian Coins'. In *Flavian Rome: Culture, Image, Text*, 103-23. Edited by A. J. Boyle and W. J. Dominik. Leiden: Brill.

Cogan, Mordecai (1974), *Imperialism and Religion: Assyria, Judah, and Israel in the Eighth and Seventh Centuries B.C.E.* Society of Biblical Literature Monograph Series 19. Missoula: Scholars Press.

—(1993), 'Judah Under Assyrian Hegemony: A Reexamination of Imperialism and Religion'. *Journal of Biblical Literature* 112: 403-14.

Cohen, Shaye (1982–83), 'Alexander the Great and Jaddus the High Priest according to Josephus'. *Association for Jewish Studies Review* 7/8: 41-68.

Collingwood, R. G. (1935), *The Historical Imagination.* Oxford: Clarendon.

Collins, John J. (1984), *The Apocalyptic Imagination: An Introduction to the Jewish Matrix of Christianity.* New York: Crossroad.

—(1998), *The Apocalyptic Imagination: An Introduction to Jewish Apocalyptic Literature.* 2nd ed. Grand Rapids: Eerdmans.

Collins, Paul Thomas (2009), *Assyrian Palace Structures.* Austin: University of Texas in cooperation with the British Museum.

Cotton, Hannah M., and Michael Wörrle (2007), 'Seleukos IV to Heliodorus: A New Dossier of Royal Correspondence from Israel'. *Zeitschrift für Papyrologie und Epigraphik* 159: 191-205.

Craig, J. A. (1974), *Assyrian and Babylonian Religious Texts: Being Prayers, Oracles, Hymns etc. Copied from the Original Tablets Preserved in the British Museum.* Assyriologische Bibliothek 13. Leipzig: Zentralantiquariat der Deutschen Demokratischen Republik.

Crossan, John Dominic (1991), *The Historical Jesus: The Life of a Mediterranean Jewish Peasant.* San Francisco: Harper.

—(2008), 'Roman Imperial Theology'. In *In the Shadow of Empire: Reclaiming the Bible as a History of Faithful Resistance,* 59-73. Edited by R. A. Horsley. Louisville: Westminster John Knox.

Croy, Clayton (2006), *3 Maccabees.* Leiden: Brill.

Cuellar, Greg (2008), *Voices of Marginality: Exile and Return in Second Isaiah and the Mexican Immigrant Experience.* American University Studies VII: Theology and Religion. New York: Peter Lang.

Curtis, John, and Nigel Tallis (eds) (1980, 2008), *The Balawat Gates of Ashurnasirpal II.* London: The British Museum Publications.

—(2005), *Forgotten Empire: The World of Ancient Persia.* Berkeley: University of California Press.

Dalley, S. (1986), 'The God Ṣlmu and the Winged Disk'. *Iraq* 48: 85-101.

Dandamayev, Muhammed A. (1984), *Slavery in Babylonia.* Dekalb, IL: Northern Illinois University.

—(1996), 'An Age of Privatization in Ancient Mesopotamia'. In *Privatization in the Ancient Near East and Classical World,* 197-221. Edited by M. Hudson and B. A. Levine. Peabody Museum Bulletin 5. Cambridge: Harvard University.

Daniels, Dwight (1990), *Hosea and Salvation History: The Early Traditions of Israel in the Prophecy of Hosea.* Beihefte zur Zeitschrift für die alttestamentliche Wissenschaft 191. Berlin: Walter de Gruyter.

Day, Peggy L. (2000), 'The Bitch Had It Coming to Her: Rhetoric and Interpretation in Ezekiel 16'. *Biblical Interpretation* 8: 231-54.

Dearman, J. Andrew (2010), *Hosea.* New International Commentary on the Old Testament. Grand Rapids: Eerdmans.

DeRose Evans, Jane (1995), 'Ancient Coins from the Drew Institute of Archaeological Research Excavations of Caesarea Maritima'. *Biblical Archaeologist* 58.3: 156-66.

Derrida, Jacques (1997), *Of Grammatology*. Translated by G. C. Spivak. Baltimore: The Johns Hopkins University Press.

Deutsch, Robert (2010), 'Roman Coins Boast "Judaea Capta"'. *Biblical Archaeological Review* 36: 51-53.

Devi, Mahasweta (1995), *Imaginary Maps*. London: Routledge.

Dijkstra, M. (2003), 'Religious Crisis and Inculturation: The Example of Post-Exilic Israel'. In *Towards an Intercultural Theology: Essays in Honor of J. A. B. Jongeneel*, 97-115. Edited by M. Frederiks, M. Dijkstra, and A. Houtepen. Zoetermeer: Uitgeverij Meinema.

Donner, H. (1964), *Israel unter den Volkern*. Supplements to *Vetus Testamentum* 11. Leiden: Brill.

—(1997), 'The Separate States of Israel and Judah'. In *Israelite and Judaean History*, 381-434. Edited by J. H. Hayes and J. M. Miller. Philadelphia: Westminster.

Donner H., and W. Röllig (1966–69), *Kanaanäische und Aramäische Inscriften*. 2nd ed. Wiesbaden: Harrassowitz.

Doran, Robert (1999), 'Independent or Co-Existence: The Responses of 1 and 2 Maccabees to Seleucid Hegemony'. *Society of Biblical Literature Seminar Papers* 38: 94-103.

—(2012), *2 Maccabees: A Critical Commentary*. Hermeneia. Minneapolis: Fortress.

Eck, Werner (1999), 'The Bar Kokhba Revolt: The Roman Point of View'. *The Journal of Roman Studies* 89: 76-89.

Erim, Kenan (1986), *Aphrodisias: City of Venus Aphrodite*. New York: Facts on File.

Fanon, Frantz (1986). *Black Skin, White Masks*. London: Pluto. Translation of *Peau Noire, Masques Blanc*. France: Editions de Seuil, 1952.

—(1963), *The Wretched of the Earth*. New York: Grove.

—(1965), *Studies in a Dying Colonialism, or A Dying Colonialism*. New York: Grove. Translation of *L'an cinq de la revolution algerienne*. Paris: F. Masperio, 1959.

—(1965), *The Wretched of the Earth*. New York: Grove. Translation of *Les damnes de la terre*. Paris, 1961.

—(1967), *Toward the African Revolution*. New York: Grove. Translation of *Pour la revolution africaine*. Paris, 1964.

Fears, J. Rufus (1981), 'The Cult of Jupiter and Roman Imperial Ideology'. *Aufstieg und Niedergang der römischen Welt* 2.17.13-141. Berlin: Walter de Gruyter.

Flusser, David (2007), 'Apocalyptic Elements in the War Scroll'. In *Judaism of the Second Temple Period*. Vol. 1, *Qumran and Apocalypticism*, 140-58. Grand Rapids/Jerusalem: Eerdmans/The Hebrew University/Magnes Press.

—(2007), 'The Roman Empire in Hasmonean and Essene Eyes'. In *Judaism of the Second Temple Period*. Vol. 1, *Qumran and Apocalypticism*, 175-206. Grand Rapids/Jerusalem: Eerdmans/The Hebrew University/Magnes Press.

Foucault, Michel (1969), *L'archéologie du savoir*. Paris: Gallimard. English edn: *The Archaeology of Knowledge*. Translated by A. M. Sheridan Smith. New York: Pantheon, 1972.

—(1971), *L'ordre du discours*. Paris: Gallimard. English edn: *The Discourse on Language*. Translated by Rupert Swyer. *Social Science Information* (April 1971): 7-30.

—(2002), *The Order of Things: An Archeology of the Human Sciences*. London: Routledge.

Fox, Robin Lane (2006), *The Classical World: An Epic History from Homer to Hadrian*. New York: Basic Books.

Foxhall, L., and H. Forbes (1982), 'Sitometreia: The Role of Grain as a Staple Food in Classical Antiquity'. *Chiron* 12: 41-90.

Fredricksmeyer, Ernst A. (1982), 'On the Final Aims of Philip II'. In *Philip II, Alexander the Great, and the Macedonian Heritage*, 85-98. Edited by W. L. Adams and E. N. Borza. Lanham: University Press of America.

—(1990), 'Alexander and Philip: Emulation and Resentment'. *Classical Journal* 85: 300-315.

—(2003), 'Alexander's Religion and Divinity'. In *Brill's Companion to Alexander*, 253-78. Edited by J. Roisman. Leiden: Brill.

Freire, Paulo (1999), *Pedagogy of the Oppressed*. New Revised 20th Anniversary ed. New York: Continuum.

Friesen, Steven (2004), 'Poverty on Pauline Studies: Beyond the So-called New Consensus'. *Journal for the Study of the New Testament* 26: 323-61.

Fuks, Gideon (2001), 'Josephus' Tobiads Again: A Cautionary Note'. *Journal of Jewish Studies* 52: 354-56.

Gabrielsen, Vincent (2008), 'Provincial Challenges to the Imperial Centre in Achaemenid and Seleucid Asia Minor'. In *The Province Strikes Back: Imperial Dynamics in the Eastern Mediterranean*, 15-44. Edited by B. Forsén and G. Salmeri. Helsinki: Foundation of the Finnish Institute at Athens.

Gadd, C. J. (1948), *Ideas of Divine Rule in the Ancient Near East*. London: Oxford University Press.

Galinsky, Karl (1969), *Aeneas, Sicily, and Rome*. Princeton: Princeton University Press.

—(1992), *Classical and Modern Interactions*. Austin: University of Texas Press.

Gandhi, Leela (1998), *Postcolonial Theory: A Critical Introduction*. Edinburgh: Edinburgh University Press.

Garnsey, Peter (1999), *Food and Society in Classical Antiquity*. Cambridge: Cambridge University Press.

Garnsey, Peter, and Richard Saller (1987), *The Roman Empire: Economy, Society, and Culture*. Berkeley: University of California Press.

George, A. R. (1993), *House Most High. The Temples of Ancient Mesopotamia*. Winona Lake: Eisenbrauns.

Gera, Dov (1998), *Judaea and Mediterranean Politics 219–161 B.C.E.* Brill's Series in Jewish Studies 8. Leiden: Brill.

Gilroy, Paul (1995), 'Diaspora'. *Paragraph* 17: 303-22.

Goldstein, Jonathan A. (1976), *1 Maccabees*. Anchor Bible Commentary. Garden City: Doubleday.

Goodblatt, David (1998), 'From Judea to Israel: Names of Jewish States in Antiquity'. *Journal for the Study of Judaism* 29: 1-36.

Goodman, Martin (1982), 'The First Jewish Revolt; Social Conflict and the Problem of Debt'. *Journal of Jewish Studies* 33: 417-27.

—(1987), *The Ruling Class of Judea*. Cambridge: Cambridge University Press.

—(1999), 'The Pilgrimage Economy of Jerusalem in the Second Temple Period'. In *Jerusalem: Its Sanctity and Centrality to Judaism, Christianity, and Islam*, 69-76. Edited by L. Levine. New York: Continuum.

—(2005), 'Coinage and Identity: The Jewish Evidence'. In *Coinage and Identity in the Roman Provinces*, 163-66. Edited by C. Howgego, V. Heuchert, and A. Burnett. Oxford: Oxford University Press.

—(2007), *Rome and Jerusalem: The Clash of Ancient Civilizations*. New York: Vintage Books.

Grabbe, Lester L. (1992), *Judaism from Cyrus to Hadrian*, vol. 1. Minneapolis: Fortress.

—(2004), *A History of the Jews and Judaism in the Second Temple Period.* Library of Second Temple Studies 47. London: T&T Clark International.

—(2008), *A History of the Jews and Judaism in the Second Temple Period.* Vol. 2, *The Coming of the Greeks: The Early Hellenistic Period (335–175 BCE)*. Library of Second Temple Studies 68. London: T&T Clark International.

—(2008), 'Sanhedrin, Sanhedriyyot, or Mere Invention?' *Journal for the Study of Judaism* 39: 1-19.

—(2011), 'Hyparchs, Oikonomoi, and Mafiosi: The Governance of Judah in the Ptolemaic Period'. In *Judah Between East and West*, 70-90. Edited by L. L. Grabbe and O. Lipschits. Library of Second Temple Studies 75. New York: T&T Clark International.

Grayson, A. Kirk (1975), *Assyrian and Babylonian Chronicles.* Winona Lake: Eisenbrauns.

Green, Peter (1990), *Alexander to Actium: The Historical Evolution of the Hellenistic Age.* Berkeley: University of California Press.

—(2007), *The Hellenistic Age: A History.* New York: Modern Library.

Groenewegen-Frankfort, H. A. (1987), *Arrest and Movement: An Essay on the Representational Art of the Ancient Near East.* Cambridge: Belknap.

Gruen, Erich (1993), 'Hellenism and Persecution: Antiochus IV and the Jews'. In *Hellenistic History and Culture*, 238-64. Edited by P. Green. Berkeley: University of California Press.

—(1997), 'The Origins and Objectives of Onias' Temple'. *Scripta Classica Israelica* 16: 48-70.

—(1999), 'Seleucid Royal Ideology'. *Society of Biblical Literature Seminar Papers* 38: 24-47.

Guha, Ranajit, and Gayatri Chakravorty Spivak (eds) (1988), *Selected Subaltern Studies.* Oxford: Oxford University Press.

Habricht, C. (1989), 'The Seleucids and their Rivals'. *Cambridge Ancient History* 8.324-87.

Hadley, R. A. (1974), 'The Royal Propaganda of Seleucus I and Lysimachus'. *Journal of Hellenic Studies* 94: 50-65.

Hall, R. G. (1989), 'Epispasm and the Dating of Ancient Jewish Writings'. *Journal for the Study of the Pseudepigrapha* 4: 71-86.

Hallo, William W. (1957), *Early Mesopotamian Royal Titles: A Philologic and Historical Analysis.* American Oriental Society 43. New Haven: Yale University Press.

—(1983), 'Cult Statue and Divine Image: A Preliminary Study'. In *Scripture in Context II: More Essays on the Comparative Method*, 1-17. Edited by W. W. Hallo, J. C. Moyer, and L. G. Perdue. Winona Lake: Eisenbrauns.

Hallo, William W., and K. Lawson Younger Jr (eds) (1997), *The Context of Scripture.* Leiden: Brill.

Hamber, Brandon (2001), 'Who Pays for Peace? Implications of the Negotiated Settlement in a Post-Apartheid Settlement in a Post-Apartheid South Africa'. In *Ethnopolitical Warfare: Causes, Consequences, and Possible Solutions*, 235-58. Edited by D. Chirot and M. Seligman. Washington: American Psychological Association.

Hanson, K. C., and Douglas E. Oakman (1998), *Palestine in the Time of Jesus: Social Structures and Social Conflicts*. Minneapolis: Fortress.

Harasym, Sarah, and Gayatri Chakravorty Spivak (1990), *The Post-colonial Critic: Interviews, Strategies, Dialogues*. London: Routledge.

Hayes, John, and Sara Mandell (1998), *The Jewish People in Classical Antiquity: From Alexander to Bar Kochba*. Louisville: Westminster John Knox.

Hayward, C. T. R. (1982), 'The Jewish Temple at Lentopolis: A Reconsideration'. *Journal of Jewish Studies* 33: 429-43.

Heckel, Waldemar, and Lawrence A. Tritle (eds) (2009), *Alexander the Great: A New History*. Oxford: Wiley-Blackwell.

Heinen, H. (1984), 'The Syrian-Egyptian Wars and the New Kingdoms of Asia Minor'. In *The Cambridge Ancient History, Second Edition*. Vol. VII, Part 1, *The Hellenistic World*, 412-45. Edited by F. W. Walbank, A. E. Astin, M. W. Frederiksen, and R. M. Ogilvie. Cambridge: Cambridge University Press.

Held, David (1980), *Introduction to Critical Theory: Horkheimer to Habermas*. Berkeley: University of California Press.

Hendin, David (1976), *Guide to Ancient Jewish Coins*. New York: Attic Books.

Hengel, Martin (1974), *Judaism and Hellenism*. Philadelphia: Fortress.

Hölbl, Günther (2001), *A History of the Ptolemaic Empire*. London and New York: Routledge.

Holladay, William Lee (1990), *Jeremiah 1 and 2*. Hermeneia. Minneapolis: Fortress.

Hollenbach, Paul W. (1981), 'Jesus, Demoniacs, and Public Authorities: A Socio-Historical Study'. *The Journal of the American Academy of Religion* 49: 567-88.

Holloway, Steven W. (2001), *Assur Is King! Assur Is King! Religion in the Exercise of Power in the Neo-Assyrian Empire*. Leiden: Brill.

Horowitz, Wayne, Takayoshi Oshia, and Seth Sanders (2002), 'A Bibliographical List of Cuneiform Inscriptions from Canaan, Palestine/Philistia, and the Land of Israel'. *Journal of the American Oriental Society* 122: 753-66.

—(2006), *Cuneiform in Canaan: Cuneiform Sources from the Land of Israel in Ancient Times*. Jerusalem: Israel Exploration Society.

Horsley, Richard (1981), 'Ancient Jewish Banditry and the Revolt Against Rome, A.D. 66–70'. *Catholic Biblical Quarterly* 43: 409-32.

—(1984), 'Popular Messianic Movements Around the Time of Jesus'. *Catholic Biblical Quarterly* 46: 471-95.

—(1985), '"Like One of the Prophets of Old": Two Types of Popular Prophets at the Time of Jesus'. *Catholic Biblical Quarterly* 47: 435-63.

—(1986), 'High Priests and the Politics of Roman Palestine'. *Journal for the Study of Judaism* 17: 23-55.

—(1986), 'Popular Prophetic Movements at the Time of Jesus: Their Principal Features and Social Origins'. *Journal for the Study of the New Testament* 26: 3-27.

—(2010), *Revolt of the Scribes: Resistance and Apocalyptic Origins*. Minneapolis: Fortress.

Howard-Brooks, Wes (2010), *'Come Out My People!' God's Call Out of Empire in the Bible and Beyond*. Maryknoll: Orbis.

Huizanga, John (1963), 'A Definition of the Concept of History'. In *Philosophy and History: Essays Presented to Ernst Cassirer*, 1-10. Edited by R. Kiblansky and H. J. Paton. New York: Harper Torchbooks.

Hyatt, James Philip (1984), 'The Deuteronomic Edition of Jeremiah'. In *A Prophet to the Nations*, 247-67. Edited by L. G. Perdue and B. W. Kovacs. Winona Lake: Eisenbrauns.

Jacobsen, Thorkild (1987), 'The Graven Image'. In *Ancient Israelite Religion: Essays in Honor of Frank Moore Cross*, 15-32. Edited by P. D. Miller, P. D. Hanson, and S. D. McBride. Philadelphia: Fortress.

James, Paula (2000), 'Essay Ten: The Language of Dissent'. In *Experiencing Rome: Culture, Identity, and Power in the Roman Empire*, 277-303. Edited by J. Huskinson. London: Routledge.

Jameson, Fredric (1991), *Postmodernism, or, the Cultural Logic of Late Capitalism*. Durham: Duke University Press.

Johnson, Janet J. (1983), 'The Demotic Chronicle as a Statement of a Theory of Kingship'. *Society for the Study of Egyptian Antiquities* 13: 61-72.

—(1984), 'Is the Demotic Chronicle an Anti-Greek Tract?' In *Grammata Demotika: Festschrift für Erich Lüddeckens zum 15. Juni 1983*, 107-24. Edited by H. J. Thissen and K. Th. Zauzich. Würzburg: Gisela Zauzich.

Jursa, Michael (2002), 'Debts and Indebtedness in the Neo-Babylonian Period: Evidence from the Institutional Archives'. In *Debt and Economic Renewal in the Ancient Near East III*, 197-217. Edited by M. Hudson and M. Van De Mieroop. Bethesda: CDL.

—(2004), 'Grundzüge der Wirtschaftsformen Babyloniens im Ersten Jahrtausend v. Chr'. In *Commence and Monetary Systems in the Ancient World*, 115-36. Edited by R. Rollinger and C. Ulf. Wiesbaden: Franz Steiner Verlag.

Kadman, Leo (1960), *The Coins of the Jewish War of 66–73 CE*. Tel-Aviv: Schocken Publishing House.

Kaiser, Aryeh. 'Further Revised Thoughts on Josephus' Report of Alexander's Campaign to Palestine (Ant. 11.304-347)'. In *Judah Between East and West: The Transition from Persian to Greek Rule (ca.400–200 BCE)*, 131-57. Edited by L. L. Grabbe and O. Lipschits. Library of Second Temple Studies 75. London: T&T Clark International.

Kamudzandu, Israel (2010), *Abraham as Spiritual Ancestor: A Postcolonial Zimbabwean Reading of Romans 4*. Leiden: Brill.

Kanael, Baruch (1963), 'Ancient Jewish Coins and Their Historical Importance'. *The Biblical Archaeologist* 26: 38-62.

Kautsky, John H. (1982), *The Politics of Aristocratic Empires*. Chapel Hill: University of North Carolina Press.

Keefe, Alice (1995), 'The Female Body, the Body Politic, and the Land: A Sociopolitical Reading of Hosea 1–2'. In *A Feminist Companion to the Latter Prophets*, 70-100. Edited by A. Brenner. Sheffield: Sheffield Academic.

Kelly, Christopher (2006), *The Roman Empire: A Very Short Introduction*. Oxford: Oxford University Press.

Kieh, G. K. (1992), 'The Roots of Western Influence in Africa: An Analysis of the Conditioning Process'. *The Social Science Journal* 29: 7-19.

Kindler, Arie (1958), 'The Coinage of the Bar-Kokhba War'. In *The Dating and Meaning of Ancient Jewish Coins and Symbols: Six Essays in Jewish Numismatics*, 62-80. Jerusalem: Schocken.

—(1974), 'Silver Coins Bearing the Name of Judea from the Early Hellenistic Period'. *Israel Exploration Journal* 24: 73-76.

King, L. W., and R. C. Thompson (1907), The *Sculptures and Inscription of Darius the Great on the Rock of Behistûn in Persia*. London: British Museum.

Kratz, Reinhard G. (2008), 'Ezra – Priest and Scribe'. In *Scribes, Sages, and Seers: The Sage in the Eastern Mediteranean World*, 163-88. Edited by Leo G. Perdue. Göttingen: Vandenhoeck & Ruprecht.

Krentz, Edgar (1975), *The Historical Critical Method*. Guides to Biblical Scholarship: Old Testament. Philadelphia: Fortress.

Kuhrt, Amélie (2007, 2009), *The Persian Empire: A Corpus of Sources from the Achaemenid Period*. 1st and 2nd ed. London: Routledge.

Kuhrt, Amélie, and Susan Sherwin-White (1991), 'Aspects of Seleucid Royal Ideology: The Cylinder of Antiochus I from Borsippa'. *Journal of Hellenic Studies* 111: 71-86.

Kurtz, Mark (1999), 'The Social Construction of Judea in the Greek Period'. *Society of Biblical Literature Seminar Papers* 38: 54-76.

Kwakkel, Gert (2009), 'The Land in the Book of Hosea'. In *Land of Israel in Bible, History, and Theology*, 167-81. Edited by J. van Ruiten and J. Cornelis de Vos. Leiden: Brill.

Landau, Y. H. (1966), 'A Greek Inscription Found Near Hefzibah'. *Israel Exploration Journal* 16: 54-70.

Landy, Francis (1995), 'Fantasy and the Displacement of Pleasure: Hosea 2:4-17'. In *A Feminist Companion to the Latter Prophets*, 146-60. Edited by A. Brenner. Sheffield: Sheffield Academic.

—(1995), *Hosea*. Sheffield: Sheffield Academic.

Larsen, Mogens Trolle (1979), 'The Tradition of Empire in Mesopotamia'. In *Power and Propaganda: A Symposium on Ancient Empires*, 75-103. Edited by M. T. Larsen. Copenhagen Studies in Assyria 7. Copenhagen: Akademisk Forlag.

Lehmann, Gunnar (1996), *Untersuchungen zur späten Eisenzeit in Syrien und Libanon; Stratigraphie und Keramikformen zwischen ca. 720 bis 300 v. Chr*. Altertumskunde des vorderen Orients 5. Münster: Ugarit-Verlag.

Lenski, Gerhard (1984), *Power and Privilege: A Theory of Social Stratification*. Chapel Hill: University of North Carolina Press.

Levine, Amy-Jill (1998), 'Visions of Kingdoms: From Pompey to the First Jewish Revolt'. In *The Oxford History of the Biblical World*, 352-87. Edited by M. D. Coogan. New York: Oxford University Press.

Lipiński, Edward (1979), *State and Temple Economy in the Ancient Near East*. Louvain: Uitgeverij Peeters.

Lipschits, Oded (2011), 'Jerusalem Between Two Periods of Greatness: The Size and Status of the City in the Babylonian, Persian, and Early Hellenistic Periods'. In *Judah Between East and West: The Transition from Persian to Greek Rule (ca.400–200 BCE)*, 163-75. Edited by L. L. Grabbe and O. Lipschits. Library of Second Temple Studies 75. London: T&T Clark International.

Lipschits, Oded, and Joseph Blenkinsopp (eds) (2003), *Judah and the Judeans in the Neo Babylonian Period*. Winona Lake: Eisenbrauns.

Liverani, Mario (1979), 'The Ideology of the Assyrian Empire'. In *Power and Propaganda: A Symposium on Ancient Empires*, 297-317. Edited by M. T. Larsen. Mesopotamia 7. Copenhagen: Akademisk Forlag.

Lloyd, Alan B. (1982), 'Nationalist Propaganda in Ptolemaic Egypt'. *Historia* 31: 33-55.

Lopez, Davina (2008), *Apostle to the Conquered: Reimagining Paul's Mission*. Minneapolis: Fortress.

Luckenbill, David Daniel (1924), *Annals of Sennacherib*. University of Chicago Oriental Institute Publications, vol. 2. Chicago: University of Chicago Press.

Lundbom, Jack R. (1999, 2004, 2004), *Jeremiah 1–20, 21–36, and 37–52*. Anchor Bible 21A, 21B, 21C. New York: Doubleday.

Lyotard, Jean-François (1984), *The Postmodern Condition: A Report on Knowledge*. Minneapolis: University of Minnesota Press.

Ma, John (2000), 'Seleukids and Speech-Acts: Performative Utterances, Legitimacy, and Negotiation in the World of the Maccabees'. *Scripta Classica Israelica* 19: 71-112.

Machinist, Peter (2003), 'Mesopotamian Imperialism and Israelite Religion: A Case Study from the Second Isaiah'. In *Symbiosis, Symbolism and the Power of the Past: Canaan, Ancient Israel and their Neighbors. Centennial Symposium of the W.F. Albright Institute of Archaeological Research and the American Schools of Oriental Research*, 237-64. Edited by W. G. Dever and S. Gitin. Winona Lake: Eisenbrauns.

Macintosh, A. A. (1997), *A Critical and Exegetical Commentary on Hosea*. International Critical Commentary. Edinburgh: T. & T. Clark.

MacKenzie, John M. (1986), *Propaganda and Empire*. Manchester: Manchester University Press.

MacMullen, Ramsay (2000), *Romanization in the Time of Augustus*. New Haven: Yale University Press.

Malamat, Abraham. 'The Twilight of Judah: In the Egyptian-Babylonian Maelstrom'. Supplements to *Vetus Testamentum* 28. Leiden: Brill.

Mann, Michael (1984), 'The Autonomous Power of the State: Its Origins, Mechanisms and Results'. *European Journal of Sociology* 25.2: 185-213.

—(1986), *The Sources of Social Power*. Vol. 1, *A History of Power from the Beginning to A.D. 1760*. Cambridge: Cambridge University Press.

Manning, Joseph G. (2003), *Land and Power in Ptolemaic Egypt: The Structure of Land Tenure*. Cambridge: Cambridge University Press.

Marcus, Ralph (1943, 1998), 'Appendix D'. In *Josephus: Jewish Antiquities Books XII–XIII*, 473-98. LCL 365. Cambridge: Harvard University Press.

Mattila, Sharon L. (2000), 'Ben Sira and the Stoics: A Reexamination of the Evidence'. *Journal of Biblical Literature* 119: 473-501.

Mattingly, David J. (1996), 'First Fruit? The Olive in the Roman World'. In *Human Landscapes in Classical Antiquity: Environment and Culture*, 213-53. Edited by G. Shipley and J. Salmon. London: Routledge.

Mbembe, Achille (2001), *On the Postcolony*. Berkeley: University of California Press.

McCane, Byron (2008), 'Simply Irresistible: Augustus, Herod, and the Empire'. *Journal of Biblical Literature* 127: 725-35.

McCarthy, Dennis J. (1978), *Treaty and Covenant: A Study in Form in the Ancient Oriental Documents and in the Old Testament*. 2nd ed. Analecta Biblica: Investigationes Scientificae in Biblicas. Rome: Biblical Institute.

McKay, John W. (1973), *Religion in Judah Under the* Assyrians *732–609 B.C.* Studies in Biblical Theology 2.26. London: SCM.

McLaren, James (2005), 'Jews and the Imperial Cult: From Augustus to Domitian'. *Journal for the Study of the New Testament* 27: 257-78.

McLeod, John (2000), *Beginning Postcolonialism.* Manchester: Manchester University Press.

Meshorer, Ya'a kov (1967), *Jewish Coins of the Second Temple Period.* Chicago: Argonaut.

Meyshan, Josef (1959), 'The Symbols on the Coinage of Herod the Great and their Meanings'. *Palestine Exploration Quarterly* 91: 109-21.

Midmead, Julye (2002), *The Akitu Festival: Religious Continuity and Royal Legitimation in Mesopotamia.* Gorgias Dissertations: Near Eastern Studies 2. Piscataway: Gorgias.

Modrzejewski, Joseph Meleze (1995), *The Jews of Egypt: From Rameses II to Emperor Hadrian.* Philadelphia: Jewish Publication Society.

Moore-Gilbert, Bart J. (1997), *Postcolonial Theory: Contexts, Practices, Politics.* London: Verso.

Mørkholm, Otto (1966), *Antiochus IV of Syria.* Classica et mediaevalia. Dissertations 8. Copenhagen: Gyldendal.

Morley, Neville (2010), *The Roman Empire: Roots of Imperialism.* New York: Pluto.

Morton, Stephen (2007), *Gayatri Spivak: Ethics, Subalternity and the Critique of Postcolonial Reason.* Malden: Polity.

Mowinckel, Sigmund (1914), *Zur Komposition des Buches Jeremias.* Oslo: Jacob Dybwad.

Müller, Hans-Peter (ed.) (1991), *Babylonien und Israel: historische, religiöse und sprachliche Beziehungen.* Darmstadt: Wissenschaftliche Buchgesellschaft.

Murray, Oswyn (2007), 'Philosophy and Monarchy in the Hellenistic World'. In *Jewish Perspectives on Hellenistic Rulers*, 13-28. Edited by T. Rajak, S. Pearce, J. Aitken, and J. Dimes. Berkeley: University of California Press.

Nicholson, Ernest W. (1974, 2008), *The Book of the Prophet Jeremiah, Chapters 1–25 and 26–52.* Cambridge Bible Commentaries on the Old Testament. Cambridge: Cambridge University Press.

Nickelsburg, George W. E. (2001), *1 Enoch 1: A Commentary on the Book of 1 Enoch Chapters 1–36, 81–108.* Hermeneia. Minneapolis: Fortress.

Oded, Bustenay (1977), 'Judah and the Exile'. In *Israelite and Judaean History*, 435-88. Edited by J. Hayes and M. Miller. Philadelphia: Westminster.

—(1979), *Mass Deportations and Deportees in the Neo-Assyrian Empire.* Wiesbaden: Dr. Ludwig Reichert Verlag.

—(1995), 'Observations on the Israelite/Judaean Exiles in Mesopotamia during the Eighth Sixth centuries B. C. E.' In *Immigration and Emigration within the Ancient Near East*, 205-12. Edited by K. van Lerberghe and A. Schoors. Orientalia Lovaniensia Analecta 65. Leuven: Peeters.

Oden, Robert A. (1977), 'Ba'al Šāmēm and 'El'. *Catholic Biblical Quarterly* 39: 457-73.

Oppenheim, A. Leo (1977), *Ancient Mesopotamia: Portrait of a Dead Civilization.* Rev. ed. by E. Reiner. Chicago: University of Chicago Press.

Parker, Bradley J. (2001), *The Mechanics of Empire: The Northern Frontier of Assyria as a Case Study in Imperial Dynamics.* Neo-Assyrian Text Corpus Project. Helsinki: University of Helsinki Finland.

Parpola, Simo (1997), *Assyrian Prophecies*. State Archives of Assyria 9. Helsinki: Helsinki University Press.

Parrot, André (1961), *The Arts of Assyria*. New York: Golden.

Paul, Shalom (1968), 'Deutero-Isaiah and Cuneiform Royal Inscriptions'. *Journal of the American Oriental Society* 88: 180-86.

PeCiikova, J. (1987), 'The Administrative Methods of Assyrian Imperialism'. *Archiv Orientální* 55: 162-75.

Perdue, Leo G. (2008), *Scribes, Sages, and Seers: The Sage in the Eastern Mediterranean World*. Forschungen zur Religion und Literatur des Alten und Neuen Testaments 219. Göttingen: Vandenhoeck & Ruprecht.

—(2008), *The Sword and the Stylus: An Introduction to Wisdom in the Age of Empires*. Grand Rapids: Eerdmans.

Petras, James (1993), 'Cultural Imperialism in the Late 20th Century'. *Journal of Contemporary Asia* 23.2: 139-48.

Pongratz-Leisten, Beate (ed) (2011), *Reconsidering the Concept of Revolutionary Monotheism*. Winona Lake: Eisenbrauns.

Portier-Young, Anathea (2011). *Apocalypse Against Empire: Theologies of Resistance in Early Judaism*. Grand Rapids: Eerdmans.

Postgate, J. N. (1972), "The Role of the Temple in the Mesopotamian Secular Community'. In *Man, Settlement and Urbanism: Proceedings of a Meeting of the Research Seminar in Archaeology and Related Subjects Held at the Institute of Archaeology, London University*, 811-26. Edited by P. J. Ucko et al. London: Duckworth.

—(1974), *Taxation and Conscription in the Assyrian Empire*. Studia Pohl: Series Major 3. Rome: Biblical Institute.

—(1979), 'The Economic Structure of the Assyrian Empire'. In *Power and Propaganda: A Symposium on Ancient Empires*, 193-221. Edited by M. T. Larsen. Copenhagen: Akademish Forlag.

—(1995), 'Assyria: the Home Provinces'. In *Neo-Assyrian Geography*, 1-17. Edited by M. Liverani. Quaderni di Geografia Storica 5. Rome: Università di Roma 'La Sapienza'.

Purcell, N. (1985), 'Wine and Wealth in Ancient Italy'. *Journal of Roman Studies* 75: 1-19.

Rajak, Tessa (1981), 'Roman Intervention in a Seleucid Siege of Jerusalem?' *Greek, Roman, and Byzantine Studies* 22: 65-81.

—(1991), 'Friends, Romans, Subjects: Agrippa II's Speech in Josephus' Jewish War'. In *Images of Empire*, 122-34. Edited by L. Alexander. Journal for the Study of the Old Testament: Supplement Series 122. Sheffield: JSOT Press.

Renger, J. (1994), 'On Economic Structures of Ancient Mesopotamia'. *Orientalia* 63: 157-208.

Rice, E. E. (1983), *The Grand Procession of Ptolemy Philadelphus*. Oxford: Oxford University Press.

Richards, Thomas (1993), *The Imperial Archive: Knowledge and the Fantasy of Empire*. New York: Verso.

Richardson, Peter (1996), *Herod: King of the Jews and Friend of the Romans*. Columbia: University of South Carolina Press.

Rigsby, K. J. (1980), 'Seleucid Notes'. *Transactions of the American Philological Association* 110: 233-54.

Robertson, J. F. (1995), 'The Social and Economic Organization of Ancient Mesopotamian Temples'. In *Civilizations of the Ancient Near East*, vol. 1, 443-54. Edited by J. M. Sasson. New York: Charles Scribner's Sons.

Rocca, Samuel (2008), *Herod's Judea: A Mediterranean State in the Classical World.* Texts and Studies in Ancient Judaism 122. Tübingen: Mohr Siebeck.

Roisman, Joseph (ed.) (2003), *Brill's Companion to Alexander the Great.* Leiden: Brill.

Roller, Duane W. (1998), *The Building Program of Herod the Great.* Berkeley: University of California Press.

Rollston, Chris A. (1999), 'The Script of Hebrew Ostraca of the Iron Age 8th–6th Centuries BCE'. PhD diss., The Johns Hopkins University.

Root, Margaret Cool (1979), *The King and Kingship in Achaemenid Art: Essays on the Creation of an Iconography of Empire.* Leiden: Brill.

Rowlandson, Jane (2008), 'The Character of Ptolemaic Aristocracy: Problems of Definition and Evidence'. In *Jewish Perspectives on Hellenistic Rulers*, 29-49. Edited by T. Rajak, S. Pearce, and J. Aitken. Berkeley: University of California Press.

Rushdie, Salman (1991), *Imaginary Homelands: Essays and Criticism 1981–1991.* London: Granta.

Safrai, Zeev (1994), *The Economy of Roman Palestine.* London: Routledge.

Said, Edward (1978), *Orientalism.* New York: Pantheon.

—(1985), 'The Rani of Samir: An Essay in Reading the Archives'. *History and Theory: Studies in the Philosophy of History* 24.3: 247-72.

—(1986), *After the Last Sky: Palestinian Lives.* New York: Pantheon.

—(1991), *The World, the Text, and the Critic.* Repr. London: Vintage. Cambridge: Harvard University Press.

—(1994), *Cultural and Imperialism.* New York: Vintage Books. Repr. New York: Knopf.

Samuel, A. E. (1993), 'The Ptolemies and the Ideology of Kingship'. In *Hellenistic History and Culture*, 168-210. Edited by Peter Green. Berkeley: University of California Press.

Sancisi-Weerdenburg, Heleen, Amelie Kuhrt, and Margaret Cool Root (1994), *Achaemenid History VIII: Continuity and Change.* Leiden: Nederlands Instituut Voor Het Nabije Oosten.

Sasson, Jack M. (ed) (1995), *Civilizations of the Ancient Near East*, vols. 1-4. New York: Simon & Schuster and Macmillan.

Scheidel, Walter, and Steven J. Friesen (2009), 'The Size of the Economy and the Distribution of Income in the Roman Empire'. *The Journal of Roman Studies* 99: 61-91.

Schmid, Hansjörg (1995), *Der Tempelturm Etemenanki in Babylon.* Baghdader Forschungen 17. Mainz: Philipp von Zabbern.

Schwartz, Daniel R. (1998), 'Josephus' Tobiads: Back to the Second Century'. In *Jews in a Graeco-Roman World*, 47-61. Edited by M. Goodman. Oxford: Clarendon.

Schwartz, Seth (2001), *Imperialism and Jewish Society 200 BCE to 640 CE.* Princeton: Princeton University Press.

Scott, James C. (1990), *Domination and the Arts of Resistance. Hidden Transcripts.* New Haven: Yale University Press.

Sefer, Hagi (2004.), 'The Priestly Leadership According to 4QMMT and the Decrees of Antiochus III'. *Zion* 69.1: 5-24.

Segovia, Fernando F. (1995), 'Toward a Hermeneutics of the Diaspora: A Hermeneutics of Otherness and Engagement'. *Reading from This Place*. Vol. 1, *Social Location and Biblical Interpretation in the United States*, 51-73. Edited by F. Segovia and M. A. Tolbert. Minneapolis: Fortress.

—(1995), 'Toward Intercultural Criticism: A Reading Strategy from the Diaspora'. In *Reading from This Place*. Vol. 2, *Social Location and Biblical Interpretation in Global Perspective*, 303-30. Edited by F. Segovia and M. A. Tolbert. Minneapolis: Fortress.

—(1996), 'In the World but Not of It: Exile as Locus for a Theology of the Diaspora'. In *Hispanic Latino Theology: Challenge and Promise*, 195-217. Edited by A. M. Isasi-Díaz and F. Segovia. Minneapolis: Fortress.

—(1999), 'Postcolonial and Diasporic Criticism in Biblical Studies: Focus, Parameters, Relevance'. *Studies in World Christianity* 5: 177-95.

—(2000), *Decolonizing Biblical Studies: A View from the Margins*. Maryknoll: Orbis.

—(2005), 'Mapping the Postcolonial Optic in Biblical Criticism: Meaning and Scope'. In *Postcolonial Biblical Criticism: Interdisciplinary Intersections*, 23-78. Edited by S. Moore and F. Segovia. London: T&T Clark International.

Setel, Drorah T. (1985), 'Prophets and Pornography: Female Sexual Imagery in Hosea'. In *Feminist Interpretation of the Bible*, 86-95. Edited by L. Russell. Philadelphia: Westminster.

Seux, M.-J. (1967), *Épithetes royales akkadiennes et sumériennes*. Paris: Letouzey et Ane.

Shaw, Brent D. (1993), 'Tyrants, Bandits, and Kings: Personal Power in Josephus'. *Journal of Jewish Studies* 44: 176-204.

Sherwin-White, Susan, and Amélie Kuhrt (1993), From *Samarkhand to Sardis: A New Approach to the Seleucid Empire*. Berkeley: University of California Press.

Sherwood, Yvonne (1996), *The Prostitute and the Prophet: Hosea's Marriage in Literary Theoretical Perspective*. Journal for the Study of the Old Testament: Supplement Series 212. Sheffield: Sheffield Academic.

Slemon, Stephen (1985), 'Modernism's Last Post'. *ARIEL: A Review of International English Literature* 20.4: 3-17.

Smith, R. R. (1987), 'The Imperial Reliefs from the Sebasteion at Aphrodisias'. *The Journal of Roman Studies* 77: 88-138.

—(1988), 'Sacra Gentium: The Ethne from the Sebasteion at Aphrodisias'. *The Journal of Roman Studies* 78: 50-77.

Smith-Christopher, Daniel L. (1990), *The Religion of the Landless: The Social Context of the Babylonian Exile*. Bloomington: Meyer-Stone Books.

—(1997), 'Reassessing the Historical and Sociological Impact of the Babylonian Exile (597/587–539 B. C. E.)'. In *Exile: Old Testament, Jewish, and Christian Conceptions*, 7-36. Edited by J. M. Scott. Leiden: Brill.

—(2002), *A Biblical Theology of Exile*. Overtures in Biblical Theology 22. Minneapolis: Fortress.

Soggin, A. A. (1997), 'רועה r'h to tend'. In *Theological Lexicon of the Old Testament*, 1246-48. Edited by E. Jenni and C. Westermann. Peabody: Hendrickson.

Spieckermann, Hermann (1982), *Juda unter Assur in der Sargonidenzeit*. Forschungen zur Religion und Literatur des Alten und Neuen Testaments 129. Gottingen: Vandenhoeck & Ruprecht, 1982.

Spivak, Gayatri Chakravorty (1985), 'Three Women's Texts and a Critique of Imperialism'. *Critical Inquiry* 12: 235-61.

—(1988), 'Can the Subaltern Speak?' In *Marxism and the Interpretation of Culture*, 271-313. Edited by C. Nelson and L. Grossberg. Urbana: University of Illinois Press.

—(1988), *In Other Worlds: Essays in Cultural Politics*. New York: Routledge.

—(1998), *Of Grammatology*. Corrected ed. Baltimore: The Johns Hopkins University Press.

—(1999), *A Critique of Postcolonial Reason: Toward a History of the Vanishing Present*. Cambridge: Harvard University Press.

—(2003), *Death of a Discipline*. New York: Columbia University Press.

Stern, Ephraim (2001), *Archaeology of the Land of the Bible*. Anchor Yale Bible Reference Library 2. New Haven: Yale University Press.

Stevens, Marty E. (2006), *Temples, Tithes, and Taxes: The Temple and the Economic Life of Ancient Israel*. Peabody: Hendrickson.

Stone, Michael (1990), *Fourth Ezra*. Hermeneia. Minneapolis: Fortress.

Stoneman, Richard (1997), *Alexander the Great*. London: Routledge.

Sugirtharajah, R. S. (2002), *Postcolonial Criticism and Biblical Interpretation*. Oxford: Oxford University Press.

Tadmor, Hayim (1981), 'History and Ideology in the Assyrian Royal Inscriptions'. In *Assyrian Royal Inscriptions: New Horizons in Literary, Ideological, and Historical Analysis*, 13-33. Edited by F. M. Fales. Orientis Antiqui Collectio 17. Rome: Istituto per l'oriente.

—(1997), 'Propaganda, Literature, Historiography: Cracking the Code of the Assyrian Royal Inscriptions'. In *Assyria 1995: Proceedings of the Tenth Anniversary Symposium of the Neo-Assyrian Text Corpus Project, Helsinki September 7–11, 1995*, 325-38. Edited by S. Parpola and R. M. Whiting. Helsinki: Neo-Assyrian Text Corpus Project.

Tarn, W. W. (1933), 'Alexander the Great and the Unity of Mankind'. *Proceedings of the British Academy* 19: 123-66.

Taylor, Joan E. (2006), 'Pontius Pilate and the Imperial Cult in Roman Judaea'. *New Testament Studies* 52: 555-82.

Tcherikover, V. A. (1999), *Hellenistic Civilization and the Jews*. Peabody: Hendrickson.

Tcherikover, Victor (Avigdor), and Alexander Fuks (eds) (1957–64), *Corpus Papyrorum Judaicarum*. 3 vols. Cambridge: Harvard University Press.

Temin, Peter (2013), *The Roman Market Economy*. Princeton: Princeton University Press.

Thiel, Winfried (1973, 1981), *Die Deuteronomistische Redaction of Jeremiah, 1–25, 26–47*. Neukirchener-Vluyn: Neukirchener Verlag.

Thiong'o, Ngugi wa (1986), *Decolonising the Mind*. Portsmouth: Heinemann.

—(1993), *Moving the Centre: The Struggle for Cultural Freedoms*. London: James Currey.

Thomas, C. G. (1968), 'Alexander the Great and the Unity of Mankind'. *Classical Journal* 63: 258-60.

Thompson, Dorothy J. (1997), 'The Infrastructure of Splendour: Census and Taxes in Ptolemaic Egypt'. In *Hellenistic Constructs*, 242-57. Edited by P. Cartledge, P. Garnsey, and E. Gruen. Berkeley: University of California Press.

Thorne, J. A. (2001), 'Warfare and Agriculture: The Economic Impact of Devastation in Classical Greece'. *Greek, Roman, and Byzantine Studies* 42: 225-53.

Todd, R. A. (1964), 'W. W. Tarn and the Alexander Ideal'. *The Historian* 27: 48-55.

Tornkvist, Rut (1998), *The Use and Abuse of Female Sexual Imagery in the Book of Hosea: A Feminist Critical Approach to Hos 1–3*. Uppsala: Almqvist & Wiksell.

Turner, Eric (1984), 'Ptolemaic Egypt'. In *The Cambridge Ancient History, Second Edition*. Vol. VII, Part 1, *The Hellenistic World*, 118-74. Edited by F. W. Walbank, A. E. Astin, M. W. Frederiksen, and R. M. Ogilvie. Cambridge: Cambridge University Press.

Udoh, Fabian E. (2005), *To Caesar What Is Caesar's: Tribute, Taxes, and Imperial Administration in Early Roman Palestine 63 B.C.E.–70CE*. Brown Judaic Studies 343. Providence: Brown University.

Unger, E. A. (1970), *Babylon: Die Heilige Stadt nach der Beschreibung der Babylonier*. 2nd ed. Berlin: Walter de Gruyter.

Van De Mieroop, Marc (2004), 'Economic Theories and the Ancient Near East'. In *Commerce and Monetary Systems in the Ancient World*, 54-64. Edited by R. Rollinger and C. Ulf. Munich: Franz Steiner.

Vanderhooft, David Stephen (1999), *The Neo-Babylonian Empire and Babylon in the Latter Prophets*. Harvard Semitic Monographs 59. Atlanta: Scholars Press.

VanderKam, James (2004), *From Joshua to Caiaphas: High Priests After the Exile*. Minneapolis: Fortress.

Van der Steen, Eveline (2011), 'Empires and Farmers'. In *Judah Between East and West: The Transition from Persian to Greek Rule (ca. 400–200 BCE)*, 210-24. Edited by L. L. Grabbe and O. Lipschits. Library of Second Temple Studies 75. London: T&T Clark International.

Van Dijk-Hemmes, Fokkelien (1989), 'Imagination of Power and the Power of Imagination: An Intertextual Analysis of Two Biblical Love Songs: The Song of Songs and Hosea 2'. *Journal for the Study of the Old Testament* 44: 75-88.

Van Seters, John (1997), *In Search of History: Historiography in the Ancient World and the History of the Bible*. Winona Lake: Eisenbrauns.

Vout, Caroline (1996), 'The Myth of the Toga: Understanding the History of Roman Dress'. *Greece and Rome* 43: 204-20.

Wacker, Marie-Theres (1996), *Figurationen des Weiblichen im Hosea-Buch*. Herder's Biblische Studien 8. Freiburg: Herder.

Walbank, F. W. (1984), 'Monarchy and Monarchic Ideas'. In *The Cambridge Ancient History, Second Edition*. Vol. VII, Part 1, *The Hellenistic World*, 62-100. Edited by F. W. Walbank, A. E. Astin, M. W. Frederiksen, and R. M. Ogilvie. Cambridge: Cambridge University Press.

—(1984), 'Sources for the Period'. In *The Cambridge Ancient History, Second Edition*. Vol. VII, Part 1, *The Hellenistic World*, 1-22. Edited by F. W. Walbank, A. E. Astin, M. W. Frederiksen, and R. M. Ogilvie. Cambridge: Cambridge University Press.

Walker, C. B. F., and M. B. Dick (1999), 'The Induction of the Cult Image in Ancient Mesopotamia'. In *Born in Heaven, Made on Earth: The Creation of the Cult Image*, 55-122. Edited by M. B. Dick. Winona Lake: Eisenbrauns.

Weems, Renita (1989), 'Gomer: Victim of Violence or Victim of Metaphor?' *Semeia* 47: 87-104.

—(1995), *Battered Love: Marriage, Sex, and Violence in the Hebrew Prophets*. Minneapolis: Fortress.

Weitzman, Steven (2004), 'Plotting Antiochus's Persecution'. *Journal of Biblical Literature* 123: 219-34.

Werline, Ridney A. (2005), 'The Psalms of Solomon and the Ideology of Rule'. In *Conflicted Boundaries in Wisdom and Apocalypticism*, 69-87. Edited by B. G. Wright III and L. M. Wills. Society of Biblical Literature: Symposium Series 35. Atlanta: Society of Biblical Literature.

Westenholz, Aage (1979), 'The Old Akkadian Empire in Contemporary Opinion'. In *Symposium on Ancient Empires*, 107-23. Edited by M. T. Larsen. A Symposium on Ancient Empires, Mesopotamia 7. Copenhagen: Akademisk Forlag.

Westenholz, Joan (2000), 'The King, the Emperor, and the Empire: Continuity and Discontinuity of Royal Representation in Text and Image'. In *Melammu Symposia*. Vol. 1, *The Heirs of Assyria*, 99-125. Edited by Sanno Aro and R. M. Whiting. Helsinki: The Neo Assyrian Text Corpus Project.

Whittaker, Charles R. (1993), 'The Poor'. In *The Romans*, 272-99. Edited by Andrea Giardina. Chicago: University of Chicago Press.

Will, Edouard (1985), 'Pour une "anthrpologie coloniale" du monde hellénistique'. *The Craft of the Ancient Historian*, 273-301. Edited by J. W. Easie and J. Ober. Lanham: University Press of America.

Williams, Patrick, and Laura Chrisman (eds) (1994), *Colonial Discourse and Post-Colonial Theory: A Reader*. New York: Columbia University Press.

Williamson, H. G. M. (1986), 'Isaiah 40, 20: A Case of Not Seeing the Wood for the Trees'. *Biblica* 67: 1-20.

Wilson, Carol (forthcoming), *For I Was Hungry and You Gave Me Food: Pragmatics of Food Access in the Gospel of Matthew*. Eugene: Wipf & Stock.

Worthington, Ian (2003), 'Alexander, Philip, and the Macedonian Experience'. In *Brill's Companion to Alexander the Great*, 69-98. Edited by J. Roiseman. Leiden and Boston: Brill.

—(2003), *Alexander the Great: A Reader*. London and New York: Routledge.

Wright, Benjamin (1999), '"Put the Nations in Fear of You": Ben Sira and the Problem of Foreign Rule'. *Society of Biblical Literature Seminar Papers* 38: 77-93.

—(2008), 'Ben Sira on Kings and Kingship'. In *Jewish Perspectives on Hellenistic Rulers*, 76-91. Edited by T. Rajak, S. Pearce, and J. Aitken. Berkeley: University of California Press.

Yee, Gale A. (1992), *Composition and Tradition in the Book of Hosea: A Redactional-Critical Investigation*. Atlanta: Scholars Press.

—(1992), 'Hosea'. In *The Women's Bible Commentary*, 195-202. Edited by C. Newsom and S. Ringe. Louisville: Westminster John Knox.

—(1996), 'Hosea'. In *The New Interpreter's Bible*, vol. 7, 195-297. Edited by L. Keck, et al. 12 vols. Nashville: Abingdon.

Young, Jason R. (2007), *Rituals of Resistance: African Atlantic Religion in Kongo and the Lowcountry South in the Era of Slavery*. Baton Rouge: Louisiana State University Press.

Young, Robert (1990), *White Mythologies: Writing History and the West*. London: Routledge

—(2001), *Postcolonialism: An Historical Introduction*. Oxford: Blackwell.

—(2003), *Postcolonialism: A Very Short Introduction*. Oxford: Oxford University Press.

Zadok, Ran (1979), *The Jews in Babylonia During the Chaldean and Achaemenian Periods According to Babylonian Sources*. Haifa: Haifa University Press.

—(1984), 'Some Jews in Babylonian Documents'. *Jewish Quarterly Review* 74: 294-97.

Zahle, Jan (1990), 'Religious Motifs on Seleucid Coins'. In *Religion and Religious Practice in the Seleucid Kingdom*, 125-35. Edited by P. Bilde, T. Engberg-Pederson, L. Hannestad, and J. Zahle. Aarhus: Aarhus University Press.

Zanker, Paul (1990), *The Power of Images in the Age of Augustus*. Ann Arbor: University of Michigan Press.

Zarrow, Edward M. (2006), 'Imposing Romanization: Flavian Coins and Jewish Identity'. *Journal of Jewish Studies* 57: 44-55.

Zevit, Ziony (2001), *The Religions of Ancient Israel: A Synthesis of Parallactic Approaches*. London: Continuum.

Index of References

HEBREW BIBLE/
OLD TESTAMENT

Genesis
1–2   101
2:5-8   101
2:18-24   101
6:1-4   168
18–19   89
22:8-10   101
40:1   122
40:2   122
40:5   122
40:9   122
40:13   122
40:20   122
40:21   122
40:23   122
41:9   122

Exodus
3–4   94
3:7-8   265
3:7   51
3:10   51
6:7   51
12:29–15:19 101
15:22–19:1   101
20:3   54
28:33-34   278
30:10   158
34:12-16   54, 207

Leviticus
16:2-34   158
27:30-33   265

Numbers
18:21-32   265
25:1-18   58
25:1-13   207

25:8   207
25:9   207
25:11   207
25:13   207
25:14-15   207

Deuteronomy
1–28   89
14:22-29   265
18:9-14   66
27–30   265
32:10-12   89
32:13-18   89

Joshua
1–12   101

Judges
1   101
8:33   54

1 Samuel
2:10   98
16:6   98
24:6-7   98
24:10-11   98
26:9   98
26:11   98
26:16   98
26:23   98

2 Samuel
1:14   98
1:16   98
7   94, 101
7:1-17   101
7:11-16   265
19:21-22   98
23:1   98

1 Kings
14:23   67
17:1-7   127
18:28   55

2 Kings
9:14-29   53
9:30-37   53
10:1-17   53
10:5   122
15   60
15:9   61
15:18   61
15:19-20   59
15:24   61
15:28   61
16–23   64
16   50
16:3   65
16:10-16   63, 65
17:1-41   38
17:7-18   61
18:1-12   38
18:5-8   67
18:13–19:36 39
21:1-5   64
21:6   66
21:7   66
22   66, 67
23   68
23:11   67
23:12   66
24:1   70
25:22   75
25:27-30   78

1 Chronicles
3:17   79
16:22   98

2 Chronicles
6:42 98
9:4 122
24:11 179
29–32 67
33–34 67

Ezra
1–7 124
1:2-4 125
1:8 120
1:11 79
2:2 79
3:2 79
4:6-16 122
4:10-11 116
4:16-17 116
4:20 116
5:14-15 126
6:3-5 94, 125
7:7 124
7:12-26 126
8:36 116
9:1-2 124

Nehemiah
1:3 122
1:11 122
2:2 122
2:5 122
2:7 116
2:9 116
3:33–4:17 123
5:2-5 119
6:1-19 123
9 120
9:2 124
9:36 121

Esther
2:5 79

Job
10:8-12 101

Psalms
2 101
20:6-7 98
23 205
24:1 246, 265
28:8 98
37 289
46 101
48 101
68:30-31 283
78:12-54 100
84:9 98
89 94, 101
89:38 98
89:51 98
104 101
105:15 98
105:16-45 100
105:18 78
106:7-33 100
107:14 78
110 101
132:10 98
132:17 98
136:10-16 100
137 79

Ecclesiastes
2:4-8 160
3:19-22 170
5:3 170
7:15-20 171
8:2-5 171
10:20 171

Isaiah
6 94, 102
7 50
10:5 281
10:33-34 283
14 281
24–27 117, 120
40–48 97, 101
40:1-11 94
40:12-31 94
40:12-18 102
40:12-17 94

40:18-24 94
40:18-20 104
40:18 103
40:21-26 102
40:23-26 102
40:25-31 94
40:29 103
41:1–42:9 95, 102
41:1-20 95
41:1-6 103
41:1 103
41:2-6 102
41:2-3 95
41:2 94
41:4 102
41:5-7 104
41:5 97
41:8 97
41:11-13 96
41:21–42:9 95
41:21-29 104
41:25 94, 95
42:1-4 97, 98, 102
42:1 97
42:5-9 98, 102
42:6 97, 98
42:7 98
42:8 104
42:10–43:8 95
42:10-16 95
42:10-12 97
42:17 104
42:18-20 95
42:21-25 95
43:1-10 102
43:1-8 95
43:1-7 100
43:1 97
43:3-4 97
43:6 78
43:9–44:5 95
44:6-23 95
44:6-8 103
44:6 102
44:8 102
44:9-20 104, 105
44:21 102

44:24–45:13	94, 95	*Jeremiah*		44:24–45:13	92	
44:24-28	98	1–39	92	46–51	90	
44:26-28	95	1:1-3	88	46	92	
44:28–45:1	114	1:3-10	102	46:2	70	
44:28	98, 103	1:5	98	46:13-26	90	
45:1	95, 98, 103	2–10	94	46:27-28	90	
45:5-8	102	2:2-9	88	47	92	
45:14-25	95	2:2-3	89	48:14	92	
45:14	78, 97	2:7	89	48:20-21	92	
45:16	104	2:20	89	50–51	91	
45:20-21	104	2:21	89	50:2	91	
45:21-22	102	4:1-2	89	51:34	281	
46–47	95	5:1-8	89	51:59	92	
46:1-7	105	5:5	89	52:30	71	
46:1-2	104	7:1-15	88			
46:1	104	7:5-10	89	*Lamentations*		
46:5-7	104	7:16-20	89	2:2	77	
47:1-15	103	8:13	89	2:11	207	
47:9-13	104	11:14-17	89	3:48	207	
48	95	14:11-12	89	4:20	98	
48:5	104	15:1-2	89	5:2-5	77	
49–55	95, 102	17:16	98	5:9-11	77	
49	95	20:15-16	89			
49:1-6	97, 98, 102	21:11–23:8	88	*Ezekiel*		
49:1	97, 98	21:13	88	1–2	94	
49:5-6	98	22:6-7	88	28	281	
49:6	97	22:15-16	88	29:3	281	
49:8	98	22:18-19	70	31–32	281	
49:23	97	23:14	89	33:23-29	77	
49:25	96	24:1-10	77			
49:26	97	24:1-7	78	*Daniel*		
50:1–51:8	95	24:8-10	78	1	201	
50:4-9	97, 98, 102	25:11-12	201	2	290	
51:9-10	102	26:1-24	88	3	201	
51:22-23	96	29:10	201	6	201	
52–53	202	30–31	78	7	202, 290	
52:2	78	31:16-20	89	8	146	
52:3	78	31:31-34	89	8:21	146	
52:9-11	102	32:37-41	89	9	208	
52:13–53:12	97, 98, 100, 102	33:15	88	9:4-19	201	
		34:13	78	9:20-27	201	
54	95	36:30	70	11:30-31	193	
54:11-12	102	40–55	92	11:31	192	
54:15-17	97	41:2-3	92	11:32-35	201	
55	95	41:25	92	11:32	201	
		44:16-18	85	11:39	189	

Daniel (cont.)
11:40-45   281
11:40   202
12:3   201
12:10   201
12:11   192

Hosea
1–3   56
1:1   50
1:2   58
1:4-5   52
1:4   53
1:5   50
1:6-7   52
1:9   52
2:2-13   54
2:2   52
2:3   52
2:5-14   54, 58
2:5-13   57
2:5   55, 58
2:7   56
2:8-9   58
2:8   55
2:12   55
2:14   52, 54
2:15   51, 52, 54, 56
2:18   50
2:19-20   56, 59
2:20   55
3:1   56, 57
3:4-5   59
3:5   54, 57, 59
4–14   56
4:1-3   52, 54, 55, 63
4:1   54, 55, 59
4:6   55, 63
4:10-19   54, 58
4:10   55, 58, 59
4:12   58
4:13   58
4:15   54, 58
5:1   50, 54, 59
5:3-4   54
5:3   55
5:4   55
5:7   51, 54, 55
5:8-12   59
5:13   51, 54, 61, 62
6:1-3   56
6:1-2   57, 59
6:1   57, 59
6:3   55
6:4   56
6:6-7   55
6:6   54, 63
6:7   51, 52, 54
6:10   54
6:11   57, 59
7:1   51, 52, 54
7:4   54, 58
7:5-7   50
7:8-13   51
7:8-9   57
7:8   54, 58
7:11-12   59
7:11   54, 62
7:13-14   54
7:13   51
7:14   51, 55
7:16   55, 59
8:1-2   51, 54
8:1   52, 54, 55
8:2   55
8:4-5   52, 54
8:4   50
8:8-10   59
8:9-10   52, 54
8:9   61, 62
8:10   61
8:12   63
8:13   54, 56, 59
8:14   55, 59, 61
9:1-9   51
9:1   54, 58
9:2   55, 59, 62
9:3   52, 56, 59, 62
9:6   61, 62
9:10   54, 58
9:11-14   56
9:11   55
9:12   62
9:13   55, 59
9:14   55
9:15   50, 51, 54, 56, 58
9:16   56, 62
9:17   52, 56, 59
10:1-2   54
10:3-10   51
10:5-6   58
10:5   54, 58
10:7   50
10:8   54, 58
10:9   55, 59
10:12   56
10:14   50, 55, 59
11:1-4   56
11:1   51, 54
11:3   55
11:5-7   51
11:5   56, 59, 61, 62
11:6   55, 59
11:8-9   59, 89
11:10-11   57, 59
11:11   56, 59
12:1   54, 59, 61, 62
12:2   59
12:6   56, 59
12:9   51, 54, 61
12:11   54
12:13   51, 54, 61
12:14   54
13:2   52, 54
13:4   51, 54, 55, 61
13:5   61
13:6   55
13:10-11   50
13:10   62
13:11   61
13:15   62
13:16   51, 54, 55, 59, 63

14:1-2	59	*Luke*		48:8	182, 183	
14:1	51	23:1-25	245	50:1-4	177	
14:3	59, 61, 62			51:12	182	
14:4	59	*John*		51:23	181	
14:4 Eng.	56	18:28–19:16	245			
14:5	56			*Baruch*		
14:7	57, 59	*Acts*		1:10-14	267	
14:9	52	12:19-23	239			
		21:38	248	*1 Maccabees*		
Micah				1:2-5	137	
6:4	78	APOCRYPHA/DEUTERO-		1:10	191	
		CANONICAL BOOKS		1:11-15	186, 188	
Nahum		*Tobit*		1:11	188, 199,	
2:12	283	1:2	122		212	
		1:6-8	258	1:15	199	
Habakkuk				1:16-22	188	
1–2	284	*Ecclesiasticus*		1:20-40	189	
1:6-11	284	4:1-10	182	1:20-28	191	
1:14-17	284	9:17–10:18	182	1:20-24	158	
3:13	98	10	183	1:21	189, 191	
		10:3	182	1:24	189, 191	
Haggai		10:4	183	1:29-40	189, 191	
1:1	120	10:6-18	182	1:41-64	190	
1:14	126	10:8	183	1:41-63	199	
2:23	122, 127	10:14-15	182	1:41-50	191	
		10:14	183	1:43	191	
Zechariah		10:19-24	183	1:57	200	
3:1	120	10:24	182, 183	1:63	199	
10:2	98	13:4-7	182	2–9	198	
11:16	98	13:9-11	182	2	198	
13:7	98	13:18-19	182	2:1-70	199	
		13:21-23	182	2:1	206	
Malachi		17:17	182	2:20-21	207	
2:10-17	119	24:23	181	2:26	207	
		26:29–27:2	182	2:29-38	200	
NEW TESTAMENT		29:8-13	182	2:34	200	
Matthew		31:4	182	2:38	200	
17:24-27	258	33:16-19	181	2:39-41	206	
20:1-16	260	38:24–39:11	181	2:49-70	207	
27:1-2	245	38:24-34	182	2:54	207	
27:11-26	245	38:24	183	3:3-9	207	
		38:34	183	3:10-26	199	
Mark		39:4	183	3:18-19	209	
15:1-15	245	39:9-11	184	3:22	207	
15:18-20	249	41:8	181	3:27–4:25	199	
15:26	249	45:11	182	3:44	208	
		48:6	182, 183	3:47	208	

318   INDEX OF REFERENCES

1 Maccabees (cont.)

3:50-54	208	16:3	208	5:11-26	189, 196
3:53	208	16:11-17	214	5:11-21	158, 188
4:10-11	208			5:11	195
4:24	208	*2 Maccabees*		5:12-14	190
4:26-35	199	2:19-22	208	5:14	188
4:30-35	208	2:50	207	5:15-21	208
4:36-61	199	3	179, 181	5:17	208
4:40	208	3:1–4:6	208	5:18	208
4:55-56	208	3:1-2	186	5:20	208
5:31	208	3:7-40	179	5:24-26	197
5:54	208	3:12	208	5:24	192
6:2	192	3:13-21	179	5:26	190
6:18-23	210	3:22-30	179	6	209
6:21-27	212	3:24-40	208	6:1-11	190, 195
7:5-7	212	4–6	192	6:1	189, 192
7:12-18	210	4:1-6	185	6:7	192
7:20-22	211	4:2	208	6:12–7:42	190
7:23-24	211	4:7-10	186	6:12	208
7:25	211	4:7-8	194	6:16	208
7:26-38	211	4:7	194	6:17	208
7:36-38	208	4:8-10	197	6:18-31	209
7:39-50	211	4:8	161, 178	6:19-20	209
9:1-22	211	4:10	186	6:28	209
9:19-21	207	4:11-17	186	6:31	209
9:32-57	211	4:11	177	7	209
9:44-46	208	4:13-15	195	7:1-42	209
9:57-73	211	4:19	208	7:2	209
10:1	211	4:22	186	7:9	209
10:8	212	4:23-25	195	7:11	209
10:18-21	212	4:24	178, 197	7:14	209
10:46-50	212	4:25	186	7:17	209
10:59-66	212	4:27-29	195	7:19	209
10:61	212	4:27	178	7:23	209
10:67-89	212	4:29	192	7:29	209
11:20-37	212	4:33-34	186	7:30	209
11:38-53	212	4:36	195	7:31	209
11:60	212	4:38	208	7:32-33	208, 209
12:15	208	4:39-42	186	7:34-35	209
12:35-36	212	4:39	208	7:38	209
12:39-53	212	4:43-50	186	8–15	198
13:12-24	212	4:50	193, 195	8:5	209
13:27-29	213	5	191	8:8-36	199
13:41	207, 213	5:1	188	9	199
13:49-53	213	5:2-3	208	9:5-6	208
14:4-15	207, 213	5:5-10	195	9:23-27	211
14:33-34	213	5:5	158	10:1-9	199
		5:11-27	195	10:1-8	208

10:4	209	38	285	89:54	205
10:11	19	38:1	285	90:2-6	205
10:24-38	208	38:2	285	90:2	205
10:29-31	208	38:4-6	285	90:6-39	205
11:8	208	42	285	90:8	206
11:13-38	199	44–57	285	90:9-17	206
12:1	210	45–57	285	90:9-10	206
12:18-25	211	46:3	285	90:18-27	206
12:22	208	46:4	285	91:11-17	203, 204
13:4-8	209	46:5	286	91:11	203, 204
13:4	193	46:6	285	91:12	204
13:22-24	210	46:7-8	286	93:1-10	203
14:3-15	211	48	286	93:2	203, 204
14:12	211	48:8	286	93:3-8	203
14:26–15:37	211	50:4	286	93:5	203, 204
14:33–15:36	208	52	286	93:9-10	204
15:27	208	52:2	286	93:10	204
15:32-35	209	52:6-9	286		
		52:9	286	*3 Maccabees*	
OLD TESTAMENT		53	286	1:1-7	158
PSEUDEPIGRAPHA		53:1	286	1:6-13	158
1 Enoch		53:5-7	287	1:11-12	158
1–36	167, 168	53:7	286	1:16-29	158
5:4-5	168	54	287	2:1-20	158
6–16	168	58–69	285, 287	2:21-24	158
7:3	168	62–63	287	6:22-41	158
8:1	168	62:1-3	287		
8:2-3	168	62:9	287	*4 Ezra*	
9:1	168	63:1	287	3:1–9:25	288
9:6	168	63:2	287	3:21	288
9:9-10	168	63:4	287	3:31	288
12–16	169	64–69	287	3:35-36	288
15:11-12	169	72–82	167	4:22-24	288
17–36	169	83–90	204	6:6	288
17–19	169	83–84	204	6:33-34	288
18:11–19:3	169	83:5	204	6:55-56	288
21–36	169, 170	83:6	205	7:16	288
21:10	169	83:7	205	7:26-44	288
22:12	169	83:9	204	7:45-61	288
25:3	169	83:11	205	7:50	288
25:5	169	84:2-6	205	8:6-19	288
25:7	169	84:5-6	205	8:46	288
27:2	170	85–90	205	9	288
37–71	284, 285,	85:3	205	10:16-17	288
	287, 425	89:17-18	205	10:19-24	288
37	285	89:35	205	11–12	288
38–44	285	89:51-53	206	11:1-35	288

4 Ezra (cont.)
11:1   288
11:2   288
11:5   288
11:6   289
11:12-21   289
11:22-23   288
11:32   289
11:34   289
11:36–12:3   288
11:39-40   290
11:40-43   289
11:45-46   289
12:1-3   289
12:4-39   288
12:7-9   290
12:14   290
12:23-24   290
12:23   290
12:32-33   290
12:32   290
12:34   290
13:1   288

4 Maccabees
6:28-30   209
17:21-22   209

Letter of Aristeas
12–14   152
83–120   167

Psalms of Solomon
1   279
1:1-3   280
1:4   281
1:5   281
1:8   281
2   279
2:1-2   280
2:7-8   281
2:25   281
2:26-30   280
2:26-27   282
2:32   282
8   279

8:1-22   279
8:1-6   280
8:9-13   281
8:15-19   279
8:16   280
8:20   279
8:21-22   279
8:22   281
9:8-9   282
17   279, 280, 282
17:5   282
17:6   281
17:7-12   280
17:7-10   281
17:9   280, 282
17:11   280
17:12   280
17:15-17   282
17:18-19   280, 282
17:21   282
17:22-29   282
17:24   282
17:32   282
17:33   282

DEAD SEA SCROLLS
1QpHab
2–4   284
2.10-16   284
2.16–3.6   284
3.7-14   284
3.17–4.2   284
5.12–6.8   284
6   284
6.8-12   284
8.13–9.7   284

1QpPs
frg 9   283

4QpIsa^a
frgs 7-10   283

4QpNah
frgs 3-4, 1. 2-4   283

War Scroll
1.2   202
1.6   202

Pesher Scroll
2.6-10   214

CLASSICAL AND ANCIENT
CHRISTIAN AUTHORS
Appian
Bella civilian
5.75   255

Syrica
1.5   176
8.50   135, 152
9.57   173
45   184

Arrian
Anabasis
2.25.4   147
3.3.2-3   142
5.19.4-6   140
7.9.8   135

Augustus
Res Gestae
1   230
3   230
7   230
12   230
13   230, 231
25   230
26   231
27   231
29   231
30   231
31–33   231

Celsus
7.25.1   188

Dio Cassius
53.12.7   135
65.7.2   258

Diodorus

1.55.5	153
16.89.1-2	140
17.4.9	140
17.72.1-6	129
18.28.3-6	137
18.43.1	139
18.56.2	142
21.5	148
28.3	179
29.15	179
40.3	167
40.3.1-7	152
40.3.8	153

Herodotus
Histories

1.178	116
3.88-95	116

Horace
Carmen saeculare

17–20	228
29–32	228
45–46	228
47–48	228
49–52	228
57–60	228
66–68	228

Josephus
Antiquities

1.121	134
3.252-57	272
4.4.205	259
4.4.240	259
4.4.68	259
4.37	272
4.203	272
4.209-11	273
8.100-105	273
8.145	192
8.147	192
10.272-81	266
11.8	121
11.154-58	273
11.304-45	145
11.317	145
11.326-339	121
11.333-34	146
11.336-39	146
11.339	161
12.1-9	167
12.6	151
12.8	152, 161
12.50	179
12.58	179
12.129-30	175
12.131-32	175
12.132-33	176
12.138-44	177, 179
12.138	158, 175, 176
12.141	177
12.142-43	177
12.144	177
12.145-46	178
12.154-236	155
12.154	176
12.158	160
12.160-61	151
12.175-76	161
12.212	160
12.246-47	189
12.246	158
12.248	189
12.249	189
12.251-56	189
12.265-434	198
12.325	273
12.362-66	210
12.379-83	210
12.384-85	210
12.384	194
12.434	273
13.28-33	211
13.34	211
13.35-36	211
13.156	211
13.213	213
13.236-49	214
13.259-66	214
13.273	214
13.301	214
13.377-86	214
13.387-92	214
14.41	215
14.67-72	158
14.74-76	215
14.74	254
14.77-78	215, 254
14.77	224
14.110-11	267
14.185-267	267
14.196	254
14.202-206	254
14.202	254
14.275-76	254
14.381-93	224
14.381	255
15.5	256
15.106	256
15.109	256
15.187-98	242
15.189	256
15.196-200	256
15.267	238
15.272-76	238
15.277-79	238
15.280-81	138
15.299-316	262
15.303	259
15.304	255, 256
15.306-16	256
15.354-59	243
15.363-69	239
15.365	259
15.380	266
15.381	266
15.387	266
15.403-405	270
15.407	270
15.423	266
16.64-65	255
16.128	256
16.136-49	256
16.153	266
16.154-56	259
16.162-65	258
16.167-70	258
16.331-34	259

Josephus, *Ant.* (cont.)

17.42	239
17.162	266
17.179-80	256
17.191-92	255
17.204-205	259
17.213-18	271
17.213-14	272
17.254-98	271
17.271-84	248
17.308-309	255, 259
17.308	259
17.318-21	254
17.342-44	243
17.355	257
18.1-2	257
18.2-3	267
18.4	257
18.26	268
18.33-35	246
18.60	275
18.90-95	270
18.90	258
18.95	246
18.117-19	247
18.172-76	246
18.257-60	240
18.257-309	158
18.273-75	257
18.274	261
19.299	258
19.326-27	275
19.328-31	255, 275
19.335-37	275
19.343-50	239
20.10-14	270
20.51-53	262
20.105-12	271
20.106	270, 272, 273
20.161-66	268, 271
20.166	266
20.169-70	248
20.181	259
20.188	248
20.197-203	269
20.203	267
20.205	268
20.206-207	259
20.211-12	257, 275
20.213	267
20.218	266
20.220-22	261
20.222	267
20.223	267
20.225-26	267
20.247	267
20.250	267
20.251	245, 267

Against Apion

1.113	192
1.118	192
1.192-93	161
1.200-204	161
1.209-11	151, 167
2.77	239
2.190	265

Life

63	259
71	257
80	259
422	258
425	258
429	258

War

1.26	272
1.33	186
1.36-47	198
1.88	270
1.143	326
1.145-51	158
1.150-51	236
1.150	223
1.152	158, 236
1.153	236
1.154	254
1.179	236
1.204	249
1.220-22	254, 255
1.304	249
1.358-59	256
1.388	256
1.400-428	256
1.403	238
1.404	238
1.414	238
1.648-55	237
1.650	236
2.4-13	271
2.39-75	271
2.42-44	247
2.55-65	248
2.57	249
2.85-86	257
2.95-99	254
2.117	244
2.118	257, 267
2.169-77	244
2.169-74	237, 247
2.175-77	237
2.192	247
2.197	239, 268
2.199	245
2.220	244
2.224-27	271
2.224	270, 272, 273
2.228-29	249
2.232-46	244, 271
2.253	244, 249
2.254-57	249, 268, 271
2.258-60	248
2.261-63	248
2.264-65	249, 261
2.271	244, 249
2.272-76	244
2.273-76	249
2.277-79	245, 249
2.280-83	271
2.293-300	237
2.293	245
2.305-308	245
2.309	243
2.315	247

2.318	245, 269	4.377-97	133, 220	157	239		
2.319-25	269	4.388	220	198	240		
2.350	243	4.395	220	207-21	158		
2.352-54	243	4.398-409	272	299-305	240		
2.356-57	243	4.402	272	306-307	158		
2.356	243	4.503	220				
2.360	243	4.544-84	220	*De specialibus legibus*			
2.365-80	243	4.545	220	1.152	259		
2.372	243	5.1-38	133				
2.383	243	5.1-20	220	Philostratus			
2.390	242, 243, 265	5.98	220	*Vita Apollonii*			
		5.105	220	1.8	261		
2.400	243	5.207-11	267				
2.404-407	257	5.222-24	267	Plutarch			
2.409-29	269	5.244	270, 272, 273	*Alexander*			
2.409-10	239			5.1-3	143		
2.425-29	271	5.255	220	6	140		
2.425	249, 273	5.257	220	15.1-2	141		
2.427-28	261	5.331-42	247	15.2-3	142		
2.433-48	248	5.367	242, 265	27.5-6	142, 143		
2.441	249	5.441	220	61	140		
2.442-48	220	6.40	220	64.4	142		
2.517-22	271	6.282	260				
2.541	249	6.285-87	247	*Moralia*			
2.563	269	6.288-315	247	327d-e	141		
2.587	249	6.300-309	247, 271	342d	141		
2.592-48	220	6.316-22	269				
2.593	249	6.333-35	264, 270	Polybius			
2.599	275	6.335	258	5.67	148		
2.614	275	6.420-29	272	5.79-87	158		
2.648	269	7.26-36	249	5.86.8-11	158		
3.123	236	7.153-57	249	5.86.8-10	158		
3.351-54	242, 265	7.216-17	258	10.27.10-13	179		
3.472-73	234	7.218	258	11.34.10-11	176		
3.475-76	234	7.260-61	263	14.11-12	148		
3.475	234			16.22a	172		
3.477	234	Macrobius		26.1	191		
3.478-79	234	*Saturnalia*		26.1.11	192		
3.480	234	2.4.11	224	28.1.4	141, 195		
3.484	234			28.18-23	188		
3.532-42	235	*Pausanius*		28.18	191		
4.133	220	5.12.4	192	29.26-27	188		
4.158-93	269			31.9.1-2	179		
4.178	269	Philo		33.18	211		
4.300-325	220	*Legatio ad Gaium*		87.5-7	158		
4.314-17	269	3.17	239				
4.323	266	156-57	258				

Tacitus
Agricola
9   233
10   233
13   233
18   233
19   233
21   233
21.1   233
21.2   233
22–25   233
29–39   233
30–32   233
30   233
33.3   233
35–38   233
42.4   234

Histories
4.64.3   233

Virgil
Aeneid
1.254-96   229
1.278-83   229
1.279   227
3.390   230
6.781-84   229
6.788-807   229
6.851-53   229
8.84   230

INSCRIPTIONS
Behistun Inscription
I.7   163
I.9   112
IV.56   112
IV.58   112
IV.63   112
IV.70   112

Demotic Chronicle
II.25   165, 166
III.1   165, 166
III.15-16   166
IV.1   166
IV.2   166
IV.6   166
IV.7   166
IV.10   166
IV.12   166
IV.21   165
IV.22-23   165
V.15-18   165
VI.19-21   165

KAI
26.C, IV.13ff   66

VAB
4 72
  I 11-14   73
4 104
  I 22-25   73
4 112
  I 13-17   73
4 122
  I 40-46   73
4 164 B
  vi 12-13   104

PAPYRI
PCairoZen
59.12   160
59004   159

Index of Authors

Abernethy, D. 133, 220
Ackroyd, P. R. 78
Aitken, J. 182, 183
Albertz, R. 69
Allen, L. 107
Amandry, M. 276
Amos, D. 263
Anderson, R. 140
Anson, E. M. 136
Aperghis, G. G. 177, 179
Ariel, D. T. 161
Ashcroft, B. 86, 218
Atkins, M. 253
Atkinson, K. 280
Austin, M. M. 137-41, 148, 161, 162

Badian, E. 138, 142
Bagnall, R. 130, 134, 148, 153
Baker, C. A. 60
Baltzer, K. 59
Bar-Kochva, B. 129, 158, 172, 180
Barag, D. 164, 165, 193
Barnett, R. D. 42
Barstad, H. M. 71
Baumann, G. 52
Behr, J. W. 96
Berger, P.-R. 74, 96
Berjelung, A. 96, 104
Berlin, A. 129, 152, 159-61, 177, 211,
    213, 214
Bernett, M. 237, 239
Bernhardt, K.-H. 98
Berrin, S. 214
Betlyon, J. W. 115
Bhabha, H. 15, 17, 19, 34, 82, 99, 131,
    132, 154, 182-84, 202, 219, 263, 290
Bickerman, E. J. 78, 177, 186, 192, 194
Bilde, P. 240
Blenkinsopp, J. 71, 125
Boer, R. 28, 31

Bonz, M. P. 228
Bosworth, A. B. 135, 138, 209
Boyce, M. 111
Braziel, J. E. 86
Brenner, S. 278
Brett, M. G. 124
Briant, P. 107
Bringmann, K. 139
Brinkman, J. A. 41, 42, 47
Brooke, G. J. 283, 284
Brownmiller, S. 154
Brueggemann, W. 49
Brunt, P. A. 138, 227, 263
Burnett, A. M. 276
Burrows, M. 275
Butler, K. D. 100

Caniotis, A. 176
Carradice, I. 276
Carter, C. E. 117
Carter, W. 133, 231, 245, 258, 262
Chrisman, L. 218
Clements, R. E. 87
Cody, J. M. 277
Cogan, M. 47, 57
Cohen, S. 146
Collingwood, R. G. 25
Collins, J. J. 203, 284
Collins, P. T. 48
Cotton, H. M. 180
Craig, J. A. 42
Crossan, J. D. 227, 262
Croy, C. 157
Cuellar, G. 100
Curtis, J. 42, 107

Dalley, S. 43
Dandamayev, M. A. 75, 78
Daniels, D. 49
Day, P. L. 52

DeRose Evans, J. 276
Dearman, J. A. 49
Derow, P. 153
Derrida, J. 20
Deutsch, R. 278
Devi, M. 21
Dick, M. B. 104
Dijkstra, M. 79, 82
Donner, H. 44
Doran, R. 185, 192

Eck, W. 226
Erim, K. 231

Fanon, F. 8, 9, 28, 131, 132, 157, 166,
    171, 175, 187, 188, 221, 250, 262, 263
Fears, J. R. 227
Flusser, D. 202, 215
Forbes, H. 261
Forman, W. 42
Foucault, M. 2, 62
Fox, R. L. 138, 144
Foxhall, L. 261
Fredricksmeyer, E. A. 138-40, 142, 143
Freire, P. 133, 175, 221
Friesen, S. 253
Fuks, A. 155
Fuks, G. 155

Gabrielsen, V. 195
Gadd, C. J. 98
Galinsky, K. 135, 229
Galling, K. 111
Gandhi, L. 218
Garnsey, P. 251, 253, 261, 262
George, A. R. 46
Gera, D. 155, 157, 172, 175, 178, 180,
    185
Gilroy, P. 33
Goldstein, J. A. 194
Goodblatt, D. 135
Goodman, M. 217, 226, 240, 241, 246,
    250, 254, 260, 263, 267, 278
Grabbe, L. L. 108, 129, 146, 150-52,
    154-56, 159, 161, 175-77, 191, 241
Grayson, A. K. 88
Green, P. 136, 148

Griffiths, G. 86, 218
Groenewegen-Frankfort, H. A. 48
Gruen, E. 172, 181, 182, 184, 190, 193
Guha, R. 19

Habricht, C. 184
Hadley, R. A. 173, 255
Hall, R. G. 188
Hallo, W. W. 39, 67, 97, 105
Hamber, B. 133, 220
Hanson, K. C. 250
Harasym, S. 19
Hayes, J. 185
Hayward, C. T. R. 182
Heckel, W. 136
Heinen, H. 148, 150
Held, D. 28
Hendin, D. 276
Hengel, M. 151, 176, 177
Hölbl, G. 135, 148, 163, 164
Holladay, W. L. 87
Hollenbach, P. W. 262
Holloway, S. W. 40, 42, 46, 47
Horowitz, W. 80
Horsley, R. 168, 169, 200, 201, 203,
    204, 248-50, 252, 267, 280, 283
Howard-Brooks, W. 168, 170, 171
Huizanga, J. 25
Hyatt, J. P. 87

Jacobsen, T. 104
James, P. 232
Jameson, F. 28
Johnson, J. J. 165, 166
Jursa, M. 75

Kadman, L. 278
Kaiser, A. 146
Kamudzandu, I. 229
Kanael, B. 276, 278
Kautsky, J. H. 251, 253
Keefe, A. 52
Kieh, G. K. 82
Kindler, A. 135, 164, 278
King, L. W. 112
Kratz, R. G. 124
Krentz, E. 25

Kuhrt, A. 107, 172-74, 191, 197, 210
Kurtz, M. 132
Kwakkel, G. 49

Landau, Y. H. 176
Landy, F. 52
Larsen, M. T. 37
Lehmann, G. 77
Lenski, G. 31, 252, 253, 259
Levine, A.-J. 224
Lipiński, E. 75
Lipschits, O. 71, 145
Liverani, M. 41
Lloyd, A. B. 165, 166
Lopez, D. 231, 232
Luckenbill, D. D. 43
Lundbom, J. R. 87
Lyotard, J.-F. 32

Ma, J. 184, 190
MacKenzie, J. M. 14
MacMullen, R. 274
Machinist, P. 102
Macintosh, A. A. 49
Malamat, A. 70
Mandell, S. 185
Mann, M. 2, 235, 241
Manning, J. G. 159
Mannur, A. 86
Marcus, R. 177, 178
Mattila, S. L. 181
Mattingly, D. J. 261
Mbembe, A. 219
McCane, B. 224, 238, 242, 266
McCarthy, D. J. 59
McKay, J. W. 57, 64
McLaren, J. 238
McLeod, J. 30
Meshorer, Y. 278
Meyshan, Y. 276
Midmead, J. 105
Mørkholm, O. 192
Modrzejewski, J. M. 158
Moore-Gilbert, B. J. 19
Morley, N. 226
Morton, S. 7
Mowinckel, S. 87

Müller, H.-P. 69
Murray, O. 162

Nicholson, E. W. 87
Nickelsburg, G. W. E. 168, 203

Oakman, D. E. 250
Oded, B. 48, 71, 78
Oden, R. A. 192
Oppenheim, A. L. 47, 63, 72
Osborne, R. 253
Oshia, T. 80

Parker, B. J. 44
Parpola, S. 37
Parrot, A. 48
Paul, S. 96-98
PeCiikova, J. 44
Perdue, L. G. 181
Petras, J. 82, 83
Pongratz-Leisten, B. 103
Portier-Young, A. 176, 178, 184, 191,
    196, 200, 201, 203, 204
Postgate, J. N. 44-46
Purcell, N. 261

Rajak, T. 214, 243
Renger, J. 75
Rice, E. E. 149
Richards, T. 41
Richardson, P. 238, 256, 266, 274, 275
Rigsby, K. J. 191, 192
Ripollès, P. P. 276
Robertson, J. F. 46
Rocca, S. 256
Roisman, J. 136
Roller, D. W. 256
Rollston, C. A. 57
Root, M. C. 107, 111
Rowlandson, J. 148149,
Rushdie, S. 33, 34

Safrai, Z. 251
Said, E. 5, 10, 11, 14, 32, 83, 130
Saller, R. 251
Samuel, E. E. 149, 163
Sancisi-Weerdenburg, H. 107

Sanders, S. 80
Sasson, J. M. 72
Scheidel, W. 253
Schmid, H. 79
Schwartz, D. R. 155
Schwartz, S. 25, 218, 279
Scott, J. C. 3, 23, 101, 149, 151, 154, 180, 197, 198, 200, 203, 205, 219, 222, 223, 235, 241
Sefer, H. 178
Segovia, F. F. 29, 86, 87, 99, 130, 131, 217, 219
Setel, D. 52
Seux, M.-J. 37, 43, 98
Shaw, B. D. 249
Sherwin-White, S. 172-74, 191, 197, 210
Sherwood, Y. 52
Slemon, S. 5
Smith, R. R. 231
Smith-Christopher, D. L. 77, 100, 124
Soggin, A. A. 98
Spieckermann, H. 57, 68
Spivak, G. C. 19, 21, 130, 219
Stern, E. 77
Stevens, M. E. 88
Stone, M. 288, 290
Stoneman, R. 135, 146
Sugirtharajah, R. S. 5, 22

Tadmor, H. 41
Tallis, N. 42, 107
Tarn, W. W. 138
Taylor, J. E. 239, 277
Tcherikover, V. (A.) 145, 146, 155, 191
Temin, P. 252
Thiel, W. 87
Thiong'o, N. wa 17, 32, 74
Thomas, C. G. 138
Thompson, D. J. 149, 150
Thompson, R. C. 112
Thorne, J. A. 176
Tiffin, H. 86, 218
Todd, R. A. 138

Tornkvist, R. 52
Tritle, L. A. 136
Turner, E. 148, 165

Udoh, F.E. 252-55, 257
Unger, E. A. 78

Van De Mieroop, M. 75
Van Dijk-Hemmes, F. 52
Van Seters, J. 25
Van der Steen, E. 159
VanderKam, J. 241
Vanderhooft, D. S. 96
Vout, C. 229

Wacker, M.-T. 52
Walbank, F. W. 129, 139, 140, 148, 162-64, 173, 195
Walker, C. B. F. 104
Weems, R. 52
Weitzman, S. 185
Werline, R. A. 280, 281
Westenholz, A. 40
Westenholz, J. 42
Whittaker, C. R. 253
Will, E. 130
Williams, P. 218
Williamson, H. G. M. 104
Wilson, C. 261
Wörrle, M. 180
Worthington, I. 136, 143
Wright, B. 182, 183

Yee, G. A. 49, 75
Young, J. R. 101
Young, R. 28, 32, 219
Younger Jr, K. L. 39, 67

Zadok, R. 76, 78, 79
Zahle, J. 173, 192
Zanker, P. 230
Zarrow, E. M. 277
Zevit, Z. 57